MARK'S
SUPERB
GOSPEL

Titles by Ivor Powell

Bible Cameos
Bible Gems
Bible Highways
Bible Names of Christ
Bible Nuggets
Bible Pinnacles
Bible Treasures
Bible Windows
Matthew's Majestic Gospel
Luke's Thrilling Gospel
John's Wonderful Gospel
The Amazing Acts
Exciting Epistle to the Ephesians
David: His Life and Times
What in the World Will Happen Next?

MARK'S
SUPERB
GOSPEL

IVOR POWELL

kregel PUBLICATIONS

Grand Rapids, MI 49501

We acknowledge with appreciation the permission to reprint material taken from *The Zondervan Pictorial Encyclopedia of the Bible*, 5 Volumes, edited by Merrill C. Tenney. © 1975 by the Zondervan Corporation. Used by permission.

Cover design: Alan G. Hartman

Library of Congress Cataloging-in-Publication Data
Powell, Ivor 1910-
  Mark's Superb Gospel

  Includes index and bibliography.
      p.   cm.
  1. Bible N.T. Mark—Commentaries. I. Title.
BS2585.3.P68   1985   226'.307   85-25615
                                                                    CIP

ISBN 0-8254-3510-2 (pbk.)

      2 3 4 5 6 printing / year 97 96 95 94 93

Printed in the United States of America

TO
BETTY
WHO FOR ALMOST FIFTY
YEARS HAS BEEN MY WIFE
AND FELLOW-LABORER IN THE
WORK OF EVANGELISM:
HER SKILLFUL EDITING, WISE
SUGGESTIONS, AND CONSTANT
ENCOURAGEMENT MADE ALL
MY MANUSCRIPTS POSSIBLE.

CONTENTS

8   CONTENTS

INDEX OF HOMILIES

PREFACE

Many of my closest friends will consider the production of this book to be a miracle. During November of 1983, a severe illness caused the cancellation of my evangelistic meetings in South Carolina, and in the following weeks, five dedicated doctors worked hard to save my life. I was in a deep coma and very near to death. When I awakened, I had a conviction that I had been sent back to earth to do something special for the Lord. I knew I had been commissioned to complete a manuscript on the Gospel of Mark. The work was commenced immediately, and now, nine months later, the task has been finished. I shall always be grateful to the Lord for allowing me to have this assignment; the work has brought a new understanding of the message beloved by all Christians.

Readers acquainted with the companion commentaries on *Luke's Thrilling Gospel,* and *John's Wonderful Gospel,* will detect changes in the structure and compilation of this new volume. Formerly, homilies were supplied at the end of each section in every chapter. This method, to some extent, has been preserved, but in addition I have tried to combine the expository notes with the special homilies. That is, almost every verse has been expounded as if it were meant to be a homily. This has been done deliberately, to help ministers in their preparation of sermons and Bible class lessons. I believe the new concept will be appreciated.

As with the earlier commentaries, most of the subject matter for this volume came from my fifty years of studying and preaching the message of the Bible. Nevertheless, I would like to pay sincere tribute to a few works which have been of inestimable worth. *The Pulpit Commentary* (Wm. B. Eerdmans Publishing Co.) has always been the background of all my studies, and in recent years, my soul has been refreshed by facts found in *The Zondervan Pictorial Encyclopedia of the Bible* (Zondervan Publishing House). My *Greek New Testament* and the expert interpretation of ancient Bible words as given by Dr. Joseph H. Thayer, have been of incalculable worth as I proceeded verse by verse through Mark's Gospel.

Finally, I shall always be indebted to Kregel Publications of Grand Rapids, Michigan whose publications are of surpassing excellence, and to Mrs. Eleanor Dzuro, who, as a service for her Lord, typed the entire manuscript of this book. It only remains to say, this volume is being sent forth with a sincere prayer that its message will inspire ministers around the world to preach the glorious gospel of the grace of God.

Santa Barbara, California
August, 1984   IVOR POWELL

INTRODUCTION

It is hardly possible to appreciate the greatness of Mark's Gospel unless we first have an understanding of its author. Mark was an impetuous, enthusiastic boy who very quickly became a man! He covered a great distance in a very short time! It was a far cry from the youngster who deserted his missionary companions, Paul and Barnabas, to the maturing man who listened to the impassioned preaching of Simon Peter; who carefully made notes of all he heard, and finally, editing those notes, produced his Gospel. Mark could not have become a Paul had he lived a million years. Mark was meant to be Mark. One of the most thrilling facts of life is that God takes a man as he is, molds and fills him with His Spirit, and then uses that man to do the impossible. Square pegs never fit round holes. Mark was never meant to be a fearless missionary, relentlessly forging ahead into hostile territory; he was meant to sit quietly listening, and then to write what he had heard. He was not a tractor ploughing difficult fields. He was more like a gentle raindrop, falling upon seeds of truth trying to germinate. He was called to become an author and not an adventurer. To follow Mark through the changing, challenging experience of his life, is a necessary prelude to the understanding of the book he produced.

Somewhere, either within or near the city of Jerusalem, was a home destined to become famous. The lady of the household was named Mary; her son was John Mark. Some scholars think that John was his Hebrew name, whereas Mark or Marcus was a Roman name acquired later in life. It has been assumed that the name Mark was derived from the Latin word *Marcus* which means "a strong hammer", a hammer capable of breaking hard rocks. There is reason to believe that Mark's home might have been the place where the Lord and His disciples ate the last supper; it is certain that it became a center for early church activities, and was the site of the famous prayer meeting to which Simon Peter went after his release from prison (Acts 12:12). John Mark therefore grew up in a home where God was honored and believers welcomed. There exists the possibility that he might have heard and seen the Lord, and that Christ's influence upon the lad was unmistakable. On the memorable night when the Savior was betrayed, "...there followed him a certain young man, having a linen cloth cast about his naked body; and the young men laid hold on him. And he left the linen cloth, and fled from them naked" (Mark 14:51-52). Possibly, the story of John Mark begins there, for as John in his gospel refers to himself as "the disciple whom Jesus loved", so Mark in these verses might be referring to himself as "the young man." Maybe he had already retired to his bed when he overheard his family speaking of the dreadful things which had happened that night, and seized by a curiosity hard to control, he silently left the house and went to see for himself the things which were taking place. What he saw, he never forgot.

Doubtless his uncle Barnabas also had a profound influence upon the boy's life. As Mark became older he exhibited an increasing desire to follow in the footsteps of his famous relative. It was not surprising therefore that when Paul and Barnabas were commissioned to become the first missionaries of the Church, they decided to take with them this young man whose enthusiasm for Christ apparently knew no limitations (Acts 13:5). When John Mark heard of the impending adventure, his eyes probably shone with delight. He was to venture forth into a pagan world as an ambassador for Christ. At that moment he seemed to be ten feet tall! It was not long before the dream of coming glory faded, and young Mark's missionary efforts came to a dramatic end. One simple statement in Acts 13:13 sounds like an epitaph! "Now when Paul and his company loosed from Paphos, they came to Perga in Pamphilia, *and John departing from them returned to Jerusalem.*" That seemed to be, and might well have been, the end of a promising career. The question has often been asked, "Why did John leave his colleagues?" There are five possible answers. (1) Had he been seasick on the ship which carried the missionary pioneers to Perga in Pamphilia? If so we can sympathize with him. To become a victim of mal-demer is sufficient to ruin enthusiasm for any cause! (2) Had he become homesick? This was in all probability his first trip away from home and the constant attention of a devoted mother. To be the pampered son of a wonderful lady was far more desirable than preparing meals and washing dishes for two men who were too busy to do anything but preach! (3) Was he fearful? They were to travel through rough country, among people who were openly hostile. Paul was unafraid. Whatever the consequences, he would advance unflinchingly. Was Mark apprehensive, and not wishing to become a martyr, did he leave while he was able so to do? (4) Had he become disillusioned? He had entertained dreams of becoming a preacher not a dishwasher! He had planned to remove sin from human hearts not stains from saucepans! The life he embraced promised fame and glory. Apparently he was only to know fear and continuing drudgery. (5) Was he jealous? Obviously Paul was assuming command of everything. His uncle Barnabas was being pushed out! Paul did what he wanted, and no one else mattered! Did Mark's eyes become clouded and his thinking a little warped as he considered what was taking place? *"And Mark departing from them came to Jerusalem."*

It was a sad home-coming. His mother welcomed him with open arms, but some of the younger brethren probably quoted a text, ". . .No man, having put his hand to the plough, and looking back, is fit for the kingdom of God" (Luke 9:62). Did Mark regret his mistake? Then, with the passing of time, the old wound was reopened. Paul and Barnabas were planning another missionary journey.

And some days after Paul said unto Barnabas, "Let us go again and visit our brethren in every city where we have preached the word of the Lord, and see how they do." And Barnabas *determined* to take with them John, whose surname was Mark. But Paul thought not good to take him with them, who departed from them from Pamphylia, and went not with them to the work. And the contention was so sharp between them, that they departed asunder one from the other: and so Barnabas took Mark, and sailed unto Cyprus; and Paul chose Silas, and departed, being recommended by the brethren unto the grace of God. And he went through Syria and Cilicia, confirming the churches (Acts 15:36-41).

Alas, Barnabas marched into obscurity, but John Mark suffered more than his uncle. Doubtless he was blamed by many for separating the two stalwarts of the faith, and he too might have disappeared in the mists of failure. Fortunately for the young man, there was another Christian leader who knew guilt born of failure. He was Simon Peter, who had never forgotten how he had denied his Lord. It is believed by all theologians that Peter welcomed Mark and, so to speak, took him under his wing. As the years passed, the bonds of love binding the two men tightened, and when long afterward, Peter wrote from Babylon, he said, "The church that is at Babylon, elected together with you, saluteth you; *and so doth Marcus my son"* (1 Peter 5:13). That one statement "Marcus my son" reveals love, warmth, tenderness unsurpassed in any other of Peter's writings.

John Mark became the traveling companion of Simon Peter, and as he sat listening to his new hero, he made copious notes of all he heard. As his collection increased, these notes were revised and edited, and finally, when his task was more or less completed, Mark's Gospel made its appearance.

"Ancient writers, as Ireneaus, Tertullian, St. Jerome, and others with one consent make him (Mark) the interpreter of Simon Peter." Eusebius, quoting from Paphos, says, "Mark, being the interpreter of St. Peter, wrote down exactly whatever things he remembered, yet not in the order in which Christ either spoke or did them; for he was neither a hearer nor a follower of our Lord, but he was afterward a follower of St. Peter." "According to the testimony of St. Jerome, he wrote a short Gospel at Rome, at the request of the brethren there; and St. Peter when he had heard it, approved of it, and appointed it to be read in the churches by his authority." Jerome says further that St. Mark took this Gospel and went into Egypt, and, being the first preacher of Christ at Alexandria, established a church with so much moderation of doctrine and life, that he constrained all those who had opposed Christ to follow his example. Eusebius states that Mark became the first bishop of the church and that the catechetical school at Alexandria was founded under his authority . . . Tradition says that the body of St. Mark was removed by certain merchants from Alexandria to Venice in A.D. 827, where he was much honoured. The Venetian Senate adopted the emblem of St. Mark—the lion—for their crest, and when they directed anything to be done, they affirmed that it was by the order of St. Mark! (*The Pulpit Commentary*, Mark, p. VII.)

To return once again to New Testament times, it is inspiring to discover that whatever misunderstanding or bitterness might have existed between Paul and the run-away Mark, all this was obliterated by the growing friendship between the two men. When certain texts are considered in sequence, much of what remained unknown becomes clear.
1. Writing to the Colossian Church (4:10) Paul said, "Aristarchus my fellow prisoner saluteth you, and Marcus, sister's son to Barnabas, (touching whom ye have received commandments: *if he come unto you, receive him).*"
2. Writing to Philemon (verse 24) Paul says, "There salute thee . . . Marcus, Aristarchus, Demas, Lucas, *my fellow labourers.*"
3. When Paul was nearing the end of his earthly journey, he wrote to Timothy and said, "Only Luke is with me. Take Mark, and bring him with thee; for *he is profitable to me for the ministry*" (2 Tim. 4:11). When we remember the bitterness which had ruined the peacefulness of that first missionary party; when we consider how disgusted Paul must have been with the deserter, we can only marvel at the change

which had taken place within both men. Paul had softened and become gentle with age; Mark had matured, and deepened in devotion to his Lord. This had become obvious to all, and it was no cause for amazement when Paul embraced the younger man and welcomed him as a son beloved.

It is necessary to remember one other detail as we seek to understand what happened long ago. There were no printing presses; no mass production of written materials. Every word of every manuscript had to be written by hand. Every copy made from an original document had to be slowly, carefully, written by scribes, and each copy became increasingly valuable as it circulated among the churches. Possibly Paul had read one of those copies of Mark's Gospel; maybe he even read the original, and instantly recognizing its worth, learned again to appreciate its author. As time passed, other Gospels made an appearance, but it is generally believed that Mark's Gospel was the first officially accepted record of the life of the Savior. Some theologians do not accept this conclusion, but all the facts appear to support the earlier statement. In any study of God's Word it is important to understand the customs and background of what the authors are dealing with. Another thing in a study of the gospels, is to see what similarities or differences there might be between them. The first three gospels are known as the Synoptic Gospels, the word "synoptic" coming from two Greek words which mean "to see together". The Synoptic Gospels, Matthew, Mark and Luke, are so very similar, in many ways, that you don't know if the three evangelists took their material from some common source or if two of the three based their writings on a third. The Gospel of Mark has 105 sections, 93 of which occur in the Gospel of Matthew and 81 in the Gospel of Luke. Only four sections are not included in the latter two. Another interesting fact is that Mark has 661 verses, Matthew has 1068 verses, and Luke has 1149. Matthew makes reference to 606 verses from Mark, and, although Matthew does change some words a little, he does reproduce 51 percent of the words used by Mark. Luke reproduces 320 verses of the 661 in Mark and uses about 53 percent of Mark's actual words. Of the 55 verses of Mark which Matthew does not use, 31 of these are found in Luke. Could we say that it seems like Matthew and Luke used Mark as the basis for their gospels? Though sometimes Matthew and Luke alter Mark's order of events they never agree together against Mark. As we study the life of Christ in this book, let us remember that it was Mark who first wrote about the events surrounding His life and ministry.

With these facts in mind, we now approach the systematic study of Mark's gospel. We might even call it "The Little-big Gospel." It only has 16 chapters, but as we read Mark's account we cannot help but see the tremendous enthusiasm filling the author's soul. He had a story to tell to the nations, and the sooner he told it, the happier he would become. If this were indeed the first Gospel to be written, we cannot help but wonder what the Lord thought, as He saw Mark bending over his parchment. Maybe when Mark had finished writing, the Lord whispered, "Well done", and with that conclusion every Christian would readily agree. Mark did a great job, and perhaps in some future time, we too will be able to thank him "face to face."

The First Chapter of Mark

THEME: *Christ Commences His Ministry*

OUTLINE:

SECTION ONE

Expository Notes on Mark's Introduction to His Gospel

The beginning of the gospel of Jesus Christ, the Son of God; as it is written in the prophets, Behold, I send my messenger before thy face, which shall prepare thy way before thee. The voice of one crying in the wilderness, Prepare ye the way of the Lord, make his paths straight. John did baptize in the wilderness, and preach the baptism of repentance for the remission of sins. And there went out unto him all the land of Judaea, and they of Jerusalem, and were all baptized of him in the river of Jordan, confessing their sins. And John was clothed with camel's hair, and with the girdle of a skin about his loins; and he did eat locusts and wild honey; and preached, saying, There cometh one mightier than I after me, the latchet of whose shoes I am not worthy to stoop down and unloose. I indeed have baptized you with water: but He shall baptize you with the Holy Spirit (vv. 1-8).

To say the least, John Mark was in a hurry! He believed in coming straight to the point. He did not like "beating around the bush!" Any psychoanalyst would have an interesting time, if he considered this introduction; then compared it with the introductions found in the other three Gospels. Using only eight verses, Mark encompasses the Old Testament, cites the prophets, describes the ministry of John the Baptist, and then introduces Jesus. Matthew, Luke and John are totally different in the approach to their accounts of the life of the Lord. Matthew had something to prove. He believed his Master was the Messiah, and went to great lengths supplying evidence to support his assertions. He does not really introduce the Person of Jesus until he reaches chapter 3, verse 13, where he says, "Then cometh Jesus from Galilee to Jordan unto John to be baptized of him." Matthew begins his Gospel by tracing the genealogy of Christ back through the generations to David and Abraham. He then proceeds to speak of the birth of the Lord and how the Wise Men came to ask, "Where is He that is born King of the Jews?" For a time, Matthew appears to be more concerned with *his facts* than with *his Friend.* Finally, after writing what we now call two and one-half chapters, he reaches the place where all attention is focused on his Master. In contrast to this, Mark had nothing to prove. His Lord had come and that was all that mattered. His wonderful Savior had been on earth doing amazing things for needy people. He had good news to tell. He might have been excused had he said, "Why waste time talking about these other things? I want to speak about Jesus, so let me get on with my job!

Luke also had something to prove. As a medical man he had already recognized Christ as the perfect specimen of humanity. There never had been, and there never would be, another to be compared with Jesus. Luke made it his business to ask questions, and there is every reason to believe he interviewed Mary and any others who could add to his knowledge of events leading to the birth of his Savior. Very carefully, Luke prepared his manuscript and took almost three chapters, before he brought Christ into the center of his story; but even then, the Lord appeared but for a brief time. Having said, "Now when all the people were baptized, it came to pass, that Jesus also being baptized, and praying, the heaven was opened, and the Holy Spirit descended in a bodily shape upon him, and a voice came from heaven, which said, Thou art my beloved Son; in thee I am well pleased," Luke reverts to his earlier style and proceeds to give a lengthy list of Christ's ancestors. Let it be candidly admitted that even today very few people take the time to read Luke's list of names. John Mark might have been excused had he read Luke's introduction; then heaving a great sigh, he said, "Brother, let's get on with it!"

mark was young and preach ed short sermons
Luke " old " " " long "

Finally, as we consider the introduction to John's Gospel, we become aware that he too went a long way back in time to find a starting point. He wrote, "In the beginning was the Word, and the Word was with God, and the Word was God. The same was in the beginning with God. All things were made by Him; and without Him was not anything made that was made" (John 1:1-2). The casual reader might—and I repeat my word—*might* wonder as to the identity of the Word. John, in verse fourteen of his first chapter writes: "And the word was made flesh and dwelt among us, (and we beheld His glory, the glory as of the only begotten of the Father), full of grace and truth." Then the author proceeds, as did Matthew and Luke to devote time and space to the record of the ministry of John the Baptist. Finally, in verse 29 he writes, "The next day John seeth Jesus coming unto him, and sayeth, 'Behold the Lamb of God, which taketh away the sin of the world'." John Mark might have been tempted *to begin* his message with that same profound statement.

Now, lest I be accused of heresy, let me hasten to explain something which is very important. Simon Peter said, ". . .holy men of God spake as they were moved by the Holy Spirit" (2 Peter 1:21). We believe the same Holy Spirit inspired the writers of the Gospels, so that a needy world could receive the Word of God. *It was both necessary and beneficial* for us all, that Matthew, Luke and John should write lengthy, detailed introductions to their Gospels, for without these messages, the world would be infinitely poorer. If, as was earlier suggested, Mark's Gospel was the *first* to make its appearance, then it is easy to understand how the later writers had opportunity to study his message. They were able to think of other things they would like to include, and when the Holy Spirit gently reminded them of more and more details, then at a later date, these were included in their memoirs of Jesus. The fact remains that John Mark was not a historian as was Matthew; nor a doctor as was Luke; not a theologian as was John. He was still a boy whose heart was filled with enthusiasm for his Lord. He had discovered Jesus the Wonderful! and if he had not talked about Him, he would have burst!

John Mark's soul was like a reservoir imprisoned behind the walls of a great dam. Suddenly the opportunity came for the life-giving waters to cascade toward a dry and dying world. Matthew, Luke and John seemingly had plenty of time to devote to lengthy descriptions of events and discourses. The first three chapters of Matthew belong to this category, and for the most part so do the first three chapters of Luke. It is noteworthy that most of John's chapters provide details of one complete story sermon. Mark, on the other hand, bursts upon the scene with descriptions of numerous stories. Once he gets started, he seems to be saying, "listen to this, this, and this" and that probably explains why his first chapter has to be divided into seven different sections. If the other evangelists were "deep-sea divers" exploring the marvelous depths of God's ocean, Mark was a youthful "water skier," skimming excitedly over the surface of the life of his Lord, and revelling in all he saw and heard. While his contemporaries were studiously reporting on obscure events and genealogies, Mark was telling people about the miracles performed by his Master. He was indeed in a great hurry; he was getting on with the task given to him by his Lord. It might well be said that John Mark set fire to his world, while his brethren looked for a match!

SECTION TWO

Expository Notes on Christ's Baptism and Temptation

And it came to pass in those days, that Jesus came from Nazareth of Galilee, and was baptized of John in Jordan. And straightway coming up out of the water, He saw the heavens opened, and the Spirit like a dove descending upon Him. And there came a voice from heaven, saying, Thou art my beloved Son, in whom I am well pleased. And immediately the spirit driveth Him into the wilderness. And He was there in the wilderness forty days, tempted of Satan, and was with the wild beasts; and the angels ministered unto Him (vv. 9-13).

A STRANGE CONFESSION

It is not known whether or not John Mark ever had the privilege of meeting John the Baptist. He was only a boy when the ministry of the Wilderness Preacher terminated. However, it would be unwise to be dogmatic on the subject for Mark affirms ". . .there went out unto him all the land of Judea, and they of Jerusalem, and were all baptized of him in the river of Jordan, confessing their sins" (v. 5). We are sure that Mark was well aware of what had taken place in the Jordan valley, and as a result, fierce excitement burned in his soul. At this early part of his narrative, he is about to introduce Jesus to his readers, but ere we consider what he has to say, it might be wise if we retrace our steps to consider a little more of his introduction to the Gospel.

THE UNFORGETTABLE PREDICTIONS

Mark, in common with other Hebrew youths, had great faith in the prophets. He had been obliged to memorize certain parts of their writings, and, long before the Baptist preacher made an appearance in the countryside, young Mark had been aware of the great predictions made centuries earlier. In retrospect, as he wrote his Gospel, it was easy for him to associate the Wilderness Preacher with what had been said concerning his ministry. "As it is written in the prophets, Behold I send my messenger before thy face, which shall prepare thy way before thee" (Mal. 3:1). John Mark had no problem associating John the Baptist with the prediction made by Isaiah: "The voice of him that crieth in the wilderness, Prepare ye the way of the Lord, make straight in the desert a highway for our God. Every valley shall be exalted, and every mountain and hill shall be made low: and the crooked shall be made straight, and the rough places plain. And the glory of the Lord shall be revealed, and all flesh shall see it together: for the mouth of the Lord hath spoken it" (Isa. 40:3-5). God meant what He had said. The Lord *had* come, and the appointed forerunner *had* prepared the way before him.

THE UNUSUAL PREACHER

"And John was clothed with camel's hair, and with a girdle of skin about his loins; and he did eat locusts and wild honey" (v. 6). He had been the only student in God's theological college. He had enjoyed private tuition from the one and only Professor—the Lord Himself! We do not know anything about the mode of teaching; nor what was taught, but we know that after John had graduated, he came to his place of ministry as a man sent from God. Probably, he was the greatest evangelist ever to minister on earth. He had no committee to prepare the way ahead of him; he had no trained workers to do "follow-up work;" he never had a choir; he never had any special musical items. He never spent money on advertising, and was never heard on radio nor television. He never took a collection, but he shook the powers of hell. These are the characteristics of all preachers "sent by God."

THE UNSURPASSED POWER

"And there went out to him all the land of Judaea, and they of Jerusalem, and were all baptized of him in the river of Jordan, confessing their sins'' (v. 5). The Valley of the Jordan was soon turned into an open-air cathedral. Oxen, wagons, tents and people were everywhere. Meeting succeeded meeting, and revival was in the air. Some people thought that Elijah had returned to earth, but everyone knew God was there. Day after day the voice of the evangelist warned of the consequences of sin, of the certainty of impending judgment, and of the necessity to repent and be forgiven. Arguments were virtually unknown, and the number of baptisms increased daily. It is of great interest, that, although eventually certain of the scribes and Pharisees questioned John's authority, no critic ever challenged his mode of baptism. Anxious as they were to stop this challenging movement, no one ever expressed surprise that he was baptizing people. Baptism by immersion was fully understood in Israel. The leaders taught, and the nation believed that they, and they alone, were the chosen people of God. They did, however, recognize that Gentiles might ''see the light'' and ask for acceptance among the people of God. Such converts were known as proselytes. They were never fully accepted into the fellowship of the nation until they were baptized, for this signified they had ''washed away their sins'' that is, they had renounced their idolatry. If such people lived in areas where water was plentiful, they were baptized in ponds or rivers; where supplies of water were scarce, the officiating priests used tubs or baths. The only surprising thing about the baptism practiced by John was the fact that *he baptized JEWS.* It was amazing that he, a Jew, was asking Jews to submit to that to which only a Gentile was supposed to submit. John realized that to be a Jew in the racial sense was not to be a member of God's chosen people. A Jew might be in exactly the same position as a Gentile; *not the Jewish life* but *the cleansed life* belonged to God.

THE UNIQUE PROMISE

John said, ''I indeed have baptized you with water, but He shall baptize you with the Holy Spirit'' (v. 8). It is noteworthy that no translator ever changes this verse. John's magnificent utterances stands alone; it could never be applied to any other, for only God can ''baptize with the Holy Spirit.'' Here we have, in all its beautiful simplicity, the foreshadowings of the great doctrines later to be expounded through the early church. God had indeed come down to tabernacle among men. To be immersed in water signified that the participant had voluntarily forsaken the old life of sin; to be immersed in the power of the Holy

Spirit indicated the same participant had sincerely embraced the deeper life offered,—to be filled and flooded with the very life of God, the Divine Spirit. The first of these might indicate a wonderful confession; the second reveals something far better—a marvelous condition!

THE UNEXPECTED PHENOMENON

"And there came a voice from heaven, saying, Thou art my beloved Son, in whom I am well pleased" (v. 11). To some, it will always be a mystery why Christ should submit to a rite reserved specially for penitent people. It must be remembered that He came to be associated with sinners, to be identified with them, and to set an example for them to follow. He had no sin of His own, but His action endorsed all that John the Baptist said. In some senses, this was an even greater confession than His being immersed in the waters of the Jordan. All of heaven was interested in what was taking place. We have been told in Genesis 1:26, that in the beginning of time, the triune God met and said, "Let US make man in OUR image." The members of the same Divine Family were at the baptism of Jesus. God the Father spoke from Heaven, God the Son stood listening, and God the Holy Spirit descended upon the Savior. At the beginning they said, "Let us make man." At the Jordan they seemed to be saying, "Let us save man." The ensuing story of the Gospels reveals how They did it.

THE UNCEASING PROTECTION

"And immediately the Spirit driveth Him into the wilderness. And He was there in the wilderness forty days, tempted of Satan; and was with the wild beasts; and the angels ministered unto Him" (vv. 12, 13). It should never be forgotten that in the two outstanding crises of the Savior's life, *the angels ministered unto Him.* Luke tells us that when, in agony, the Lord prayed in Gethsemane, ". . .there appeared an angel unto Him from heaven, strengthening Him" (Luke 22:43). Was there physical danger in the desert where Christ was being tempted? Did the "wild animals" present a threat? We do know that it was Satan, who would have liked to kill Christ in the garden of Gethsemane; Satan who suggested that the Lord should cast Himself down from the pinnacle of the temple; Satan who also used a mob to thrust Christ toward a precipice in Nazareth: that same evil One, had it been possible, would have used the wild animals to tear the Lord's body apart. We are told in Hebrews 1:14, "...the angels are ministering spirits sent forth to minister for them who shall be heirs of salvation." It is comforting to know that as they stood by the Savior in His hour of trial and temptation; so also they stand by those who trust in Him. We are never alone! It is gloriously possible to

> Turn your eyes upon Jesus
> Look full in His wonderful face:
> And the things of earth will grow strangely dim
> In the light of His glory and grace.

SECTION THREE

Expository Notes on the Call of the First Disciples

Now after that John was put in prison, Jesus came into Galilee, preaching the gospel of the kingdom of God. And saying, The time is fulfilled, and the kingdom of God is at hand: repent ye, and believe the gospel. Now as He walked by the Sea of Galilee, He saw Simon and Andrew, his brother, casting a net into the sea; for they were fishers. And Jesus said unto them, Come ye after Me, and I will make you to become fishers of men. And straightway they forsook their nets, and followed Him. And when He had gone a little further thence, He saw James the son of Zebedee, and John, his brother, who also were in the ship mending their nets. And straightway He called them: and they left their father, Zebedee, in the ship with the hired servants, and went after him (vv.14-20).

A STIRRING CALL

There are but two divisions in this passage—His Message and His Men. Let us consider them in that order. As was said earlier, John Mark did not *set down in order* the things spoken and performed by Christ. Obviously there is a break in time here, for these events happened *after John was imprisoned*.

HIS EARLY PREACHING...Christ's Message

"Jesus came into Galilee, preaching the good news of the kingdom of God, and saying, The time is fulfilled, and the kingdom of God is at hand: repent ye, and believe the gospel" (vv. 14, 15). *The Living Bible* translates the latter portion in a most attractive way: "*God's*

kingdom is near. Turn from your sins, and act on the glorious news!''
It would seem from a study of the entire Bible that God's message in
all ages could be summed up in two words: *repent* and *believe*. . .Paul,
in reminding the Ephesian elders of his doctrines said, ''I testified both
to the Jews, and also to the Greeks, *repentance toward God, and faith
toward our Lord Jesus Christ''* (Acts 20:21). If one should ask, ''How
do we act on the glorious news?'' Paul surely supplies the answer:
''Believe on the Lord Jesus Christ'' (see Acts 16:30, 31). It is the
consciousness of need which begets a desire for help. Faith without
repentance is hardly faith; repentance without faith is the harbinger of
sorrow. Repentance indicates disease is rampant in the heart; faith is
the hand that opens the door to admit the Great Physician.

Alas, in these modern days, the church seems to have emphasized
faith in Christ at the expense of repentance. There is always the lurking
fear that folk might be upset if they are touched on sensitive subjects.
We are fearful they may never return if we offend them with our
teaching. Many preachers think it is better to speak of heaven than of
hell; of God's mercy than His wrath. But, however debatable this point,
it is impossible to escape the fact that every preacher, used by God
throughout the centuries, emulated the example set by the ancient
prophets. They affirmed, that, unless people repented of their sin,
entrance into God's kingdom was an impossibility. It was not surprising
that Jesus commenced His ministry in Galilee by urging listeners to
repent of their sins and to exercise faith in the good news of the kingdom.
He said, ''The time is fulfilled, and the kingdom of God is at hand.''
He was announcing the all important fact—THE KING HAD COME!

HIS FIRST CONVERTS. . .Christ's Men

How surprising His choice. Throughout the Bible, God followed a
pattern in choosing His prophets. Seldom, if ever, did He choose an
important, well known, or famous man. He always made His servants
great, but at their beginning, they were nothing! Abraham was the son
of a man who worshipped idols in Ur of the Chaldees. Joseph was an
insignificant boy despised by members of his own family. Saul was a
farm-hand ploughing with oxen. David was a boy who lived with his
flocks. Amos was a herdman. Saul of Tarsus was a graduate student
without a job; he was hired as a hit-man for the priest! Why did God
always choose insignificant people? Perhaps it was that no flesh should
glory in His presence. The Lord Jesus obviously needed assistants to

carry His message throughout the land—the entire nation lay before Him. There were many educated and sincere men who might have been better equipped for the tasks ahead. Why then did He choose unlearned, unknown fishermen? With all his prestige and knowledge, Nicodemus might have become an influential disciple. Joseph of Arimathea, with all his wealth, could have underwritten the daily expenses of sending preachers on a full-time basis to city after city. Surely there must have been many sincere people who were equipped to help any good cause. Yet Christ went to the seashore to find uneducated, and probably poor fishermen, and these He called to be His first disciples. They were nothing; they brought nothing to Him but devotion and eagerness to serve, and these insignificant men He turned into giants! To know this is to find excitement hard to suppress. If He did it then, He can do it now. There is hope for us!

How splendid their response. "And straightway they forsook their nets, and followed Him" (v. 18). To say the least, this was remarkable. We remember another man who, when confronted by a similar call said, "Suffer me first to go and bury my father" (Luke 9:59). Everything for which those fishermen had labored remained in the deserted boats: their livelihood, their future, the future of their families, their father Zebedee, and any thought of providing for retirement. Those men had worked long and hard to establish themselves as commercial fishermen; and then in one seemingly impulsive moment, they abandoned everything! *"And at once they left their nets and yielding up all claim to them, followed with Him, joining Him as disciples and siding with His party" (The Amplified New Testament, p. 120).* We remember another young man who was also called by Jesus. He possessed great riches, but when confronted by the challenge to forsake his wealth, he decided to stay where he was—in his boat! (Matt. 19:16-26).

We all possess "boats," and most of what is valued on earth may be found in them. To turn our backs upon family and friends, to renounce all personal ambitions, our longing for fame and fortune, is seldom, if ever, easy. Yet this is the test of true discipleship. Jesus said, "He that loveth father or mother more than me is not worthy of me: and he that loveth son or daughter more than me is not worthy of me. And he that taketh not his cross, and followeth after me, is not worthy of me. He that findeth his life shall lose it: and he that loseth his life for my sake shall find it" (Matt. 10:37-39). It is much safer to rest in the arms of the living God than to be rocked to and fro in an expensive fishing boat!

How suggestive their jobs! ". . .he saw Simon and Andrew his brother *casting a net* into the sea for they were fishers" (v. 16). In contrast to this we read: "he saw James. . .and John his brother. . .*mending their nets*" (v. 19). We are reminded here that these accounts came from an eye witness. Had anyone challenged these details, Peter would have replied, "I was there when it happened!" Did Simon Peter ever reminisce, nod his head and say, "Surely, coming events were casting their shadows before?" The respective stories of their Christian service were all mirrored in those two short statements. Peter was casting his net—*he was concerned with getting fish into the net*—it was to be ever thus. As an evangelist he was destined to cast his net into the sea of life in the great endeavor to catch men for Christ. On the other hand, John was *mending* his net—*he was more concerned with keeping the fish in the net*. It would be quite useless if Peter caught fish, only to find they escaped through the unrepaired parts of a torn net. With unending patience, John examined the net inch by inch; he was determined to keep what Peter caught! John was the pastor who recognized that evangelism would be useless if the converts were not retained for the Lord.

The tragedy of modern evangelism is that converts are hard to find when the special evangelistic services terminate. Eloquent speakers influence and invite vast numbers to accept the challenge of the Gospel, but alas, six months after the special meetings terminate, it is difficult to find those who responded. Pastors and evangelists must work together; sometimes they might share each other's tasks, but casting and mending nets are two different jobs. It is comparatively easy to cast a net; it is extremely exacting to sit down examining every strand in a net meant to hold fish! Today, alas, there are times when the pastors and the evangelists do not share each other's favor. Long ago, Peter and John loved and helped each other, and that was the reason they did not go bankrupt either *before* or *after* the Lord called them! "He that hath an ear, let him hear what the Spirit saith unto the churches" (Rev. 2:11).

SECTION FOUR

Expository Notes on the Expelling of the Demons

And they went into Capernaum; and straightway on the sabbath day He entered into the synagogue, and taught. And they were astonished at His doctrine: for He taught them as one that had authority, and not as the scribes. And there was in their synagogue a man with an unclean

spirit; and he cried out, saying, Let us alone; what have we to do with thee, thou Jesus of Nazareth? art thou come to destroy us? I know thee who thou art, the Holy One of God. And Jesus rebuked him saying, Hold thy peace, and come out of him. And when the unclean spirit had torn him, and cried with a loud voice, he came out of him. And they were all amazed, insomuch that they questioned among themselves, saying, What thing is this? what new doctrine is this? for with authority commandeth He even the unclean spirits, and they do obey him. And immediately His fame spread abroad throughout all the region round about Galilee (vv. 21-28).

A SERIOUS CHALLENGE

HIS GLORIOUS PREACHING. . . explaining

"He taught them as one that had authority, and not as the scribes" (v. 22). *The Living Bible* translates this passage in a most interesting way: "The congregation was surprised at his sermon because he spoke as an authority, *and didn't try to prove his points by quoting others—* quite unlike what they were used to hearing." Readers of this or any other commentary will soon become aware of quotations from other writers. No modern author considers himself to be the absolute authority on any subject. There are other scholars who, at times, express thoughts in what is considered to be a clearer, and perhaps a better way. Such extracts are often quoted in books and at the same time an acknowledgement of the source of such information is offered to readers. The Lord had no need to supply corroborating evidence from anyone— He was the Absolute Authority on every subject. There were times when He reminded His audience of certain things which the prophets had spoken, but this He did to prove that He was not an exponent of heresy. As He said, "If ye believed the prophets, ye would have believed the words which I have spoken unto you."

HIS MIGHTY POWER. . . exorcising

The Lord's encounter with the demon-possessed man in the synagogue introduces a provocative subject. There are scholars who scoff at the mention of evil spirits. This doctrine, they declare, is a throwback to the dark ages! The fact that the man in the synagogue was thrown into convulsions is explained as an attack of epilepsy. Basically, the only thing that really matters here is that *the people of Christ's day believed in demons*, and in order to understand this scripture, that fact must be considered. The Jews had all kinds of strange ideas connected with demonology. Often, if a man's behavior was abnormal, his neighbors accused him of being demon-possessed. Many theologians believe the existence of demons upon the earth dates back to antideluvian times when angels fell from heaven. Some of these were said to have engaged in forbidden intercourse with women, and that as a result of their indiscretion, ". . .the angels which kept not their first estate, but left their own habitation, God hath reserved in everlasting chains under darkness unto the judgment of the great day" (Jude v. 6). The other evil spirits which did not commit that sin, remained free to roam the earth, and were responsible for the tragedies apparent on the earth during the life of Jesus. Such a tragedy was seen when Jesus entered into the synagogue.

I have never met a missionary who had worked in Africa or China *who did not believe in demon-possession*. I could give many examples, but one will suffice. It was my inestimable privilege to be the national evangelist for the South African Baptist Church, and in that capacity, I visited every Baptist Church from Capetown to what was then known as the Belgian Congo. A friend had presented me with a movie camera, and my desire for unusual missionary pictures knew no bounds. During my visit to an American mission station in Southern Rhodesia, I heard of a place in the mountains where witchcraft was practiced; where the witchdoctors of various tribes seemingly did the impossible. I asked one of the missionaries if he would take me to the place, but his reactions shocked me. His face became pale; his eyes filled with fear when he replied, "I would not take you there for all the money in the world." I was disappointed, but he went on to speak of a colleague who had defied a witchdoctor. That very keen missionary had somehow obtained a drum used in witchcraft, and this he planned to take back to America to use in receiving offerings at his meetings. He thought it would be an excellent idea if people could place their gifts on a drum which once had belonged to a real witchdoctor. When the African heard of the white man's intention, he became very angry and issued a warning. Unfortunately, the missionary was determined to do as he had planned. The witchdoctor thereupon placed a curse on him. My friend hesitated and shivered, then quietly said, "Within a few weeks he was stricken by a malady which we could not cure. He returned to America, but alas, soon he was dead. No Sir, I would not take you to that place for all the money in the world." Many stories of this type could be told, but we must be content with the incident mentioned by Mark.

The Amplified New Testament translates verses 23 and 24: "Just at that time there was in their synagogue a man who was in the power of an unclean spirit, and now immediately he raised a deep and terrible cry from the depths of his throat, saying. . ." To say the least, this hardly sounds like a man undergoing an attack of epilepsy. This was a face-to-face confrontation with the powers of evil. In ways beyond our finite understanding, the Son of God was being tested and challenged. When the Lord delivered the demoniac, it was another illustration of how coming events cast their shadows before. He came to set the captives free, and what He did in the synagogue, in one way or another, He has been doing ever since.

HIS MARVELOUS POPULARITY. . . expanding

Phillips modern translation of verse 28 is rather attractive. . . "And his reputation spread like wild-fire through the whole Galilean district." Everywhere, people talked about the new preacher. Surely God was visiting His people, but alas, the plaudits of the crowd are never a reliable indication of the spirituality of the people. Within three years those same people were clamoring for His crucifixion. Perhaps we should add a new beatitude to the list already in Matthew's gospel. . . "Blessed are they who last!"

SECTION FIVE

Expository Notes on Christ's Visit to Simon's Home

And forthwith, when they had come out of the synagogue they entered into the house of Simon and Andrew, with James and John. But Simon's wife's mother lay sick of a fever, and anon they tell Him of her. And he came and took her by the hand, and lifted her up; and immediately the fever left her, and she ministered unto them. And at even when the sun did set, they brought unto Him all that were diseased, and them that were possessed with devils. And all the city was gathered together at the door. And He healed many that were sick of diverse diseases, and cast out many devils; and suffered not the devils to speak, because they knew Him (vv. 29-34).

A SPLENDID CONVERT

If I were a pastor, I would like to preach a series of sermons on the subject "Homes Visited by Jesus." The Lord delighted in the opportunities of addressing crowds, but He loved to visit homes. John describes how the Master attended a wedding that surely was held in a home, and there are other examples to be found in the Gospels. This visit to the home of Simon and Andrew is among them. Perhaps it will be wise if we consider the account under three headings.

THE MASTER. . .healing

It has been stated that the main Jewish service in the synagogue generally ended just before noon. If that be the case, it would be safe to assume that Simon and Andrew took the Lord home to lunch. That is the kind of thing we would do if we were placed in similar circumstances. Perhaps they had ulterior motives! Peter's mother-in-law was very sick with a burning fever. The Greek word translated "in a fever" is *puressousa*, which according to Dr. Thayer means "a fiery heat." Elsewhere, words from the same root word are translated "flushed or glowing" or "to be on fire!" It follows therefore that Simon's mother was seriously ill; this was not just a common cold. Her illness seemed to be burning her up; her face was very flushed, and her immediate outlook was bleak. "And *anon*, they tell Him of her." The *Englishman's Greek Testament* translates this in a much stronger way: "And *immediately*, they told Him of her." The best thing to do with any problem is to bring it to Jesus. If He is unable to handle the situation, no one can. . . Gently, the Savior took her hand, and lifting her, completely healed her. Jesus can solve every problem—if He gets a chance!

When I am asked if I believe in all the faith healing movements which are in the world today, I answer, "I do not." Some healing meetings are more like a circus; events which are claimed as modern miracles are spurious, and the people who claim such things in Christ's Name are charlatans doing harm to the Master's cause. I think it is disastrous to claim that a woman has been healed of cancer; to publicize throughout a community that God has done the impossible, when a few months after the press announcement, comes a further announcement that the funeral of the late Mrs. — will take place on Tuesday! The New Testament never reveals that a man healed of lameness had to buy a new pair of crutches after he had discarded the old pair. Bartimeus never had to employ a guide after he had received his sight. The leper never returned to live in his hovel after Christ had made him whole. Furthermore, when Christ placed His peerless hands upon the head of a sufferer, He did not proceed to half-strangle the victim. Not even a hypnotist would do the things now being practiced by healing preachers. Suffering people are punched, squeezed, prodded, and twisted in all sorts of ways in a valiant effort to obtain healing. I do not think the Lord ever did this. I believe He was gentle, good, and kind. *He was never a high-pressure showman.*

During my stay in Africa I often watched *healers* at work in their meetings. I saw how they drove devils from people who believed themselves to be devil-possessed. The display was so disgusting that I greatly desired to deal drastically with the man concerned. The poor victim was punched—yes, punched again and again—, and I left horrified, wondering if this were a softening-up process meant to warn the indwelling devil that worse would follow unless he decided to change his lodgings! I believe that when Jesus approached a man or woman, He did so quietly with dignity and confidence. I believe that living faith shone through His eyes; that His captivating smile encouraged and promoted confidence in the sufferer who struggled against doubt. I believe that when Jesus placed His hand upon the needy, life flowed into the sick frame, and without any sensational show of professional showmanship, the works of Christ glorified God. Furthermore, I believe He could, and would do it again through His people, if certain conditions were fulfilled. His church must be clean (taken from my earlier book, *This I Believe*, pp. 167-168).

THE MOTHER-IN-LAW . . . helping

". . . and immediately the fever left her, *and she ministered unto them*" (v. 31). Martha of Bethany would have loved this woman, for she also believed the best way of showing gratitude to Christ was to feed Him!" Some ill-advised friends might have tried to restrain that mother-in-law. They might have said, "Sit down and rest awhile. Jesus has come to your aid; don't undo all the good He has done. Feed him tomorrow, but for now, be patient and take things easy." That dear woman with one thrust of her resolute arm would have pushed them aside saying, "Get out of my way, I have a job to do." I like her; everybody should like her, for she taught the world an important lesson. The most effective way to pay a debt is to do it as soon as possible with loving service. If the church could sit at her feet for a series of lessons on dedicated service, the world would soon be ablaze with revival fires. Unfortunately, at the present time this is wishful thinking. Christendom is suffering from an acute attack of sleeping-sickness, and for us the malady presents far more problems than the case of a mother-in-law with a burning fever. (See the homily at the end of this chapter.)

THE MULTITUDE...hoping

"And at even, when the sun did set, they brought unto Him all that were diseased, and them that were possessed with devils. And all the city was gathered together at the door. . . ." (vv. 32, 33). The flame of enthusiasm had been lit; the fires were now spreading near and far. Alas, the crowds only came because they wanted something! Few of the people ever came because they loved Him. It is significant that others believed to be possessed of demons were now brought to Jesus. Probably the news of the events in the synagogue had spread, and this resulted in a rush of relatives anxious to see the synagogue miracle repeated.

As a young Christian in Wales, I was privileged to know the influence of two remarkable men of God. Both were medical doctors. Dr.Martyn Lloyd-Jones, before his removal to London, exercised a very successful pastorate in Aberavon, Glamorganshire. To me, and to many others, Dr. Jones was a prince of preachers, and crowded churches awaited his every appearance. Dr. Rendle Short of Bristol was equally great, but he was a teacher—the greatest many had ever heard. For me, particularly, it is interesting to remember again Dr. Short, and to mention something from one of his books. As a surgeon he was interested in all branches of medicine, and his research shed significant light on the ancient belief in demons. The people of the New Testament era appeared to be very interested in the ancient art of trephining. This was the method used in boring a round hole in a person's head. A crown saw was used to remove a piece of bone from the skull in order to relieve pressure. There were occasions when this ancient art was called *trepanning*. Dr. Short cites the fact that in many ancient cemeteries, skulls have been, and are still found with evidence of trepanning. He spoke of one cemetery where, out of the 126 skulls found, six had been trepanned. Furthermore, it was clear from the bone growth that the surgery had been performed during the lifetime of the patient. It was also evident that the hole in the skull was too small to be of any surgical value. The small circular piece of bone was worn as ornament around the neck. It seems the reason for trepanning was to provide means by which demons could escape from the body of the man. It is perfectly logical to assume that if primitive surgeons were prepared to undertake that operation, and if men were prepared to undergo it, their belief in demon possession must have been exceedingly great. This would explain why the news of the exorcising of the demon in the synagogue spread like wild-fire, and all people knowing of a similarly distressed person, hurried to bring that one to Jesus. They were not disappointed, for the Savior was able to meet every demand made upon Him. The scene at the door of Simon's house must have been entrancing. One sun was slowly sinking in the Western sky; the Other was slowly rising with healing in His wings! Happy are they whose eyes are able to recognize beauty in both sunset and sunrise. Sad indeed is the lot of those whose cataracts blind them to both.

SECTION SIX

Expository Notes on Christ's Moments of Solitude

And in the morning, rising up a great while before day, He went out, and departed into a solitary place, and there prayed. And Simon and they that were with him followed after Him. And when they had found Him, they said unto Him, All men seek for thee. And He said unto them, Let us go into the next towns, that I may preach there also: for therefore came I forth (vv. 35-38).

A SACRED COMMUNION

There are four vital details in these few verses, and all should be considered. They are (1) His Problem, (2) His Place, (3) His Prayer, and (4) His Power.

HIS PROBLEM

Although He was the Son of God, Jesus could not live without prayer. This may beget difficulties for some readers, but the fact remains, the Lord, prior to every major decision, talked with God. He enjoyed unlimited power, He was the embodiment of wisdom; yet it was obvious that to Him prayer was an essential for the continuance of His ministry. Every day people followed Him until privacy was an impossibility, and even when He tried to find a solitary place, His disciples followed Him to say, "All men seek for thee." Even today this is the high price that every famous person has to pay for popularity. Members of a Royal Family, every famous film star, every politician or television personality is recognized in the street, on a beach, at a resort or in any other public place. Their patience is often destroyed by reporters, photographers, and even by autograph hunters who persistently follow their hero. If this is still true with modern people, it was much more with Jesus of Nazareth. Each morning, and even after He had retired for the night, people clamored for attention. Relaxation was an impossibility. His problem was very acute, but He solved it by rising to pray when other people were still in bed! When we are tempted to say, "We are too busy to pray," we should remember our Lord. If we are too busy to pray, then we are too busy!

HIS PLACE

". . .a solitary place!" (v. 35). A solitary place is never overcrowded; it is never a holiday resort, and is only known to those persistent souls who look for it. The Psalmist said, "He that dwelleth in *the secret place* of the most High shall abide under the shadow of the Almighty" (Ps. 91:1). *There is such a place, but since it is secret, it must be diligently sought.* It is interesting and thought-provoking to discover that this became a pattern during the Lord's life. When He went to His baptism, He was praying (Luke 3:21). On the Mount of Transfiguration, ". . .as he prayed, the fashion of His countenance was altered. . ." (Luke 9:29). We are also informed that when confronted by the responsible task of choosing His disciples, "He continued all night in prayer to God" (Luke 6:12). When an excited crowd would have made Him their king, "He went up into a mountain apart to pray" (Mark 14:23). We are also told in Mark 14:34 that Jesus prayed in the Garden of Gethsemane. In fact, He prayed at every important phase of His ministry. The Lord knew, and we should know, it is far easier to preach than to pray, but without real prayer, preaching is hot air! Dr. Jowett, the famous British preacher, used to say, "A minister's study should be an upper room, not a lounge." The pastor who kneels in his study stands tall in his pulpit. When a preacher is *run-ragged* all week, from Dan to Beersheba, his congregation easily recognizes "his battery is flat!" When he tries diligently to preach on Sunday morning, he succeeds in getting nowhere! It is always wise to behold the face of God before we even look at church members!

HIS PRAYER

Sometimes in the Gospels, we are allowed to read the words used in the Lord's prayers; at other times we are not given that privilege.

When Jesus prayed, He *prayed*; that is, *He really talked with God*. "Real prayer is not a marvelous display of oratory meant to impress a listening audience; nor is it an appeal for financial assistance when wealthy people are in the meeting. Prayer is the outpouring of a worshipping soul, a confession before God of man's deepest needs. It is very true that God knows our frame and remembers that we are dust; but even so, His superb patience must be greatly tried at times. I have endured many prayer meetings only with a considerable effort. I have silently groaned as certain people recited their news bulletin for Heaven's listening audience. I remember the Christian who used to take God and any other interested party for an excursion each prayer-meeting night. First we were informed what she had told the milkman; then we went down the street to appreciate the trials of the soul as the cost of potatoes went higher; then we had a blast of the husband's irritable nature; and after going here, there, and everywhere, invariably arrived back in time for the benediction. I have often waited to break the bread at the Lord's Table, but I have had to wait a very long time. Brother So-and-So was asked to return thanks for the bread, but in so doing, he managed to pray for missionaries, parliamentarians, crooks, swindlers, house-keepers, tradesmen, and all other sinners. I have known prayers which were not prayers—they were meeting killers..." (taken from *This I Believe*, pp. 162-163). When the Lord prayed, Heaven listened and Hell trembled. "Lord, teach us to pray."

HIS POWER

"And he said unto them, Let us go into the next towns, that I may preach there also; for therefore came I forth" (v. 38). The Reader's Digest *Great Encyclopedic Dictionary* defines *power* as "the right, ability, or capacity to exercise control." That definition covers a large area of life. There is the power to think; the power to live; the power to act. There is the power to achieve great victories and endure crushing disappointments. There is the power to speak wisely and to remain silent, which may be infinitely harder and a lot wiser! The list could be endless, but every detail of our existence may be linked with real prayer. To *love* God is to desire communion with Him; to *share* His desires is to help establish His Kingdom. Real prayer keeps our spiritual batteries fully charged; dedicated service permits the stored energy to shine in the darkness of a needy world. The church of today may organize great movements, raise huge sums of money, and use the most sophisticated equipment; but nothing can ever replace the power of the Holy Spirit operating through the dedicated lives of real Christians. Dr. Graham Scroggie used to say, "It is easier to organize than to agonize," and the quality and success of Dr. Scroggie's ministry proved he knew what he was talking about—he was very close to his Lord and to reality.

SECTION SEVEN

Expository Notes on the Cleansing of the Leper

And He preached in their synagogues throughout all Galilee, and cast out devils. And there came a leper to Him, beseeching Him, and kneeling down to Him, and saying unto Him, If thou wilt, thou canst make me clean. And Jesus moved with compassion, put forth His hand, and touched him, and saith unto him, I will; be thou clean. And as soon as He had spoken, immediately the leprosy departed from him, and he was cleansed. And He straightly charged him, and forthwith sent him away; and saith unto him, See thou say nothing to any man: but go thy way, shew thyself to the priest, and offer for thy cleansing those things which Moses commanded, for a testimony unto them. But he went out, and began to publish it much, and to blaze abroad the matter, insomuch that Jesus could no more openly enter into the city, but was without in desert places: and they came to Him from every quarter (vv. 39-45).

A SUBLIME COMPASSION

Commenting on these verses, Bishop J. C. Ryle writes: "Of all our Lord's miracles of healing, none were probably more marvelous than those performed on leprous people. Two cases only have been fully described in the Gospel history. Of these two, the case before us is one . . . Leprosy is a complaint of which we know little or nothing in our northern climate . . . In Bible lands it is far more common. It is no mere skin infection, as some ignorantly suppose. It is a radical disease of the whole man. It attacks not merely the skin, but the blood, the flesh, and the bones, until the unhappy patient begins to lose his extremities, and to rot by inches. . . . To use the words of Aaron, when he interceded for Miriam, the leper was, 'as one dead, of whom the flesh is half consumed'" (Num. 12:12).

The Hebrew word that is used in Leviticus for leprosy is *tsaraath*. Leviticus 13:47 speaks of a *tsaraath* of garments; and a *tsaraath* of houses is dealt with in Leviticus 14:33. This kind of blemish on a garment would be like a mold or fungus. On a house, it could be a dry-rot in the wood or a destructive lichen in the stone. According to Jewish custom, the word "leprosy" included any type of skin desease. This disease made the sufferer unclean and thus he was turned away from having anything to do with others. He had to stay outside the camp, go with rent clothes, a bare head, and a covering on his upper lip. No matter where he went in this condition, he had to cry out, "unclean, unclean!" During the Middle Ages, lepers were permitted to attend church services, but they were required to stay outside the building and to look through peep-holes specially made for this purpose. Such *lepers'* peep-holes may be seen even today in some of the preserved churches of Norway.

One of the greatest men I ever met was a leper named Paul. I journeyed three thousand miles into the heart of Africa to meet him, for his fame as a Christian counselor had reached the entire continent. He had neither hands nor feet, but his heart was aflame with the love of Christ. When I first saw this remarkable man, my emotions overwhelmed me, and it was very difficult for me to speak. Palestine had many lepers; and at any turn in the road, one could appear uttering the mandatory warning. There was no known cure for leprosy apart from an intervention by God. When the leper came asking help from Jesus, certain things became obvious. Knowing the challenge of the coming day, the Lord had prepared for it by communing with His Father.

DISEASE LEADING TO DEATH

Lepers were required to live apart from all others, except lepers. We do not know how this man heard about the Savior. Had he left his hovel in search of food? Had he been attracted by the shouts of the excited crowd? Was it a coincidence that he happened to be passing near the road upon which Jesus was traveling? We do not know, but, "There came a leper to him, beseeching him . . ." Luke 5:12 adds that the man was "full" of leprosy, which probably means the disease was in a very advanced stage—enough to make the man utterly repulsive. Matthew 8:2 says the "leper came worshipping him." This indicates a degree of faith and love. How this developed within the leper's soul we have not been told. The man was desperate; for unless Jesus came to his assistance, there remained no hope for him. He was dying. There is a modern leprosy called sin; happy indeed is the soul who knows that in such a situation only Jesus of Nazareth has a cure!

DESIRE LEADING TO DELIVERANCE

"And Jesus, moved with compassion, put forth His hand, and touched him, and saith unto him, I will; be thou clean. And as soon as He had spoken, immediately, the leprosy departed from him, and he was cleansed" (v. 41, 42). What compassion! The man had no right to approach any clean person; he had broken the law, and was in great danger. He had, by his rash act, endangered the health of clean people. Jesus did not condemn him; He saw not a law-breaker but a human in great need. The Lord actually touched him which was tantamount to committing suicide! Probably that poor man had not felt another human touch, since the day he became afflicted. The leper's rash action endangered his own life, but probably he decided he had nothing to lose—he was dying anyway! The old philosophy has always been true—nothing attempted, nothing gained! The best thing to do with any problem is to bring it to Christ. If He cannot help, no one can.

DISOBEDIENCE LEADING TO DIFFICULTIES

According to the Levitical law, a leper who believed he had been cleansed, was required to present himself before the priest for an official examination. Real leprosy was incurable, but some of the other skin diseases could be cured. When this took place, official recognition had to be obtained, before the leper was permitted to take his place among men. Certain offerings had to be made, and it was for this reason that Jesus commanded the man to "offer for thy cleansing those things which Moses commanded, for a testimony unto them" (v. 44). Unless the man did as he was required, he could have been arrested by the authorities. Jesus was careful to remind the fellow of his duty. In addition, his testimony would carry the Good News to priests who might otherwise never hear it. That the man disobeyed the Lord brings mixed emotions to our hearts. The cleansing of a leper was certain to create great excitement. Thousands of people crowding narrow streets might bring danger to individuals, and anger from the authorities. Therefore, the Lord wisely commanded the man to remain silent. The man's disobedience made it necessary for the Lord to retire into the desert. His enthusiastic testimony hindered other sufferers who might have found it difficult to travel. There are times when enthusiasm runs away with brains! Happy and wise are they who know when to speak, and when to say nothing.

HOMILIES

Study No. 1

REPENTANCE...The First Word in the Gospels

"John did...preach the baptism of repentance for the remission of sins" (v. 4). When he did this, he followed in the footsteps of all the preachers God ever sent to sinful men. We are told in 2 Peter 2:5 that Noah was *a preacher of righteousness*, and when we remember the type of people among whom he lived and ministered, it is easy to understand why he denounced the sins rampant in his day. We are also informed in Jonah 1:2 that the unwilling prophet was commissioned to "...cry against Nineveh, for their wickedness is come up before me." Jonah ran away, only to discover he could not outrun God. That he was brought back to complete his assignment is evidence that the longsuffering of God is tremendous.

GOD'S CONCERN...Requesting

One of the most delightful verses in the Bible is found in Isaiah 1:18 where God says, "Come now, and let us reason together, saith the Lord: though your sins be as scarlet, they shall be as white as snow; though they be red like crimson, they shall be as wool." When we consider the holiness of God and compare and contrast it with the sinfulness of man, it must be an everlasting cause for wonderment that He should ever love humans. That He should appeal to us to draw near and to reason with Him is something difficult to comprehend. He is so great; we are so small. He has everything; we have and are nothing. Surely, He must love us immensely. It suggests that Solomon in all his splendor would invite a penniless, dirty tramp into the palace to discuss what should be done about life's problems. God said "Come." People who refuse are very stupid!

GOD'S COMMAND...Repenting

During the speech which Paul made at Mars' Hill, the apostle said, "Now while it is true, that God has overlooked the days of ignorance, He now commands all men everywhere to repent. For He has fixed a day on which He will judge the whole world in justice by the standards of a man whom He has appointed. That this is so He has guaranteed to all men by raising this from the dead'' (Acts 17:30-31, PHILLIPS). Repentance is based upon the indisputable fact that man in his sinful condition is totally unacceptable to God. This state of affairs cannot be permitted to continue eternally, so, obviously, there must be a day when God will terminate what is now being permitted. There will be a day of judgment when sinners reap what they have sown. The only means of escape from the eternal catastrophe is supplied by forgiveness, and since this is only made possible by repentance, the concern of God commands all men, everywhere, to repent. This has always been the first step toward Heaven. The Pharisee, who stood and prayed thanking God he was not as other men, never reached the first milestone on the heavenly highway. The Publican who exclaimed, ''God be merciful to me a sinner,'' was halfway there even before he took a step (Luke 18:9-14).

GOD'S CONDITION. . .Resolving

"And the Lord appeared unto Solomon by night, and said unto him. . .If my people, which are called by my name, shall humble themselves, and pray, and seek my face, *and turn from their wicked ways*; then will I hear from heaven, and will forgive their sins, and will heal their land" (2 Chron. 7:12-14). It is impossible to over-emphasize the little word *If*. There is much blessing which God desires to bestow upon humans. There is much spiritual wealth He desires to share, but there is a very simple condition with which we must comply. Repentance not only means *remorse*; it also demands *resolve*. John's mode of baptism was by immersion in which the candidate was buried in water. This signified the termination of one kind of life and the birth of another. This, and only this, was *the baptism of repentance unto the remission of sins*. If a man professed he was forsaking his idolatry, only to return to his idols at the first opportunity, then his baptism was foolish and a waste of time. Similarly, the convert who shed many tears as evidence of his sincerity, and who later returned to his former practices, was only making a mockery of the most sacred things in the Christian faith. Remorse must be followed by resolve. . .never to worship idols again. This was the essence of every message preached by God's anointed messengers.

GOD'S COMPASSION. . .Receiving

During one of His discourses, the Lord said, "whosoever shall receive me, receiveth Him that sent me. . ." (Luke 9:48). It is true that this was mentioned in connection with the value of a child, but nevertheless, that simple statement sums up the Gospel. Jesus taught that He had the full and complete confidence of God; that He spake as God, and that all He said and did was in alignment with the will of the Father. He affirmed that He only was the way to the realms of the blessed. He said, "I am the way, the truth, and the life; no man cometh unto the Father, but by me" (John 14:6). If remorse reveals sickness, resolve indicates a determination to do something about the problem. Christ completes the cycle by instructing where to go to find what is needed. He said, "Come unto me, all ye that labour and are heavy laden, and I will give you rest" (Matt. 11:28). The penitent soul turning from sin, embraces the Savior. Repentance toward God leads to faith in our Lord Jesus Christ. This was the Gospel preached by Paul (Acts 20:21) and as far as the Word of God is concerned, *there is no other Gospel able to meet man's need.*

HOMILIES

Study No. 2

GOD-GIVEN OPPORTUNITIES

Mark in his Gospel provides one of the most entrancing scenes in all New Testament history. His writings take us into the home of Simon Peter. The household was hushed! Jesus had been taken into the mother-in-law's bedroom. The lady was very sick, but some of the people believed Jesus could restore her health. Could it be true? And then the door opened, and they saw her, radiant with health and purpose. Her old cheerful self, she elbowed the onlookers out of the way as she walked toward the khtchen. The Master was hungry; she had a job to do. Doubtless, she did it well. Other Bible characters were not as industrious!

A LOST MAN. . .Dying

Calvary's Hill had become strangely quiet! The crowd which had demanded Christ's death, now seemed fascinated as they watched their victim. Even the soldiers were staring hard at the One whose hands they had nailed to the cross. One of the criminals crucified with Jesus had electrified the crowd with a strange request. He had asked for admittance to Paradise, and Jesus, acknowledging the request, had given peace to the suppliant. It was all so strange. How could He possibly do such a thing? Was He not another common criminal? But there was another man whose raucus voice disturbed the silence. He was swearing at everybody. Why did he not keep his mouth shut? He was disturbing everyone; he was a nuisance. A soldier should quiet the fellow! There was no need; death was about to silence him for ever. What a shame! His companion had found eternal peace, and that same peace might have filled the soul of the second thief. Alas he might have become famous, but he lost his opportunity. He was at the very door of Heaven, but his stupidity, not the nails, prevented his entrance.

A LEARNED MAN. . .Delaying

The Supreme Court was hushed! An outstanding Doctor of the Law was about to address the Assembly. Those pesky Jewish preachers should be taken to the waiting room; why should their presence defile the chamber? "The honorable Member will now speak:" "Then stood there up one in the council, a Pharisee, named Gamaliel, a doctor of the law, had a reputation among all the people, and commanded to put the apostles forth a little space." The man was a genius; his knowledge of historical events was vast and unassailable. The audience listened carefully, as he proceeded to explain his philosophy. What a speaker! What a man! He was nearing conclusion. "And now I say unto you, Refrain these men, and let them alone: for if this counsel or this be of men, it will come to nought. But if it be of God, ye cannot overthrow it; lest haply ye be found to fight against God. Gentlemen; be wise, do nothing. Just wait and see." And, apparently, that is exactly what he did for the rest of his life. When the power of the risen Christ turned the world upside down, Gamaliel remained in the background. He watched the game; he even appreciated some of the players; but he never became a participant; he was too scared of getting hurt (see Acts 5:34-42).

A LITTLE MAN. . .Deciding

The street was crowded with excited people, and the little businessman could not conceal his curiosity. What in the wide world was happening?

And Zaccheus, went out of his office to meet the most wonderful Man he had ever seen. "And he sought to see Jesus WHO HE WAS!" We cannot help but ask where had Zaccheus been during the amazing three years of Christ's ministry. Surely all people knew WHO JESUS WAS! No, the tax-gatherer, so hated by the citizens because he worked for the accursed Romans, had reciprocated; he hated them also. He only saw people; and because he was so short, they probably appeared to be very tall—and very big, hypocrites. But the excitement in the street was irresistible. Something was happening, and suddenly he ceased looking at Jews. He was sick of them anyway. Thank God for making trees; they were perfect grandstands from which to see the show! "And Jesus...saw him.... And Zaccheus made haste, and came down, and received him joyfully." And that night they had dinner together. Simon's mother-in-law would have loved the little tax-gatherer. He seized his opportunity (see Luke 19:1-10).

A LIBERATED MAN...Declaring

The former demoniac was climbing the hill; he was intensely grateful, very puzzled, and a little apprehensive. He paused to look back, and his face reflected a keen disappointment. His Friend, Jesus of Nazareth, was in that little fishing boat going further and further away. Those stupid people and their swine! They had asked Him to go away, and He had gone. "Why could I not also be in that boat?" No, he had a job to do. Jesus had asked him to testify in the village and he would do it, if it killed him! He would never be able to forget the Lord, Who said, "Return to thine own house, and shew how great things God hath done unto thee." Yes, he was determined to do it even though he got laryngitis! "And he went his way and published throughout the whole city how great things Jesus had done unto him" (see Luke 9:37-39). If that man had ever met Saul of Tarsus, they would have talked for hours! Real opportunities for service may seem rare, and yet they are all around us—they are everywhere. Perhaps we need to have the cataracts removed from our eyes, and the lethargy from our souls. We remain tired and inactive. Let us remember the words spoken by God to Moses, "Speak unto the children of Israel that THEY GO FORWARD!" (Exod. 14:15).

HOMILIES

Study No. 3

THE PRIESTS...Who Became Converts

(Acts 6:7)

"And the work of God increased; and the number of the disciples multiplied in Jerusalem greatly; *and a great company of the priests were obedient to the faith.*" It is not unlikely that the final statement in this verse represents a triumph of patient perseverance in the art of soul-winning.

TESTIMONY No. One...Matthew 8:4

Perhaps some of the priests were sitting around their table, when the ominous knock sounded at the door. Someone was in a hurry! When one of the number opened the door, he saw a rather dilapidated beggar—or so he thought. Here was another fellow who thought all priests were millionaires! "Yes, and what do you want?" "I want to give you something, Sir. Moses said that if a leper were cleansed, he should offer certain things according to the law, and I want to do that." The words tumbled from the man's lips, and he seemed possessed by a strange excitement. The priest looked at him. A leper—cleansed! What nonsense! "Yes, Priest, I was a leper without hope when Jesus found me. Perhaps I should say that I found Him, for I ran and fell at his feet, and said, 'Lord, if thou wilt, thou canst make me clean', and He touched me and I was cleansed immediately. Then he reminded me of my duty to go to the priests, and here I am." When the priest had attended to the requirements of the stranger, he returned to his colleagues; and that evening, they surely had great discussions. Then, as always, it was one thing to dismiss Jesus of Nazareth as a fanatical imposter, but quite another to account for the wonder of His miracles.

TESTIMONY No. Two...Luke 17:14

The priest could hardly believe his ears! Nine men standing around the doorway maintained they had all been lepers. They were very poor; their garments were tattered, and everything about their appearance suggested hardship—but lepers! No! "Yes Sir, we were all lepers and we stood and cried, 'Jesus, Master, have mercy on us'. He heard us and told us to come and see you." "And were you cleansed then?" "No Sir, we heard His voice but we were still lepers. Yet, He commanded us to come. We obeyed, and as we walked along the street, power came into our bodies and we were made clean." Some time later, the priest was recalled to the door to find another man who claimed he was the tenth member of the original party. He had returned to Christ to give thanks, and was a little late in presenting himself to the priest. He reiterated all that had already been told to the priest, and once again the great men of the temple faced the challenge of the Nazarene. We shall never know how close they came to believing in Christ at that time; but when Jesus died, it seemed the new movement would die with Him.

TESTIMONY No. Three...Acts 3:1-8

It was the hour of prayer and some of the priests would be officiating within the sacred house. Outside, the city was agog with excitement. People were saying that Jesus of Nazareth had risen from the dead, and great public meetings had brought the enthusiasm of the crowds to fever pitch. Everywhere men and women talked of the great occurrence, and it was rumored that thousands of converts had been won for the new movement. The priests waited expectantly, for some of the strange preachers would be coming to pray. Suddenly there was a loud commotion outside the building, and as the door opened, the waiting men saw a great crowd being led by an apparently hysterical man who jumped, and danced, and shouted. "And they knew that it was he which sat for alms at the Beautiful gate of the temple; and they were filled with wonder and amazement at that which had happened to him." When Peter explained how the lame man had been made whole, the priests realized that once again the power of Jesus had been made manifest. And this time, the great leaders refused to postpone their decision. They could not remain secret followers of Christ, when their hearts thrilled at the mention of His Name. That day, they left all and followed the Savior. And the moral of the story for all soul winners is: "If at first you don't succeed, try, try again" (taken from the author's commentary, *Luke's Thrilling Gospel*, pp. 126-127).

The Second Chapter of Mark

THEME: *The Winds of Criticism Begin to Blow*

OUTLINE:
   I. The Lord's Enemies Criticize His Claim
      (Verses 1-12)
  II. The Lord's Enemies Criticize His Conduct (Verses
      13-22)
 III. The Lord's Enemies Criticize His Companions
      (Verses 23-28)

SECTION ONE...CRITICIZING HIS CLAIM

Expository Notes on the Healing of the Sick Man

**And again He entered into Capernaum, after some days; and it was
noised that He was in the house. And straightway many were gathered
together, insomuch that there was no room to receive them, no, not
so much as about the door; and He preached the word unto them
(vv. 1-2).**

When the leper's indiscreet testimony made it necessary for the Lord
to retire to the desolate areas in the locality, Jesus and all who
accompanied Him, began to recognize the impossibility of escaping the
crowds. They followed Him everywhere. How He managed to return
unnoticed to Capernaum we have not been told. "...*after some days,
it was rumored that He was in the house...*" (v. 1). We cannot avoid
the question, "Whose house?" *The Amplified New Testament* suggests
it was Peter's house, but there are difficulties in accepting this theory.
Other translators simply refer to it as "a house" that is, the Lord had
obtained a place in Capernaum, and this was his home during the frequent
visits to that city. There are reasons for believing this is more acceptable
than the earlier suggestions. Matthew wrote: "Now when Jesus had
heard that John was cast into prison, he departed into Galilee. And
leaving Nazareth, *He came and dwelt in Capernaum*, which is upon

the sea coast, in the borders of Zabulon and Nephthalim'' (4:12-12). Furthermore, Matthew placed this ahead of the call of Simon and the other fishermen (4:18-22). Probably the home of Simon and Andrew was not large; it belonged to fishing folk, and might have been a little overcrowded! Simon's mother-in-law lived with her daughter, so the possibility exists that already two bedrooms were occupied. It is a little difficult to envisage a three bedroom home belonging to an ordinary fisherman. If the Lord *stayed* in Simon's home, and if as was the case later, He was accompanied by His disciples, it would have been an inconvenience to those already occupying the home. It seems more likely, as Matthew suggests, that when Jesus left Nazareth, he obtained a home somewhere in Capernaum, and this for a time at least, was the place in which He stayed when visiting the city. It will be remembered that many years later, Paul similarly rented a house in Rome (see Acts 28:30). By doing this, perhaps he was emulating his Lord's example.

That the Savior had been able to enjoy a time of seclusion and rest suggests He had reached his home unnoticed; maybe He had returned during hours of darkness. Eventually someone either saw Him, or heard about His presence there, and soon the news of His arrival spread. One translator says, ''it spread like wildfire!'' Among the working class people there were very few pretentious homes. Often there was no entrance hall; the door opened to the living room. Most Palestinian homes consisted of one split-level room. At the end was a raised platform-like section which the family used as a sleeping place. During the day, the lower section was used for living and dining purposes. When the members of the family retired to sleep, the lower section was occupied by any animals which could be brought through the doorway. Thieves were abundant in the country, and whenever possible, animals were brought indoors at night to prevent their being stolen. If the house to which the Lord came—whether it were his own or the home of Simon, is not of great importance—if the house were one of the usual homes found in the Middle East, it is easy to understand why it became so crowded. The increasing number of people from Capernaum soon filled the building, the entrance, and even any courtyard which might have been there. Usually, even today, in those very hot lands, doors are left open for ventilation purposes. The people rushed forward until movement was almost impossible.

''. . .and He preached the word unto them'' (v.2). This is truly significant. The healing of a man's soul is always far more important than the restoration of his health. We are informed elsewhere in the

Gospels that a man who had been healed was told "...Behold, thou art made whole: sin no more, lest a worst thing come upon thee" (John 5:14). At best, physical healing lasted only until death finally claimed the body. Spiritual healing, which emancipated a soul from the grip of sin, continued for ever. There was excitement, thrills, and attraction in healing meetings. People flocked to see "signs and wonders," but soul-stirring sermons were not as popular. The Lord was very conscious of that danger when He said, "Except ye see signs and wonders, ye will not believe" (John 4:48). We must remember the words spoken to Thomas: "...Thomas, because thou hast seen me, thou hast believed: *blessed are they that have not seen, and yet have believed*" (John 20:29). The sincerity of souls can always be measured by what they are willing to give, and not by what they hope to receive.

And they come unto Him, bringing one sick of the palsy, which was borne of four. And when they could not come nigh unto Him for the press, they uncovered the roof where He was; and when they had broken it up, they let down the bed wherein the sick of the palsy lay (vv. 3-4).

One translator explains that "*they were discussing the Word!*" We have not been told what part of the Scriptures was being considered, but suddenly, in the midst of their discussion, a small party of people arrived bringing a man sick with the palsy. They had either found their neighbor, or had responded to his request for assistance. Later in the story we are told how Jesus recognized *their faith*. It is, therefore, obvious that these men, having heard about the miracle performed by Jesus, were not convinced He could heal their friend. The very large crowd momentarily challenged them. Either they had to abandon their plans, or find a way by which they could bring the sufferer to the Lord. The roof of a Palestinian house was flat, and was a place where the family could enjoy a siesta. Sometimes it was used as a place of storage. Among the working class people, homes were primitively constructed. Wooden beams, about two or three feet apart, were placed across the stone walls of the structure, and between these beams, brushwood was tightly packed. The whole thing was finally cemented together by mud dried in the sun. This helped to insulate the interior against cold in winter and heat in summer.

I have seen such buildings where earth had been deposited all over the roof where grass grew plentifully. Always an outside stairway led to the roof, and obviously this was the type of house in which the Lord was teaching. Someone in the small party of five people looked at the stairway and suggested a way of bypassing the excited crowd. Vincent, in *The Amplified New Testament* writes, "And when they could not get him to a place in front of Jesus because of the throng, *they dug through the roof above him, and when they had scooped out an opening*, they let down the (thickly padded) quilt or mat, upon which the paralyzed man lay."

Today in Middle Eastern countries, tremendous changes have taken place. The homes are modern and the architecture vastly different from what was normal two thousand years ago. Yet, when visitors to Israel, Jordan and Egypt take time to travel into country areas, the same kind of home can still be seen. It would be a simple task to do exactly what the four men did when they "dug" through the roof. They found the space between the beams, and commenced digging. Breaking the covering of clay or dried mud, they removed the closely packed brushwood, and there beneath them was the interior of the home. Furthermore, when the job was finished and their purpose gained, it would be comparatively easy to repair the damage.

It must have been a strange and wonderful moment when dirt began falling on the heads of that household congregation; when looking up, they saw the faces of men silhouetted against the sky. Everybody watched as the sick man was gently lowered to the floor, and some were surprised when Jesus, having ceased teaching, said, "*Son, thy sins be forgiven thee*" (v. 5). Recognizing that the sufferer and his companions shared a common faith, "when he saw THEIR faith," Jesus responded by absolving the palsied man from guilt. Then and now, pardon is always better than the palsy! Nevertheless, it must be recognized that the man had not come to obtain forgiveness for sin. He sought healing for his body and not his soul. Here we have a rare insight into the amazing knowledge of the Savior. John wrote: "Jesus saw Nathanael coming to him, and saith of him, Behold an Israelite indeed, in whom is no guile. Nathanael saith unto Him, whence knowest thou me? Jesus answered and said unto him, Before that Philip called thee, when thou wast under the fig tree, I saw thee" (John 1:47-48). As Christ was able to see Nathanael under the tree, so He saw all that had happened in the life of the palsied man. We all know that sickness came into the world because of Adam's sin, but it does not necessarily follow that all sickness is the direct outcome of an individual's personal shortcomings. To say or even infer that a man is suffering because he has violated a law of God is wrong. Sometimes God permits His children to walk in the darkness, so that they might cling all the more to His outstretched hand. During the stilling of the storm, the disciples learned

more in the boat than they ever would have, had they stayed on the
beach. Daniel would never have known God's power to shut the mouths
of lions had he not been sent into the den. History attests the simple
fact that some of God's best saints have suffered most, and yet, their
affliction brought them nearer to Christ.

The man sick with the palsy was different. He had sinned; he knew
it, and so did Christ. Somewhere in the man's past was a regrettable
mistake; the memory of his indiscretion, whatever it might have been,
had remained with him. Worry, frustration, guilt, increased his anguish,
and one thing led to another until the man's health was undermined.
He seemed to be beyond aid. There is nothing too hard for Jesus, but,
to use a modern illustration, before the Lord commenced the mopping
up operation within the man's heart, He carefully turned off the running
faucet, the cause of all the trouble! "Thy sins be forgiven thee." Let
it be carefully noted that never at any time did the man deny or protest
what had been inferred by the Lord. It is extremely difficult to argue
against anyone who is sure of his facts.

**When Jesus saw their faith, He said unto the sick of the palsy, Son,
thy sins be forgiven thee. But there were certain of the scribes sitting
there, and reasoning in their hearts, Why doth this man thus speak
blasphemies? who can forgive sins but God only? (vv. 5-7).**

The Jewish Sanhedrin was the supreme court of the nation; its members
were responsible for the enforcement of the Mosaic law, and any man
accused of violating the fundamentals of the Jewish faith was tried and
sentenced by this council. Their basic teaching claimed that God was
Supreme; that He alone could authorize pardon for an offender. People
accused of blasphemy could expect no sympathy. It was this Court which
was responsible for the trial and sentencing of the Savior, and later,
this same Assembly brought accusations against Paul and the other
leaders of the early Church. Probably the leaders of the nation had heard
of the ministry and message of Jesus, and believing a threat to their
own authority and prestige might be forthcoming from the new Preacher,
they sent out a scouting party to ascertain what was taking place in
Capernaum. Luke informs us that: " . . . as He was teaching, there were
Pharisees and doctors of the law sitting by, which were come out of
every town of Galilee, and Judaea, and Jerusalem; and the power of
the Lord was present to heal them" (Luke 5:17) (see the homily at the
end of this chapter). These emissaries of the Sanhedrin, had in all
probability occupied seats where they could hear everything spoken by

Jesus. When He announced the palsied man had been forgiven, they were astounded; for this, to them, was evidence of blasphemy. Luke says "they were *thinking* about the problem." Matthew says "...they were thinking evil in their hearts." It would appear that nothing was said; that the concern, the criticism, at that point in time, was unspoken. That Jesus challenged them even before they uttered a word, suggests His ability to read minds. It was a staggering thought that a Carpenter from Nazareth should have the audacity to take the place of the Almighty. Had we been in their place, we might have acted as they did. Their condemnation was deserved, not because they questioned the Lord's sincerity, but because they rejected evidence that was shortly to be forthcoming. There is a vast difference between *doubt* and *rejection*. Doubt, under some circumstances may be tolerated, but rejection of truth is inexcusable.

And immediately when Jesus perceived in His spirit that they so reasoned within themselves, He said unto them, Why reason these things in your hearts? Whether it is easier to say to the sick of the palsy, Thy sins be forgiven thee; or to say, Arise, and take up thy bed, and walk. But that ye may know that the Son of man hath power on earth to forgive sins, He saith to the sick of the palsy, I say unto thee, Arise and take up thy bed, and go thy way into thine house. And immediately he arose, took up the bed, and went forth before them all; insomuch that they were all amazed, and glorified God, saying, We never saw it on this fashion (vv. 8-12).

The critics must have been most embarrassed when they were suddenly confronted by a very simple challenge. That the larger audience listened to every word only deepened and intensified their embarrassment. Any man, either sane or insane; innocent or blasphemous; wise or foolish, could say, "Thy sins are forgiven." However outrageous the statement, in the final analysis, it would be one man's word against another man's questioning. Yet, if a teacher said, "Take up thy bed and walk" only to see the sick man remaining on his bed; that teacher would appear to be foolish. Actions sometimes are more eloquent than words, and knowing this to be true, Jesus said to the palsied man, "Arise, and take up thy bed, and go thy way into thine house" (v. 11). The greatest evidence for Christ has been, and always will be, His power to transform men. One miracle is worth a thousand sermons!

The Lord's statement, "Thy sins be forgiven thee," has caused endless discussion. Church Councils, large and small, have engaged in debates which sometimes were extremely bitter. Sects of many kinds have propagated their own brand of doctrine, and today, ordinary listeners hardly know what to believe. It might help readers if the possibilities are briefly summarized.

1. Did Christ utter those words because He had been empowered by God to forgive sins? Did He act as *the representative* of God in forgiving the sins of the palsied man? There can only be one king in a kingdom; but if that king should appoint a trusted friend to act in his stead, then the word of the appointee would represent the desires of the monarch. The king would honor what the designated official said and did. Similarly, if God's representative had announced a pardon, then the man was surely forgiven.

2. Was Christ merely explaining a very simple fact? The Grace of God has always responded to faith—*real faith*. It was obvious that this man had already believed, for otherwise it would have been folly to break up the roof of a home which was not his own. Recognizing true faith, did Christ announce that forgiveness was granted because faith had made pardon possible? "If we confess our sins, He is faithful and just to forgive us our sins" (1 John 1:9). If therefore a pastor or priest, or any other person hears a penitent confessing sin to God, the Christian worker is justified in telling the suppliant that his sins have been forgiven. This is so, not because some special power has been vested in the clergyman, but because that Christian worker has enough wisdom to know that God will not break His promise. When a counselor introduces a man to Christ, he is authorized to inform the convert that God has accepted him. Such a statement should never be criticized. Christ said, "Him that cometh unto me, I will in no wise cast out" (John 6:37), and that promise is sufficient authorization for a pastor to say to his charge, "Thy sins are forgiven." When he does this, he is not usurping the authority or power of God by rash statements; he is simply relying on the promises of the Almighty, Who cannot lie.

3. If God only can forgive sins, did Jesus make His statement because He did have that power—*for He was God*? In the eyes and ears of the critics, this seemed blasphemy, when in reality, He was only speaking the truth. John said, "In the beginning was the Word, and the Word was with God, and the Word was God" (John 1:1). The charge made against Jesus was, "This man maketh himself equal with God" (see John 5:18). Let it be fully considered that never on any occasion did the Lord deny the accusation. Although temporarily He had laid aside the robes of His majesty, He nevertheless remained as He had always been—"He whose goings forth have been from of old, from everlasting" (Micah 5:2).

There is every reason to believe that the man sick with the palsy would have had little interest in the theological questions asked by the critics. Since they could not refute his healing, their arguments were unimportant. It is better to "get up and walk" than to remain in bed solving puzzles!

SECTION TWO...CRITICIZING HIS CONDUCT

Expository Notes on the Supper in Matthew's Home

And He went forth again by the sea side; and all the multitude resorted unto Him, and He taught them. And as He passed by, He saw Levi the son of Alphaeus sitting at the receipt of custom, and said unto him, Follow me. And he arose and followed Him (vv. 13-14).

The cold winds of criticism were indeed beginning to blow. The authorities in Jerusalem had become suspicious of the Nazarene preacher, and their spies were following Him everywhere. The doors of the synagogues were closed to Him, and it had become evident that "He had come unto His own, and His own had received Him not" (John 1:12). From this time onward His parish would be along the seashore; the open air would be His cathedral, and the common people his congregation. If He could not occupy the Jewish pulpit, then He would borrow a fisherman's boat!

A GRATEFUL MAN...inviting

Apart from Jerusalem, Capernaum was probably the most important place in the country. Situated at the north-west corner of the Sea of Galilee, it was a most strategic place for the collection of customs dues. A main highway, built by the Romans ran north and south; another ran east and west. Along these main arteries came caravans carrying the wealth of the nations. Gold, silver, precious spices, cloth, silk, ivory, and many more desirable commodities were brought in abundance, and this presented a tremendous opportunity for the tax gatherers to become wealthy. Capernaum was one of a group of nine cities, each with a population of 15,000 or more inhabitants. Every industry connected with fishing such as the making and repairing of nets and boats, the catching and preservation of fish, the production of sails, etc., provided employment for a host of people. Determined to reap a financial harvest, Caesar had commissioned his tax gatherers to get as much money as possible from everybody. The officials were given a franchise; they were expected to reach a certain quota, but anything in excess of the stated figure, they kept. Many of the more unscrupulous tax gatherers had become wealthy at the expense of their victims. Everybody detested the tax collectors, for the officials were experts at swindling their own people. Yet, there was not much that ordinary folk could do about the matter, for the tramp of soldiers was a constant reminder that the power of Rome was there to suppress insurrection. One of the detested tax gatherers was named Levi. He was the son of Alphaeus. Matthew in his gospel (9:9) says the name of the man was Matthew. Luke (5:27) uses the name Levi. It would seem that the tax-gatherer was known by two names...Matthew-Levi. This was not uncommon in those days. It was possible to stand in the doorway of Matthew's custom house and watch the world go by.

The fact that Jesus had made his headquarters in the city brought Matthew or Levi in close proximity to the work of the new movement, and it is probable that sometimes the tax man watched Jesus either going or returning from some mission. Matthew knew he was despised; he worked for the enemy, and had surrendered every claim to moral integrity. No one could do as he had done, without inviting the taunts and jeers of other citizens. All tax gatherers were regarded as traitors to their country; their money was considered to be tainted, and it would not be accepted in the synagogue. Even their testimony was refused in the courts. In some senses they were as defiled as were the lepers! What Matthew-Levi thought when he considered Jesus, we may never know. Perhaps his heart yearned for a peace seemingly beyond his grasp, but his position seemed hopeless. And then one day, the Lord stopped before Matthew's seat of custom. His penetrating eyes looked into the depth of the tax gatherer's soul, and Matthew's heart was stirred. When Christ invited him to become a disciple, the official left everything. His conversion was a miracle; he probably gave up more than any other disciple. Peter, John, and the others could always return to their fishing boats, but when Matthew left his job, there could be no return. His position would be taken by another man. It has been said, "He left all, *but his pen*," to follow Jesus.

This in itself is thought-provoking. Throughout the rest of this and the other Gospels, Matthew is never mentioned by name again, except in those places where the disciples are named together. We are told that on the day of Pentecost, "...Peter, standing up with the eleven, lifted up his voice..." (Acts 2:14) and preached. Matthew is not mentioned by name, but he was there with the others to give moral support to his gifted fisherman-brother. Matthew was not a preacher, nor an administrator; he was a man of the pen, a keeper of records. He was accustomed to working as he sat at a table, and not when he stood in a pulpit. Probably, when he left his customs house, he put his pen in his pocket, and ever afterward he knew where to find it!

We might be tempted to ask why the Lord called a man who obviously would be of little use in evangelizing the world. It is not difficult to supply an answer. Matthew had a special talent not possessed by the others. He was a gatherer of facts, and this became increasingly obvious as he wrote the details of the Lord's messages, and eventually produced his gospel. The Sermon on the Mount; the Parables of the Kingdom are unique in Matthew's Gospel, and to that author the Christian church will always be indebted. The Lord knew exactly what He was doing when He paused that day, at the seat of custom in Capernaum. When the tax gatherer responded and issued an invitation to supper, the Lord's eyes became pools of delight. If the rulers of the synagogues had closed their doors, then somehow, somewhere, God would open other doors. Matthew's response indicated this was already beginning to happen.

And it came to pass that, as Jesus sat at meat in his house, many publicans and sinners sat also together with Jesus and His disciples; for there were many, and they followed Him. And when the scribes and Pharisees saw Him eat with publicans and sinners, they said unto His disciples, How is it that He eateth and drinketh with publicans and sinners? When Jesus heard it, He saith unto them, They that are whole have no need of the physician, but they that are sick: I came not to call the righteous, but sinners to repentance (vv. 15-17).

A GREAT MURMURING. . .increasing

That Matthew acted as host for a great many guests suggests he was a wealthy man. Maybe, as a gatherer of taxes he had made a lot of money. On the other hand, he might have been wealthy in his own right; he could have inherited the money. We cannot be sure. We know that as soon as he became a follower of Jesus, he longed to share his Lord with his friends. That all these could be called *publicans and sinners* suggests he had no friends among the scribes and Pharisees. They hated him. He had deliberately associated himself with the enemies of his nation, and had accepted a job which automatically severed him from all respectable and orthodox citizens. When Jesus accepted the invitation to join the outcasts of society, He actually challenged all that the Pharisees considered to be essential and sacred. The strict law-keeper could not have fellowship with the Pharisees nor could he do any business in any way with them. Of course, he could not have his daughter marry a Pharisee. By having fellowship with Matthew and his friends, Christ was going against the Jewish customs of His day.

Thus, in this undisguised manner, Christ declared war on traditions, systems and practices which had been made by men and were in open conflict with everything suggesting the all-embracing mercy of God. It was to be expected, therefore, that His enemies would criticize His actions. When they expressed surprise that He should join such people, Jesus responded by saying only sick people sought the aid of a physician. That is, He was trying to tell them that only people *WHO KNEW THEIR PHYSICAL NEEDS* sought aid from a physician. This did not infer that the Pharisees had no need, but it did suggest that their eyes had never been opened to see that fact. Smug in their conceit and self-righteousness, they would resent any insinuation that they were displeasing to God. Let it be candidly admitted that many of their descendants live today! To recognize spiritual need is tremendous, but to discover where that need can be met is probably the greatest discovery man will ever make. Matthew had no illusions about this matter. He had met Jesus of Nazareth, and what had happened in the depths of his own soul could easily take place in the experience of his friends. With that in mind he invited them to supper. Happy and wise are they who share the desire to bring others to Christ. When the Lord said, ''I came not to call the righteous, but sinners to repentance'' (v. 17), He expressed the heart of His message and the sole purpose of His mission.

If the critics had known the Scriptures, they would have realized instantly that in God's sight, there were no people who could truly be classed as righteous. David had written, ''The Lord looked down from heaven upon the children of men, to see if there were any that did understand, and seek God. They are all gone aside, they are altogether become filthy: there is none that doeth good, no, not one'' (Ps. 14:2-3). Quoting this scripture, Paul said, ''As it is written, there is none righteous, no, not one: there is none that understandeth, there is none that seeketh after God. They are all gone out of the way, they are together become unprofitable; there is none that doeth good, no, not one'' (Rom. 3:10-12). The scribes were in greater danger than the people they abhorred. Alas, they were too blind to recognize that important fact.

And the disciples of John and of the Pharisees used to fast: and they come and say unto Him, Why do the disciples of John and of the Pharisees fast, but thy disciples fast not? And Jesus said unto them, Can the children of the bridechamber fast, while the bridegroom is with them? As long as they have the bridegroom with them they cannot fast. But the days will come, when the bridegroom shall be taken away from them, and then shall they fast in those days (vv. 18-20).

Fasting was an integral part of a Pharisees's life, but often the practice was only meant to draw attention to personal piety. Jesus cited an example: "Two men went up into the temple to pray; the one a Pharisee, and the other a publican. The Pharisee stood *and prayed thus with himself*, God, I thank thee, that I am not as other men are, extortioners, unjust, adulterers, or even as this publican. I fast twice in the week, I give tithes of all I possess. . . ." (Luke 18:10-12). It should be noted that the parable was given "to certain *which trusted in themselves, that they were righteous*, and despised others" (v. 9). Orthodox Jews regularly fasted twice every week. This took place on Mondays and Thursdays but the ritual was not as exacting as one might expect. They went without food from 6 a.m. until 6 p.m. but afterward they were sometimes gluttons. Fasting, for many, was just a way of exhibiting self-righteousness. That the man in Christ's parable stood and prayed *with himself*, suggests he stood alone—even God was absent!

To understand the Lord's message one must appreciate the customs of those times. A wedding in the Middle East was vastly different from weddings as we know them. Sometimes the festivities continued for seven or more days. The bride and groom did not hurry away for a honeymoon; they lingered to share happiness with their closest friends who were known as "*children of the bridechamber*." The married couple would possibly never know another week to be compared with this one. Earning a living in the desert was wearisome. It was customary, therefore, "to make hay while the sun shone"—they enjoyed to the full, a week without work, and to have fasted during those times of joy would have been foolish. When Jesus spoke about the futility of the children of the bridechamber fasting, His hearers knew precisely what He meant. Bonds of eternal love were being forged between the disciples and Himself; it was not a time for legalism and sadness. Eventually fasting would be wise and beneficial, but until that time arrived, the disciples should rejoice with joy unspeakable!

No man also seweth a piece of new cloth on an old garment: else the new piece that filleth it up taketh away from the old, and the rent is

made worse. And no man putteth new wine into old bottles; else the new wine doth burst the bottles, and the wine is spilled, and the bottles will be marred; but new wine must be put into new bottles (vv. 21-22).

A GLORIOUS MESSAGE. . .inspiring

The scripture here is most interesting, for the Lord was careful to use illustrations easily understood by the people. The word translated ''new'' is *agnaphou* which according to Dr. Thayer means ''unmilled, unfulled, undressed.'' The cloth was still unshrunk; it had not been worked-over by the mill. No man would ever think of sewing a piece of unshrunken cloth on an old garment. If rain fell, the new cloth would shrink; the old piece would remain as it was, and the result would be disastrous. The shrinking piece would pull at the rest of the cloth, and the garment would be ruined.

The Lord went on to speak of the foolishness of putting new wine into old bottles. The terminology used is equally interesting; *oinos neos* means ''recently made.'' The same expression is used elsewhere to signify, *recently made, born,* or even *youthful* as in Titus 2:4. The Lord spoke of freshly made wine being placed in old leather skins. Glass bottles were not known in those days. A new wineskin, under pressure could expand; that is, it could stretch, but an old skin was hard and rigid with no elasticity. New wine was still capable of fermenting, and the gas would need an expanding skin. If the skin did not respond, the pressure would cause an explosion. New wine needed new skins; just as unshrunken cloth needed to be sewn on garments made of the same type. What had Christ in mind when He used these illustrations? Throughout the centuries theologians debated that question. Many ideas have been expressed, but only one satisfies.

During the supper in Matthew's home, the new ideas were being challenged by the old traditions. The attitude, actions, and message of Jesus were at variance with all that the Pharisees taught, and this invited criticism. The disciples of Jesus were not fasting; the Jews fasted twice a week and expected all men to follow their example. Jesus and His followers had fellowship with publicans and sinners; the Scribes and Pharisees detested this fact and said so. The old and the new orders were in open opposition. War had been declared. The statements of the Lord must be considered against that background. Jesus was announcing the simple fact that a new order had been initiated. The new life, fellowship and joy which He was introducing could hardly be contained in unexpanding, unyielding, unchanging traditions of the

Pharisees. God's *new wine* would increase in intensity and power until
the entire world would hardly be able to contain it. How then could
it be imprisoned within precepts and traditions which never yielded to
anything? Already the critics were showing signs of strain! If that
continued, inevitably there would be an explosion! The new order would
be contained within a new skin; the new life would be expressed within
a new movement, the church would replace the synagogue in the Divine
pattern of things to come.

Two scenes appear before us. (1) The synagogue filled with pious
Jews whose miserable faces betrayed the cynicism of their minds. (2)
The dinner party in Matthew's home where men known for their greed
were suddenly exhibiting a new kind of interest. They had found more
happiness during one meal than all their ill-gotten gains could purchase.
The synagogue audience were chanting psalms; the dinner guests were
beginning to sing the praises of Jesus. The Pharisees affirmed that God
could only be found in the Temple; that sin and sinners alone were in
the house of the tax gatherer. Somehow they seemed to have erred in
their judgment. Jesus had accepted Matthew's invitation; His act was
thought-provoking! It seemed easier to find God at the supper table than
at any other place. Perhaps He knew that being with the publicans and
sinners, He was mingling with potential saints! He had made His choice;
He had burned His bridges; there could be no turning back. The fact
that all the details of His arguments and illustrations are recorded,
suggests the man with the writing materials did a great job.

The Lord did not make a mistake in calling Matthew. He had seen
His man busy at a job, and He liked what He saw. If you want anything
done, ask someone whose time is fully occupied. The transformation
wrought in Matthew is clearly evident throughout his writings. When
we remember he had been a money-grabber at heart, it is wonderful
to see how he stresses the principle of giving without expecting a return.
It is thrilling to read his emphasis on the virtue of secret giving without
sounding a trumpet. It is surely inspiring to see how he wrote about
taking no thought for the morrow, and the advisability of complete trust
in God. Here is a revolutionized Matthew—a wonderful testimony to
the power of Christ's transforming grace.

Matthew was the business man, and, from the moment he arose from
the table; gave his testimony to his friends; and went out to follow Jesus,
he remained faithful. All business men should recognize, in this great
disciple, one of their own class. Matthew had come from a world of
jingling coins into a new sphere of joyful consecration in which ''he

could lay up treasure in heaven.'' His gift as a writer made him invaluable to his Lord, the church, and their world.

SECTION THREE...CRITICIZING HIS COMPANIONS

Expository Notes on the Incident in the Cornfields

And it came to pass, that as He went through the corn fields on the sabbath day; His disciples began, as they went, to pluck the ears of corn. And the Pharisees said unto Him, Behold, why do they on the sabbath day that which is not lawful? (vv. 23-24).

It is necessary to differentiate between the laws of God and the traditions of men. God gave His commandments for the guidance of Israel, but to those laws were added thousands of other requirements which were completely unnecessary and man-made. Legalism can be extremely deadly, and the Lord knew He would be criticized for many of the things He permitted.

CRITICISM ON THE SABBATH

When the disciples began to pluck the ears of corn, the watching Pharisees immediately questioned Christ concerning the action. They said it was illegal to do this. Obviously they had misinterpreted the commandment given in Deuteronomy 23:24-25. ''When thou comest into thy neighbor's vineyard, then thou mayest eat grapes thy fill at thine own pleasure; but thou shalt not put any in thy vessel. When thou comest into the standing corn of thy neighbor, then thou mayest pluck the ears with thine hand; but thou shalt not move a sickle unto thy neighbor's standing corn.'' The action of the disciples was perfectly legal, but the Pharisees had super-imposed their own teaching upon the ancient commandment. They taught that it was illegal to do any work on the Sabbath, and some of their teaching was ludicrous. For example, we have been told that no work or deed of healing could be done on the Sabbath. Only certain medical attention could be given if life were in danger, but a fractured bone, for instance, could not be taken care of on the Sabbath.

People were only permitted to walk a certain number of miles on a Sabbath day, and this was classified as ''a sabbath day's journey.'' This seems very strange and even outrageous to people of our age, but the Jews were very strict about all their rules and regulations. Their legalism had become chains of bondage which impeded every movement. Thus, they were ready to criticize and ask questions when they saw the disciples "working" on the Sabbath. This same crippling legalism is still with us. Our traditions and self-made laws have hindered the cause of God. Long ago in writing to the Galatian Church, Paul said, "But now, after that ye have known God, or rather are known of God, how turn ye again to the weak and beggarly elements, whereunto ye desire again to be in bondage. Ye observe days, and months, and times, and years. I am afraid of you, lest I have bestowed upon you labor in vain" (Gal. 4:9-11). If the apostle were with us today, he would repeat his message.

There are sincere people who argue as to whether it is right to worship on Saturday or Sunday; there are others who believe that a communion service should be held only on Sunday mornings. I remember when I was denounced publicly because I worshipped on Sunday, my critic said, "*You will land in hell*, and it will be your own fault because you have been warned!" On another occasion I was criticized because I preached in a church on a Sunday morning. I was told my presence was necessary at the "Breaking of Bread" service because worship was more important than service! When I said there was no Bible commandment which insisted that I attend a communion service every Sunday morning, I was considered an uninformed backslider! The Lord said, "AS OFT AS YE DO THIS, do it in rememberance of me" (1 Cor. 11:25). Furthermore, within the New Testament church, the believers looked upon every meal as a communion service. When they met together as an assembly, they broke bread at NIGHT. After one of these services, Paul continued preaching until midnight, when a young man fell from a window and was killed (see Acts 20:7-12).

It is a great privilege and most inspiring to break bread every Sunday morning—or any other morning for that matter. It is a privilege to worship the Lord on Saturday or Sunday or any other day, but we must remember that love is better than legalism. If a course of obedient action is demanded because men insist on that procedure, then the real spirit of worship is missing. "Where the Spirit of the Lord is, there is liberty" (2 Cor. 3:17). The ancient Pharisees did not accept those principles; their descendants today make the same mistake.

CLARITY IN THE SCRIPTURE

When the critics expressed indignant surprise at the action of the hungry disciples, the Lord asked a question of His own. He said, "Have ye never read what David did, when he had need, and was an hungered, he, and they that were with him? How he went into the house of God. . .and did eat the shewbread, which is not lawful to eat but for the priests, and gave also to them which were with him.'' That story is found in 1 Samuel 21:1-6. David the fugitive, had come to the high priest of Israel to seek food for his hungry followers. When he discovered that no supplies were available, he took the shewbread which was never eaten except by the priests (see Exodus 25:23-40). Apparently David violated the laws of God when he took the food and gave it to his hungry followers.

The Lord was very wise when He mentioned this incident from David's life. The Pharisees professed to believe their scriptures and taking advantage of that fact, the Lord directed their attention toward the shewbread incident. First Kings 15:4-5 said, ''Nevertheless for David's sake, did the Lord his God give him a lamp in Jerusalem, to set up his son after him, and to establish Jerusalem. Because David did that which was right in the eyes of the Lord, *and turned not aside from anything that he commanded him all the days of his life*, save only in the matter of Uriah the Hittite.'' *If the verse were true*, then David had no guilt in eating the shewbread. If David were guilty, the scripture was unreliable! If David were innocent, they had no justification in criticizing the disciples for plucking corn on the sabbath. The shewbread in the tabernacle was considered to be holy, as it had been consecrated. The corn in the fields had not been chosen for sacred service; so why should the Pharisees be making a fuss about so little a matter? This was a storm in a teacup! They were substituting their pre-conceived ideas for the expressed will of God. He desired not sacrifices and conformity to unnecessary rules; He desired contrite spirits and broken hearts. The Pharisees were soon entangled in a web of their own making. They had no answer to the Savior's question.

It is extremely noteworthy that in every difficulty or moment of danger, the Lord referred to the Scriptures. For Him, it was a source of unfailing help and guidance. The preacher without an inspired Bible can never be a prophet!

CLAIMS OF THE SAVIOR

It is easy to appreciate the greatness of Christ's message when we look in retrospect over two thousand years of church history. The people who stood in His presence that day in the corn fields did not enjoy this privilege. They were hearing things which shocked them. That a carpenter should make such statements suggested he was mentally deranged. "And He said unto them, The sabbath was made for man, and not man for the sabbath" (v. 27). He was teaching that man made in the image and likeness of God was infinitely more important than any day or ordinance. When He said: "Therefore, the Son of man is Lord also of the sabbath" (v. 28), His hearers thought He was mad!

This outstanding utterance demands attention. A king had authority and power to do with his household and kingdom whatever he desired. The head of a family had absolute authority in the ruling or changing of family procedure. The head of a firm could do with his business anything he desired. Similarly, if Jesus were Lord of the sabbath; then He could do with it as He pleased. He could work; He could permit His disciples to pluck corn; or in the final analysis, *He could change it*. And that is precisely what He intended to do. The synagogue was to be replaced by the church; the laws of Moses were to give way before new laws of grace which would be supreme within the kingdom about to be established. Later, the followers of Christ only went into the synagogues on the seventh day *to preach the Gospel* to the assembled audience. They did not wish to lose a glorious opportunity of extending the kingdom of Christ. When they came together to worship and remember their Lord, they did not do it on the seventh day but on the first day of the week (see Acts 20:7). Furthermore, as the years passed, it became the unfailing custom for all Christians to follow the example set by the apostles. Writing to the church at Corinth, Paul said, "Upon the first day of the week, let every one of you lay by in store, as God hath prospered him, that there be no gatherings when I come" (1 Cor. 16:2). *The Amplified New Testament* renders this as follows: "On the first day of each week, let everyone of you (personally) put aside something and save it up as he has prospered—in proportion to what he is given—*so that no collections will need to be taken after I come*."

Even today, after nearly two thousand years of Christian teaching, there are many people who state that the apostles went out of the will of God by encouraging these actions. The sabbath, they teach, was and still is, an institution given by God, and no man had, or has, authority to change an ordinance of God. This is correct, but Jesus was not an ordinary man. He was *Lord of the sabbath*, and could do anything He chose to do. He had been there at the beginning when the sabbath was first conceived as a "Rest Day" for mankind. He had instituted that special day and had never intended it to become a wearisome burden. He set aside the day at the beginning, and later He had authority to change it. Had the disciples violated divine principles; had they displeased their Savior, He could not have given them the power to turn the world upside down! God cannot bless that which is sinful; He never uses disobedient people. When the Lord works in unfamiliar, unexpected ways, it is better to kneel at His feet to learn, than to stand at His side to criticize.

HOMILIES

Study No. 4

THE GREAT LEADERS...Who Missed God's Blessing

Matthew 9:2-8; Mark 2:1-12; Luke 5:17-26

"And it came to pass on a certain day, as He was teaching, that there were Pharisees and doctors of the law sitting by, which were come out of every town of Galilee, and Judea, and Jerusalem; and the power of the Lord was present to heal *them*." This verse suggests certain questions. (1) What attraction brought together this select company of religious dignitaries from every town in the country? Why did these celebrated people converge on one central spot? I have often thought of our denominational assemblies, to which all the churches send their representatives. I have wondered if something of the sort was being held in this town, and if these ministers, far from their congregations, seized the opportunity of hearing the new Teacher—a privilege they would have shunned nearer home. (2) Why did God specially prepare for the coming of these men?—"...the power of the Lord was present to heal *them*." (3) What hindrances prevented the receiving of the blessing?

A PERSONAL NEED

Somewhere in the district, the Lord Jesus addressed His audience; and it must have been a wonderful meeting. The building was packed to its utmost capacity, and it is not too much to suggest that the special visitors arrived early. A late-comer found it necessary to enter through the ceiling! They claimed their seats and waited for the sermon. It would be most interesting to know their reactions to His message. Ignorant of the fact that God had planned to draw near to them, they listened critically and went away unblessed. (1) Were they too blind to recognize their own need? Were they watching others and not considering that they might have been His first converts? (2) Even if they knew their need, were they too proud to admit it? Did the dignity of the synagogue forbid bowing before a Carpenter? (3) Did the fear of men hold them back? Were they conscious of the presence of colleagues, and mindful of the consequences that would follow any rash action? These questions are interesting because all these types still exist.

A PERSONAL APPEAL

The story provides a glorious contrast. Elsewhere in the district a man lay at home sick of the palsy. He was desperately anxious to meet Jesus of Nazareth, but had no means of transport until four friends volunteered to carry him to the meeting. (1) Unlike the priests, he already knew his own personal need of Christ. His case had baffled other healers. (2) He was not too proud for other men to know of his desires. He chose to enter the service in such a novel way that the world has never ceased talking about him. (3) He also knew that his actions would lead to expensive repercussions. He was damaging the property of some other man—a man who in all probability would have much to say concerning it. In blissful abandon, the sufferer urged his friends to lift the tiles. Perhaps even God smiled as He watched from heaven.

A PERSONAL SAVIOR

This man had determined to meet Christ. He intended to present his own petition whatever the cost. The Lord Jesus ceased preaching when the plaster or dirt began to fall. It would have been futile to speak when the audience stared upward at an ever-increasing hole in the ceiling. "And when He saw their faith, He said unto the sick-of-the-palsy, Man, thy sins are forgiven thee. And the scribes and Pharisees began to reason, saying, Who is this that speaketh blasphemies? Who can forgive sins, but God alone?" Thus their Bethel became a debating chamber. The power of God was present to heal them—and not one was healed. I do not know if the convert was ever required to pay damages; nor do I know what harsh words might have been spoken to him. Yet, however great his account, it never equalled the other account settled when Christ said, "Thy sins are forgiven thee." How sad is the thought—a man may only be a step from the Kingdom, and yet miss it by a mile! (reprinted from the author's book, *Bible Cameos*, pp. 107-108).

HOMILIES

Study No. 5

THE SECRET OF REAL HAPPINESS

King David, because of his position and wealth, was able to obtain most of the world's pleasures. He had everything! Yet even he knew that in comparison with eternal happiness, the world had nothing to offer. When he wrote, "...in thy presence is fullness of joy; at thy right hand there are pleasures for evermore" (Ps. 16:11), he expressed truth which in all ages has thrilled millions of people. This sublime fact is exhibited all through the gospels.

JOY...through His Preaching

"...and the common people heard Him gladly" (Mark 12:37). It was well said, "...Never man spake like this man" (John 7:46). He was so simple and so direct in all His utterances, that no one had difficulty in understanding what He said. He never used words hard to understand, and people knew they could trust Him. His charm attracted lepers; His arms encircled children. When the pulpits in the synagogue were closed to Him, He borrowed a fisherman's boat, and from it taught the congregation assembled on the beach. He never uttered a harsh word except to those who loved their sin. He used illustrations they understood, and described God as the loving, welcoming Parent waiting to throw His arms around a returning prodigal son. He was different in all He said, and did, and it was no cause for amazement when crowds hurried to His meetings.... Even the disciples learned that in His presence there was indeed fullness of joy, and at His side were pleasures for evermore. He never denounced sin without hastening to add that God could and would forgive the penitent. He never appealed for financial assistance, but was careful to commend a widow who placed "all that she had" into the treasury. He was the busiest Man who ever lived, and yet had time to welcome to His arms the children the disciples were sending away. Unlike the rulers of His times, He saw the real needs of the people. When they were hungry, He fed them: when they were sad, He comforted them; when they were fearful, He drew near to solve their problems and lift their burdens. He was different! No one ever shed tears in His presence unless they were tears of remorse or gladness.

JOY...through His Predictions

Matthew remembered every word of that memorable Sermon on the Mount, and in after days, his eyes glowed when he enumerated the "blessed" from that immortal message. "Blessed are the poor in spirit;...Blessed are the merciful...Blessed are the peacemakers...." These and the others thrilled his soul, but perhaps the greatest was the last. "Blessed are ye when men shall revile you, and persecute you, and shall say all manner of evil against you falsely, for my sake. *Rejoice, and be exceeding glad: for great is your reward in heaven...*" (Matt. 5:11-12). When the Lord ministered on earth, positions of importance were usually bought. Bribery and corruption were common practices of the day, and therefore, ordinary people had no chance of reaching places of eminence. The two extremes of wealth and poverty were so far removed from each other, that no bridge could be built between them. Yet the Lord addressed His remarks to the common people; the poor, the destitute, the outcasts. Even they could be absolutely sure that God was aware of what was taking place, and nothing they did for righteousness' sake could ever be lost. Even the poorest person was able to lay up "treasure in heaven." The Lord never promised an easy road through life; He could, and did promise a glorious ending. They would have riches in heaven, and these would last eternally. His prediction encouraged them; they were beginning to feel wealthy even before they received a penny!

JOY...through His Presence

"Then the same day at evening...came Jesus and stood in the midst, and saith unto them, Peace be unto you. And when He had so said, He shewed unto them His hands and His side. *Then were the disciples glad* when they saw the Lord" (John 20:19-20). The Cross at Calvary had ruined their hopes of a kingdom. They had expected a crown of gold and not one of thorns. Their Messiah had not expelled the Romans; instead the enemy had nailed their Lord to a tree. They had been devastated, and then came the news that Jesus had risen from the dead. The small band of disciples hardly knew what to believe. Some of the number had become enthusiastic; others were critical and unbelieving. And then, thank God, the Lord came to stand in their midst. They stared in wonder; they could hardly speak or breathe! Their Lord had conquered death; He was alive! They had seen the nail prints in His hands, and the horrible wound in His side. It was true; it was gloriously true; their Master was alive. "Then were the disciples glad when they saw the Lord" (John 20:20). Surely, they remembered His words, "Let not your heart be troubled: ye believe in God, believe also in me. In my Father's house are many mansions; if it were not so, I would have told you. I go to prepare a place for you. And if I go and prepare a place for you, I will come again, and receive you unto myself; that where I am, there ye may be also" (John 14:1-3). Life suddenly had new meaning for the disciples. Their joy increased by leaps and bounds! If they were to be persecuted, at least, they could be sure of His presence. When they were reviled, at least He would be aware of what was taking place. If they were to die, He would be with them when they walked through the valley of the shadow of death. The Lord was alive and with them. They were thrilled: their cup was running over!

These truths shed light upon the Lord's statement: "Can the children of the bridechamber fast, while the bridegroom is with them? As long as they have the bridegroom with them, they cannot fast" (Mark 2:19). The most effective advertisements for Christ are a radiant life, a joyous countenance, and a soul resplendent with a loveliness that only God can bestow.

HOMILIES

Study No. 6

LIFE'S MOST IMPORTANT CHOICE...
What Shall I Do With Jesus?

Life is filled with the necessity of making decisions; they are inescapable! At the gas station we choose between regular and non-leaded. At the supermarket we decide between dozens of brands of everything each claiming to be the best. Those on diets choose between no sugar or low sugar. If necessity demands no sugar, then we consider various brands of saccharin. Life insurance; health insurance; home and fire insurance; all claim priority, and as a result many people would love to reach an isolated island where pressures would decrease. Yet, even there things would remain unchanged, for sooner or later they would have to decide whether to leave or remain! Some decisions may be postponed; others may be ignored, but always there remains the most important decision of all... What shall I do with Jesus?

LEGALISM OR LOVE...Christ and the Sabbath (Mark 2:24-28)

It was the sabbath day; there was rest upon the countryside. The Lord and His disciples were strolling through the cornfields, when casually some of the disciples began to pluck the corn. They were hungry; perhaps they had been too busy to eat. It was permissible to take a neighbor's corn; Moses had said so in the law. The birds could take some; and men were more precious than birds! The watching Pharisees sneered; their eyes had become slits! They always thought Jesus to be a law-breaker, but now they were sure. He had not restrained his foolish disciples. Even though He had not shared their action; He was at least guilty of being an accomplice, for He had uttered no words of condemnation. Yes, they had caught Him red-handed. "And the Pharisees said unto him, Behold, why do they on the sabbath day that which is not lawful?" Their man-made laws had obscured the truth of God. They had substituted tradition for truth. Elsewhere we have been told "the letter of the word killeth; it is the Spirit that giveth life" (2 Cor. 3:6). Sometimes when people repeat lies, ultimately it becomes easy to believe they are telling the truth. The Pharisees had done this for centuries, and their traditions were as important as the laws of Moses. They might have been excused had they kept their convictions to themselves. When they enforced their will upon others, they became dictators; self-made gods who worshipped at their own shrine.

It is to be regretted that such people still exist. Legalism dominates their every thought. Commandments have replaced suggestions; insistence has replaced persuasion; a dictatorship has banned democracy! Unless others do as I do, they are utterly and completely condemned. Law not love has characterized every act; every thought; every word. It is wonderful to observe the sabbath and to keep it holy whether it be on Saturday or Sunday. *It is infinitely better to keep all seven days holy.* Hard, unrelenting, unsympathetic personalities are not attractive. The most wonderful thing this side of heaven is *love*. "Love suffereth long, and is kind...love rejoiceth in the truth; beareth all things, believeth all things, hopeth all things, endureth all things. Love never faileth..." (1 Cor. 13:4-7).

THE SWINE OR THE SAVIOR...Christ and the Crowd

"Then went the devils out of the man, and entered into the swine; and the herd ran violently down a steep place into the lake, and were choked...They which also saw it, told by what means he that was possessed of the devils was healed. Then the whole multitude . . . besought him to depart . . .'' (Luke 8:33-37). The people were staring at the man who was sitting at the feet of Jesus. They could hardly believe that yesterday he had been demon possessed. The light of sanity shone in his eyes; his face had been transformed. It was unbelievable! But alas, their swine had gone. They had paid a great price for this miracle, and there was no possibility of claiming damages against anyone. It was wonderful to see the transformed man, but other things had to be considered. If Christ continued to work His miracles in this fashion, within twenty-four hours, every farmer would be bankrupt! The thought was frightening. Such a tragedy had to be prevented whatever the cost. Jesus could not be permitted to repeat His action. It would be very nice to entertain Him, but He had no respect for other people. Then suddenly someone expressed what they were all thinking. "Go away. Jesus of Nazareth, we have no wish to be rude, but your coming here has cost us a fortune. Please do not have any hard feelings, but we cannot afford to lose our swine.'' "And He went into the ship and returned back . . .''

That probably is one of the saddest, strangest stories in the Bible. The world will never know how many other folk might have been healed had the Lord been invited to stay. Alas, the cost was too great. Two thousand years have passed since that memorable day, but things have not changed. The swine might represent money; evil associations of many types; they might mean anything which we permit to exist within our hearts. Christ challenges anything which is not according to the will of God. Our swine must go out if He is to enter, and that is the problem with many individuals. They would like to welcome the Savior, but it would be easier if He would mind His own business! "Jesus, You will be welcome, but please don't interfere with our profits!" The Lord never accepts such terms, for if He be not Lord of all, He is not Lord at all.

POPULARITY OR PEACE . . .
"Lord, what wilt thou have me to do?" (Acts 9:6)

Things were looking up! At last, Saul of Tarsus had found employment; it promised to be lucrative. He was working for the High Priest, the most influential man in the nation. Furthermore, he liked his job. These Christians were a menace to society and an insult to God. Their Leader, Jesus of Nazareth was an imposter, and those fishermen who said He had risen from the dead were liars. The more he thought about it, the more enraged he became. He had become a dragon to defend the faith. ''And Saul, yet breathing out threatenings and slaughter against the disciples of the Lord, went unto the high priest, and desired of him letters to Damascus to the synagogues, that if he found any of this way, whether they were men or women, he might bring them bound unto Jerusalem'' (Acts 9:1-2). There would be a handsome reward, and if he succeeded in this mission, doubtless there would be others of its type. His future was bright with prospect and hope; he was made!

And then he met the Lord! He remembered that one blinding flash of heavenly light before he plunged into the darkness. All his plans; all his hopes for the future; everything had been ruined. ''And he said, Who art thou, Lord. And the Lord said, I am Jesus. . .'' And suddenly, although he was still in the dark, a strange glow illuminated his soul. He had met his match! No man could fight successfully against One Who commanded the sun to shine with such intensity. His lifestyle had been wrong. What could he do? The Lord smiled, for He knew that Saul was swiftly becoming Paul. Saul realized he would lose favor with the high priest; he would never be great in the eyes of the officials; he was finished! But at least, he had found peace. He would have no home; very little money; he would be stoned, whipped, and imprisoned; but his peace would never diminish. Some day, a long, long way ahead, he would reach the end of his pilgrimage and reminisce. He would look back and say, ''The time of my departure is at hand. I have fought a good fight; I have finished my course; I have kept the faith. Henceforth there is laid up for me a crown. . .'' (2 Tim. 4:6-8). He would have no regrets. Surely he had paid a great price for his peace of mind, but he never regretted his action. Outside the gates of Damascus, Saul had fallen at the feet of his Lord. Often during his long ministry, he had done likewise, and as soon as he reached Heaven, he would do exactly the same thing! Some things should never change!

The Third Chapter of Mark

THEME: *Christ Continues His Ministry*

OUTLINE:
    I. The Man in the Synagogue (Verses 1-6)
    II. The Multitude by the Sea (Verses 7-12)
    III. The Master Chooses His Servants (Verses 13-19)
    IV. The Murmuring of the Scribes (Verses 20-30)
    V. The Message to the Skeptics (Verses 31-35)

SECTION ONE

Expository Notes on the Incident in the Synagogue

And He entered again into the synagogue; and there was a man there which had a withered hand. And they watched Him whether He would heal him on the sabbath day; that they might accuse Him. And He saith unto the man which had the withered hand, Stand forth. And He saith unto them, Is it lawful to do good on the sabbath days, or to do evil? to save life or to kill? But they held their peace. And when He had looked round about on them with anger, being grieved for the hardness of their hearts, He saith unto the man, Stretch forth thine hand. And he stretched it out; and his hand was restored whole as the other. And the Pharisees went forth, and straightway took counsel with the Herodians against Him, how they might destroy Him (vv. 1-6).

It is interesting to note that the word translated "synagogue" comes from the Greek word *sunago* which means "to gather together." It is used in Matthew 13:47 to indicate *a drawing together, or the catching of many fish in a net.* John 11:52 uses the word to suggest a gathering together of people previously separated. It did not relate to any building. The synagogue was a gathering together of men who could meet on a mountain, along the seashore, or in any other convenient place. Scholarship has been unable to ascertain any specific date when buildings became associated with the term. Originally there was but one recognized meeting place in Israel. Erected by Moses, the Tabernacle in the wilderness was the place in which God was said to dwell, and to which the people went to worship. Eventually, that building was replaced by Solomon's temple, but when this was destroyed, the Jews hardly knew where to go, or what to do, to preserve their ancient heritage. As time passed, the Jews circulated throughout the world and the desire to preserve their culture and faith inspired them to erect, in central locations, buildings in which they could do the things considered necessary for the growth of their nation. Synagogues were erected in market places, or any other location readily accessible to the people. These buildings were used as schools where qualified elders instructed the young; they often contained a library, and were the administration centers where trials were held, verdicts passed, and sometimes punishment administered to offenders. Joseph H. Thayer suggests, "Synagogues seem to date their origin from the Babylonian exile. In the time of Jesus and the apostles, every town, not only in Palestine, but also among the Gentiles, if it contained a considerable number of Jewish inhabitants, had at least one synagogue. The larger towns had several or even many."

These facts enable us to understand that the synagogue had become the local senate or university. The leaders of every community could be found there, and all matters of serious religious jurisprudence were handled within the building. Each leader was committed to the preservation of the laws of God and Moses, and the worst charge which could be made against any man was that of blasphemy. If he were found guilty of that offense, the punishment was death by stoning. When Jesus deliberately entered again into the synagogue, it was tantamount to entering into a lion's den. His action not only suggested bravery of the greatest kind; it also indicated His complete confidence in God.

"... *and there was a man there which had a withered hand*" (v. 1). Luke, with the exactitude of a doctor, says in his gospel that it was the man's *right* hand which was withered. This infers the man's capability in regard to earning a living had been seriously impaired. A fragment from an ancient manuscript informs us that the man was a stone mason who had been injured in an accident. There is no authentic way of deciding whether the information is accurate, but at least it lends credence to the idea that he was unable to work. His *right hand* was incapable of movement. The fact that Jesus healed this man is somewhat inconsequential. The thing of vital significance was the challenge to tradition issued by the Lord on that memorable day. He knew His enemies were watching Him, and from a human point of view, it would have been wise to postpone helping the afflicted man until the sabbath was over. He could have easily healed the man the following day, and had this been the case, the objection about healing on the sabbath day would not have been made. Christ was aware of their close scrutiny.

"And they watched Him, whether He would heal on the sabbath day; that they might accuse Him" (v. 2). Visiting dignitaries were always offered seats at the front of the synagogue, where they were able to see and hear everything that took place. Even their attitude within the house of God was hypocritical. Commentating on this scripture, Ellicott says the passage suggests two things: 1) The Pharisees *expected* the Lord to heal the afflicted man. They had already discovered that suffering of this kind appealed to His sympathy. 2) That they had resolved, if He did so heal, to make it the ground for a definite accusation before the local tribunal, the judgment of Matthew 5:21. The casuistry of the rabbi allowed the healing art to be practiced on the sabbath in cases of life and death, but "the withered hand" did not come under this category.

It is not without significance that the afflicted man was already in the synagogue when Jesus arrived. He did not go to the place of worship in order to meet the Lord and be healed. It would appear he went because this was his custom. As far as he was concerned he had no knowledge that a special visitor would be there that day. He had come *to give*, and had no expectation of receiving anything. It was certainly not customary for people to be healed in the regular services! "Jerome informs us that, in an apocryphal gospel in use among the Nazarenes and Ebionites, the man whose hand was withered is described as a mason, and is said to have asked for help in the following terms: 'I was a mason, seeking my living by manual labor. I beseech Thee, Jesus, to restore to me the use of my hand, that I may not be compelled to beg my bread.' This is consistent with Mark's description that the malady was the result of disease or accident, and not congenital. Luke informs us it was the right hand. The disease probably extended through the whole arm...It seems to have been a kind of atrophy, causing a gradual drying up of the limb; which in such a condition was beyond the reach of any human skill." (*The Pulpit Commentary, Mark's Gospel*, p. 115.)

"And He saith unto the man which had the withered hand, Stand forth. And He saith unto them, Is it lawful to do good on the sabbath days, or to do evil? to save life or to kill? But they held their peace" (vv. 3, 4). The words in the original Greek Testament are important. *Egeirai eis to meson.* Literally translated these would be "Arise, and come into the midst." There is no mention of any compelling faith in this man's

soul; but the fact that he was in the house of God surely suggests qualities of devotion and trust. He did not stay away from the sanctuary because God seemingly had been unkind toward him. Even though he may not have been able to understand why calamity had fallen upon him, he was still able to trust his Maker. The Lord would know all this, and with divine pity reflected on His face, commanded the sufferer to come forward. The man's eyes must have been alight with hope and expectancy when he discovered himself to be the center of attraction. Ultimately when he was told to stretch forth his hand, he made the effort to obey even though the very idea seemed ludicrous. His act of obedience brought healing. Faith is excellent, but it is always wise to remember that healing comes, not because of the greatness of our faith but because of the immensity of God's love for suffering people. Faith enables us to cling to Him; but when our faith is woefully weak, it is then we discover how He clings to us!

Dumbfounded by the Lord's direct questions, the watching critics had nothing to say. The people who were trying to entangle the Lord in His words and deeds were suddenly caught in a web of their own making. Everyone knew it was commendable to do good at any time, and to refuse to do good on God's day would have been unpardonable. Men were of more value than animals, and since they would rescue a sheep fallen into a ditch on the sabbath, it was far more important to save a human life on the same sacred day. The Greek word *orges*, translated "anger," denotes "a movement or deep agitation of the soul; impulse, desire; any violent emotion; anger" (Thayer). This was one of the rare times when the anger and the pity of the Lord were seen together. He was intensely grieved that religious men could be so blind, sinful, and arrogant. He was ready and willing to help them, but He was angry that sin had been permitted to blind them to everything which was honorable and good. The fact that they were soon planning with the Herodians to kill Him, more than indicated His anger was justified. There are no people so blind as the people who do not wish to see.

SECTION TWO

Expository Notes on the Multitude by the Sea

But Jesus withdrew himself with His disciples to the sea; and a great multitude from Galilee followed Him, and from Judea, and from Jerusalem, and from Idumea, and from beyond Jordan; and they about Tyre and Sidon, a great multitude, when they had heard what great

things He did, came unto Him. And He spake to His disciples, that a
small ship should wait on Him because of the multitude, lest they should
throng Him. For He had healed many; insomuch that they pressed upon
Him for to touch Him, as many as had plagues. And unclean spirits,
when they saw Him, fell down before Him and cried, saying, Thou art
the Son of God. And He straightly charged them that they should not
make Him known (vv. 7-12).

The impact made by Jesus of Nazareth upon the population of Palestine
can only be described as sensational. Four centuries had passed since
the appearance of Malachi, the last of the Old Testament prophets, and
apart from the military activity of the Maccabees and the more recent
appearance of John the Baptist, there had been no evidence of any true
spiritual activity. Then suddenly, the Preacher from Nazareth had
revolutionized the entire country. His preaching was startling, and His
deeds far exceeded anything the people had known. Every caravan which
travelled along the great highways leading north, east and west carried
tidings of the miracles which had thrilled a country. The traders spoke
more of the events in Palestine than of the goods being carried on the
backs of the camels. Everywhere people were astonished, and Mark's
statement, "a great multitude came to Him," hardly did justice to the
thrilling spectacle. People came from every quarter, and "pressed
[rushed] upon him for to touch him, as many as had plagues" (v. 10).

The overwhelming excitement of the people caused consternation and
gave rise to problems. It seemed the Lord was being pressed on every
side. He could hardly move, and therefore the necessity of having a
small boat near at hand became acute. There appeared to be the danger
of physical harm, but in any case, to preach under such circumstances
was an impossibility. It is worthy of attention that Mark wrote (v. 7)
that prior to these events, "Jesus withdrew himself with His disciples
to the sea." This suggests His earlier miracles had been performed *away*
from Capernaum, which stood on the shores of the Sea of Galilee. The
most important city in Galilee was Sepphoris which Herod Antipas had
made his capital. There were many Herodians in the locality, and this
explains how easy it became for the Pharisees to go and discuss with
them *"how they might destroy Jesus."* Herod's city contained five
important synagogues, and as a result many Jews lived in or near the
city. A timid preacher would have avoided at all costs this place where
his life would certainly be threatened.

*"And unclean spirits, when they saw Him, fell down before Him and
cried, saying, Thou art the Son of God. And He straightly charged them*

that they should not make Him known" (v. 11, 12). Many and varied
have been the explanations of these verses, but, although men may debate
the possibilities, some things are evident. These demon-possessed men
recognized in Jesus the Son of God—*they knew Him.* A voice from
Heaven had spoken at the Lord's baptism; and afterward many miracles
attested the fact that Jesus was no ordinary man. There is no suggestion
within the Bible that demons have powers of reproduction, and therefore,
these evil spirits had fallen with Satan from Heaven. If that were the
case, they had seen Him at the beginning and had not forgotten what
they saw. Dr. E. H. Bickersteth writes: "It is probable that they (the
evil spirits) were ignorant of the end and fruit of this great mystery,
namely, that mankind were to be redeemed by the Incarnation, the Cross
and the Death of Christ; and so their own kingdom was to be overthrown,
and the kingdom of God established. Blinded by their hatred of Jesus,
Whom they perceived to be a most holy Being, drawing multitudes to
Himself, they stirred up the passions of evil men against Him, *little
dreaming that in promoting His destruction, they were overthrowing
their own kingdom*" (*The Pulpit Commentary*, Mark, p. 117).

There was always the possibility the great crowd would get out of
control. Furthermore, should the zealous patriots be swept away by their
fierce hatred of the Romans, and launch an insurrection, the revolt would
provide reasons for the soldiers of Caesar to attack the people. Bloodshed
would banish blessing, and the entire purpose of Christ's coming to
earth would be thwarted. This had to be avoided at all costs, and so
the Lord "straightly charged the evil spirits that they should not make
Him known." The question has often been asked if such conditions exist
today. Is demon possession still a reality anywhere in this world? The
Chinese Church Research Center in Hong Kong has published a folder
in which is the following story: "Chang suffered from demonic
possession. Though he was young and strong, he could not work in
the rice fields, because the demons controlled his body and mind. His
strange outbursts and irrational behavior worried his family. One day
an itinerant preacher came to his village in rural China. Chang's
neighbors encouraged him and his family to come and listen. 'Maybe,
the preacher can heal you' they said. Chang agreed to go. Suddenly,
the demons inside him became enraged. As Chang raved and thrashed
about, his family half-carried him to the secret meeting held in a house
church. Seeing the man so obviously controlled by demons, the preacher
prayed in the name of Jesus for them to leave Chang. Everyone watched
as Chang gradually relaxed and blinked in amazement. 'I feel like a

new person' he said. Chang's family were astonished. They asked, 'Who is this Jesus? What kind of healing power does He have? This is a miracle!' They listened as the preacher explained who Jesus was; why He died for them, and how much He loved the Chinese people. With wrapt attention they heard the good news and wept. Chang and all his family asked forgiveness for their sins, and opened their hearts to receive Jesus. Again and again they returned to the house church for more teaching. Hope for a new life surged through them. They told their friends about the miracle and about Jesus. Even the threat of harassment or arrest by the communists did not shake their faith. Encouraged by older Christians, they became even bolder and more enthusiastic about sharing the exciting truth about Jesus with others. And soon the whole village walked with new faith in Christ.''

Many people may scoff at this story, but the fact remains that when Christ ministered on earth, He and the people around Him, believed the powers of evil constituted a threat to the happiness and liberty of the human soul. He came to set men free; to proclaim liberty to the captives. Happy are they who help complete what He commenced.

SECTION THREE

Expository Notes on the Choosing of the Twelve Apostles

And He goeth up into a mountain, and calleth unto Him whom He would: and they came unto Him. And He ordained twelve, that they should be with Him, and that He might send them forth to preach, and to have power to heal sicknesses, and to cast out devils. And Simon He surnamed Peter; and James, the son of Zebedee, John, the brother of James; and He surnamed them Boanerges, which is, The sons of thunder; and Andrew and Philip, and Bartholomew, and Matthew, and Thomas, and James the son of Alphaeus, and Thaddaeus, and Simon the Canaanite, and Judas Iscariot, which also betrayed Him; and they went into an house. (vv. 13-19).

The Lord had now reached a very important and vital time in His life. Already He had commenced His mission, but He was aware of an acute need. Eventually reaching the end of His earthly journey, He would return whence He had come. If the kingdom of God were to be extended throughout the earth, then somebody would need to assume responsibility of making known God's message to people who had never heard it. Jesus knew He would have to entrust this work to trained and willing missionaries. He had already found such men, but now it was necessary to impress upon those disciples the share they would have in evangelizing the nations. They had to be trained for the greatest task they would ever have; and since there was not a seminary to which they might be sent as students, His would be the task of educating those future missionaries.

"And it came to pass in those days, that He went up into a mountain to pray and continued all night in prayer to God. And when it was day, He called unto Him His disciples: and of them He chose twelve, whom also He named apostles..." (Luke 6:12-13). Are we justified in emphasizing, "and when it was day"? It appears the Lord never did anything without prior consultation with His Father. Continually throughout His ministry, He deliberately went aside to speak with God, and every major decision was made in harmony with the will of the One Who had sent Him. The choice of the twelve apostles was among the greatest of all decisions ever to be made. This becomes all the more evident when we consider that one of the chosen men would be Judas the betrayer. Was there any doubt in the Savior's mind? Was there need to make absolutely certain of what God wished to be done? Throughout the hours of darkness, did Jesus and His Father deliberate on these matters, and "when it was day," everything had become clear? There may be no authoritative answers to our questions, but at least we may be sure of other things. There will always be need to make communion with God a priority in our lives. If two heads are better than one, the truth becomes increasingly obvious when one of those heads belongs to the Lord! The people who walk in darkness often stumble. It is better to wait for the day to dawn.

And He ordained twelve, that they should be with Him, and that He might send them forth to preach, and to have power to heal sicknesses, and to cast out devils (vv. 14-15).

Here we have three important phases to consider: 1) *The Great Consent*—"He calleth whom He would...and they came unto Him", 2) *The Gracious Communion*—"...that they should be with Him", 3) *The Glorious Commission*—"...that He might send them forth to preach,...to have power...to cast out devils." Here we have the divine order of service. It was important and very essential that *FIRST,...* they would be with Him. Communion with Christ charges our spiritual batteries. The preacher who tries to serve God when his batteries are dead, quickly discovers that his tires are also flat! If, as was the case with John the Baptist, he emerges from the presence of God, his ministry will be charged with the invincible power of the Almighty. Yet, however attractive and desirable it might be to perform miracles, the first objective must be the preaching of the Gospel, for a man's soul outlives his body. Finally, if he be absolutely convinced that healing is the will of God for an individual; then the minister should pray in faith, and God will honor His promises.

SIMON PETER...The Big Fisherman

And Simon He surnamed Peter (v. 16). Simon's life was divided into two categories. The first was dominated by fish; the second by faith. He who had spent years endeavoring to get fish in his nets, was ultimately caught himself in the net of Christ's compassion. Impulsive, indignant, and only sometimes inspired, a less-likely candidate to become a great preacher could hardly have been found. His hands were toughened from the hauling of nets; his self-assuredness was beyond question. He was a big fisherman capable of holding his own with any other along the shores of Galilee. When Jesus saw him, He recognized those rough hands would some day hold a pen and write epistles. Those strong arms so accustomed to pulling large and small fish to the shore, would also pull fish of a different kind to the shores of God's kingdom. All he needed was special instruction in the noble art of catching men. Although Peter would deny his Lord and reveal an inexcusable weakness through boasting, Jesus knew that, at the end of life's road, that rough, tough fisherman would gladly lay down his life for his Savior. The weak, vascillating man could be made a ROCK, the strength of whose example would support and hold the people won through his testimony. Although to all others, Simon Peter appeared to be a poor candidate for Heaven's honors, Jesus looked at him, loved him, called him, and then went to work to make him one of the greatest Christians who ever lived. Ever afterward Peter knew he had been caught by the greatest Fisherman Who ever walked along the shores of Galilee.

JAMES...The Second of the Big Three

And James the son of Zebedee... (v. 19). I have never preached a sermon exclusively about James, and now that I think about it, I have never heard any other minister do so. Whenever James was mentioned, he was linked with his two companions. The Bible often refers to Peter, James, and John. That order never changes. We never read of John, Peter and James. There must be a reason for this interesting fact. The grace of God turned Peter into an explosive preacher; the same grace turned John into a quiet, contemplative pastor, but what of James, the man destined to become the first Apostolic martyr? He was the strong cement-like man whose presence solidified and united the brethren. He spoke only when it was necessary, but when he did, he said something! His fishing partner Peter often said things, which afterward, he wished he had not uttered. Peter generally spoke first and thought afterward. James thought first, and thought and thought again. He only spoke when he knew what needed to be said. He had not always been that type of man, for he had earned a title, ''The Son of Thunder.'' The grace of God within his soul had changed and sanctified those natural characteristics, and used them for the Lord's glory.

Commissioner W. A. McIntyre of the Salvation Army, writing of James, said, ''He possessed three outstanding, natural, human characteristics, which although they needed to be purified, refined, and controlled, did not have to be completely eradicated. These were ZEAL, JEALOUSY and AMBITION. Used as means to earthly ends, they were more or less ignoble; but, having been sanctified through contact with Christ, *they became Zeal for His cause; Jealousy for His honor, and Ambition to follow in Christ's footsteps.* Herod selected James to be the first victim of his own fanatical hate.''

JOHN...The Youngest of Them All

There is a great amount of evidence to prove that John lived until the times of Hadrian, who was Emperor of Rome from 98-117 A.D. Therefore, John must have been a teenager when he was called to follow Jesus. James, his brother, was considerably older, and in all probability, the elder brother had taken John under his wing to instruct him in the art of becoming a prosperous fisherman. Zebedee the father, was a well known businessman along the Sea of Galilee. His fleet of vessels was surely large, for we have been told it was necessary to employ hired servants (Mark 1:20). John, doubtless, was very enthusiastic about learning the family business, but his association with John the Baptist produced changes in his attitude. We have not been informed as to why he left the wilderness preacher to return to his father's fishing boats. John, at first had a fiery disposition, and the possibility exists that the two Johns did not make admirable companions. In some senses, the hot tempered young man never changed. Ultimately, he was given the nick-name of ''Son of Thunder.'' This may or may not have referred to his fiery temperament which on occasion became volcanic! Later, when he realized his Master had been slighted by the people in a Samaritan village, John became so annoyed that he desired the cremation of the entire population. At that moment his eyes had become pinpoints of infuriation, his face was scowling, and lightning flashed across his soul. In some senses he never lost those startling characteristics, for even when he had become an old man, there were still rumblings from his stormy soul. His tongue never lost its sharp edge, and four times in his epistles, he refers to his opponents as "liars." Constantly he wrote of the necessity *to overcome, to fight, to endure.* The young fisherman from Galilee had become an Old Testament prophet! He had been at the feet of Jesus, and the overwhelming, tempestuous torrents of emotion had been effectively harnessed, as the waters of a mighty river. That glorious change brought guidance to the early church and light to a world sitting in darkness. The Lord was well aware of the fiery disposition of that young teenager, and knew He could handle the problems. The rough, untutored young man could become a saint to be revered by all the churches. The nick-name, "Son of Thunder," is extremely interesting. Some theologians think it was given because both John and his brother had rich, deep tones in their voices. When they spoke, people could hear clearly and easily; when they shouted, even hell trembled! Be that as it may; the fact remains that John, young and inexperienced, became a man of whom even the Lord could be proud. Even marred, ugly vessels can be transformed by the touch of a master potter's hands.

ANDREW...The Go-getter!

And Andrew (v. 18). W. A. McIntyre wrote: "Andrew never witnessed the great miracles that others did. He was never at the Speakers Table...Yet we cannot conceive of Andrew being jealous of Peter, James and John. He had no part in the angry wrestling for place and power that disfigured the character of some of the other disciples. He was content to fill a subordinate's place, thereby exhibiting one of the brightest gems among the Christian graces—a meek and a quiet spirit."

Andrew was a go-getter; he stopped at nothing. To attain his ends, he would remove mountains, cross oceans, turn the world inside out, laugh at impossibilities, and finally set a city on fire while other people looked for a match. Other men became Great Generals in the holy war, but Andrew planned the campaigns, removed the difficulties, and prepared the way for every new advance. Andrew is mentioned on three specific occasions within the sacred record. The day after his conversion

Andrew became a soul winner. His power consisted of the intensity of spirit which Christ had stirred within him. He had one great gift; he was an expert at bringing others to Jesus. John alone supplies the insight into the character and work of his gentle friend (see "ANDREW...The Patron Saint of Personal Workers" in my book, *John's Wonderful Gospel*, pp. 47-49).

PHILIP...The Persistent Plodder!

And Philip (v. 18). The more one reads the accounts of the disciples, the more obvious it becomes that each disciple was one of a kind. Peter was a man of fiery temperament; an enthusiast. John unquestionably became a dreamer, a visionary, but unlike all the others, Philip was a down to earth, practical, matter-of-fact man. Often it took him a long time to reach an objective, but he never failed in the end. Once again I quote from those exceedingly attractive essays written by Commissioner McIntyre. "Thoroughly at home with the hard facts of life, Philip was as careful with details as the paying teller in a bank. His mind was precise, methodical and accurate. What it lacked was originality, imagination and spiritual perception." The possibility exists that since Philip, Andrew and Peter all belonged to the same town, they might have known each other, even before Christ called them. Andrew and John came to the Savior; Philip did not. He lingered at home, weighing carefully the pros and cons of the whole matter, and it became necessary for Jesus to go in search of him (see John 1:43). There is something specially attractive about this lesser-known disciple. Although sometimes he seemed to get "stuck in the mud," somehow he always managed to dig himself out and get to wherever he wanted to go. Other enthusiastic disciples could seemingly outrun him as if they were hares; but later, in some miraculous fashion, it was Philip, like a turtle, that crossed the finishing line first. He made up for his lack of overflowing enthusiasm by the amazing perseverance with which he followed every project to a successful conclusion. He was one of the first to succeed in mastering the mechanics of successful evangelism.

NATHANIEL BARTHOLOMEW...
Who Had Two Names and Two Opinions

"It is very commonly believed that Nathaniel and Bartholomew were the same person. The evidence for that belief is as follows: John, who twice mentions Nathaniel, never introduces the name of Bartholomew. Matthew (10:3), Mark (3:18), and Luke (6:4) all speak of Bartholomew, but never of Nathaniel. It may be, that Nathaniel was the proper name, and Bartholomew was the surname of the same disciple'' (*Unger's Bible Dictionary*, p. 778). Other authors do not agree with this conclusion, but as D. Edmond Hiebert says, "If Bartholomew is not the same as Nathaniel, he remains a mere name among the Twelve'' (*The Zondervan Pictorial Encyclopedia of the Bible*, vol. 1).

It is assumed that Nathaniel had been influenced by John the Baptist, and that he was sitting beneath the fig tree thinking about spiritual things, when Jesus passed by and saw him. This might explain why Jesus said to him, "Before that Philip called thee, when thou wast under the fig tree, I saw thee.'' Nazareth and Cana were about eleven miles apart, but alas, Nazareth did not have a good reputation among Jews. All Galileans were despised by the rulers in Jerusalem, because they freely traded with the heathens in Tyre and Sidon. In addition to this fact, the Nazarenes did not attend the feasts in Jerusalem, stating the distance to be travelled was too great. Consequently, they were considered to be as undesirable as the people with whom they traded. Possibly all this was in the mind of Nathaniel when, in response to Philip's testimony of Christ, he disdainfully asked, "Can any good thing come out of Nazareth?'' Philip was not easily dismissed, and his "Come and see'' finally overcame the doubt and prejudice of his listener. When Nathaniel ultimately met the Lord, he cried, "Rabbi, thou art the Son of God; Thou art the king of Israel'' (John 1:49). This was a glorious confession, which for spontaneity of purpose, and intensity of spirit, ranks with the confessions of Simon Peter and Thomas. Peter cried, "Thou art the Christ, the Son of the living God.'' Thomas said, "My Lord and my God.'' It is impossible to remain silent when one's heart is bursting. Nathaniel was one of the men who returned to the fishing boats after the resurrection, but was back with the other disciples, when they met for prayer in the Upper Room. Tradition says that he died as a martyr in India.

MATTHEW...The Book Man

Consideration has already been given to the conversion of Matthew, the tax collector (see the expository notes on Chapter Two). There are certain truths expressed in this great story of Matthew which might reward a little closer study.

No man is beyond the reach of God's love

Matthew, in all probability, had earned the disrespect of his fellow citizens. He had not only given himself to the service of the enemy; he had exploited his race and probably had become wealthy at their expense. At least, the people of his city believed this was the case. The tax-gatherer was in their esteem lower than the heathen; a disgrace to the Jewish race, and an abomination in the sight of God. Had they been asked to nominate a person for inclusion in any of their respected committees, Matthew's name would never have been mentioned. He was a renegade; an outsider beneath and beyond the realms of decency. Yet, the Lord stopped one day, at the door of Matthew's office, and invited him to become a disciple.

No man can escape hearing God's call

It is not possible to hide from God. He knows where we are, and how best we might be reached for His kingdom. We may not wish to participate in any of the divine purposes; we may even strive to forget what we hear about those purposes, but it is very difficult to close our ears to the voice of God. He loves the entire world; and every person in it is the object of His gracious desire. If God gave His Son to redeem us, then He loved us a great deal. Such love is sure to seek us wherever we might be.

No man can avoid the responsibility of either accepting or rejecting God's call

Had Matthew remained at his seat of custom, he would have lost the greatest opportunity of his life. Yet, that possibility surely existed. The Lord did not drag him from his place of employment; He called him, and in those electrifying moments, Matthew made his decision. Would he stay with his chances of making more money, or would he abandon everything and start a new banking account in Heaven? It did not take Matthew many moments to make his decision. Alas, many people lose their lives while they try to decide what to do with Jesus. It is God's business to find and call men; but it is their responsibility to avail themselves of the God-given opportunity which comes when Christ stops at their door!

No man is devoid of the opportunity to express gratitude to God

When Matthew hurriedly called his friends to supper, he proved the greatness of the transformation which had changed his life. He was not only grateful to Christ for the happiness flooding his soul; he wanted all his associates to meet his Savior. This really is the test of the new life in Christ. We cannot hide our lights under a bushel. We may not have the means with which to provide a sumptuous banquet for great numbers of people, but Jesus declared that even a cup of cold water given in His Name would not pass unnoticed. We may not be able to preach as did Peter and Paul, but our lives can be more eloquent than any spoken word. Everybody has the means to tell God how much His grace is appreciated. Alas, many people have lockjaw!

No man is completely without a talent, which, when dedicated, can be used to extend God's kingdom

It has already been said that Matthew left everything except his pen. God took Matthew, and his pen, and did for the world far more than anyone would have thought possible. There is no detailed record that Matthew ever preached a great sermon. Doubtless he tried, for when Jesus sent out seventy disciples to preach the Gospel of the Kingdom, Matthew was among the number. There must have been many places in which he gave his testimony; but the fact remained, he found it easier to write what he heard others saying. This was particularly true with the messages Jesus preached. The tax-gatherer was never called to be a great orator. He knew where his gift lay, and with great determination, dedicated that gift so that the world could know about Christ. We have talents; what are we doing with them?

THOMAS... The Hard-to-convince Man

Historians tell us that the real name of Thomas was Judas or Didymus, which means "a Twin." Tradition says that he had a twin sister whose name was Lydia. Other writers maintain he had a twin brother who was also a disciple. These are traditions which have never been established as truth. We know that he was born at Antioch and was closely associated with Matthew and Philip. We have deduced from the Gospel records that Thomas was a man slow to believe; refusing almost to go anywhere until he could see clearly the path before him. Today we remember him mostly for his faults! The term "Doubting

Thomas'' has become part of our language. Any person slow to accept a given explanation is immediately called "a doubting Thomas." This fact has spoiled the portrait of a great man, for Thomas was *A GREAT MAN*. Maybe it would be wise to change the description of this disciple. He would be better known as THE MAN WHO WANTED TO BE SURE. Perhaps John mentioned Thomas so frequently because he found many of his type in Ephesus and throughout Asia. The Ephesians had shrewd minds, and to them John was able to say, "One of the Lord's disciples was of your kind. Let me tell you about him."

We see Thomas at his best in the story written for us in John, chapter 11. When Jesus indicated his intention to return to Bethany, the whole idea seemed ludicrous. It was only when He explained that Lazarus was dead, that the disciples realized their friend in Bethany had succumbed to illness. When Jesus indicated He was going back to Bethany in order to awaken Lazarus from "the sleep of death," the disciples realized that nothing could make their Master change His mind. It seemed so futile; it was tantamount to committing suicide, for on the previous visit to that locality the Lord's life had been threatened. It was then that Thomas said, "Let us also go that we may die with him" (John 11:16). It is true that he did not utter the cry of the martyrs, "We will die FOR Him," but at least he was willing to die WITH Him. In his own round-about way, Thomas was telling everyone that life without the Lord would be death! If Christ went, nothing would be left. The world would be empty, the days unbearably long, and the nights endless. "No, no," he seemed to say, "If my Master is going to die, I do not wish to live. So let us go that we may die with Him." Thus we see in him a depth of spiritual devotion that could not be associated with a man of little faith. Thomas was a definite asset to the disciples. When the others in exuberant excitement drove their spiritual wagon at break-neck speeds, Thomas was an expert at putting on the brakes!

JAMES THE LESS. . .The Apostle of the Little People!

We do not have very much information concerning this disciple; and what there is, has caused endless debate. Most of the theologians believe James was called "the Less" because he was either much younger than James "the Great" or that his call was of less importance than that of his more famous namesake. "This James, the son of Alphaeus, or Clopas (not Cleophas); called 'the Less' either because he was junior in age, or rather in his call, to James the Great, the brother of John. This James, the son of Alphaeus, is called the brother of our Lord. St. Jerome says his father Alphaeus, married Mary, a sister of the Virgin Mary, which would make him the cousin of our Lord. This view is confirmed by Bishop Pearson (Art. iii on the Creed). He was the writer of the Epistle which bears his name, and became the Bishop of Jerusalem" (*The Pulpit Commentary*, Vol. 16, p. 118).

Commissioner McIntyre has expressed a different thought. His interpretation may not have the scholastic backing of the earlier idea, but at least its originality invites consideration. He says: "James...was called 'the Less' not because he was of lesser importance...than the other James, but because he was small of body. Evidently, he was a little man! In the days of the Roman Empire, a man's worth was measured largely by his inches! Every human body was regarded as a possible engine of war. A man to be worthy of the name, must be ready for battle, where he faced his foe at close quarters, and where every inch counted. That was the Roman viewpoint, but Jesus brought an entirely new idea to bear upon that situation. He looked at the insignificant little James, and judged him to be worthy of a place among the chosen twelve."

This interpretation, at least, would find a response in the hearts of countless numbers of God's people—ordinary people with few talents! They take little part in public affairs, and enjoy no preeminence in this life. They nevertheless find a niche in which to pull their weight for the Lord. In all probability they count just as much as the clever people who live their lives in the limelight of popularity. If James the Less had been placed before a large audience to give his testimony, there would be a large group who would say, "James, you are our man. You belong to our type. If Jesus could love you, then surely He will love us." James was, and ever will be, *The Apostle of the Little Men and Women*. We are told in the Book of Revelation, that in the last days, the twelve apostles will sit on twelve thrones to judge their own tribes. There we shall find James the Less sitting on his throne, judging his group with as much authority as any other of that illustrious company.

THADDAEUS OR JUDE...Who Always Pulled His Weight!

We do not know very much about this seldom mentioned disciple. The early church writers suggested that he had three names: Thaddaeus; Lebbaeus, and Judas. He later became known as Jude to differentiate him from Judas Iscariot who betrayed the Lord. Now what can possibly be said about anyone of whom nothing is known? Let us classify him as being one of the back-room boys! His greatest characteristic and asset was that *he was always there*, whether he was needed or not! When Simon Peter stood up to preach on the day of Pentecost, the eleven stood with him, and one of that number was Thaddaeus. He was ready to share the moral responsibility of Peter's action. If stones were to fly, then Thaddaeus would be there to shelter Peter with his own body. If death were to come because of Peter's utterances, then Brother Peter would not die alone! If we can express this in modern terms, Thaddaeus never drove the car, but as a faithful mechanic, he attended to needs, and made it safe for other better qualified "drivers." I like Thaddaeus. If the church today had more of his type, our machinery would function more efficiently. The Epistle of Jude begins with the words: "Jude, the servant of Jesus Christ, and brother of James..." These words are very significant. James was the head of the church at Jerusalem, he was the brother of the Lord and the author of the epistle bearing his name. Jude must have been a younger brother both of Jesus and James. Evidence of this can be found in Matthew 13:55-56 where the people said, "Is not this the carpenter's son? Is not His mother called Mary? and His brethren, James, and Joses, and Simon, *and Judas*? And His sisters, are they not all with us? Whence then hath this man all these things?" That Jude was the young brother of the Lord, and that he wrote: "Jude, *the servant* of Jesus Christ" (Jude 1) indicates the true humility which filled his soul. Had he been as many of today's followers, he would have exploited his family connections with Christ to assert his own importance. Jude or Thaddaeus was able to appreciate the words of John the Baptist who said, "He must increase; I must decrease." With Paul the Apostle, Jude would have exclaimed, "That in all things, He might have the preeminence" (Col. 1:18).

SIMON THE ZEALOT...Who Had Fire in His Bones!

Luke calls this man "Simon Zelotes" or Simon the Zealot (6:15), and in that one eloquent title we find the life story of the disciple. Some years before Christ came to earth, a band of die-hard revolutionaries came together with the avowed intention of expelling the Romans from their country. They were led by a wild man, Judas of Gamal, who hated the Romans with a wild, unrestrained bitterness. His followers did many terrible things and consequently were among the most irresponsible of Rome's enemies. The Roman legions attacked these outlaws constantly, but in spite of many losses there remained a band of men known as Zealots. Their smoldering animosity was ready to erupt at a moment's notice. Simon was one of this band of hot-heads. The fact that he was called Simon the Canaanite has really been misinterpreted. He was not a Canaanite as was the woman mentioned in Matthew 15:22. It is more likely that the term refers to his birthplace—Cana in Galilee. Simon was officially linked with this army of death. No scheme was too wild; no deed too abhorrent for his hand. He and his collaborators were desperate men ready and willing to die for their cause.

When Jesus met and captured this man, he performed one of the greatest miracles of all time. What happened to those tongues of fire which leaped as wild beasts from the caverns of his soul? Were they destroyed for ever? Certainly not. Simon remained "The Flaming One" long after he became a disciple. The burning desire to destroy had assumed new proportions. Simon now wanted to build a new kingdom in which both Jews and Romans would dwell as brethren. If the old Simon had addressed a meeting, his voice would have been raised; his arms flying, and his feet stomping. Zeal was his specialty, and every one knew it. The new Simon still had the same passion, but his overflowing energy had been directed into new channels of service. The old Simon would have shattered the Gospel into a thousand pieces. The transformed Simon was content to occupy an obscure part in the ongoing work of Christ's kingdom. The new man was distinguished by nothing but the even glow of his personality and the warmth of the fellowship which he enjoyed with those who shared his overwhelming love for the Lord.

JUDAS ISCARIOT...The Lonely One!

Throughout the centuries men have questioned the choice of Judas to be one of Christ's disciples. Church Councils argued for long periods, and assemblies divided by theologians whose viewpoints differed. Few people ever considered the possibility that the Lord had no choice in the matter. Maybe Jesus chose Judas *because he had to do so.* Could Jesus, the Son of God live triumphantly with a snake in His bosom!? Perhaps Judas was thrust upon Christ. He became Satan's challenge to the sinless Son of God. Obviously there came a moment when Jesus knew what was to happen in regard to His betrayal. Probably He knew the details of that terrible act even before they were committed, but never at any time did He reveal bitterness toward His false friend. The tranquility of His soul remained undisturbed. He was calm and serene in all that He did, and this surely infuriated the powers of evil.

Judas was called "The Son of Perdition" and this term was never given to any other except the Antichrist, the Man of sin who will terrorize the earth in the last days of time. It has been said that when Judas died, "he went to his own place" and that statement was never made of any other human. Judas was Satan's man, and unfortunately this characterized his entire life. Doubtless, he followed Jesus because he honestly believed that through Him the Kingdom would be established, and the Romans expelled from the land. He became the Treasurer of the disciple band and handled the finances which became available. That he stole some of the much needed money reveals he probably thought he should be paid for his services! There is no evidence that he ever truly loved his Leader. On the other hand, there is no evidence that Jesus ever lost His love for Judas. The only place of honor within the disciple band was given to Judas, and the last act of Jesus was to give "the sop when he had dipped it, to Judas" (John 13:26). This was the traditional way of bestowing favor upon a friend—it was the special portion given by a host or hostess to an honored guest. It has been recorded for us that "Judas went his way," and that probably sums up his entire life. He always went *his* way. As long as following Christ fitted into his plans, and promised to bring what Judas most desired, there was no problem. Unfortunately, when it became obvious that Jesus would not live up to his expectations, Judas decided he had had enough, and forsaking his Leader, went out to make the best of a bad job! Even thirty pieces of silver were better than nothing! "And Judas went out and it was night!" It became a very long night; it had no dawning!

JESUS...The Incomparable!

Those twelve disciples came from varying walks of life; they were temperamentally different. Apart from the uniting power of the love of Christ, they would not have lasted two weeks. The depressing attitude of Thomas would have angered the ebullient Peter. The methodical Philip would have irritated the Zealot, and James and John sooner or later would have created a civil war! Why did these men leave everything to follow a Carpenter? There must have been a compelling charm about the Nazarene Preacher. He was irresistible. The following paragraph is exceedingly interesting, and might supply the answer, at least in part, to the question just asked. It is said to be a description of Jesus by Publius Lentulus, Governor of Judea, addressed to Tiberius Caesar, the Emperor of Rome. It was found in an excavated city, and was written in Aramaic on stone.

There lives, at this time, in Judea, a man of
singular virtue whose name is Jesus Christ, whom
the barbarians esteem as a prophet, but His
followers love and adore Him as the offspring of
the immortal God. He calls back the dead from
the graves, and heals all sorts of diseases with
a word or a touch.

He is a tall man, and well shaped, of an amiable
and reverend aspect; His hair of a color that
can hardly be matched, the color of chestnut
full ripe, falling in waves about His shoulders.
His forehead high, large and imposing; His
cheeks without spot or wrinkle, beautiful with a
lovely red; His nose and mouth formed with
exquisite symmetry; His beard thick and of a
color suitable to His hair reaching below His
chin. His eyes bright blue, clear and serene,
look innocent, dignified, manly, and mature. In
proportion of body, most excellent and captivating,
His arms and hands most delectable to behold.

He rebukes with majesty, counsels with mildness,
his whole address, whether in word or deed,
being eloquent and grave. No man has seen Him
laugh, yet His manner is exceedingly pleasant;
but He has wept in the presence of men. He is
temperate, modest, and wise; a man, for His
extraordinary beauty and divine perfections,
surpassing the children of men in every sense.

King Solomon also knew this man, for of Him he wrote: "...He is
altogether lovely..." (Song of Sol. 5:16).

SECTION FOUR

Expository Notes on Christ's Answers to the Murmuring Scribes

**And the scribes which came down from Jerusalem said, He hath
Beelzebub, and by the prince of the devils casteth He out devils (v. 22).**

Obviously, the Pharisees had now declared war on the Preacher from
Nazareth. His message, to say the least, constituted a threat to the
traditions of the Fathers; His increasing popularity was undermining

their own authority. Something had to be done to embarrass the upstart Preacher! That the Scribes came all the way from Jerusalem, seems to imply purpose; they had been sent to do what had to be done. Their initial statement lends credence to the idea that they had been specially commissioned and had a definite plan of action. No one could deny the reality of the Lord's miracles, for in every town were people whose lives had been transformed by either His touch or His word. Perhaps some hired attorney had dictated the course of action. The common people believed sincerely in the existence of demons and lived in daily dread that they themselves might become victims of evil spirits. If somehow, Jesus could be associated with the very things to be feared, then it might be possible to keep the congregations away from the Man Who wished to preach to them. Probably, with this in mind, the scribes said Jesus was in league with the prince of the devils. They recognized His power, but attributed it to help given by the powers of darkness. This was doubtless a sly, devious approach, but there was little else they could do. The people who had been healed or delivered did not care who had healed them; *they had been healed*, and that was all that mattered! It was an impossibility to prevent Christ from preaching, but it might be possible to prevent people from listening! Therefore, they did their utmost to associate the words and works of Jesus with the evil spirits so very much feared by the men and women of the country. This new challenge might have been devastating, but Jesus knew how to offset its implications.

And He called them unto Him, and said unto them in parables, How can Satan cast out Satan? And if a kingdom be divided against itself, that kingdom cannot stand. And if Satan rise up against himself, and be divided, he cannot stand, but hath an end. No man can enter into a strong man's house, except he will first bind the strong man; and then he will spoil his house (vv. 23-27).

These verses introduce readers to what might be called *The Battle of Implications*! The scribes had suggested possible associations between Christ and the prince of demons. The Lord retaliated with undeniable facts. Internal discord and dissension is bad for anything. A civil war splits a country. A warring household can only alienate members of a family from each other. If Christ by expelling demons did so by the power entrusted to Him by Satan, then Satan himself was at war with his followers! If this were the case, he could expect insurrection among his subjects. If, as had been inferred, Satan was helping Jesus to exorcise devils, then he was at war with his own community, and his kingdom was about to perish. Allowing this to sink into the thoughts of His listeners, the Lord then proceeded to reveal another possibility. He spoke of a *strong* man's house. This fellow was no weakling; he was a man of muscle capable of defending his property. If he were overcome, and bound with cords, then surely, *A STRONGER POWER* had arrived on the scene. Christ's presence and power had already defeated the strongest agency they knew. Satan and his helpers had been overcome, and this was all the evidence necessary to prove the absurdity of the scribes' insinuations. The emissaries from Jerusalem must have been dumbfounded by the answers of the Lord, but as they listened, He proceeded to utter one of His most serious warnings:

> **Verily I say unto you, All sins shall be forgiven unto the sons of men, and blasphemies wherewith soever they shall blaspheme. But he that shall blaspheme against the Holy Spirit hath never forgiveness, but is in danger of eternal damnation; because they said, He hath an unclean spirit (vv. 28-30).**

It is worthy of note that Matthew places this utterance after the deliverance of a demon possessed man (see Matthew 12:22-32). He then proceeds to quote the Lord as having said, "And whosoever speaketh a word against the Son of man, it shall be forgiven him; but whosoever speaketh against the Holy Spirit, it shall not be forgiven him, neither in this world, neither in the world to come." Let it be admitted that these statements have caused great problems throughout the entire history of the Church. Unfortunately, men and women, lacking adequate understanding of the Scriptures assumed responsibility for committing this unpardonable sin, and later, became inmates of mental institutions.

There is such a thing as the Unpardonable Sin, but what it is, and how it is committed, are things we must clearly understand. Let us begin by emphasizing there is *ONLY ONE* sin. There is not a second, nor a third, nor a fourth. The Bible clearly teaches that if a man dies without Christ, he is lost forever. The Lord said, "I go my way, and ye shall seek me, and shall die in your sins: whither I go, ye cannot come" (John 8:21). If there be only ONE unpardonable sin, *then the rejection of Christ and the blasphemy against the Holy Spirit must be identical.* John reminds us that the Lord said of the Holy Spirit, "When he, the spirit of truth is come, he will guide you into all the truth: *for he shall not speak of himself*; but whatsoever things he shall hear, that shall he speak; and he will shew you things to come. *He shall glorify me*; for he shall receive of mine, and shall shew it unto you" (John 16:13-14).

If the Holy Spirit is NOT TO SPEAK OF HIMSELF, then the main purpose of His mission would be to present Christ, and that is exactly what the Savior predicted. To suggest that Jesus could be identified with evil was tantamount to blasphemy, for it contradicts all the Holy Spirit taught. It has been said that if a man repeats a lie often enough, ultimately, in his eyes, the lie becomes truth. This represents a hardening of his attitude; an advance from which there can be no return. It is possible to bend a young sapling; but it is impossible to bend an old oak!

Unfortunately, many people have lifted these statements out of their original settings and have become victims of error. It cannot be overstressed that the Lord was not referring to any gifts of the Spirit; nor any teaching concerning the same. Let it be emphasized that no true Christian can ever commit the unpardonable sin, for his name is written in Heaven; his eternal salvation is assured; and his great High Priest ever liveth to make intercession for him (see the homily at the end of the chapter).

One of the most pathetic sights ever to be seen is the man or woman who sincerely believes the unpardonable sin has been committed. There is no rest by day nor night, for constantly the haunting whisper of guilt torments the soul, and threatens sanity. Any prayer for forgiveness is silenced by the thought that God will not listen; any thought of the future becomes bleak as the soul increasingly fears eternal condemnation. Considering this pitiable situation, Thomas Fuller wrote: "The sin against the Holy Spirit is ever attended with these two symptoms: absence of all contrition, and of all desire of forgiveness. Now, if thou canst truly say that thy sins are a burden to thee—that thou dost desire forgiveness, and wouldst give anything to attain it, be of good comfort. Thou has not yet, and, by God's grace, never shall commit that unpardonable offence. I will not define how near thou hast been unto it. As David said to Jonathan, 'There is but a step between me and death,' so may be, thou hast missed it very narrowly; but assure thyself, thou art not as yet guilty thereof" (Thomas Fuller, *Cause and Cure of a Wounded Conscience*).

SECTION FIVE

Expository Notes on Christ's Reference to His Family

And when His friends heard of it, they went out to lay hold on Him; for they said, He is beside himself. . . And the multitude sat about Him,

and they said unto Him, Behold, thy mother and thy brethren without seek for thee. And He answered them, saying, Who is my mother, or my brethren? And He looked round about on them which sat about Him, and said, Behold my mother and my brethren! For whosoever shall do the will of God, the same is my brother, and my sister, and mother (vv. 21 and 31-35).

Let us refrain from criticizing Mary. She was doubtless a very precious soul, who, in common with the rest of us, made a mistake. Momentarily she took her eyes from Christ and listened to the complaints of His critics. Some of the early church writers could not forgive this error. "Theophylact taxed her with vain-glory and guilt in endeavouring to draw Jesus from teaching the Word. Tertullian pronounced her guilty of incredulity. Chrysostom, of vain-glory, infirmity and madness for this very thing" (J. C. Ryle *Expository Thoughts on the Gospels*, Mark, p. 60). Mary had been the stay-at-home mother who daily heard neighbors speaking about the words and deeds of her Preacher-Son. Some of the leaders of the nation claimed he was mad for saying, "Before Abraham was, I am." Others drew attention to the fact He claimed to have placed the stars in the sky, and no man could thus speak without indicating a serious lapse in mental competence. Mary had watched her Son fashioning farm implements, but the mention of his pre-creation acts suggested insanity. The more she considered the complaints being made against Jesus, the more she forgot the miraculous nature of His birth. Like Peter, she took her eyes from the Lord, and immediately began to sink beneath waves of doubt. It is not clearly stated that she considered Him to be mad, or "beside himself," but that she came with others of her family to take Jesus home, suggests she feared He might suffer a nervous breakdown!

Luke says it was difficult to get close to the Lord, for great crowds were around Him. Someone recognized the family of Jesus and carried the news to the Savior, saying, "Behold, thy mother and thy brethren without seek for thee." The Lord was very thoughtful when He replied, "Who is my mother, or my brethren?" This was one of the rare occasions when He compared His spiritual and earthly families. There are times when a brother or sister in Christ is infinitely nearer, and maybe, even dearer, than a brother or sister in the flesh. Those who share love for the Savior, also share a common understanding, a mutual sympathy and interest, and a consuming desire to do the will of God. Members of an earthly family may have no knowledge of Christ; they may at times resent bitterly His interference in usual family loyalties.

Matthew quotes the Lord as saying, "For I am come to set a man at variance against his father, and the daughter against her mother, and the daughter-in-law against her mother-in-law. And a man's foes shall be they of his own household" (10:34-36). There have been occasions when the claims of Christ were at variance with the demands of one's family, and in those moments of crucial decision, Christians have been forced to make a painful choice. Here, quite clearly, the Lord explained that to do the will of God was of far more importance than to conform to any earthly requirements of family and friends. Blessed are they who know the will of God and do it (see Luke 11:28).

HOMILIES

Study No. 7

THE CHOICE BETWEEN COMPROMISE AND CONFLICT

Even an elementary study of the New Testament reveals a very thought-provoking fact—the Lord was never far from His Father, and Satan was never far from the Lord. God was ever present to help; Satan was always there to hinder, and consequently, each day became a battlefield upon which Jesus chose between compromise and conflict.

The Lord Jesus Christ came into this world with a passion to win the lost. He had no illusions as to what this might mean, and even from the beginning, contemplated His crucifixion. Yet, in one sinister moment, Satan unfolded a plan to solve all the problems of evangelism. "Again, the devil. . .sheweth him all the kingdoms of the world, and the glory of them; and sayeth unto him, All these things will I give thee, if thou wilt fall down and worship me" (Matt. 8:9). In those vital moments, the world seemed to be as a map spread before the Lord. He saw India, China, and Japan. He saw the jungle villages of Central Africa; He saw the crowded cities of Western Civilization; He saw the lonely islands of the sea, and realized that in all these places, Satan would resist the eternal purposes of God. Bitter would be the conflict; long would be the campaign before the world would be won, and even then the victory would hardly be complete, for many souls would have passed into eternity. It was against this background that Satan made his insidious offer.

PURITY. . .the foundation of all true usefulness

Satan said, "All this will I give thee." We do well to consider that Christ never denied Satan's ability to do as was suggested. The account as described by Luke is very pointed. "And the devil said unto him, All this power will I give thee, and the glory of them, *for that is delivered unto me; and to whomsoever I shall give it*. If thou therefore wilt worship me, *all shall be thine*" (Luke 4:6-7). The temptation suggests that Satan offered to withdraw all his opposition. There would be no more surging passions; no more vice, wickedness, godlessness. The heart of Africa would be free from superstition; the underworld of the great cities would become clean overnight; and the entire world would be released from the thraldom on sin and brought back to God. "All this will I give thee, if—." From every human angle the offer was most attractive; but the Lord Jesus refused. It, therefore, became clear that He considered the integrity of His soul to be of more importance than winning the world. The end never justifies the means, *if the means destroy the sanctity of the soul*. The evil one offers many attractive rewards, but his condition—if—is always the prelude to disaster.

PREACHING. . .the forerunner of all true blessedness

After his triumph, Jesus returned in the power of the Spirit into Galilee (Luke 4:4). "And from that time began to preach, and to say, Repent. . ." (Matt. 4:17). There can never be any effective substitute for preaching in the power of the Holy Spirit. When the Church loses this dynamic; when the services become glorified entertainments; when the message is secondary in importance to other superficial things, the Church is on the road to suicide. "And Jesus, walking by the sea of Galilee. . .called Peter and Andrew. . .and He saith unto them, Follow me, and I will make you fishers of men." These men were only converts themselves, and yet already before them was the prospect of catching men as they had often caught fish. The Lord meant to train these converts, so that as quickly as possible, they could go in search of kindred souls. Evangelism has been the greatest striking force in the history of the church. A church without a pulpit becomes a hall!

POWER. . .the feature of all true godliness

"And Jesus went about all Galilee, teaching in their synagogues, and preaching the gospel of the kingdom, and healing all manner of sickness, and all manner of disease among the people. And His fame went throughout all Syria; and they brought unto him all sick people that were taken with diverse diseases and torments, and those that were possessed with devils, and those which were lunatic, and those which had the palsy; and he healed them'' (Matt. 4:23-24). And against all these remarkable statements, we must consider another promise. ''And greater things than these shall ye do, because I go unto my Father'' (John 14:12). It would seem that something has gone wrong with the church. We may talk about opening the eyes of blind unbelief, of cleansing the moral leprosy from our cities; but are these the final word in the fulfilment of Christ's promise? The power of the church would be increased immeasurably, if we resisted every attempt to impair the sanctity of our souls. Preaching is a great weapon; holiness is also a great weapon, but when these two are combined and used by the Holy Spirit, even the gates of hell cannot prevail against us (taken in part from the author's book, *Bible Highways*, pp. 89-90).

HOMILIES

Study No. 8

THE UNPARDONABLE SIN
AND THE OTHER SIDE OF THE PICTURE!

The most frightening truth in all the Bible is that God might ultimately abandon efforts to save a lost soul. The Savior taught it is possible to sin against the Holy Spirit, a sin for which there can never be forgiveness. Almost at the beginning of time, God warned that His Spirit would not always strive with men, and this fact was demonstrated when God sent the flood upon the earth. Nevertheless, that is only one side of a very interesting picture. It is wise to consider that in spite of the sinfulness of man, God never abandons him, until the rescue operation becomes useless.

METHUSELAH AND THE FLOOD

Genesis 5:21-27

HOW THRILLING THE METHODS OF GOD

''And Enoch lived sixty and five years, and begat Methuselah. And Enoch walked with God *after he begat Methuselah* three hundred years, and begat sons and daughters.'' It is significant that the beginning of Enoch's walking with God dates from the birth of his first child. The sacred record is content to say that Enoch merely lived for the first sixty-five years of his sojourn upon earth. He was like any other man, merely fulfilling the normal functions and requirements of existence. He lived as a man among men. Then suddenly everything changed. The expected baby arrived and from that moment, the father was amazingly transformed. The glad event transported him to heights of joy hitherto unknown; and when the unprecedented ecstacy had passed, the proud father was left with a consuming desire to keep in step with God. The Almighty had sent this inestimable gift, and gratitude could only be expressed in holy conduct. How strange are the ways of God! A baby accomplished in one moment what sixty-five years of living failed to do.

HOW TRANSCENDENT THE MAN OF GOD

The child was named Methuselah. Many and varied interpretations of this strange name have been given. Certain scholars say it means, "Man of the dart or javelin." Another startling suggestion is that the name Methuselah means, "It shall not come till he die" (Lange's Commentary). A. R. Fausset says it means, "He dies, and it is sent" (*Bible Dictionary*, p. 470). Jude in the 14th and 15th verses of his short epistle, says that Enoch, the seventh from Adam, was a prophet who predicted an outpouring of judgment upon sinful people. Thus, it would appear that when he named his child, the father indicated a great spiritual revelation had been linked with the birth of his baby. It is even more startling to notice that the prediction was fulfilled. Methuselah was destined to become famous for he lived longer than any other person. He reached the age of 969 years, but in the year of his death, the great flood devastated the earth. This awesome truth was clearly seen by Enoch long before it happened, and although the name Methuselah had never been given to any child, no other name could possibly meet the requirements of the new arrival.

HOW TREMENDOUS THE MERCY OF GOD

"And all the days of Enoch were three hundred, sixty and five years: And Enoch walked with God; and he was not; for God took him." Amid the increasing corruption of the earth, this saint was out of place, and ultimately God translated him to higher and nobler society. But Methuselah lived on and on. Possibly some men thought he would never die; that he had discovered the secret of perennial youth. Yet we know the length of the patriarch's life was an indication of the overwhelming mercy of God. "It shall not come till he die." The Homecall of the aged man would coincide with the closure of God's offer of mercy to a guilty world. Thus he was allowed to linger. When other people were taken away, he remained, and every day of his long life proved to be another opportunity for men to repent. Alas, the spiritual condition of the people constantly deteriorated, and finally the Lord repented that He had ever made man. During that year, Methuselah died, and his death was followed by outpoured judgment. It is true that particular generation ultimately reached the place where forgiveness became an impossibility, but before God abandoned His rescue operation, He explored every possible avenue by which they might have been brought to repentance. That same fact is also expressed in the story of the destruction of Sodom and Gomorrah, when God sent angelic evangelists to warn Lot and his family of the impending doom (see Genesis 19). It is clearly seen in the destruction of the first born in Egypt (Exodus 12), when God provided a way by which all believers could find safety. It is a glorious truth running throughout the Scriptures. God never abandons anyone unless it is too late to do anything else (taken in part from the author's book, *Bible Treasures*, pp. 3-4). (See also "Paralysis in the Pew" . . . The Man whose right hand was withered, pp. 144, 145, and "The Unpardonable Sin," pp. 284-286 in *Luke's Thrilling Gospel*, by Ivor Powell.)

The Fourth Chapter of Mark

THEME: *Christ Becomes an Open-Air Preacher*

OUTLINE:
  I. Christ's Expanding Ministry (Verse 1)
  II. Christ's Entrancing Methods (Verse 2)
  III. Christ's Enthralling Message (Verses 3-34)
  IV. Christ's Enduring Majesty (Verses 35-41)

SECTION ONE

Expository Notes on the New Meeting Place

And He began again to teach by the seaside; and there was gathered unto Him a great multitude, so that He entered into a ship, and sat in the sea; and the whole multitude was by the sea on the land (v. 1).

This verse is a milestone on the journey through Mark's Gospel. Until that moment, the ministry of the Lord had been confined almost exclusively to the synagogues of the nation (see Mark 1:21, 1:39, and 3:1). On a few occasions, He had also entered into homes to instruct and heal those gathered there (see Mark 1:29; 2:1, and 3:19). Mark 2:13 says: "And He went forth again by the seaside; and all the multitude resorted unto Him, and He taught them." That first occasion was but the prelude of what was to follow. Two facts had become obvious. (1) The rulers of the synagogues, and the authorities they represented, had made it clear they had no sympathy for the Preacher from Nazareth. (2) The ministry and miracles of Jesus were attracting very large audiences, and no building within the land could accommodate all who wished to hear Him. It was, therefore, necessary to move to some other location where everybody could see and hear what was taking place.

As the Lord considered the possibilities, two places seemed suitable. (1) The mountains bordering on the Sea of Galilee where He could look up at the audience seated on the rising slopes, and (2) the seashore, where people could sit on the beach and listen as He spoke to them from a boat. Thereafter, the greater part of His ministry was exercised in the open air. A boat became His pulpit, the realm of nature His cathedral, and the blue sky the roof of the God-made auditorium. The boat mentioned here was probably the same one mentioned in chapter 3, verse 9. *The Amplified New Testament* translates the verse, "And He told His disciples to have a little boat in constant readiness for Him because of the crowd, lest they press hard upon Him and crush Him." *Phillips' Modern English Translation* of the Bible says: "Then once again He began to teach them by the lakeside. A bigger crowd than ever collected around Him, so that He got into a small boat on the lake, and sat down, while the crowd covered the ground right down to the water's edge . . ." Obviously, the fame of Jesus had spread throughout the land, and the tremendous interest generated by his continuing miracles brought thousands of people to His meetings. This was indeed revival at its best, something unknown in the nation for centuries.

SECTION TWO

Expository Notes on the New Type of Teaching

And He taught them many things by parables, and said unto them in His doctrine, Hearken; Behold there went out a sower to sow (v. 2).

To appreciate the new style of message delivered by Jesus, it is necessary to understand the difference between speaking in the open-air and addressing an audience indoors. For the most part, people who attend a service either in a church or a synagogue, do so because they want to be present. They are, more or less, *a captive audience*. For better or worse, they enjoy or endure a sermon to its end. Very seldom will any man or woman leave the service because the speaker has become uninteresting. A service in a park or at the beach is totally different. There, a man may leave at any moment; furthermore, some listeners might arrive when the sermon is half over. The psychological approach of the speaker needs to be flexible to meet situations as they arise. The early part of my own preaching career was spent with a band of itinerant evangelists known throughout Great Britain as The Pilgrim Preachers. Our leader was an old saint known affectionately as Daddy Luff. He was Mr. Ernest Luff, who owned a Bible Store in Frinton-on-Sea in Essex. He did more to mold my young life than any other person I ever knew! I shall always remember the day when he took me aside to deliver his usual advice to a new "boy." The other members of the party merely smiled, for they too had received the same lecture. The old man told me never to preach about hell unless I had a sob in my voice. He reminded me that some preachers appear to be glad there is such a place, so that hecklers, someday, may be rewarded for interrupting a good speaker! He told me I should never tell long drawn-out stories. A man passing on the top of a tram-car would only be within range of my voice long enough to hear two sentences. I should have enough Gospel in either sentence to point him to Jesus. I owe such a lot to that wise old counselor.

Let it be admitted that the audience which listened to the Lord had come of their own volition; they could hardly be termed "a captive audience." Many of those people had walked great distances just for the privilege of hearing Jesus of Nazareth. Some might have been picnicking on or near the beach, but at least, they were free to leave whenever they desired. Professor Garvey, my instructor in homiletics, always emphasized that the first two minutes of a sermon are crucial. He said that after the hymn preceding the sermon, the congregation would sit down, shift around to get a comfortable position, and then begin listening to see if the minister would be any good! The speaker, so said Professor Garvey, had just one or two minutes in which to capture the thoughts of the listeners. If he failed, the ladies would be thinking about the Sunday dinner, and the men would be playing a round of golf! Readers of the professor's books were reminded that it did not really matter what the first two minutes of the sermon contained. The speaker could talk about anything as long as he gripped the minds of the audience. This was excellent advice. Obviously, the Lord was a Master of the art of preaching.

Calmly He sat in His floating pulpit and looked, first at His audience, and then at the farmer sowing seed in the fields alongside the sea of Galilee. "Listen," He said, "Behold there went out a sower to sow" and probably as He uttered those words, His outstretched hand pointed to His living illustration. It has been said that a parable is an earthly story with a heavenly meaning. Be that as it may, the fact is readily understood that very few people fail to respond to a good story. If the tale be simply told, and gripping in its details, every listener will award the speaker with rapt attention. The Lord realized this truth, and seeing a sermon spread out before Him, He proceeded with His message.

SECTION THREE

Expository Notes on the Parable of the Sower

. . . Behold, there went out a sower to sow: And it came to pass, as he sowed, some fell by the wayside, and the fowls of the air came and

devoured it up. And some fell on stony ground where it had not much
earth; and immediately it sprang up, because it had no depth of earth,
but when the sun was up, it was scorched; and because it had no root,
it withered away. And some fell among thorns, and the thorns grew
up, and choked it, and it yielded no fruit. And other fell on good ground,
and did yield fruit that sprang up and increased; and brought forth,
some thirty, and some sixty, and some an hundred fold. And He said
unto them, he that hath ears to hear, let him hear (vv. 3-9).

All the listeners understood this parable for they were accustomed
to the topography of the district. Often between the boundaries of
properties there was a narrow footpath made hard by the constant
treading of feet. Occasionally, small stones were pressed into the soil
to give added stability. The corners, or more inaccessible parts of the
field, were often neglected and there the weeds and thistles flourished.
The larger roads running through the country, and close to the fields,
completed the picture described by the Lord. There was nothing wrong
with the seed, and neither was the farmer inexperienced. The results
of the sowing was governed by the circumstances in which the seed
was received. When given a fair chance, it germinated and grew; when
hindered by all kinds of enemies, there was danger that it would die.

This was a masterpiece in the art of preaching. The Lord could have
spoken these words in less than one minute, and yet within that short
span of time, He divided the congregation into several categories. His
unspoken question could have been, "To which of these do you belong?"
The *first* seed produced nothing, for the fowls of the air came and
consumed it. The *second* seed produced only the blade for there was
no depth of soil to sustain growth. The *third* seed made real progress
and was almost ready to produce fruit, but, unfortunately, the
surrounding thistles choked it. The *fourth* seed produced fruit and
rewarded the farmer for all his effort. It is doubtful if any other man
could have said so much, in such a short time, with so few words.

It would have been easy for anyone to identify the *first* of these
categories. The scribes and Pharisees were hearing the word, but were
seizing every opportunity to find something to criticize. They had no
intention of believing; they disliked the Speaker, and detested all He
said. Satan had no difficulty whatsoever in snatching away the seed as
soon as it fell on their stony, unresponsive hearts. The *second* type was
also easily recognized, for there were many people who had been swept
off their feet by exuberant enthusiasm. They had never heard such a
Preacher; they were enthralled by His miracles; this certainly was the
King of Israel. Most preachers would have been thrilled with this

responsive an audience, "But Jesus did not commit himself unto them, because He knew all men, and needed not that any should testify of man, for He knew what was in man" (John 2:24-25). The same crowd which would have crowned Him one day was ready to crucify Him the next day. It is easy to be a good Christian when everything seems favorable, but the test of true faithfulness comes when problems make continuance difficult. "But when the sun was up, it was scorched; and because it had no root, it withered away" (v. 6).

The *third* type at first appeared to be more reliable than the others. The seed germinated, developed, showed excellent signs of growth, but then, suddenly began to wither. Other plants were stealing the moisture; the corn was slowly being starved to death. If the thistles had been removed, the end result would have been different. Weeding is an essential part of every aspect of good gardening. Pruning is an essential part of all wise fruit-growing. The same truth applies to the growth of spirituality within the souls of men and women. The Bible tells of a very fine young man whose name was Demas. He had listened to Paul on innumerable occasions, and the seed of the Gospel within his life gave excellent promise of a bright future. Alas, the young man forgot to "weed" his garden, and it was written by Paul at a later date, "...Demas hath forsaken me, having loved this present world, and is departed unto Thessalonica..." (2 Tim. 3:10). Unfortunately, it would appear that most of the crowd which heard Jesus that day beside the sea, failed to graduate to class four. Mark says later in his gospel (14:50), "And they all forsook Him and fled." Others remained to bear fruit, some thirty fold, some sixty fold, and some even a hundred fold; and from these brave and wonderful souls sprang the church in all its beauty. It is most significant that as far as Mark was concerned, that first sermon in the open-air, envisaged all that was to take place throughout the centuries ahead (see the homily at the end of the chapter).

"And when He was alone, they that were about Him with the twelve, asked of Him the parable" (v. 10). Mark, unlike Matthew and Luke, seems to emphasize that the questions were put to Jesus *when He was alone*! This could hardly have been the case had He been sitting in the boat. Mark seems to be interested in *the timing* of the questioning rather than *the substance* of the question. The other writers seem to stress the reason for the story-telling. Mark alone remembers the Lord had ceased his preaching, probably had returned to the shore, and was accompanied only by His more intimate friends. Puzzled by His new approach to witnessing, the disciples asked, "Why speakest thou unto them in parables?" (Matt. 13:10). They had listened to His preaching in the synagogue; they appreciated His fearless utterances, but the change to story-telling amazed them. They were asking, "Master, what has happened to you? You are always decisive in your statements; you never flinch from denouncing sin and warning sinners, but now you have lost your punch!" If we may be permitted to use another modern saying, they were unaware that the longest way around, sometimes, is the shortest way home!

And He said unto them, Unto you it is given to know the mystery of the kingdom of God; but unto them that are without, all these things are done in parables: that seeing they may see, and not perceive; and hearing, they may hear, and not understand; lest at any time they should be converted, and their sins should be forgiven them (vv. 11-12).

Let it be candidly admitted, this has always been one of the most difficult scriptures to understand. At the first reading, one would think God had deliberately veiled His truth, so that certain people would be incapable of understanding what was being said. It is very necessary to make haste slowly in trying to decide the true meaning of this scripture.

1. There are preachers who affirm that the guiding principles of the Bible teach acceptance with God is something predestined from eternity; that election overrides any choice made by a human. They affirm that unless God predestines a man to salvation, he can never be saved. They believe that the doctrine of "The Whosoever Will" is erroneous, misleading, and unscriptural. I remember being asked by one of the proponents of these doctrines, to imagine a tray filled with grains of sand and steel filings. I was told that if a powerful magnet moved over the tray, the steel filings would "jump" while the grains of sand would remain unresponsive. The speaker went on to explain that the "Call of God" works in a similar fashion. When the Holy Spirit moves among men, the elected ones respond by yielding to the Savior; the others do not, and die in their sins. When I affirmed that in such a case, sinners were not responsible for their rejection, as they never had a chance; the speaker answered, "Well, that is how it is." This I totally reject. Let us be honest and give God credit for having said exactly what He meant: "whosoever will may come."

2. Whatever this scripture may, or may not mean, let us remember it was, first and foremost, a quotation from Isaiah 6:9-10 ". . . Go and tell this people, Hear ye indeed, but understand not; and see ye indeed, but perceive not. Make the heart of this people fat, and make their ears heavy, and shut their eyes; lest they see with their eyes, and hear with their ears, and understand with their heart, and convert and be healed."

Obviously, since both Isaiah and the Lord used identical words, there must have been a similarity between their audiences. Isaiah and the other contemporary prophets ministered to people who loved their idols; stoned God's messengers, and who ultimately paid for their sins by being slaves in Babylon. Jesus ministered to people who rejected His teaching; sanctioned and even clamored for His death, and who ultimately were massacred by the legions of Rome. Isaiah was specially commissioned to preach to his people, so it must be obvious that God was leaving no stone unturned in a valiant effort to reach people before they reached a point of no return. Similarly, the Lord went throughout Palestine preaching and teaching the gospel, but the moment arrived when He had to say, "If thou hadst known, at least in this thy day, the things which belong unto thy peace! *but now they are hid from thine eyes*" (Luke 19:42).

3. The Lord, Isaiah, and all the prophets recognized there comes an end to God's offer of mercy, and once His door of opportunity closes, it cannot be reopened. Did the Savior realize that such a moment had come, and was sorrow reflected in His voice, when He seemed to say, "What is the use? You will not believe, whatever I say." The Bible teaches that as there are degrees of responsibility, so there will be degrees of punishment (See Matthew 11:23-24). If at the day of judgment, it will be more tolerable for Sodom and Gomorrah than for other cities, then added condemnation belongs to those who having heard more, are consequently responsible for their actions. Sodom never had a church, nor a Sunday school, nor a Preacher like Jesus. Sodom never witnessed lepers being cleansed, nor the blind being made to see. Is it not true that when people continually harden their hearts, even God recognizes the futility of trying to bring them to repentance? It is the hand of mercy and not judgment which closes the door of opportunity. To continue pleading with hardened sinners would only increase their responsibility and punishment. Did not such conditions exist in the times of Isaiah and Jesus of Nazareth? Is not this the reason for the messages given by both God's messengers? (see also Matthew 13:14-15).

And He said unto them, Know ye not this parable? and how then will ye know all parables? The sower soweth the word. And these are they by the wayside, where the word is sown; but when they have heard, Satan cometh immediately, and taketh away the word that was sown in their hearts. And these are they likewise which are sown on stony ground; who, when they have heard the word, immediately receive it with gladness. And have no root in themselves, and so endure but for

a time; afterward, when affliction or persecution ariseth for the word's sake, immediately they are offended. And these are they which are sown among thorns; such as hear the word, and the cares of this world, and the deceitfulness of riches and the lust of other things entering in, choke the word, and it becometh unfruitful. And these are they which are sown on good ground; such as hear the word, and receive it, and bring forth fruit, some thirty fold, some sixty, and some an hundred (vv. 13-20).

Probably this parable of the Savior has been more widely used than any other of the Lord's story-sermons. Preachers in every age understood its message, and easily found in their congregations each class of people represented. I shall always remember preaching at a Baptist church in London, England. The services continued nightly for two weeks, and one special man attended regularly. I learned that often he had to come through very dense fog, but each night he traveled fourteen miles in order to hear what I had to say. His interest was apparent, and one night I was delighted to see him in the counseling room where I introduced people to Christ. That night, although many people accepted the Lord as their Savior, he did not. Later, when we were alone, I tried to influence him to change his decision, but I failed. He was adamant when he said, "I do not want Christ; I love my sin and will not give it up." Although he continued to attend the services, he became increasingly unresponsive, and finally I had to admit I was wasting my time.

FROM SUNDAY SCHOOL TO SCAFFOLD

Perhaps it would be wise not to mention his real name. Let us be content to refer to him as John, and to remember that he was well known to my old colleague, ex-Police Constable, Fred Dawes, of the London Police Force. He belonged to a Sunday school in the poorer part of London, and was one of five boys who formed a class. Nearly every Sunday he sat with the others and listened as the teacher expounded the Word of God. He seemed to be very interested, and the teacher hoped he would soon surrender himself to Christ. Then came the Sunday, when impelled by strong desires, the leader urged the boys to yield to the call and claims of Christ. Four of the scholars agreed to do so. John refused to follow their example; he was hesitant and ill at ease. . . He watched as the other boys wrote in the teacher's Bible. Beneath the words, "I will trust the Lord Jesus today," they wrote their names. When John's turn came, he took the pen and wrote: "I will trust Jesus some day."

Within a few weeks, John became an absentee, and after some months, other associations led him into evil practices. Apparently, he forgot the lessons learned in Sunday school, and his criminal activities increased. Finally, he was arrested and charged with murder. The evidence against him was overwhelming; he was found guilty and sentenced to death. Yet, before he paid the penalty for his crime, he heard once again from his former teacher...On the last fateful morning, accompanied by several of the senior scholars, the teacher visited the prison. He was not permitted to see John; the Prison Chaplain was already with the condemned man. The teacher asked the Governor if he would take the Bible and show the prisoner what he had written therein. Would he tell him that his old Sunday school teacher and some friends were outside, and would he ask if there's a hymn they could sing for him? The governor hesitated; this was unusual procedure. He had no wish to violate prison regulations...He took the Bible and went away. Prayerfully, the small group of Christians waited...When he came back, the teacher asked, "Did you tell him we were here?" "Yes." "What did he say?" "Nothing." "Did you ask him if he would like us to sing a hymn?" "Yes, he would like you to sing the hymn he used to sing in Sunday school, 'When I survey the wondrous Cross on which the Prince of glory died'." The small group of workers stood with their backs to the wind, as they sang lustily, hoping the condemned man would be able to hear. Alas, the prison bell announcing the execution rang as they were singing,

> See from His head, His hands, His feet,
> Sorrow and love flow mingled down:
> Did ere such love and sorrow meet,
> Or thorns compose so rich a crown?

John had paid the penalty for his crime.

When my friend had finished telling his story, I asked what became of the other boys in that same class. He replied, "Yes, I thought you would ask that question. I can tell you. Two of them became missionaries; the other two became prominent Christian businessmen in the city of London. Their decision for Christ led to years of fruitful Christian service; John's indecision led to crime and retribution on a murderer's scaffold" (from the author's book, *Bible Windows*, pp. 51-52). We are reminded again that some seed fell by the wayside and was stolen; some sprang up but did not endure; some were choked by things of this world, but other seed became fruitful. The question should be inescapable, "What will happen to us?"

> And He said unto them, Is a candle brought to be put under a bushel, or under a bed? and not to be put on a candlestick? For there is nothing hid, which shall not be manifested; neither was anything kept secret, but that it should come abroad. If any man have ears to hear, let him hear. And He said unto them, Take heed what ye hear; what measure ye mete, it shall be measured to you; and unto you that hear, shall more be given. For he that hath, to him shall be given; and he that hath not, from him shall be taken even that which he hath. And He said, So is the kingdom of God, as if a man should cast seed into the ground; and should sleep, and rise night and day, and the seed should spring and grow up, he knoweth not how. For the earth bringeth forth fruit of herself; first the blade, then the ear, after that the full corn in the ear. But when the fruit is brought forth, immediately he putteth in the sickle, because the harvest is come. And He said, Whereunto shall we liken the kingdom of God? or with what comparison shall we compare it? It is like a grain of mustard seed, which, when it is sown in the earth, is less than all the seeds that be in the earth. But when it is sown, it groweth up, and becometh greater than all herbs, and shooteth out great branches; so that the fowls of the air may lodge under the shadow of it (vv. 21-32).

We have now reached what to some readers might seem a strange and bewildering section of Mark's manuscript. Within the short space of twelve verses, the writer gives extracts from several sermons, and they have little, if any, connection with each other. It is interesting to discover that Matthew and Luke also mention these sayings, but unlike Mark, they have them in several different places. This is particularly so with Matthew's gospel. For example, Mark 4:21 is found in Matthew 5:15. Mark 4:22 is found in Matthew 10:26. Mark 4:24 is found in Matthew 7:2. Verse 25 is found in Matthew 13:12 and is repeated in Matthew 25:29. To say the least, this is interesting. It suggests certain things:

1. These, apparently unrelated statements, must have been extracts from sermons repeated several times. As the Lord moved throughout the country, He often used material used on former occasions. There was nothing wrong with this procedure. People suffering from the same disease often receive the same medicine!

2. As Simon Peter listened to his Lord, certain features of the sermons made profound impressions upon his mind. He did not remember all that was said, but he never forgot certain outstanding features of each message. Later when he shared his memoirs with John Mark, those sayings came flooding into his mind, and Mark, as a faithful emanuensis, recorded what Peter said.

3. Luke at the beginning of his gospel, explained he was setting forth *in order* the things which he knew had happened (see Luke 1:1, 3). Mark made no such claim. He was not concerned with *when* Christ uttered these words; he was more interested in the fact that Christ *had* said them.

4. There remains the possibility, that under the guidance of the Holy Spirit, the various sayings of Jesus came simultaneously to Peter and Mark, so that we should have the benefit of considering them together. If that be true, then the following headings might be helpful.

THE LAWS OF RADIANCE...
the candle must be allowed to shine! (vv. 21-22)

Its main purpose in life is to shine in the darkness, and unless it be permitted to do this, its existence is unjustified. When a man lights a candle and then covers it with a snuffer, such as a peck measure, the man only advertises his stupidity. Similarly, the Gospel of Truth was the light to shine into the darkness of the world's sin. That light had been entrusted to the Lord, and later would be given to those representing Him. Nothing should ever be allowed to interfere with its ministry of illumination.

THE LAWS OF RECOMPENSE...
a man gets what he gives! (vv. 24-25)

I remember the late Dr. Frank Boreham, that prince of preachers, saying, "If you have anything you cannot live without, give it away!" Nothing is so important that it should dominate one's life. The Lord taught, "Give, and it shall be given unto you; good measure, pressed down, and shaken together, and running over, shall men give into your bosom. For with the same measure that ye mete, withal it shall be measured to you again" (Luke 6:38). A man will doubtless be rewarded according to the sacrificial service rendered. It behooves him then, to give to his utmost ability.

THE LAWS OF REWARD AND RETRIBUTION...
the harvest is coming (vv. 26-29)

Here, there is an indirect reference to the Parable of the Sower, for the Lord speaks of the seed sown. However, there appears to be a difference. Formerly, attention was focused on a man who went forth to sow; here the sower is said to have wasted a lot of time sleeping! The earth, and not the farmer, is given credit for the growth of the seed. Other forces were at work in spite of the laziness of the slumbering man. Come what may, it was inevitable that at the end of the season, there would be a harvest. If the man continued to sleep, the day of harvest would proclaim his foolishness. If he decreased his time of sleeping, and attended to the needs of the farm, then harvest time would be a period of intense rejoicing. It was incumbent on all sowers of seed, not to sleep when they should be working!

THE LAWS OF REDEMPTION...
the Kingdom of God will grow (vv. 30-32)

The Savior said, "Whereunto shall we liken the kingdom of God? or with what comparison shall we compare it? It is like a grain of mustard seed..." (vv. 30-31). Since God was the first to sow the seed, it should be obvious that He would complete what He commenced. The days of small beginnings would be followed by times of unprecedented triumph. The tiny mustard seed would become a towering tree, giving shelter to all who sought it. Within the land of Israel, it is possible to see mustard trees growing to great heights. In some senses, it remains inconceivable that, from the infinitesimal mustard seed, should grow a tree of such proportions. The people who listened to the Lord knew exactly what He meant. They knew the birds were very partial to the small mustard seeds. To see many of them over the trees was a common sight. Jesus likened the Kingdom of God to that seed, and the resultant tree. One might ask, how this could possibly be? The unmistakable answer lies in the irrepressible life within the seed. This would germinate and continue to grow until all men would be aware of its presence. Here we have the history of the Church. Insignificant men and women within whose breasts God's new life had been implanted, would defy the difficulties of a hostile terrain, and in all parts of the world, their message would begin to influence hearers. Redeemed by the love of God, those heralds of the Cross could not rest until others shared their happiness. They climbed mountains; they descended into valleys; they crossed oceans; they laughed at impossibilities, and wherever they planted the seed of the Gospel, it took root and grew. Today, thank God, the sun never sets upon the church, and millions of people find rest in its shadow.

And with many such parables spake He the word unto them, as they were able to hear it. But without a parable spake He not unto them;

and when they were alone, He expounded all things to his disciples (vv. 33-34).

HIS SPECIAL PREACHING

"...with parables...He spake the word..." (v. 33). What a window is to a building, an illustration is to a sermon—it admits light. A building without a window resembles a prison or a vault. A sermon without an illustration becomes boring and unattractive. The Savior became the Master of story-preaching. He enshrined eternal truth in every-day happenings, and when He preached in parables, even the children remembered what He said.

HIS SPECIAL PERCEPTION

"...as they were able to hear it" (v. 33). He recognized their capabilities of understanding, and made absolutely sure He was not *"preaching above their heads."* The same thought is expressed in John 16:12. Jesus said to His disciples, "I have many things to say unto you, but ye cannot bear them now." Any message which is to change the lives of men and women must have three necessary qualities. (1) It must *convey* truth. If it be but an expulsion of hot air, an expression of the favorite ideas of a forceful, enthusiastic speaker, it will never accomplish anything of eternal value. A sermon must convey the truth of God; it must reveal to hearers something totally wonderful. Every God-inspired sermon should begin with "Thus saith the Lord." (2) It must *convict* hearers. When God speaks to men, they become either guilty or glad. If guilty, it is because the word of God has made them aware of grievous shortcomings; they have done that which should not have been done. If glad, it is because the message has reminded them of the faithfulness of the Savior. Under no circumstances could He ever fail those who trust Him. (3) It must *convince* everybody that the wisest way to travel is to go God's way! This is the meaning of conversion. God has said, "If my people, which are called by my name, shall humble themselves, and pray, and seek my face, and *turn from their wicked ways*; then will I hear from heaven, and will forgive their sin, and will heal their land" (2 Chronicles 7:14). When the Lord had finished preaching, it was never difficult for hearers to remember what He had said. He talked to them, *"as they were able to hear it."*

HIS SPECIAL PUPILS

"...and when they were alone, He expounded all things to His disciples" (v. 34). The word translated "expounded" comes from the

Greek *epiluo* and is not found anywhere else except in 2 Peter 1:20 where the verse reads: "Knowing this first, that no prophecy of the scripture is of any private *interpretation*" (*epiluseos*). Literally, this means the unloosening of a knot! The Lord took that which was inexplicable to the disciples, and carefully loosened the difficult parts of the story, explaining every detail. When He had finished, they were able to appreciate the message, and were ready to repeat His words wheresoever He might send them.

SECTION FOUR

Expository Notes on the Stilling of the Storm

And the same day, when the even was come, He saith unto them, Let us pass over unto the other side. And when they had sent away the multitude, they took Him even as He was in the ship. And there were also with Him other little ships (vv. 35-36).

"They took Him even *as He was,*—in the boat" (v. 36). They did not go ashore to obtain provisions. This would have presented problems as the immense crowd would be everywhere. If there were shops in the vicinity, each one would have been besieged by hungry customers. Therefore, as soon as the preaching ceased, the disciples announced there would be no more preaching until the next day, and urging the audience to go away and rest, they set sail across the lake. The presence of many other ships suggests local boat owners had used their small vessels to get closer to Christ; something almost impossible on the beach. Perhaps the crowd did not believe what the disciples said, and hoping there would be additional activity on the other side of the lake, they formed a flotilla to accompany the Lord. Some of those boat owners might have lived on the other side and were returning to their homes. It was certainly a most picturesque ending to a perfect day. Alas, that beautiful evening was destined to be ruined.

And there arose a great storm of wind, and the waves beat into the ship, so that it was now full. And He was in the hinder part of the ship, asleep on a pillow: and they awake Him, and say unto Him, Master, carest thou not that we perish? (vv. 37-38).

There was a time when liberal theologians dismissed this account as fantasy, but their criticisms were unjustified. The science of meteorology now gives warning of approaching weather conditions, and as a result, the fishermen of Galilee know when it is best to refrain from fishing. Long ago, before weather forecasters started practicing their art, the ancient Palestinians did not enjoy today's privileges. They looked at the sky, and tried to decide what might happen before their work ended. Alas, it was possible to set sail beneath a blue sky, when the lake was perfectly calm, and before many minutes had passed, they could be fighting for their lives against forces beyond their control. Thompson in his fascinating volume, *The Land and the Book*, p. 375, says, "Storms of wind rush wildly through the deep mountain gorges which descend from the north and north-east, and are not only violent, but sudden; they often take place when the weather is clear." Norval Geldenhuys, quoting Plummer, says of the hills around the lake, "These are furrowed with ravines like funnels, down which the winds rush with great velocity" (*The New International Commentary on the New Testament, The Gospel of Luke*, p. 243). Probably the most awesome description of that stormy scene comes from *The Amplified New Testament* which says: "But as they were sailing, He fell off to sleep. And a whirlwind revolving from below upward swept down on the lake, and the boat was filling with water, and they were in great danger" (Luke 8:23).

The Reader's Digest *Great Encyclopedic Dictionary*, in explaining the meaning of the word "tornado," says, "A whirlwind of exceptional violence, accompanied by a pendulous, funnel-shaped cloud marking the narrow path of greatest destruction." All residents of the mid-western and eastern States of America are painfully aware of the destructive power of tornadoes. During one of my visits to Florida, Dr. Harold Horne, in whose home I was staying, invited me to go fishing in the Gulf of Mexico which bordered his property. He had been given a beautiful fishing net, and together we strung this out from the land to a distance of perhaps one hundred feet. After two hours we returned, not to land fish but to try and rescue the net from the turbulent waters of the bay. For some inexplicable reason, the calm sea had become stormy and with each moment, conditions were getting worse. I never worked so hard in my life pulling on the oars, and rowing against the tide to give my friend a chance to retrieve his net. With one hand, Dr. Horne held the boat; with the other, inch by inch, miraculously, he succeeded. Finally, together we brought the ship to the shore. If fish can laugh; they had a carnival that day! Later, the radio announced a tornado had touched down only a few hundred yards from our location. We had been too busy even to see it!

The Greek word translated "storm" is *lailaph* and, according to Schmidt, ". . . it is never a single gust, nor a steadily blowing wind, however violent, but a storm breaking forth from black thunder-clouds in furious gusts with floods or rain, and throwing everything topsy-turvy.'' What we had experienced was a minor tornado in five feet of water. I shudder to think what would have happened to us had we been in the middle of Tampa Bay. It is not difficult, therefore, to appreciate the terror which filled the hearts of the disciples when they were suddenly swamped by a raging tempest. The amazing feature about the entire experience was that Jesus slept through the storm. At the back of all such boats was a small seat upon which a passenger could be seated. There was also a small carpet and a cushion. That Jesus could use the cushion as a pillow and sleep so soundly, cannot be less than amazing. The thunder was crashing; lightning flashing through the air; waves were hitting the boat and the water rising so quickly, that all attempts to bail it out were futile. The voices of the desperate men fighting for their lives were loud and filled with fear, and yet Jesus remained asleep! He must have been extremely weary with the exertions of the day, for the shattering sounds of that fierce storm failed to awaken Him. And yet, in contrast, the moment one of the disciples asked for help, He was awake and able to respond to the desperate request. The parallel passage in Luke 8:24-25 reads: "And they came to him, and awoke him, saying, Master, Master, we perish. Then he arose, and rebuked the wind and the raging of the water; and they ceased, and there was a calm." The word translated "rebuked" is *epetimeesen*, and this is very suggestive. *The Amplified New Testament* renders the passage, "And He, being thoroughly awakened, *centured*, and *blamed*, and *rebuked* the wind and the raging waves . . ." "It is impossible to censure an insensible thing; to scold, as it were, an inanimate object. To blame the wind for blowing would be ludicrous, and, therefore, we are obliged to give added consideration to the text. Could it have been that the Lord recognized in the unfriendly elements the handiwork of His greatest enemy, Satan? Was this another attempt to kill him, this time by drowning? Throughout the itineraries of the Lord, the devil constantly tried to end Christ's life prematurely. This text suggests the Lord rebuked not the storm itself, but the hand which controlled the elements . . ." (taken from the author's commentary on *Luke's Thrilling Gospel*, pp. 193-194).

And He arose, and rebuked the wind, and said unto the sea, Peace, be still. And there was a great calm. And He said unto them, Why are ye so fearful? How is it that ye have no faith? And they feared

exceedingly, and said one to another, What manner of man is this, that even the wind and the sea obey Him? (vv. 39-41).

The word translated "still" is very interesting. It means *to be muzzled*, as if the Lord were commanding a threatening dog to be muzzled; that is, He was making it incapable of biting or harming anyone. I remember a personal experience during a storm in Wales. My church had a corrugated roof, and every time hailstones fell, the sounds underneath were deafening. We had prepared a special program with which to celebrate Christmas; our children had been well rehearsed and although some of them were only four or five years old, they were ready for the big occasion! We had dressed them in the national costumes of other nations, and were planning to depict "Christmas Around the World." The church was packed to capacity with adoring parents who had come to see their children perform, and then came the storm! I stood in the pulpit and shouted to the audience, and even then, they could hardly hear what I was saying. The entire town was being devastated by a hail storm and the effect within our church was paralyzing. I shouted, asking the people to pray, and doubtless, they did, for suddenly there was a great silence. The hailstones had ceased falling. We began our program, and the results exceeded our expectations. The proceedings lasted about one hour and a half, but all the time I was mindful of the miracle which God had performed. When the time arrived for the closing hymn, I decided to express publicly my gratitude to God for answering our prayers. Alas, I hardly had an opportunity, for as we were singing, the hailstones began falling again, and I was unable to carry out my intentions. The noise once more had become deafening, and no one could hear what I was trying to say. Later, when I mentioned the lull in the storm, the people of the community asked what I meant—there had been no lull! When I asked questions throughout the area, I discovered that homes had been damaged; telephone poles were down, and there had been no let up in the storm's activity all night. Some people looked at me rather skeptically when I recounted what had happened in our church. Yet, what I said was undeniable, for I had a packed congregation to corroborate my testimony.

It is in this connection we best understand what happened on the sea of Galilee. We know that the miracle was real, but what happened just once on that lake, has happened millions of times in the storm-filled lives of Christians. Before we embark on any voyage through life, it is well and wise to be sure Christ is in the boat. We cannot sink when He is near, for even *"the winds and the waves obey Him."*

HOMILIES

Study No. 9

THE CHURCH. . .The Mighty Mustard Seed (Mark 4:31-32)

It is interesting to know that Jesus was mindful of small things. Doubtless, He loved to speak to crowds, and was aware of immensity in every possible way. Nevertheless, He saw what others were apt to miss. The individual was never lost in the crowd; the inconspicuous was never overshadowed by the obvious! He was aware of the value of a sparrow, and said one never fell but what God saw it. He spoke of a widow's gift, and although it only amounted to two farthings, said it superceded the lavish gifts brought by wealthy Pharisees. He loved small children, and when the disciples would have sent them away, countermanded the order, and welcomed those boys and girls to His arms. Perhaps the most eloquent commentary in support of this assertion was the Lord's interest in, and reference to, the very small mustard seed. He said it resembled the Kingdom of God; it was an embryonic picture of the Church.

HOW SMALL AND INSIGNIFICANT

". . .a grain of mustard seed. . .when it is sown in the earth, is less than all the seeds that be in the earth" (v. 32). W. E. Shewell-Cooper, writes: "Most Bible students agree that the plant is the black mustard, *brassica nigra*. This is the plant grown for the production of the normal mustard, but in our Lord's day, it was grown possibly for its oil content. Plants, when isolated, may grow to a height of fifteen feet, and have a thick main stem, with branches thick enough to bear the weight of a bird. . . Mark 4:32 describes the plant as 'greater than all herbs', and *the black mustard* certainly fits this description. The seeds are black and very small; so small that they appear almost as nothing."

The idea that such a small seed is capable of producing a large tree seems ludicrous. When the Lord likened it to the kingdom of God, He was indirectly predicting the future. His disciples, untrained by universities, were completely unequal to the task of overthrowing pagan superstitions. That these men should start a movement which one day would spread throughout the world, was unbelievable. No one would have given the idea a second thought.

HOW STRONG AND INVINCIBLE

Jesus said, "...I will build my church, and the gates of hell shall not prevail against it" (Matt. 16:18). It will be remembered how Satan made the kingdoms of the world to pass before the Lord, and offered them as a gift if Jesus would worship him (see Matthew 4:8-9). The Lord preferred to win the world another way, and to make that possible, took man's sin to the Cross, and there laid the redemptive foundations of the kingdom He intended to create. His Gospel—the message at which the scholastic world laughed—would be as the seed of the mustard tree. It would become large enough to shelter the entire world.

HOW SAFE AND INVALUABLE

Jesus said, "But when the grain of mustard seed is sown, it groweth up, and becometh greater than all herbs, and shooteth out great branches; so that the fowls of the air may lodge under the shadow of it" (Mark 4:32). The fowls of the air were the finches, linnets, and sparrows found throughout the land. These birds do not nest in the tree; they eat the seeds, and find shade from the relentless heat of the eastern sunshine. When the Lord used this illustration He indicated that in the centuries ahead, within His Church, countless souls would find refuge, and food for their deepest longings. It would be their hiding place from the storms of life.

O where are kings and empires now
Of old, that went and came?
But Lord, Thy Church is praying yet,
A thousand years the same.

We mark her goodly battlements,
And her foundations strong:
We hear within the solemn voice,
Of her unending song.

For not like kingdoms of this world
Thy holy Church, O God:
Though earthquake shocks are threatening her
And tempests are abroad.

Unshaken as eternal hills
Immovable she stands
A mountain that shall fill the earth,
A House not made with hands.

Samuel J. Stone (1839-1900)

HOMILIES

Study No. 10

JESUS THE SON OF GOD... What They Thought About Him

"For where two or three are gathered in my name, there am I in the midst of them" (Matt. 18:20). Jesus always planned to be in the midst of His people. The Lord was in the midst of the camp of Israel (See Psalm 46:5). Christ on that memorable resurrection day stood in the midst of His disciples (John 20:19). He stood in the midst of the seven golden lampstands (Rev. 1:13). He will be in the midst of the heavenly throng (Rev. 5:4). Throughout the ages, Jesus, the Son of God has been at the center of world opinion, and from time to time, all kinds of people have testified concerning Him.

THE CONFESSION OF DEMONS...A Testimony of Remembrance

Heaven was shocked; there was insurrection among the angels of God. The impossible had taken place; the unbelievable had happened. Lucifer, Son of the Morning, had sown seeds of dissension, and like Absalom of a much later time, had gathered his forces around him. He was intent on making himself equal with God, but his plans were thwarted from the beginning. "How art thou fallen from heaven, O Lucifer, son of the morning! how art thou cut down to the ground, which did weaken the nations? For thou hast said in thine heart...I will exalt my throne above the stars of God...I will be like the most High" (Isa. 14:12-15). "And there appeared another wonder in heaven; and behold a great red dragon...And his tail drew the third part of the stars of heaven, and did cast them to the earth" (Rev. 12:3-4). The evil powers which were expelled from Heaven never forgot what they saw at the beginning of time. They had excellent memories, for when confronted by the One Who had come to earth to save men, they cried in fear, "What have I to do with thee, Jesus, THOU SON OF GOD most high? I beseech thee, torment me not" (Luke 8:28).

THE CONFESSION OF JOHN THE BAPTIST...
A Testimony of Recognition

"And I knew Him not; but He that sent me to baptize with water, the same said unto me, Upon whom thou shalt see the Spirit descending, and remaining on Him, the same is He which baptizeth with the Holy Spirit. And I saw and bear record that this is THE SON OF GOD'' (John 1:33-34).

The enormous crowds wishing to hear John the Baptist were increasing daily; his fame had spread abroad. Each day, the watchful eyes of the preacher searched for the One soon to make an appearance. But how could the Newcomer be recognized among the thousands of new faces? John smiled and remembered. His Teacher in that wonderful school in the desert had supplied the signs by which recognition would be easy. "The Holy Spirit will descend upon Him, and stay with Him." John could never forget those words, and daily he waited and watched. And then came Jesus to the Jordan, and in the moments which followed the baptismal ceremony, John saw clearly what had been promised. He knew this was THE SON OF GOD. They who hear clearly the Word of God have no difficulty in recognizing God's Son.

THE CONFESSION OF NATHANAEL. . .A Testimony of Respect

"Nathanael answered and said unto him, Rabbi, thou art THE SON OF GOD; thou art the King of Israel" (John 1:49). It was not always thus. Nathanael had been an unbeliever, and had asked, "Can any good thing come out of Nazareth?" It was easy to jump to conclusions when he had never met Jesus. Preconceived notions were evidence of a biased mind. His friend, Philip, from Bethsaida, was a persistent man. He never gave up easily! His "Come and see" led to great things. Nathanael came to discover the most wonderful man he had ever met. The Lord's statement, "Behold an Israelite indeed, in whom is no guile!", prepared the way for the conquest of Nathanael's heart. "Master, how do you know me?" "Nathanael, before Philip called thee, when thou wast under the fig tree, I saw thee" (John 1:45-49). Poor Man! This was too much! Whoever He was, this Jesus was no ordinary person. Surely, with such knowledge and insight, he could only be THE SON OF GOD, and Nathanael who took such a long time to come, refused to leave. This generally happens when the love of Christ conquers a man's heart.

THE CONFESSION OF GOD. . .A Testimony of Relationship

That day, everything was very still. The skies were blue; the atmosphere serene, and the watching crowds absolutely still. The intense stillness was broken only by the gentle flow of the Jordan and the songs of the birds in the trees. All eyes were focused on that strange but wonderful preacher who was about to baptize the Carpenter from Nazareth. For a few moments, the preacher seemed a little reluctant to continue the ceremony; he and the Candidate were quietly speaking out there in the water. "But Master, why should I baptize You?" "Suffer it to be so. . . ." "And Jesus was baptized of John in the Jordan" (Matt. 3:13-17). "And lo, a voice from heaven, saying, THIS IS MY BELOVED SON, IN WHOM I AM WELL PLEASED." Jesus was not merely a servant, however dignified and wonderful that privilege might have been—HE WAS THE SON OF GOD. Who else but God the Father could adequately give testimony concerning that glorious fact? This was a "family matter," in which God not only owned His Son, but expressed pride and pleasure in their relationship. When God uttered those wonderful words, He was surely smiling! Perhaps we can take a hint from His testimony, and copying it, say, "This is my wonderful Savior; in Him I am perfectly satisfied."

THE CONFESSION OF MARTHA. . .A Testimony of Reliance

The happiness of the home in Bethany had been shattered; Lazarus was dead; Jesus had not responded to an urgent request for help, and even God seemed to have forgotten the two sisters who trusted Him daily. The funeral had devastated their hearts; the house was now empty; the future seemed meaningless and bleak. Poor Martha! And then she heard Jesus had entered the town. "Then Martha, as soon as she heard that Jesus was coming, went and met Him. . .and said unto Him. . .Lord, if thou hadst been here, my brother had not died. But I know, that *even now*, whatsoever thou wilt ask of God, God will give it thee. . .Jesus said unto her, I am the resurrection and the life; he that believeth in me, though he were dead, yet shall he live. . .Believeth thou this? She saith unto him, Yea, Lord, I believe that thou art the Christ, THE SON OF GOD, which should come into the world" (John 11:20-28). There are many wonderful words in Martha's testimony, but none are more suggestive than her "even now." There were things beyond her comprehension; there were things breaking her heart, but even then, Jesus her Savior could solve her problems. If He asked of God anything, His prayer would be answered. Her brother surely could and would live again, but if only Christ would intercede in the matter, the resurrection of her brother *would be sooner not later*! Happy are they who turn away from the shadows of the tomb in order to see the face of Jesus.

THE CONFESSION OF SIMON PETER...
A Testimony of Revelation

The disciples were watching their Lord. He appeared to be anxious to listen to their words. He had problems; He wanted to know what people were saying in the market place. He had asked, "Whom do men say that I am?" Yes, He seemed genuinely concerned, and of course they would help Him. "Some say that thou art John the Baptist; some, Elias; and others, Jeremias or one of the prophets." He was looking straight into their eyes, when He asked quietly, "But whom say ye that I am?" So that was it! He wanted to know what they thought. "And Peter answered and said, Thou art the Christ, THE SON OF THE LIVING GOD. And Jesus answered and said unto him, Blessed art thou Simon Barjona: for flesh and blood hath not revealed it unto thee, but my Father which is in heaven" (Matt. 16:16-17). John Wesley said, "You cannot organize conversion; it is a work of God's grace in a man's heart...it is a miracle within a man's soul." Paul said, "...it pleased God...to reveal his Son in me..." (Gal. 1:15-16). Each true conversion begins with God, and that is the reason why Christians only boast in the Cross of the Lord Jesus Christ. Conversion is a matter of personal revelation. The light of the glorious gospel shines into human hearts, but, alas, there are none so blind as they who do not wish to see!

THE CONFESSION OF THE CENTURION...
A Testimony of Redemption

It was beginning to get light again. Mercifully, God had thrown His cloak over the ugly scene which man had created on the hill of Calvary. The crown of thorns; the nails in the hands; the blood gushing from a gash in the side of Jesus; all had been veiled in darkness when the sun ceased to shine. That period was now ending; light was beginning to appear in the sky. The Captain of the Guard was a little relieved; it had been an eerie experience not being able to see. Suddenly a piercing cry echoed from the center cross, "And when the centurion, which stood over against him, saw that He so cried out, and gave up the ghost, he said, Truly this man was THE SON OF GOD" (Mark 15:39). We shall never know all that passed through the mind of that soldier. He had been there from the start of that grim execution; he had heard every word uttered by the condemned Carpenter. At that moment, a more unlikely Son of God there could not be. And yet, in some mysterious way, the Centurion was sure. We cannot help but ask if he were the same man mentioned in Luke 7:1-10. Centurions of this kind must have been few and far between. He had been privileged to witness the greatest scene ever to be enacted beneath the skies.

> Well might the sun in darkness hide,
> And shut His glories in;
> When Christ the mighty Maker died
> For man, the creature's sin.

Perhaps, he was one of the most privileged people on earth; he had been given a place at the front to behold the greatest evidence that God so loved the world!

THE CONFESSION OF THE READER...
A Testimony of Responsibility

I am sorry I cannot complete the paragraph. I have no idea what your opinion would be. Would you like to answer for yourself?

The Fifth Chapter of Mark

THEME: *Christ Demonstrates His Power Over Demons, Disease and Death*

OUTLINE:
- I. Christ's Pity . . . *He Rescued the Demoniac* (Verses 1-19)
- II. Christ's Perception . . . *He Responded to the Distressed* (Verses 25-34)
- III. Christ's Power . . . *He Raised the Dead* (Verses 21-24 and 35-43)

SECTION ONE

A Necessary Introduction to the Study of This Section

There are three schools of thought in regard to the interpretation of this scripture.

1. *Denial*. Some teachers scoff at the message and emphasize it could not have happened. Rejecting the *miraculous* within the Bible, they affirm that such an account is an exaggerated version of superstitions shared by people in those days. The suffering man could have been a victim of epilepsy or some other ailment, but the idea of a human being inhabited by demons is preposterous!

2. *Dilution*. Some theologians have expressed an idea which has been welcomed by liberal elements within the churches. They feel that the Lord was both a psychologist and a psychiatrist, and that His treatment of this particular patient was sensational. Actually, so they suggest, the man was not possessed by demons, but unfortunately, *he thought he was!* The terrible obsession had ruined his life, and even the word of Jesus would have been unconvincing without some visible proof to persuade the man that evil spirits had been expelled from his body. Therefore, the Lord supplied the external evidence when he allowed the demoniac to associate his deliverance with the death of the swine.

3. *Defense*. The conservative section of the church, the

fundamentalists, insist that men must believe and accept the Bible just as it is; any "private interpretation" is completely unacceptable. They believe this man was truly possessed by powers of evil, and that deliverance was only possible when Christ's power expelled the forces subjugating the man's life. Furthermore, they insist that unless this be the truth, Mark was very stupid when he wrote in verse 12 of his fifth chapter, "And all the devils besought Jesus, saying, Send us into the swine, that we may enter into them. And forthwith, Jesus gave them leave."

Expository Notes on the Deliverance of the Demoniac

And they came over unto the other side of the sea, into the country of the Gadarenes. And when He was come out of the ship, immediately there met Him out of the tombs a man with an unclean spirit, who had his dwelling among the tombs; and no man could bind him, no, not with chains; because he had been often bound with fetters and chains, and the chains had been plucked asunder by him, and the fetters broken in pieces; neither could any man tame him. And always, night and day, he was in the mountains, and in the tombs, crying, and cutting himself with stones (vv. 1-5).

Describing the importance of the sea of Galilee in the ministry of the Lord, Bishop J. C. Ryle wrote: "The Sea of Galilee, or Tiberias, on which the circumstances recorded in this passage took place, is an inland lake, through which the river Jordan flows. It is about fifteen miles long and six broad. It lies in a deep valley, much depressed below the level of the sea, its surface being 652 feet below that of the Mediterranean. It is surrounded on most sides by steep hills. Owing to these last circumstances, sudden squalls or storms are reported by all travelers to be very common on the lake. The Sea of Galilee and the country surrounding it, were favored with more of our blessed Lord's presence, during His earthly ministry, than any other part of Palestine. Capernaum, Tiberias, Bethsaida, and the country of the Gergesenes were all on its shores, or in the immediate neighborhood of this lake. It was on the Sea of Galilee that our Lord walked. It was on this shore that He appeared to His disciples after His resurrection. Sitting in a boat on its waters, and in a house close by, He delivered the seven parables recorded in the thirteenth chapter of St. Matthew. On its banks He called Peter, and Andrew, James and John. From it, He commanded the disciples to draw the miraculous draught of fishes. Within sight of it, He twice fed the multitude with a few loaves and fishes. On its shore, he healed the man possessed with devils; and into it the two thousand swine plunged headlong after that miracle had been wrought. Few localities in the Holy Land were so immediately connected with our Lord's ministry as the Sea of Galilee and the country around it'' (J. C. Ryle, *Expository Thoughts on the Gospels*, Mark, pp. 87-88).

It is important to remember the time and place of this incident. Mark 4:35 tells us the Lord and His followers set sail for the other side of the lake, ''when the even was come.'' Then came the storm, and when calm had been restored, the party reached the country of the Gadarenes. Either they arrived as it was getting dark, or the seashore must have been bathed in the light of a full moon. Mark goes on to say that ''there met him *out of the tombs* a man with an unclean spirit.'' The hillside abounded in caves and in some of these, dead bodies had been buried. The hilltop was actually the local cemetery, and for most of the time was as isolated as a leper camp. When funerals were taking place, the people went there to bury their dead; at other times they never went near unless unwelcome circumstances dictated their actions. After dark, it was a prohibited area from which people stayed away. That two wild, irresponsible maniacs chose to dwell among the tombs only heightened the fear of the community.

It is not difficult to visualize the scene when the devil-possessed man rushed down the hillside to accost Jesus. Darkness had either come or was swiftly approaching; the disciples were ill-at-ease, for to say the least, to visit a cemetery after dark was not usual procedure! The silence was intense; the surroundings were gloomy, and the less brave among the party were very apprehensive! Superstitious people would have said it was a place for ghosts and goblins! Suddenly a horrible cry echoed down the hill, and out of the darkness rushed this wild, tormented man. Paralyzing fear gripped the hearts of the disciples, and they were horrified as they wondered what was to happen to their Master. Describing this poor man, *The Amplified New Testament* translates the passage: ''Night and day among the tombs, and on the mountains he was always shrieking and screaming, and beating and bruising and cutting himself with stones.'' The sight confronting the disciples was enough to scare them to death! The madman possessed superhuman strength, for when the people of the village chained his hands and feet, exerting himself, he snapped those fetters as if they had been made of flimsy cotton. He was dangerous; he was a man to be avoided.

But when he saw Jesus afar off, he ran and worshipped Him (v. 6).

The Greek word translated "worshipped" is *prosekuneesen*, and it does not mean worship in the sense of adoration to God. According to Dr. Thayer, the root word *proskuneo* means "to prostrate oneself; sometimes, to kiss the hand; by kneeling or prostration, to do homage or make obeisance, whether in order to express respect or to make supplication. Among Orientals, to touch the ground with the forehead as an expression of profound reverence." The demon-possessed man was not motivated by love, but fear; he came not to adore the Lord Jesus, but recognizing a greater than he had arrived, the evil spirit desired to ask a favor.

> **And cried with a loud voice, and said, What have I to do with thee, Jesus, thou son of the most high God? I adjure thee by God, that thou torment me not. For He said unto him [Jesus was commanding him], Come out of the man, thou unclean spirit (vv. 7-8).**

"Now as soon as he saw Jesus in the distance, he ran and knelt before him, yelling at the top of his voice, What have you got to do with me, Jesus, Son of the Most High God? For God's sake, don't torture me!" (*Phillips*). It should be easily recognized that the hysterical shrieking was hardly evidence of true worship. The man had not sent for Jesus, and as far as we know, the townsfolk had not interceded on his behalf. Why then had the Lord arrived at this unusual time of the evening or night, in this eerie place on the hillside, just to meet a bewildered, beleaguered man? Their meeting could not have been accidental. Had this thing happened on a normal highway, there would be no problem in understanding the story. The fact that the meeting took place in a strange, outlandish location implies that the Lord had gone there deliberately. He was aware of the demoniac's existence, and since no other could help, the Lord was constrained to go Himself to rescue one of God's unfortunate creatures. Pity, love, and power were echoing in the voice of Jesus when He commanded the evil spirit to vacate the man's body. It was the same matchless love of God that brought Christ to earth. Many other souls were suffering beneath the thraldom of evil, and it was in God's plan to rescue them that the Lord left His home in heaven.

> Out of the ivory palaces, into a world of woe:
> Only His great eternal love, made my Savior go.

And He asked him, What is thy name? And he answered, saying, Legion: for we are many. And he besought him much that He would not send them away out of the country. Now there was there nigh unto the mountains a great herd of swine feeding. And all the devils besought Him, saying, Send us into the swine, that we may enter into them. And forthwith Jesus gave them leave (vv. 9-13).

There are two ways of interpreting this scripture, and readers must judge for themselves which is the more acceptable. Was the man identifying himself with the demons, or was one special demon acting as the spokesman for the others?

1. It is written that the Lord asked, "What is thy name? and he answered, saying, *My name* is Legion, for *we are many*." The afflicted man was aware of the strange impulses controlling his actions, but the possibility exists his thinking was also colored by things he had seen. A legion of Roman soldiers numbered six thousand men, and these could often be seen marching through the land. During times of insurrection, those soldiers had been guilty of very brutal behavior; they had terrorized the nation, and had only been opposed by a band of fanatical patriots known as "the Zealots." Had this man witnessed atrocities, and aware of the pressure from within, did he assume that a legion of evil spirits was responsible for his condition?

2. Were there literally 6,000 demons inhabiting the man's body, and did one of their number act as spokesman for the group? It is obvious that evil was there in strength; this was a head-on confrontation between the powers of Hell and the Prince of Heaven. We have not been informed how this terrible situation arose. Had the man sinned? We may never fully understand the situation, but to say the least, it was a tragedy that a man made in the image of God should ever become the abode of demons. That the Lord could love the man in spite of his condition, and go out of His way to deliver him from bondage, must forever be a cause for wonder and praise. Luke in his chapter 8 and verse 31 reminds us that the demons feared the possibility of being sent out into "the deep." The Greek word used is *abusson*, and is the same word used in Revelation 20:1. The demons feared being banished to the bottomless pit where they would be imprisoned and helpless. It is thought-provoking that the Lord asked for a name which was not supplied. "What is THY name?" The poor fellow was unable to reply accurately, for even his tongue was controlled by the evil within him. Yet we must inquire why the Lord asked the question. Surely, He knew

already. Probably the Lord was trying to focus attention on the fact
that the man, although subjugated by demons, was nevertheless, still
a man. He did have a name; he did possess an individuality. A soul
may be submerged by evil, but no man can sink out of God's sight (taken
from the author's commentary, *Luke's Thrilling Gospel*, pp. 197-198).

> **And the unclean spirits went out, and entered into the swine; and the
> herd ran violently down a steep place into the sea (they were about two
> thousand) and were choked in the sea. And they that fed the swine,
> fled, and told it in the city, and in the country. And they went out to
> see what it was that was done (vv. 13-14).**

It is very interesting that Matthew says there were TWO demoniacs.
Readers are urged to study the homily at the end of this chapter. The
law as given by Moses forbade the eating of swine flesh, but little had
been said about the production of swine-flesh for Gentile consumption.
"After the conquest of Syria, the Romans had rebuilt ten cities, and
these were called Decapolis (Mark 5:20). The name is self-explanatory.
Deka means ten; *polis* means city. The ten cities included in this rebuilt
area were: Scynthololis, Pella, Dion, Gerasa, Philadelphia, Gadara,
Raphana, Kanatha, Damascus, and Hippos. Each of the ten cities
controlled surrounding territory, and perhaps separated enclaves of land.
This probably accounts for the confusion between the various readings,
'Gadarenes' 'Gerasenes' and 'Gergasenes' in the various texts of
Matthew 8, Mark 5, and Luke 8." (*The Zondervan Pictorial
Encyclopedia of the Bible*, Vol. 2, p. 82).

Many Gentiles are known to have lived in the area and the swine
mentioned in this story were probably owned by Jews, and were to have
been sold to the Gentile neighbors. When the animals were drowned,
the farmers suffered a great financial loss, and this, of course, led to
serious repercussions.

It would seem that the swine preferred suicide to bondage, and their
doom gave rise to another question. What happened to the demons who
had desired sanctuary within the ill-fated animals? Perhaps they were
sent to the one place they feared; it is certain that the Lord would never
permit a repetition of what they had already done in the life of the
enslaved demoniac.

> **And they came to Jesus, and see him that was possessed with the devil,
> and had the legion, sitting, and clothed, and in his right mind: and they
> were afraid. And they that saw it, told them how it befell to him that**

was possessed with the devil, and also concerning the swine. And they began to pray Him to depart out of their coasts (vv. 15-57).

The crowd was very silent; their faces reflected the anxiety filling their hearts. One of their neighbors had been a wealthy man; now he was bankrupt. It was splendid to see the evidence of Christ's miracle; it was thrilling that the man they had feared so much could now become an honored citizen, but the grim specter of further financial losses terrified them. If the visiting Preacher were more sensitive to their losses; if He had used other means to deliver the afflicted, He would have been welcomed with open arms; they might have made him an honorary freeman of their cities. He had destroyed their swine; years of hard work lay buried in the sea. Who would compensate them for their tragedy? Who would help the impoverished farmer to regain what had been taken from him? The most paralyzing thought of all was that it might be their turn next!

The swineherders were telling their story once more, but the farmers were swiftly losing their interest; they were desperately apprehensive. They had their future to consider; their families would need food, and their bills had to be paid. This Jesus was a menace! Yes, they preferred to have a demented man rather than an empty larder. ''And they began to pray Him to depart from their coasts.'' And all the time they were trying to decide what to do with this Visitor, the delivered man sat calmly at the feet of his Savior. Peace was upon his face; heaven was in his heart, all was well! It is interesting to note that whereas on a former occasion he had torn clothing to pieces, now he was clothed, and doubtless was thrilled with the fact. But we might ask, ''Whence came the garments?'' The miracle had been performed out in the country at the edge of the Sea of Galilee. There were no shops in the vicinity, and therefore it would have been impossible, immediately, to purchase clothing. Surely, the Lord came prepared for the convert's need. Maybe He removed one of His own garments, and ''without money, and without price,'' gave it to the grateful convert.

What would have happened had the Lord been invited to stay? It might be well to compare and contrast this account with an Old Testament story. We have been told in 2 Samuel, chapter six, that when David and his men went to bring again the ark of God from Baale of Judah, an unexpected catastrophy overwhelmed David to the extent that he abandoned his plans and returned to Jerusalem. Then we read, beginning at verse 10, ''So David would not remove the ark of the Lord unto him in the city of David; but David carried it aside into the house of

Obededom the Gittite. And the ark of the Lord continued in the house of Obededom the Gittite three months; AND THE LORD BLESSED OBEDEDOM, AND ALL HIS HOUSEHOLD.'' God knew how to pay His debts! David probably considered the death of Uzzah, and believed this price was too high to pay for any project of restoring the ark to its rightful place. David was frightened, but another man who witnessed the same sight, rejoiced at the privilege of entertaining God! ''And God blessed Obededom and all his house.'' There is reason to believe God would have blessed the people of Gadara, had they been sufficiently wise to welcome the Lord Jesus. They were not expert business men. They were careful in assessing the cost of allowing Christ to remain on their shore; they forgot to count the cost of asking Him to leave. With Christ, they had everything; without Him, they had nothing.

> **And when He was come into the ship, he that had been possessed with the devil prayed Him that he might be with Him. Howbeit, Jesus suffered him not, but saith unto him, Go home to thy friends, and tell them how great things the Lord hath done for thee, and hath had compassion on thee. And he departed, and began to publish in Decapolis how great things Jesus had done for him; and all men did marvel (vv. 18-20).**

We are now to study one of the most fascinating sections of Mark's narrative. It was perfectly natural for the healed demoniac to ask permission to accompany Christ on His travels, but the fact that the Lord denied the request encourages search for His reasons in so doing. To appreciate the refusal it is necessary to understand more of the ten cities restored by Caesar. Nine of them were to the East of the Sea of Galilee, and only one to the West. This was in some ways, a bridgehead in Palestine for the culture of the Decapolis region. Although Jews lived throughout the area, the population was largely made up of Gentiles.

Professor E. M. Blaiklock has said, ''Of chief interest to the student of the New Testament is the influence of the Decapolis on Galilee. 'The Decapolis' writes G. A. Smith, 'was flourishing at the time of Christ's ministry. Gadara, with her temples and amphitheatres, with her art, her games, and her literature, overhung the lake of Galilee, and the voyages of its fishermen' (G. A. Smith, *The Historical Geography of the Holy Land*). Across the lake, five to eight miles wide, the farmers of Galilee could see a Gentile world. That world had a bridgehead in their territory at Scynthopolis, and the roads converging on that center, and radiating thence, must have had an attraction for many Jews. Perhaps the story of the Prodigal illustrates the fact, with *the far country* remote only in outlook and way of life. Swine, a Gentile food, was among the farm stock of the Gadarene territory, and the wanderer of the story, trapped and ruined by an alien society, may have been no more than a hard day's journey from home." Two different worlds were separated only by the blue waters of the Sea of Galilee, and the Gentile one, for the most part, had been unreached by the Lord and His followers. We can now consider four simple, but vital headings.

A DESIRE . . . Denied

"He that had been possessed with the devil, prayed Him that he might be with Him" (v. 18). This is not difficult to comprehend. The convert had been rescued from a living nightmare; his soul had been freed, and his mind cleared of pressures which had ruined his life. Jesus had brought new life to a man who had been practically dead, and it was to be expected the convert would desire the continuation of this happiness. He could think of nothing more desirable than to spend the rest of his life in the company and service of his Benefactor.

A DUTY . . . Described

" . . . Jesus saith unto him, Go home to thy friends, and tell them how great things the Lord hath done for thee, and hath had compassion on thee" (v. 19). Luke reports the Lord as having said, "Return to thine own house." It would be nice if we could identify his nationality or race. Was the man a Jew or a Gentile? If he were a Jew, did he have among his friends those who were not Jews? The most significant thing about this strange commission was that Jesus was making this man *the first missionary to the Gentiles*. Later, the Apostle Paul would carry the torch of the Gospel into the darkest places of the Gentile world, but the first to attempt this kind of task, was the man whose heart had been the abode of demons. It is interesting to note that Matthew does not report this command. Maybe—maybe, had he done so, his gospel would not have been so pleasing to his Jewish readers!

A DISCIPLE . . . Determined

"And he departed, and began to publish in Decapolis how great things Jesus had done for him . . ." (v. 20). He had a story to tell; a testimony to give, and nothing in the world would prevent his obeying what the Lord had commanded. Doubtless, he began as Luke suggests "in his own home," but afterward, the circle of ministry widened, until his story was known throughout the ten cities of the region. He became a traveling evangelist in his own right, and his example is something all Christians should emulate. Perhaps he never became an expert in theological interpretation; but his soul-thrilling testimony captivated every listener. Had he been able to compare notes with the beggar of John 9, both men would have had a marvelous time of fellowship (read John 9:28-34).

A DEVOTION. . . Displayed

". . . and all men did marvel" (v. 20). We know this man succeeded in his mission. Later, Mark says: "And again, departing from the coasts of Tyre and Sidon, he came unto the Sea of Galilee, *through the midst of the coasts of Decapolis. . . .* In those days the multitude being very great. . ." (Mark 7:31 and 8:1). The Lord had asked the convert to witness to *his friends*; we know he did this, but having done this, he surely told others, until his testimony was known throughout the Decapolis area. This was evangelism at its best. His story, and the warmth of the devotion inspiring it, prepared the way for the Lord, and when Jesus once again passed through the district, great crowds were waiting to see and hear him. It is not said that He ever returned to the village from which He had been asked to leave, but, in a country where villages and towns were close together, it would not be difficult to travel the twenty or thirty miles to adjacent places where Jesus could be heard again. If one voice could accomplish so much, what would happen if every Christian displayed similar determination in taking the Gospel to the nations?

SECTION TWO

Expository Notes on the Woman Who Touched the Hem of His Garment

And a certain woman, which had an issue of blood twelve years, and had suffered many things of many physicians, and had spent all that she had, and was nothing bettered, but rather grew worse, when she heard of Jesus, came in the press behind and touched His garment. For she said, If I may touch but His clothes, I shall be whole. And

straightway the fountain of her blood was dried up; and she felt in her body that she was healed of that plague (vv. 25-29).

F. L. Godet quotes Eusebius as saying "this woman was a heathen who dwelt at Paneas, near the source of the Jordan, and that in his time her house was still shown, having at its entrance two brass statues on a stone pedestal. One represented a woman on her knees, with her hands held out before her in the attitude of a suppliant; the other, a man standing with his cloak thrown over his shoulder and his hand extended toward the woman. Eusebius had been in the house himself, and had seen this statue, which represented, it was said, the features of Jesus" (F. L. Godet, *Commentary on Luke*, p. 250). There is reason to believe that of all the women mentioned in the Gospels, this one is more deserving of pity than any other. "The fifteenth chapter of the book of Leviticus has much to say of a woman in this condition. She was not only considered to be unclean herself; she also defiled anything or anyone she touched. If she were a Jewess, she would be an unfortunate woman with whom no one would wish to associate. . . If she were a Gentile, a heathen, as Eusebius suggests, then she would be even more unclean in the estimation of her Jewish neighbors. Thus, viewed from any angle, this woman was an object of pity, a desolate dejected case for whom the physicians could do nothing" (taken from the author's commentary, *Luke's Thrilling Gospel*, p. 203).

HER CASE-HISTORY

"There was a woman who had suffered terribly from severe bleeding for twelve years, even though she had been treated by many doctors. She had spent all her money, but instead of getting better, she got worse all the time" (v. 25, 26) (*Today's English Version of the Bible*). This woman was indeed in a very pitiable state. Her condition caused pain and intense embarrassment, and before she went into the streets to buy food, or for any other reason, it was necessary to take precaution, lest she be further embarrassed before onlookers. If she were a Jewess, it would have been logical to seek refuge in her faith, but alas, the Talmud, the Jewish "Bible" dealing with civil and religious laws, had little if any good advice to offer.

Probably, she had been required to work very hard to obtain money to pay her doctors' bills, but everything of value had been sacrificed in her vain search for relief. It is significant that Mark refers to *many physicians*; his information came from Simon Peter, and Peter knew about doctor's bills, for he had cared for a sick mother-in-law! When one physician failed to improve her condition, the woman sought the advice of another; probably changed her medication, and eventually received another bill. This continued for twelve, seemingly-endless years, and finally she had become completely impoverished and depressed.

HER CONTINUING HELPLESSNESS

". . . She had spent all she had and there had been no improvement; on the contrary, she had grown worse" (v. 26) (NEB). It is not difficult to imagine her sitting at home, waiting to die! Her religion had no comfort to offer; the doctors were apparently useless; her neighbors kept their distance, life had become meaningless. Many people with such an outlook committed suicide, and perhaps we shall never know how often this thought occurred to her. Would it not be better to die and be released from her troubles? Who can tell whether or not in those acute moments of depression, the love of God prevented tragedy? Later in her life she was destined to meet the Great Physician, and only then, as she looked in retrospect over her life, would she be able to understand that He knew and saw her long before she even heard of Him. If this be true, it is the expression of experiences known by all who trust the Savior. Alas, for one reason or another, most of us only seek help from Christ when we have "run out of doctors and cash!" It is, and ever will be, a cause of regret that God never gets a chance to help us until all other sources have failed. We resemble a man sinking in a quicksand. A would-be rescuer throws a rope, but disdaining the offered assistance, the man says, "Thank you, I can get out myself." And he continues to sink! Should we blame his pride or his stupidity?

HER CALCULATING HOPEFULNESS

"When she heard about Jesus, she came up behind Him in the crowd, and touched His cloak, because she thought, If I just touch His clothes, I will be healed" (vv. 27, 28) (NIV). Some theologians suggest her act was more in keeping with heathen superstition; that she sought to touch Him by stealth, believing some magical process would cure her ills. There is nothing to support this theory, for even the Lord commended her faith. The Greek word translated "the border" of His garment is *kraspedou*, and this, according to Dr. Thayer, means "a little appendage, hanging down from the edge of the mantle or cloak, made of twisted wool; a tassel or tuft.'' The Jews wore these in accordance with the commands of God. ''Speak unto the children of Israel, and bid them that they make them fringes in the border of their garment. . . And it shall be unto you for a fringe, that ye may look upon it, and remember all the commandments of the Lord, and do them'' (Num. 15:38-39). The robe customarily worn by the Jews resembled in some ways a woman's shawl. Two corners hung down at the back and to these would be attached the tassels. Whether she were a Jewess or a Gentile there was very grave danger in what the woman contemplated. The laws of God emphasized that anyone in her condition had to stay away from people; contact meant defilement. If she were a Gentile, then the Jews would be infuriated by her nearness; if she were a Jewess, and her search for healing ended in failure, there would be those who would blame her for endangering their own cleanliness. Probably the woman had reached the place where she no longer cared. The laws of God and Moses were very strict (read Leviticus 15:19-33). She could be fined; she could be imprisoned, but the worst thing they could possibly do was to stone her for deliberate violation of the law. Perhaps in her perverted way of thinking, she decided that either way, she would be rid of her scourge.

She had surely heard of His exploits; perhaps she had even heard someone singing His praises. Was it possible that He might be able to do what the doctors had found impossible? In the event of His failure, would it be wise to make her effort a secret one? If no one knew about her act, whether it led to success or failure, future reprisals would be avoided. Maybe we shall never fully fathom her motives. She watched as He approached, and then suddenly reaching a decision, she pushed her way through the crowd, and reaching out her arm, somehow succeeded in touching one of the tassels hanging from His cloak. ''And straightway the fountain of her blood was dried up; and she felt in her body that she was healed of that plague'' (v. 29).

And Jesus, immediately knowing in himself that virtue had gone out of Him, turned Him about in the press, and said, Who touched my clothes? And His disciples said unto Him, Thou seest the multitude thronging thee, and sayest thou, Who touched me? And He looked round about to see her that had done this thing. But the woman fearing and trembling, knowing what was done in her, came and fell down before Him, and told Him all the truth. And He said unto her, Daughter, thy faith hath made thee whole; go in peace, and be whole of thy plague (vv. 30-34).

HER COMPLETE HAPPINESS

His question must have seemed ludicrous! "Master," said the disciples, "In the last few yards, dozens have touched You, and yet you ask, 'Who touched me!' Master, isn't that silly?" "No," replied Jesus, "Somebody *touched* Me—*somebody really touched me*, for I felt virtue, life, going out of my body." Faith had been the life-line between the Lord's sufficiency and the woman's need. Life had gone out of Him to solve the very real problem of an impoverished soul. Had she not come to Him, she would have carried her burden to the grave. Faith is excellent; but faith expressed in public confession is better. Faith leads to healing; confession leads to joy. Hiding in the crowd, she heard His question, and momentarily trembled. Her secret was no longer a secret; He knew about her act; would He consider her to be a thief? Had she stolen the blessing? "And when the woman saw that she was not hid, she came trembling, and falling down before him, she declared unto him *before all the people* for what cause she had touched him, and how she was healed immediately" (Luke 8:47). There was no escape; the Lord was aware of her action; she felt guilty! The Savior's smiles must have been very attractive when He looked at the kneeling woman. She was making her first confession and the people were listening. At that moment blessing came to her in triplicate: 1) faith in her soul, 2) health in her body, and 3) peace in her mind. Thus would Christ teach His followers that they who are healed by His grace should tell their story to a waiting world. The woman's happiness was now complete. She was thrilled because: 1) she was no longer suffering from embarrassing hemorrhages, 2) she no longer had to pay doctors' bills, 3) she was no longer considered to be unclean; she could worship God in His temple, 4) she could face her future confidently, and 5) she had come to know and love the Savior. Life had taken on a new meaning. It always does when Christ becomes its center.

SECTION THREE

Expository Notes on the Raising of Jairus's Daughter

And behold there cometh one of the rulers of the synagogue, Jairus by name; and when he saw Jesus, he fell at His feet and besought Him greatly, saying, My little daughter lieth at the point of death: I pray thee, come and lay thy hands on her, that she may be healed; and she shall live (vv. 22-23).

To appreciate what Jairus did, and to understand the kind of man he was, it is necessary to know something about the position he held within the synagogue. "The ruler of the synagogue had the care of external order in public worship, and the supervision of the concerns of the synagogue in general. This officer was found in the entire sphere of Judaism, not only in Palestine, but also in Egypt, Asia Minor, Greece, Italy, and the Roman Empire in general. . . The Hebrew word means 'The minister of the synagogue'. . . This office differed from that of an elder of the congregation, although the same person could fill the offices of both. The ruler of the synagogue was so called, not as head of the community, but as conductor of their assembly for public worship. Among his functions is specially mentioned that of appointing who should read the Scriptures and the prayer, and summoning fit persons to preach; to see that nothing improper took place within the synagogue, and to take charge of the synagogue building. Although it was customary to have but one ruler of the synagogue, yet sometimes more are mentioned (Acts 13:15)" (*Unger's Bible Dictionary*, p. 1053). "The evidence indicates that at first this was an elective office, only becoming hereditary, and finally perfunctory after centuries of the synagogue's existence" (*The Zondervan Pictorial Encyclopedia of the Bible*, Vol. 5).

It will be understood from these facts that to be a ruler of the synagogue conferred upon a man one of the highest honors the Jewish community could bestow. He became the chief administrator in all things connected with faith and practice; he was a judge, advisor, attorney, and sometimes the confidant of everybody. Jairus had been elected to this position, and thus we may be sure he enjoyed the respect and admiration of the entire Jewish population. The people looked to him for guidance; what he did was an example for young and old. He was a man set apart for the spiritual guidance and growth of his people. We are now able to follow a progressive outline of his development.

HIS DIGNITY

Jairus was no ordinary man. When heresy threatened the integrity of the synagogue, it would be his duty to warn and advise the congregation. Possibly he had already found it necessary to do this in regard to Jesus of Nazareth. The teachings of the Carpenter appeared to endanger the authority of the Jewish leaders; the chief Council in Jerusalem was infuriated by what had taken place, and throughout the nation, warnings were being issued against something which appeared to be dangerous and hostile to Judaism. At first, there could not have been any reason why Jairus should be different from other rulers of synagogues. He would stand before his congregation and do what was expected of him. His influence was undeniable; he commanded the support and respect of all who listened. All rulers of the synagogue were men of learning for in part at least, the education of the children was their responsibility.

HIS DAUGHTER

Jairus was a father; he had one girl, and she was twelve years of age. This was the time, when according to Jewish custom, the child was on the threshold of womanhood. There is a striking contrast here. The woman who touched the hem of Christ's garment had been slowly dying for twelve years; this girl had been living for twelve years. The woman had been terribly ill; the girl had been radiantly happy. We have not been told whether or not Jairus had any other children; if this girl were his only child, then she must have been the delight of her father's life. Her illness was serious; the outlook was bleak indeed. The best medical skill available had been summoned, but apparently the girl was beyond human aid. Her father said, "My little daughter lieth at the point of death." Perhaps he had watched as the doctors shook their heads in frustration, and listened as they announced their inability to save the child's life. Then he thought of the strange Man against whom he had warned his congregation. People throughout the land were saying that Jesus of Nazareth could heal the sick; could it be possible that He could heal this child? We shall never know how fierce was the conflict that turned his heart and mind into a battleground.

HIS DISTRESS

Mark says, "And, behold, there cometh one of the rulers of the synagogue, Jairus by name" (v. 22). We cannot help but wonder why he came at all. Since his child was so gravely ill, why did he not send one of his friends? What if his child died during his absence? Is there a possibility that his friends refused to go to Jesus? Did they frown when Jairus even mentioned the Name of the detested Preacher? Had their ruler not urged people against the very thing he was now contemplating? Was Jairus left alone with his problem? Did he realize that unless he swallowed his pride and refuted all he had said, his wonderful little daughter would die? There is no language which can adequately describe the mental anguish of such a situation. He was caught on the horns of his greatest dilemma. He was fighting to save his child's life, but God was also endeavoring to save a father's soul.

HIS DECISION

"I must go to Jesus." That surely was the most important decision he ever made, and for the remaining years of his life, he was glad he made it. His gratitude knew no bounds when the Lord began the journey toward the Ruler's home; but when the woman caused an interruption in the proceedings, the faith of that desperate father was surely shaken. His daughter was at the point of death; every moment was vital, but the Lord seemed determined to discover the identity of the person who had touched Him. Poor Jairus; his thoughts were with his child. Was she still alive? "And while Jesus was yet speaking, there came from the ruler of the synagogue's house, certain which said, Thy daughter is dead: why troublest thou the Master any further?" (v. 35). The father was shocked beyond words. His heart almost died within him; his child was dead! There was now no cause for hope. He should have come to Jesus earlier. Why had he waited so long? And Jesus said, *"Be not afraid, only believe"* (v. 36). *The Living Bible* translates this passage, "Don't be afraid, just trust Me."

> While he yet spake, there came from the ruler of the synagogue's house certain which said, Thy daughter is dead: why troublest thou the Master any further? As soon as Jesus heard the word that was spoken, He saith unto the ruler of the synagogue, Be not afraid, only believe. And He suffered no man to follow him, save Peter, and James, and John the brother of James. And He cometh to the house of the ruler of the synagogue, and seeth the tumult, and them that wept and wailed greatly (vv. 35-38).

HIS DENUNCIATION

It is not difficult to imagine the reaction of the Jewish leaders when their trusted friend apparently became a hypocrite. Their lips probably curled with contempt; their eyes reflected the cynicism of their hearts. The ruler was inconsistent! They watched as the procession moved along the street. The Carpenter was actually going to the Ruler's home! The professional mourners were already filling the place with their wailing.

Within our western world it seems strange to read the account of this sad story. It was customary in Jewish times that immediately after the death of a person, a loud wailing took place to let others know that someone had passed away. The wailing was repeated at the graveside with the mourners beating their breasts and tearing at their hair as they lay over the dead body. Flute players were also part of the act, and no matter how poor the loved one of the deceased was, he had to have two flute players at the funeral. There were musicians who thrived on funeral performances, and their actions sometimes were revolting. They screamed and performed in such a way as to impress upon all who heard, how great they were in making a spectacle of the death procedure. The greater the noise, so it was believed, the greater the performance. When Jesus and his faithful followers arrived on the scene; the musicians had turned the death chamber into a circus! The fact that the people present were ready and waiting to criticize the Lord, only indicates the resentment they felt toward His presence and toward the Ruler who had requested His help.

And when He was come in, He saith unto them, Why make ye this ado, and weep? the damsel is not dead, but sleepeth. And they laughed Him to scorn. But when He had put them all out, He taketh the father and mother of the damsel, and them that were with him, and entereth in where the damsel was lying (vv. 39-40).

HIS DESIRE

With an arm around his wife's shoulder, the ruler probably stood watching. Hope shone in his eyes; dread maybe filled his heart. Could Jesus possibly raise his little girl? He saw and heard the sneering mourners. Their mirth seemed out of place; their laughter was offensive. He was glad when the Lord asked them to leave. They had no sympathy; they were only waiting to collect their fee. *The Amplified New Testament* says, "They jeered at Him." Deliverance and derision cannot live together. "Faith is the substance of things hoped for; the evidence of things not seen" (Heb. 11:1). The silence which followed the departure of the cynics prepared the way for what was to follow. The Ruler's eyes were focused on the ashen countenance of his dead child; his heart seemed to be crying aloud, "Lord, can you do it, even now?"

And He took the damsel by the hand, and said unto her, Talitha cumi; which is, being interpreted, Damsel, I say unto thee arise. And

straightway, the damsel arose, and walked; for she was of the age of twelve years. And they were astonished with a great astonishment. And He charged them straightly that no man should know it; and commanded that something should be given her to eat (vv. 41-43).

HIS DELIGHT

Perhaps the father was unable to speak; his eyes were filled with tears; his arms were now around his restored child. She was alive again! Amazement was spreading through the hearts of all who had witnessed the miracle; they were excited, and even the crowds in the street were astonished, for the Preacher had done the impossible. *Talitha cumi* is Aramaic for "Maid arise" and it seems strange to find this little bit of another language squeezed in among the other words of the Gospel. Probably, Mark learned from Peter these words of Jesus could never be forgotten. As the Lord had spoken them, so Peter and Mark reproduced them. The parents were overjoyed; the others were excited, but with care so characteristic of the Friend of children, Jesus remembered that little girls can be hungry! He commanded that she should be given something to eat. Doubtless His command was obeyed, and when the parents saw their child happily eating what was provided, their cup was full and running over! Thus did the Lord reward a man, who throwing aside his preconceived notions, came desperately to ask for help. "No good thing will He withhold from them that walk uprightly" (Ps. 84:11).

"Possibly, the Lord commanded the parents to refrain from broadcasting the news of the miracle, because He knew His enemies would only endeavor to make this event another cause for sarcastic comment. If they were capable of laughing when the parents were breaking their hearts, they would also be capable of saying the girl was never dead. The entire episode might have become an object of ridicule as embittered men accused the parents of being sensationalists, fools, people who hastily jumped to conclusions. There are times when silence can be golden" (taken from the author's commentary, *Luke's Thrilling Gospel*, p. 209).

HOMILIES

Study No. 11

THE MAN...Who Vanished! (Matthew 8:28)

There is an apparent discrepancy between the accounts of Matthew, Mark, and Luke. Matthew firmly insists there were two demoniacs awaiting the coming of Christ. Mark and Luke do not deny the presence of the second man, but are content to tell the story of the one. For some unknown reason, the second man failed to reappear, and we are left wondering what happened to him. Your guess is as good as mine, but if we share our thoughts, we might discover truth.

WAS HE FORGETFUL?

He could never forget the wonderful moment when the Savior brought relief from inward horror. Yet, in his thrilling excitement, did he rush to his home and loved ones; and in the tranquility of the new calm, did he forget the One who had rescued him from the storm? If this were the case, he resembles many modern people. Men and even nations are apt to flee to God in their distresses. Prolonged periods of prayer are the usual means to win from God those things most desired. Yet in the triumph of subsequent days both man and nation are apt to forget their indebtedness, and to return to ways of sin. Some of us could hardly blame the demoniac.

WAS HE FEARFUL?

Some unknown farmer had lost a herd of two thousand swine. The savings of years had vanished in a moment. He would not be pleased. There would be no compensation, and after due consideration he would have many things to say. If other people were involved in the loss, then quite a number of impoverished citizens would give vent to their anger. Was the delivered demoniac scared of the charges which might be brought against him, and as a result, did he stay in hiding? Who can tell? It is at least a possible solution, and no one can deny that such calculated action may still be witnessed. There are many people who recognize their indebtedness to Christ. They secretly acknowledge that they should publicly confess their allegiance to Him, yet they shrink from open discipleship. Fearful of what people might say, they remain secret disciples. Their example is not good.

DID HIS FAMILY INTERFERE?

It would have been most natural had he returned to his home, to share the great news of his deliverance. Probably he had been estranged from his people for a considerable time. The coming of Christ opened new possibilities; home and family were once again within reach. We could never blame him for his action in going to them; we are concerned with his failure to return later in thankfulness to the Master. Did his family talk him out of this idea? Were his objections overcome by the persuasions of his own loved ones? Alas, man has always been failing at this point. Perhaps we shall never know how many people have secretly said, "Lord, I will follow thee, but let me first go bid them farewell which are at home at my house." Then they vanished from the scene.

DID THE FUTURE TROUBLE HIM?

If this were the case, we are able to appreciate his difficulties. He would know that Christ had a band of disciples. Had they not been present that same morning? Would the Savior make great demands in return for His act of delivering grace? Would He expect the former demoniac to forsake all and to follow whithersoever He might lead? And greatest of all the problems, would the convert be able to maintain such high and holy standards of life and service? Was the man afraid to come near to Jesus lest he should be confronted with these demands? People still excuse their staying away from Christ. They say, "I could never live that life; I should fail." This sounds sincere, but actually it lacks reality. Our starting point for deliberation should be what He has already done for us, and not what He might yet require. To try and to fail is at least more satisfactory than never to try at all. The demoniac lived ever-afterward with a troublesome conscience. Poor fellow! (Taken from the author's book, *Bible Cameos*, pp. 85-86.) (See also "Which Shall I Choose—The Swine or the Savior?" in author's book, *Luke's Thrilling Gospel*, pp. 200-202; "The Woman Who Paid Doctor's Bills," in *Luke's Thrilling Gospel*, pp. 205-207; "Jairus...Who Probably Broke All His Vows," in *Luke's Thrilling Gospel*, pp. 209-210.)

The Sixth Chapter of Mark

THEME: *Triumphs and Tragedies in Galilee*

OUTLINE:

SECTION ONE

Expository Notes on Christ's Experiences in Nazareth

And He went out from thence, and came into His own country; and His disciples follow Him (v. 1).

Luke 4:16-30 describes the earlier visit Jesus made to His home city. The fact that He returned in spite of the earlier threat to His life, suggests courage and purpose of great intensity. Yet there appears to be a difference between the two homecomings. The first occasion was marred by the assault made after His message in the synagogue. Then, He had been as a local man returning after a short absence; He was coming home! The second visit appears to have been more auspicious. He came, as any rabbi would have done, followed by a band of devoted assistants. He was indeed coming to His own; but alas, His own would receive Him not (John 1:11).

And when the sabbath day was come, He began to teach in the synagogue; and many hearing Him were astonished, saying, From whence hath this man these things? and what wisdom is this which is given unto Him, that even such mighty works are wrought by His hands? Is not this the carpenter, the son of Mary, the brother of James, and Joses, and of Juda, and Simon? and are not His sisters here with us? And they were offended at Him (vv. 2-3).

The citizens of Nazareth could not have been unaware of the miraculous nature of the Lord's ministry, and His return to their synagogue was met with guarded interest and suspicion. Formerly, He had come alone, and they had planned to assassinate Him. This time He had strong men at His side; it might not be safe nor wise to repeat their earlier indiscretion. Many of the older people could easily remember His childhood; they had watched as He grew to manhood; some of them doubtless had been His customers. They knew His family; they knew the limited schooling He had received from the local teachers, and it seemed incomprehensible that He Who had received so little, could now offer so much. The ancient writer, Chrysostom, described how the Savior made ploughs and yokes for oxen, and if we can accept his testimony, it is safe assume that farmers of the district had often sought the help of the One they were now about to criticize. He had walked along their streets; had listened to their problems and requests for help; had received their money and returned their change. They had seen Him at work in the carpenter's shop and had often passed the time of day with the other members of the family. He was just one of their own citizens Who had no legal authority to be an official rabbi. They resented His standing in their synagogue to tell them what they ought to do. It is worthy of attention that Mark expresses so much in a few words: 1) They were astonished, 2) they were offended, and 3) they were unbelievers. It has often been said the same sunshine melts wax and hardens clay. We may also say that the same gracious, wise and loving words of the Lord had similar effects. To the blind, the leper, the infirm, the hopeless, the message of Christ brought help and happiness. To the cynical critics, His words meant nothing, and as a result, "... He could there do no mighty work, save that He laid His hands upon a few sick folk, and healed them."

Throughout the centuries, much discussion has taken place concerning the family of the Lord, "Some have thought that these were literally brethren of our Lord, sons of Joseph and Mary. Others have considered they were his legal half-brothers, sons of Joseph by a former marriage.

This view is held by many of the Greek Fathers, and has something to recommend it. But on the whole, the most probable opinion is that they were cousins of our Lord—sons of a sister of the Virgin Mary, also called Mary, the wife of Cleophas. There is evidence that there were four sons of Cleophas and Mary, whose names were James and Joses, Simon and Judas. Mary the wife of Cleophas is mentioned by Matthew (27:56) as the mother of James the Less, and of Joses. Jude describes himself as the brother of James (Jude 5), Simon is mentioned in Eusebius, as the son of Cleophas. It must be remembered also that the Greek word *adelphos*, like the Hebrew word which it expresses, means not only a brother, but generally, a near kinsman. In the same way, the "sisters" would be cousins of our Lord. According to a tradition recorded by Nicephorus (2:3) the names of these sisters or cousins were "Esther and Tamar" (Dr. Bickersteth in *The Pulpit Commentary*, Mark, p. 244).

Some students will be quick to point out that the word *adelphos*, according to Dr. Thayer, means primarily "from the same womb" (*Greek-English Lexicon of the New Testament*, p. 10). Dr. Thayer also reminds his readers that the term also applies to a brother, whether born of the same two parents, *or only of the same father or the same mother*. Protestants and Catholic students may be at variance on this issue, but let us not miss the central fact that, whatever their personal relation to Jesus might have been, the members of the family of Christ were all known to the inhabitants of Nazareth, and as we have seen already, were among those who fell before the onslaught of doubt and prejudice (see Mark 3:21 and 31).

But Jesus said unto them, A prophet is not without honor but in his own country; and among his own kin, and in his own house. And He could there do no mighty work, save that He laid His hands upon a few sick folk, and healed them. And He marvelled because of their unbelief. And He went round about the villages teaching (vv. 4-6).

The key statement in these verses is "He could there do no mighty work." This cannot mean that it had become an impossibility for Jesus to perform miraculous deeds, for had this been the case, He could not have healed the people upon whom He placed His hands. It must mean that within the Kingdom of God, certain laws are always in operation, and that even the actions of Jesus were more or less governed by those requirements. "Without faith, it is impossible to please God: for he that cometh to God, must believe that He is, and that He is a rewarder of them that diligently seek Him'' (Heb. 11:6). Alas, the people of Nazareth had permitted familiarity to breed contempt, and in the absence of real faith, the Lord found it difficult to release powers which could have solved their problems, healed their sick, and turned the night of their personal sorrows into a day of unprecedented joy. Yet here and there among the unbelieving crowd, were a few people within whose hearts hope existed. They looked, they believed, and thanked God, and they were not unnoticed. Jesus saw them, loved them, understood them, sympathized with them, and responding to their faith, reached out His hand to touch them, and they were healed immediately. Happy indeed are those people who see not the crowd but the Christ in the crowd— for them, anything is possible.

SECTION TWO

Expository Notes on the Commissioning of the Disciples

And He called unto Him the twelve, and began to send them forth by two and two; and gave them power over unclean spirits; and commanded them that they should take nothing for their journey, save a staff only; no scrip, no bread, no money in their purse; but be shod with sandals; and not put on two coats. And He said unto them, in what place soever ye enter into an house, there abide till ye depart from that place. And whosoever shall not receive you, nor hear you, when ye depart thence, shake off the dust from under your feet for a testimony against them. Verily I say unto you, It shall be more tolerable for Sodom and Gomorrha in the day of judgment, than for that city (vv. 7-11).

THE GREAT ADVANCE

It is worthy of note that Mark alone mentions this commission. Luke records how, "after these things, the Lord appointed other seventy also, and sent them two and two before His face into every city and place whither He himself would come" (10:1). Obviously this became the Lord's strategic plan of operation, but originally, and perhaps prior to the enlargement of the disciple band, the Lord had only twelve men to commission. Jesus knew the time for a major advance had come. If the world were to be reached for God, then an acceleration of effort was necessary. Hitherto, the disciples had stayed close to their Master. Jesus had solved their problems and satisfied their every need. They had been as young birds fed by a devoted parent! The time had come when they should spread their wings and fly into the wide, open skies of opportunity. Jesus would not always be with them in Person; they would have to manage on their own, so calling them unto Him, He commissioned them and sent them out, two by two, to further the cause of God's kingdom. The entire world would like to know the identity of the couples. Did Peter go with John, or did Christ find it necessary to send the impulsive, fiery Peter with Thomas whose sober reflections would prevent Peter's reckless enthusiasm from ruining the project? Had James and John gone together, one small disappointment might have caused such an explosion that repercussions would have gone throughout the empire. Maybe the Lord deliberately veiled His act in secrecy, so that today we might look for greatness in everyone whom He places at our side. When the Lord sent out those six evangelistic couples, He realized that six times as many villages would be reached than would have been the case had they all gone together. Doubtless, they were not as experienced as He would have wished, and the possibility exists that, before they had gone very far on their journeys, they encountered perplexing problems. Yet, they had to learn sometime, and Jesus thought that moment had arrived.

THE GLORIOUS ASSURANCE

"He gave them power over unclean spirits" (v. 7). They were not to expect an easy time as they travelled from place to place. Evil would confront them at every turn of the road. There was no need to fear. The Lord would never ask them to go forth unprepared to meet the difficulties of the life to which He had called them. With each new day would come new power, and even the devils would be subject unto them. Their trust in God had to be complete. They were to go forth as poor men, and this had to be obvious to all with whom they came into contact. They were not to carry excessive changes of raiment; they would need no "suitcases." They were not to carry supplies of money nor food; constantly, they were to be completely dependent upon God to meet their needs. Today, we live in a different world. To make great advances for Christ, enormous sums of money have to be spent on television and radio coverage, etc. Modern preachers reach more individuals within one half an hour segment than the disciples would have reached in many years of untiring service. Today's television personalities find it necessary to appeal constantly for the financial aid which makes their programs possible; the disciples of Jesus never appealed for anything—

except listening ears. Evangelists often have suits of various colors for every service; their fellow laborers must be clad in matching outfits to appeal to the watchful eyes of the audience. The disciples of Jesus had but one garment and probably that was a dirty, dust-filled, unattractive cloth draped from shoulders to ankles. The New Testament preachers had no money to buy snacks or anything else, but they possessed within their souls a power that shook Hell!

Every day, the itinerant evangelists had to trust God moment by moment. They never begged, but they never ceased praying. There is reason to believe that what they *were*, had as much influence upon their hearers as anything they ever said.

THE GRATEFUL ACCEPTANCE

These men who learned to laugh at impossibilities, were not above accepting help. The giving of hospitality was considered to be a sacred responsibility and privilege through Bible Lands, for people believed that in entertaining strangers they might be welcoming angels. It was to be expected, therefore, that someone would invite the preachers into their home, and the request was not to be refused. Only those who have been in a similar position can fully appreciate what this meant. The entertaining host could be a poor man; his home might be impoverished and totally lacking in comfort. The disciples were told not to complain, nor move to a more luxurious dwelling. Their entire stay in a village, as far as it was possible, had to be spent beneath the same roof. It would then be impossible for the host to be offended if his hospitality were exchanged for better things. Furthermore, there would never be any doubt in the minds of the listeners concerning the reasons for the visit of the strangers. The preachers thought not of themselves, but of the message they preached. They had no desire to get, but to give.

THE GRIEVOUS ANNOUNCEMENT

The Jews were very strict in their laws and practices concerning shaking off unclean dust. They insisted that when a foreigner entered the country, his first act would be to shake off the dust brought from the Gentile world. It was their means of proclaiming that orthodox Jews could have no dealings with unclean people. When Jesus instructed the disciples to follow this procedure, He was using a practice well known in every community. He was proclaiming the simple fact that a man

who refused to entertain the preacher of the Gospel, was as unclean
in the sight of God as Gentiles were in the estimation of the Jewish
rabbis. When Christ compared Sodom with "that city," His words of
condemnation provided food for thought. Doubtless, the disciples entered
many respectable communities where sincere people endeavored to
observe the laws of God, and be faithful in the practice of their religious
beliefs. Apparently, this would be of little worth, if they rejected the
preachers and the message they brought. That Jesus compared those
places with Sodom and Gomorrah, the filthiest of all the ancient cities,
might appear to be surprising. However, it is necessary to remember
that Sodom never enjoyed the advantages of hearing the Gospel. The
ancient people never possessed a Bible, and since God can only judge
people according to the light they have received, the city which has
received much, will be expected to give more.

**And they went out, and preached that men should repent. And they
cast out many devils, and anointed with oil many that were sick, and
healed them (vv. 12-13).**

The Amplified New Testament renders this passage as, "So they went
out and preached that men should repent, that is, that they *should change
their minds for the better, and heartily amend their ways with abhorrence
for their past sins.*" And thus did Christ organize and initiate the first
systematic evangelistic crusades the world ever knew. The disciples went
forth conquering and to conquer, and it must have been for them the
most thrilling moments of their lives, when they discovered His power
went with them. They were carrying their Master's message, and
everywhere they urged listeners to repent. This was, still is, and ever
will be the first priority of the church, for unless sinners turn from their
sins to seek the living God, all hope of their entering the eternal kingdom
will be lost.

SECTION THREE

Expository Notes on Herod's Relationship With John the Baptist

**And King Herod heard of Him [Jesus]; (for His name was spread
abroad:) and he said, That John the Baptist was risen from the dead,
and therefore mighty works do shew forth themselves in Him (v. 14).**

The complicated marriages of the Herod family, and the murderous intrigues leading to the death of John the Baptist have been described in detail by the historian, Josephus (see the *Works of Flavius Josephus*, Book 18, Chapter 5, paragraphs 1 and 2, p. 382). The Herod of this passage, known as Herod Antipas had married the daughter of Aretas, the king of Arabia. Later, after a visit to Rome where he met the wife of his brother, Philip, he not only seduced her, but persuaded her to leave her husband and to come to him in Palestine. All this led to a terrible war between the father of his former wife, and the armies of Herod. Woven into the fabric of the story is the action of the wilderness preacher known as John the Baptist. Herod had violated the Levitical laws. "Thou shalt not uncover the nakedness of thy brother's wife; it is thy brother's nakedness" (Lev. 18:16). His action was known and condemned throughout his domain, but no one had the courage to denounce the monarch. This apparently was John's problem. To him, sin was sin whether it were in a king's heart or in the life of the poorest peasant. How could John preach repentance to the common people when Herod blatantly ignored the consequences of wrong-doing? When John publicly denounced the immorality of Herod, he brought upon himself the wrath of a detestable woman, who never forgave the preacher. As we shall see, Herod murdered John, but could never forget him. The king had to live with a troubled conscience, and his problems increased immeasurably when he fearfully believed John had risen again from the grave. Doubtless, he expected the slain man to appear in the palace to execute vengeance upon his murderer. He was harassed, haunted, worried. A guilty conscience is the most terrible companion in the world.

Others said, That it is Elias. And others said, That it is a prophet, or as one of the prophets. But when Herod heard thereof, he said, It is John, whom I beheaded: he is risen from the dead (vv. 15-16).

It is not too difficult to understand Herod's problem. The entire nation was speaking about the exploits of the Nazarene Preacher. The market places had become centers of discussion where people exchanged the latest stories of His exploits. The old and the young; the poor and the wealthy; the educated and the common people, all were speaking about Jesus. He had captured the attention of all the citizens. Herod knew this, but in spite of his determination to forget John the Baptist, he was unable to do so. John had surely reappeared among men. When Herod asked questions concerning the age and appearance of the new messenger, all the answers seemed to fit into the general picture. When he inquired about the content of the preacher's message, he seemed to be hearing again the man who feared none but God. Of course, this had to be John the Baptist! When he continued to think of what he had done to God's servant, paralyzing fear gripped his soul and life became unbearable. The other ideas expressed by the common people were stupid! The folk in the streets should know better. No other prophet could possibly fit the description given of this new preacher. Yes, any one in his right mind would know this had to be John! And Herod relived the scenes next described for us by Mark.

> **For Herod himself had sent forth and laid hold upon John, and bound him in prison for Herodias' sake, his brother Philip's wife; for he had married her. For John had said unto Herod, It is not lawful for thee to have thy brother's wife. Therefore Herodias had a quarrel against him, and would have killed him; but she could not for Herod feared John, knowing that he was a just man and an holy, and observed him; and when he heard him, he did many things, and heard him gladly (vv. 17-20).**

Poor Herod seems to fit perfectly into the picture described in the lines of Studdart Kennedy, the poet of World War I. He wrote:

> There's summat the pulls us up;
> And there's summat that pulls us down;
> And the consequence is that we wobble,
> Twixt muck and a golden crown.

It is incredible that Herod could hate the message and yet admire the messenger. It is almost beyond comprehension that he should incarcerate the preacher and still go out of his way to hear more of the message he disliked. Yet such was the case, and let us admit there is a little bit of Herod in us all. We know what we ought to do, but we resent anyone who reminds us of our shortcomings. Again and again Herod thought, "If only that stupid preacher would compromise and forget my sin, I could do a lot for him. I could even make him my official Chaplain!" But John was totally unyielding; he recognized one Master, and to Him, he was determined to be faithful, even unto death. The end was never in doubt. From the moment John stood on the steps of the palace to denounce the sin of the monarch, he was a marked man. Herodias was incensed with the preacher who dared to drag her name through the gossip of the market places. She would get even with him even though it were the last thing she did.

The ballroom in the palace was crowded; haunting music filled the room. Half-drunk, Herod sat on his throne gloating over the surprise he had in store for his honored guests. Suddenly, his step-daughter glided through the drapes to begin an unforgettable performance. That particular role was generally played by professional prostitutes who were accustomed to sacrificing their souls on the altar of personal gain. That Herodias was willing to allow her daughter to occupy such a dastardly role, indicates the intensity of her bitterness toward John. Nothing had to be left to chance; the dancer would perform precisely as she was instructed. Oblivious to the staring eyes of lustful men; insensitive to the twisting, twirling body of her naked daughter, Herodias saw only the head of the man she detested. It was worth sacrificing her daughter's honor, if she could procure in exchange the head of that interfering, meddlesome preacher.

It was all over except the shouting. The performance had been completed; the guests were applauding, and Herod, hardly knowing what he was doing, said, "Ask of me whatsoever thou wilt and I will give it thee." Poor Herod; he had carelessly stepped into sand; now he was discovering it to be a quicksand!

And when a convenient day was come, that Herod on his birthday made a supper to his lords, high captains, and chief estates of Galilee; and when the daughter of the said Herodias came in, and danced, and pleased Herod and them that sat with him, the King said unto the damsel, Ask of me whatsoever thou wilt, and I will give it thee. And he sware unto her, Whatsoever thou shalt ask of me, I will give it thee, unto the half of my kingdom. And she went forth, and said unto her mother, What shall I ask? And she said, The head of John the Baptist (vv. 21-24).

Students may want to consider, 1) his Party, 2) his Pleasure, 3) his Pride, and 4) his Prisoner. The man who becomes a heavy drinker is quickly lulled into the sleep of indiscretion and foolishness; the man who continues to drink, often dies in his ill-fated sleep. Herod was suddenly trapped between the people and his pride. If he agreed to any request to be made he would lose half a kingdom; if he refused, the people would broadcast the news that he had broken his word, and as a result, the birthday celebrations would be ruined. Herodias was delighted; her husband would not break his promise; her carefully-made plan had succeeded. When she married Herod, she lost her previous husband. When she gained the head of John the Baptist, she lost her soul. In all probability she never considered those consequences, until it was too late to do anything about them. Her descendants are still with us!

> **And she came in straightway with haste unto the king, and asked, saying, I will that thou give me by and by in a charger the head of John the Baptist. And the king was exceeding sorry; yet for his oath's sake, and for their sakes which sat with him, he would not reject her. And immediately the king sent an executioner (one of his guards), and commanded his head to be brought; and he went and beheaded him in the prison, and brought his head in a charger, and gave it to the damsel; and the damsel gave it to her mother. And when his disciples heard of it, they came and took up his corpse, and laid it in a tomb (vv. 25-29).**

It is said that the castle where John was imprisoned stood on a lonely ridge overlooking the Dead Sea. Because of the large ravines which surrounded it, the prison was regarded as one of the most invincible and desolate strongholds in the world. If one travels to this citadel today, he can see the iron hooks in the wall to which John was probably bound.

It is not too difficult to appreciate the predicament in which Herod found himself. He had given his word, and had promised anything to the value of half his kingdom. How could he possibly escape from the mess into which he had gotten himself? At this moment I cannot help but think of an incident which took place during the four years I was privileged to serve the Baptist churches in South Africa. A native teacher had been telling the story of Herod's folly and of the promise made to the dancing girl. She asked her class of small children, "What would you have done had you been in Herod's place?" One little boy lifted his hand, and then said, *"Miss, I would have said that the head of John the Baptist belonged to the other half of the kingdom I had not promised."* Surely, John knew what to expect, and as he sat awaiting the arrival of the executioner, a strange and wonderful peace filled his soul. He had said of Christ, "He must increase; I must decrease," and what he had predicted was certainly coming to pass. He would soon be leaving the work to which God had called him, but the future lay in good hands. And who can tell what happened as the footsteps of the coming guard sounded on the stony steps? Perhaps John slipped to his knees, and from that position probably obtained a clearer view of the celestial city.

The ballroom was filled with a strange, horrible quietness. The musicians had stopped playing their instruments; the guests were no longer dancing. Salome, near the throne, with ashen face and staring eyes, looked at the grisly head being brought by the guard. If John's eyes were still open, they were gazing sightlessly into the depths of Herod's soul. He was destined never to forget that awful moment. He shuddered and, to cover his embarrassment, ordered the prize to be given to the girl who had requested it. But the zest for enjoyment had died; the party had ended prematurely, God's curse was resting upon the entire proceedings. Alone, Herodias gloated over her triumph. She had gotten even with that pesky preacher; he would never denounce her again. Alas, she was either too blind or too stupid to realize that God and history would unite to condemn her.

The floor of John's cell had turned, in places, to scarlet; the lifeless body lay where it had fallen. "And John's disciples came, and took up the body, and buried it, *and went and told Jesus*" (Matt. 14:12). What else could they do? Their master was dead; their world had suddenly ended; the future was utterly bleak. Then they remembered that at least Jesus would understand, and together they took their problems to the Savior. Happy indeed are all people who, learning from this example, also find their way to the One Who said, "Him that cometh unto me, I will in no wise cast out" (John 6:27).

SECTION FOUR

Expository Notes on the Invitation to a Private Retreat

And the apostles gathered themselves together unto Jesus, and told Him all things, both what they had done, and what they had taught. And He said unto them, Come ye yourselves apart into a desert place, and rest a while: for there were many coming and going, and they had no leisure so much as to eat (vv. 30-31).

The disciples were radiant; their cup of happiness was full and running over. Their first missionary journey had been a resounding success. Their earlier fears of failure had been unfounded; they had succeeded beyond their wildest dreams. Their Master would be pleased with them. Their return would be all that a "homecoming" should be.

A TIME TO REPORT

"...*they told Him all things, both what they had done, and what they had taught*" (v. 30). We cannot help but wonder what reports were given, for the disciples were not always wise in their actions and speech (see Mark 9:38). If all that had been done by the disciples had been described or recorded on tape, the entire church would have an interesting time listening. Perhaps they had said things which afterward they regretted; on the other hand, they could have been jubilant as they told of their triumphs. It is always wise to tell the Lord about everything. Dr. A. J. Gordon once had a dream in which he saw a stranger entering the church. As the pastor delivered his message, instinctively his eyes looked in the direction of the stranger. At the end of the service, Dr. Gordon hurried to the door to speak with the visitor. Alas, he was too late; the man had already left. The same procedure was repeated at the evening service, when frustrated at being unable to interview the new listener, the pastor said to an elder, "Did you see that man sitting over there? Who was he?" The elder replied, "Pastor, that was Jesus of Nazareth." Instantly, Dr. Gordon awakened with the realization that he had preached to the Lord. His first reaction was to ask a simple question, "What did I say?" That dream changed the life of that famous minister, for he realized as never before that Jesus of Nazareth was in every service. It behooved the pastor to be very careful in what he said, for the Lord was an attentive listener.

A TIME TO REJOICE

Later, when seventy disciples returned to give a similar report (Luke 10:17), they came "...with joy, saying, even the devils are subject unto us through thy name." It is always wise to check with the Lord concerning the nature and value of the services rendered to Him. At the end of each day, every Christian should ask, "Lord, what have I done for you today? Were you satisfied with my efforts? Could I have accomplished more had I tried a little harder?" The service of Christ should always be the happiest sphere of life, but it is wise to remember that true joy does not necessarily rest upon successful service. If it were so, many of God's dearest children might remain unhappy. We cannot all be successful, but even the most feeble can be faithful. It should be considered our highest and greatest privilege just for the chance to do something for Him Who did so much for us. If devils are subject unto us in Christ's Name; if our preaching be sensationally successful; if our service, whatever its type, be thought excellent, so much the better, but other things must be considered. We may not be outstanding preachers, missionaries, teachers, doctors or any such like, but if our hands should offer a cup of water to the thirsty; help to the needy, or even advice to the despairing, we might be ministering to the Lord. This consideration makes service a continuing joy. It is not what follows our effort that counts, but rather what prompts it in the first place. To speak His Name; to carry His blessing; to represent His cause, anywhere or at any time, is a privilege every angel would covet.

> There is joy in serving Jesus,
> As I journey on my way
> Joy that fills the heart with praises,
> Every hour and every day.
>
> There is joy in serving Jesus
> Joy that triumphs over pain.
> Fills my soul with heavenly music
> Till I join the glad refrain.
>
> There is joy in serving Jesus,
> As I walk alone with God;
> 'Tis the joy of Christ my Savior,
> Who the path of suffering trod.
>
> There is joy in serving Jesus,
> Joy amid the darkest night,
> For I've learned the wondrous secret,
> And I'm walking in the light.
>
> There is joy, joy, joy in serving Jesus,
> Joy that throbs within my heart,
> Every moment, every hour,
> As I draw upon His power,
> There is joy, joy, joy that never will depart.

A TIME TO RELAX

When the sick woman touched the hem of Christ's garment, the Lord said, "Somebody touched me. I perceive that virtue has gone out of me." Sacrificial service for the Lord leads to a draining of one's spiritual resources. Successful efforts beget thanksgiving, but often difficult and unrewarding tasks lead to strained nerves, and sometimes strained feelings. It is easy to become irritable and upset when things are not going as we desire. Then either anger or despondency grips the soul, and scowls replace the smiles on the face of the worker. Too much work leads to exhaustion, and if this continues, it is often followed by a nervous breakdown. After a severe illness, a doctor advises his patient to rest. For example, when my wife had undergone very serious surgery, the physician said, "Mrs. Powell, each afternoon, you must rest. You may be washing dishes, when suddenly you will feel very tired. Do not argue with yourself about finishing the dishes, go immediately and stretch yourself on your bed. Completely relax for half an hour, and you will feel better." His advice and my wife's cooperation worked wonders in her body. The same rule applies in the Christian life of service. Too much continuing service leads to strain and inefficiency; too much rest leads to indolence. Happy is the man who hears the Savior saying, "Come ye apart...*and rest awhile*..." To rest, does not necessarily mean one's permanent retirement! A battery that is always charging never gives light. A battery that is charged and then used, supplies light and power to the owner. There are times when even our desert place may become a health resort, *but we must make the time to go there.*

A TIME TO REFLECT

When David was a fugitive being hunted by King Saul in the wilderness of Judea, he wrote a Psalm (63) in which he reflected upon his past, and then considered his immediate future. He said, "*Because thou hast been my help, therefore in the shadow of thy wings will I trust*" (63:7). Frightening events were happening all around David; danger lurked at every turn in the road, and his future was ominous. How could he possibly escape from Saul when thousands of soldiers sought him, and almost every villager seemed willing to betray him? David lay upon his bed of ferns, and each night looked through the branches of the trees toward the stars shining brightly in the heavens. He knew he was looking into God's country, and slowly he realized that His God was not far away; He was in the wilderness with him. God had never failed to help his servant; why should David be discouraged? To reflect on the goodness and faithfulness of God is the greatest of all tonics for a weary soul. The Lord knew and practiced this each time He climbed the mountain to enjoy fellowship with His Father. So often we share David's experience and amid the failures of life exclaim, "Why art thou cast down, O my soul? and why art thou disquieted in me?" David's answer was clear and simple, "...hope thou in God: for I shall yet praise him for the help of his countenance" (Psalm 42:5). Perhaps the best advice ever offered to men comes in the words of the Negro spiritual. "Steal away, steal away, steal away to Jesus." This is the only way to discover rest in a restless world.

A TIME TO REPLENISH

After every shopping week, the shelves in a store must be restocked. After every major military advance, an army must pause to regroup, build up its reserves and prepare for the next phase of its onward march. Similarly, after each and every crusade for Christ, the missionaries need to rest and re-equip themselves for the next phase in their crusade against evil. The mind must be filled with fresh materials; the soul must be filled with new inspiration, and this is only accomplished by being alone with Christ. Many years ago I attended the Keswick Convention in England and listened to Dr. W. Graham Scroggie giving a testimony. He told his audience of a period in his ministry when he believed himself to be a colossal failure. Experiencing problems within his church, his soul was disturbed, and his mind seemed unable to cope with the demands being made upon him. He contemplated quitting the ministry and finding employment in some other sphere of education. Instead, he climbed a mountain and sat beneath a tree. There he told the Lord he was an absolute failure, and quite incapable of continuing his ministry. Then the Lord seemed to reply, "You are just the man I am seeking. I think I can do something with you now." And Dr. Scroggie, referring to the Breaking of the Bread, went on to say, "He took me, broke me into small pieces, and gave me back to my people. And that was the beginning of my present ministry." So many enthusiastic young preachers are totally exhausted within six months of their ordination, because they fail to replenish their minds. They are busy doing all kinds of things, but too busy to go out into the desert to sit at the feet of Jesus. We must never forget that what we are to Christ is infinitely more important than anything we shall ever do for Him. Unless the pastor looks first into the face of his Lord, he should never enter a pulpit to look into the faces of his congregation. As Dr. Jowett once said, "A minister's study should be an upper room and not a lounge."

A TIME TO REDEDICATE

All Christians should remember that however marvelous recent achievements seem to be, the crusade will never be over, until the world has been brought to Christ. Let us thank God for victories, but let us seize every opportunity to prepare for the next phase of the battle. When we leave our place of recuperation, we shall go back into the battle-lines to fight against all forms of evil, and we must be ready. With the same fresh enthusiasm which we knew at the beginning of our work, we must go forth as people renewed in the grace and power of our Lord. Paul said, "Let us not grow weary in well doing, for in due season we shall reap *if we faint not.*" The vessels which were dedicated for use in the temple were never used for any other purpose, until they were taken as spoils of war into Babylon. Their kind of dedication was forever! It is disappointing and sad to see men who once were great preachers and outstanding workers for Christ, finishing their lives in all kinds of secular jobs. It is understandable when physical ailments force a man to leave a church or some other area of Christian service, but when a man leaves the work to which God called him in order to become wealthy in some lucrative area of activity, one wonders if he were ever really called of God in the first place. No decision of any importance should ever be made by a Christian worker, until he has discussed the matter alone with his Lord. If there the Lord reveals He wants us elsewhere, we shall be safe in moving. If there be any doubt about the matter, it is wise to remain where we are, and determine to do our best for the Savior.

SECTION FIVE

Expository Notes on the Feeding of the Thousands

And they departed into a desert place by ship privately. And the people saw them departing, and many knew Him, and ran afoot thither out of all cities, and outwent them, and come together unto Him. And Jesus, when He came out, saw much people, and was moved with compassion toward them, because they were as sheep not having a shepherd; and He began to teach them many things (vv. 32-34).

It has often been said that the best made plans of mice and men are apt to be ruined, and so it was with Jesus and His followers. Possibly the Lord had in mind some quiet spot on the far side of the Sea of Galilee, but in order to reach it, their little boat had to cross the lake, which at that point was about four miles wide. Ordinarily there would have been no problem, but if an adverse wind were blowing that day, the progress of the boat would have been impeded. The watching crowds, anxious to hear and see more, ran around the top of the lake, perhaps about eight to ten miles, and they obviously arrived before the boat reached the beach. When the Lord disembarked, He saw not the peacefulness of a quiet retreat, but an expectant crowd waiting on the shore. Their presence, in itself, might have become a source of irritation. Leaders of less spiritual stature might have exclaimed, "Why cannot you leave us alone. We are tired; we must rest; come back tomorrow." Unruffled and serene, the Savior looked at the multitude, and loved them. To Him, they seemed as sheep without a shepherd. They were lonely; they were hungry; they were lost. "And He began to teach them many things." Did He use Isaiah 53:6 as a text? "All we like sheep have gone astray; we have turned every one to his own way; and the Lord hath laid on him the iniquity of us all." We cannot tell, but some things about sheep are obvious.

Often they need to be found. Sheep are among the most stupid animals in the world; they are prone to wandering. Cows will return to the sheds at milking time; horses return to the barns at feeding time; pigs, goats, dogs, cats and all other animals seem to be aware of their natural habitats, but sheep seemingly have no sense of direction; they just wander further and further away. They resemble humans. Men know where they should be; they even know the direction in which they should travel, but alas, they love to wander further and further away from God. Unless the Good Shepherd seeks them, they seldom return.

Always they need to be led. Throughout the countries of the Middle East, all sheep have their own shepherd. Sheep know how to eat, but unfortunately they appear to have no ability to find fresh pasture. Horses can smell water and so can other animals, but unless a shepherd leads the flock to green pastures, the sheep would die in the wilderness. Perhaps this thought was amplified when the Lord, seeing the hungry multitude, "taught them many things." They needed the bread of life, and Christ was willing to postpone his plans for a quiet vacation with the disciples in order to meet that need.

Constantly they need to be protected. Sheep have no natural defenses. Sometimes in a vain effort to protect a lamb, an old ewe may try to give a measure of protection, but the effort is very feeble. During my visit in Western Australia, I stayed with a farmer who found it necessary to wage a constant battle against the foxes which were destroying his flocks. Probably the large mountain sheep with their curling horns might be able to display force, but the ordinary sheep known throughout Palestine, were among the most helpless of all creatures. The Lord surely knew this and saw in the people the same characteristics. They needed a friend who would protect them, feed them, comfort them, and quite obviously His great heart was moved with compassion the moment He saw them waiting on the shore. It is so stimulating to remember that time has not changed Him. He remains the same, "yesterday, and today, and forever."

And when the day was now far spent, His disciples came unto Him, and said, This is a desert place, and now the time is far passed. Send them away, that they may go into the country round about, and into the villages, and buy themselves bread; for they have nothing to eat. He answered and said unto them, Give ye them to eat. And they say unto Him, Shall we go and buy two hundred pennyworth of bread, and give them to eat? (vv. 35-37).

The Greek word *ereemos* translated "desert" means "isolated, lonely, desolate, uninhabited" (Thayer). It is therefore easy to appreciate the reasonableness of the disciples' suggestion. Within fifteen to twenty miles there were several communities, and although the evening was approaching, it would still be possible to obtain food at some of the stores. Nevertheless there was a problem. There were five thousand men present, and Matthew adds, "beside women and children" (Matt. 14:21). Probably there were aged people and also very young children present. If all those people had been sent hurriedly to purchase provisions, the crowd might have become a mob, in which hungry, frustrated people would have been hurt. When Christ commanded His disciples to feed the multitude, the disciples gasped with amazement. They replied, "Two hundred pennyworth of bread would be insufficient to feed such a crowd." The question inferred in their statement was, "Where at this late hour could we obtain such an amount of food, even if we had the money to buy it?" It should be remembered that a penny represented the daily wage for a workman who toiled twelve hours in the vineyard (see Matthew 20:1-16). To earn two hundred pennies, a man would have to work 200 days, and since labor was forbidden on the sabbath, then it would be necessary to toil for almost nine months to earn the money necessary to purchase the amount of food needed. The entire disciple band, twelve men in all, would have to work twelve hours a day for almost three weeks to earn that amount of money. Where then could they find enough cash at a moment's notice to do the impossible? Let us not be too critical of their reactions; probably we also would have been dumbfounded.

He saith unto them, How many loaves have ye? go and see. And when they knew, they say, Five, and two fishes. And He commanded them to make all sit down by companies upon the green grass. And they sat down in ranks, by hundreds and by fifties. And when He had taken the five loaves and the two fishes, He looked up to heaven, and blessed, and break the loaves, and gave them to the disciples to set before them; and the two fishes divided He among them all. And they did all eat, and were filled. And they took up twelve baskets full of the fragments, and of the fishes. And they that did eat of the loaves were about five thousand men (vv. 38-44).

"The importance of this miracle is emphasized by the fact that all the evangelists record the event. The four records vary a little but this only endorses the individuality of each author. Each reported the event as he was able to understand its implications. Probably this has been the hardest of all the miracles to refute; there were so many reliable witnesses of the event. Following the oriental custom by which women and children were apart, only the men were counted. However the presence of a great number of women and children was indicated by Matthew (14:21).

"Christ was careful to have the audience seated before He performed His miracle. Had He neglected to do this, the scene might have beggared description. Had they been standing in a closely packed throng all around Him, the startling news of what He was doing might have turned that crowd into a rushing multitude of fanatics. The people would have pressed from all sides to see what was taking place; children might have been injured in the crush, and the whole scene would have become an object of criticism. Therefore, with the aid of His disciples the Lord arranged that the people be seated in groups of fifty (Matthew) or by double rows of fifty—hundreds (Mark). This exhibited orderliness in the Master's methods; it provided an easy way by which the people could be counted, and each individual was able to see clearly what Christ was doing. Thus a catastrophe was averted, and a benediction rested upon the scene.

"John supplies the information that the food was provided by a lad. The basket was probably the small receptacle carried by strict Jews. Unwilling to purchase provisions from pagans, orthodox Jews took bread on every journey. Certain critics suggested the miracle was fraudulent; each traveler surrendered his small store of provisions, and the people had a basket lunch! This absurd suggestion is unworthy of comment, except perhaps for one detail. The critics might have told us if any of the donors ever claimed their portions from the abundance left over in the twelve baskets. The surplus was probably used to help people who had special needs. The account provides a picture of a greater faith. Christ the Bread of Life sees the multitude before Him, and dispensing the Good News to His disciples, commands that they go forth to supply what is needed. The disciples, the Church, can only give what they first receive from Him. Their own resources are too small and inadequate. Unless the preacher obtains the food from the hand of Christ, congregations go home hungry. Furthermore, the provision of Christ and the cooperation of His followers cannot avail unless hungry people accept what is offered. Christ supplies the banquet, but He never *FORCES* His guests to eat'' (taken from the author's book, *Luke's Thrilling Gospel*, p. 220).

SECTION SIX

Expository Notes on the Rescue of the Disciples in the Storm

And straightway He constrained His disciples to get into the ship, and to go to the other side before unto Bethsaida, while He sent away the people. And when He had sent them away, He departed into a mountain to pray (vv. 45-46).

To understand this action, it is necessary to consider John's version of the incident. He wrote: ''Then those men, when they had seen the miracle that Jesus did, said, This is of a truth that prophet that should come into the world. When Jesus therefore perceived *that they would come and take Him by force, to make Him a king,* He departed again into a mountain himself alone'' (John 6:14-15). The appreciative, spellbound thousands who had witnessed the great miracle were about to take the law into their own hands. The fiery Zealots who were in the crowd were ready to arrange a hasty coronation, and come what may, were ready to fight for the liberation of Israel. The best for which they could hope was an untrained army without weapons; their enthusiasm was about to run away with their brains! This was the very thing Christ did not desire. Even the disciples might be carried away by the popular movement and the false enthusiasm. Even if they tried to convince the people to leave, their persuasions would leave much to be desired. They might volunteer to become officers in a hurriedly-formed army. Knowledge of such a movement would soon be known to the Romans, and within a few hours, detachments of soldiers would be sent to suppress any uprising. Many people would be massacred, and the entire cause for which Christ had come to earth would have been ruined. It was, therefore, considered unwise to leave the dispersal of the crowd to the disciples. The Lord Himself had to handle the difficult situation, and this could hardly be done when the disciples were present and ready to countermand any order given. So, "straightway, He constrained His disciples to get into the ship, and to go to the other side." All thought of the quiet retreat had to be temporarily abandoned. A crisis had arisen, and any personal pleasure the Lord had been anticipating had to be sacrificed in the interest of the kingdom of God.

After their departure, the Lord calmed the multitude, and urged them to seek shelter for the night. There would always be another day; He would meet them again in the morning! The serenity of His presence and the soothing tones of His voice quieted their turbulent spirits, and as their eyes began to droop, they recognized the wisdom of His advice, and left Him alone on the beach. Jesus also was tired; He had had a very busy day, but He was never too tired to pray. Slowly He climbed the hillside where, in the silence of the night, His Father would be waiting. God is always waiting for those who diligently seek Him. Dr. G. Campbell Morgan, in one of his brilliant books, illustrated what it meant *to walk circumspectly*. He described an old tom-cat walking across the top of a garden wall where hundreds of pieces of broken glass had been embedded in the cement. Very, very carefully, the cat stepped in between the cutting edges, and in spite of the surrounding danger somehow reached the end of the wall without incident.

The scripture now before us reminds of that illustration. The Lord was literally surrounded by very dangerous people and circumstances. The Pharisees, and especially the chief priests, were plotting to kill Him; the scribes were seeking evidence to refute the veracity of His message; the Zealots were determined to make Him their king, and Satan was the commander-in-chief of all the forces arrayed against Him. One false step; one unwise action; one untimely word could have caused a national conflagration. He needed to be alone with God; to consider every detail in communion with His Father. With such a load on His mind, sleep would have been completely impossible. Resolutely, He climbed the hillside, and doubtless, the higher He climbed, the lighter became His burden. Happy are they who emulate His example.

And when even was come, the ship was in the midst of the sea, and He alone on the land. And He saw them toiling in rowing; for the wind

was contrary unto them; and about the fourth watch of the night He cometh unto them, walking upon the sea, and would have passed by them (vv. 47-48).

We have not been informed as to the time of day or night when the Lord climbed the mountain; we only know "the even had come." The Jewish night began at 6 p.m. and lasted until 6 a.m. The intervening time was divided into four watches which lasted from 6 p.m. until 9 p.m.; 9 p.m. until midnight; 12 p.m. until 3 a.m.; and 3 a.m. until 6 a.m. It would appear as if a moon was illuminating the area, for "about the fourth watch" He saw His friends toiling in very rough seas. Probably the time was about 4 a.m. and it was obvious that the boatmen were experiencing difficulties in keeping their craft under control. They were pulling hard on the oars, but unfortunately, they were not making much progress. The waves were getting higher; the wind showed no sign of abating; the disciples were fighting against tiredness and fear. Their muscles were aching, their lives were in jeopardy, but "He saw them" and, instantly, His prayer reached an abrupt end. Soon He was walking over the water toward the little boat in which the disciples were fighting for their lives. The little statement, ". . .and would have passed by them" is so interesting, especially when it is compared with Luke 24:28. Describing the walk with the disciples to Emmaus, Luke indicates that as the travelers approached the village, ". . .he made as though he would have gone further." Compared also with Revelation 3:20, where the Lord said to the church at Laodicea, "Behold I stand at the door and knock. . .", it becomes clear that the Lord loved to be invited to enter—a boat, a home, or a church. He was never oblivious to the need of His people, but sometimes help was delayed so that folk could have the privilege of saying, "*Come into my heart Lord Jesus.*"

But when they saw Him walking upon the sea, they supposed it had been a spirit, and cried out: For they all saw Him, and were troubled. And immediately He talked with them, and saith unto them, Be of good cheer; it is I; be not afraid. And He went up unto them in the ship; and the wind ceased: and they were so amazed in themselves beyond measure, and wondered. For they considered not the miracle of the loaves: for their heart was hardened (vv. 49-52).

HOW SERENE

It is not easy to describe nor even to understand the supreme majesty of the Lord, as He calmly walked across the troubled waters. This was something beyond human comprehension. The disciples could only stare in unbelief; it seemed impossible to find a logical explanation for His ability to do the impossible. That He was demonstrating to them the fact that He was Lord of Creation, they had no idea. Their only explanation was that He was a ghost; a spirit; anything but a human. Many years afterward a poet wrote:

> "No waters can swallow the ship where lies
> The Master of ocean, and earth, and skies."

HOW SCARED

"For they all saw Him, *and were troubled*" (v. 50). The boat apparently was trying to go in all directions at the same time; the waves were pouring into the frail craft; their muscles were aching beyond measure; death seemed imminent. Yet all this seemed insignificant as they grimly held on to the heaving vessel and stared at what they considered to be an apparition. They were afraid, and in all honesty let it be admitted, we would have been as scared as they. Life is filled with stormy situations when everything appears to be going against us. It becomes easy in such moments to despair; to feel we have reached the end. Sometimes our Divine Rescuer appears to arrive very late; but as we look back we have to admit He always arrived in time!

HOW SAFE

Actually, those storm-tossed men were as safe in that boat, as if they were at home in bed. It is unthinkable that they could have drowned, when they were so precious in the eyes of their Master. It is true that in all probability they had earlier lost sight of Him, but He had never lost sight of them. He had seen them from the hillside and had hurried to their assistance. It is wise to remember that although occasionally He permits our boat to be rocked, He never allows it to sink! I am reminded of the lady who in the midst of a terrible storm at sea, asked the captain, "Sir, what will happen if this boat sinks?" Calmly he replied, "Madam, I do not know what will happen to you, but if this ship sinks, I shall fall into the everlasting arms of my heavenly Father."

HOW STUPID

"They were amazed. . .beyond measure. . .For they considered not the miracle of the loaves: *for their heart was hardened*" (vv. 51, 52).

The Amplified New Testament translates this scripture as follows: "For they failed to consider, or understand the teaching and meaning of the miracle of the loaves; in fact, their hearts had grown callous—had become dull, and had lost the power of understanding." This always happens when *we fail to consider what He has done for us in the past.* Had He ever failed to respond to their urgent needs? Had He ever abandoned them when they were in urgent need of help? No. Yet they forgot what He had done, and only considered what they wanted done then. Those disciples were as stupid as the rest of us. Faith is better than fear. It is safer to be in a storm-tossed ship with Christ than to be on solid ground without Him.

SECTION SEVEN

Expository Notes on Christ's Return to Gennesaret

And when they had passed over, they came into the land of Gennesaret and drew to the shore. And when they were come out of the ship, straightway they knew Him, and ran through that whole region round about, and began to carry about in beds those that were sick, where they heard He was. And whithersoever He entered, into villages, or cities, or country, they laid the sick in the streets, and besought Him that they might touch, if it were, but the border of his garment; and as many as touched Him were made whole (vv. 53-56).

Perhaps we are able to understand here, as nowhere else, the tremendous effect made by the Lord upon the localities in which He ministered. Revival fervor had swept through the land, and everywhere, people waited to see the Miracle-worker. His presence was as refreshing as a Spring morning; His voice echoed the music of the Eternal, and His touch was as the Balm of Gilead applied to an aching body. The people were extraordinarily thrilled, but His enemies were intensely bitter and apprehensive. They considered Jesus to be a menace, threatening all they had ever believed or taught.

HIS PRESENCE...how exciting

"And when they were come out of the ship, straightway, the people knew Him, and ran throughout the whole region..." (vv. 54, 55) telling the good news of His arrival. People knocked on doors, rushed to tell their friends, prepared sick people for a journey to the marketplace, and their actions set villages agog with excitement. There was prospect that the arrival of Jesus would make the day the most memorable time in the entire history of the community. Anything seemed possible now that He had come. We read the account, and sigh. Somehow, somewhere, with the passing of the centuries, we have lost that glorious excitement which characterized the early days of the Christian era. There is deadness in our orthodoxy, boredom in our services, and often unattractiveness in our presentation of the greatest story ever told. Our churches are cold and uninspiring; our sanctuaries are filled with empty pews; and instead of excited people running through the streets to announce the arrival of Jesus, even those who claim to be His disciples find more attraction in a ball game. Surely, somewhere, something has gone wrong.

HIS PEOPLE. . .how expecting

". . .they began to carry about in beds those that were sick. . .And whithersoever He entered, into villages, or cities, or market places, they laid the sick in the streets, and besought Him that they might touch if it were but the border of His garment" (vv. 55, 56). The entire district was stirred; it seemed as if a human ant-hill had been disturbed; everybody was moving in the direction of the market place where Jesus was expected to appear. *They ran*—there was no time to lose. *They brought in beds those that were sick* — faith without works is dead. They did all they could possibly do, and then left the rest to Christ. *"They besought Him"*—they were not presumptuous; they asked permission to touch His garment. This was not a fanatical mob; it was an assembly of excited, but respectful, sincere citizens. Naturally, they were hoping to receive a blessing, but their increasing anticipation did not make them discourteous. They gave Him respect even before they asked for assistance.

HIS POWER. . .how exhilarating

". . .and as many as touched Him were made whole" (v. 56). This simple sentence describes the greatest benediction ever to fall upon that countryside. The marketplace became an open-air cathedral, from which the healing power of Christ reached those who had the faith to touch Him. It was no cause for amazement that "the common people heard him gladly." This was truly the Son of God. The text says, "as many as *touched* Him were made whole." Does that infer there were others who did NOT touch Him? We cannot tell. The distance between the fullness of God's efficiency and the depths of man's need is but the length of an out-stretched hand. Alas, some people suffer from the paralysis of doubt and are unable to lift an arm. People have not changed. It is still possible "to look and live," but if men prefer to keep their eyes closed, God can do nothing for them.

HOMILIES

Study No. 12

KING HEROD...The Only Man to Whom Christ Refused to Speak (Luke 23:9)

The royal ballroom was hushed. Uneasy stillness reigned supreme as a host of guests watched a startled king. Herod, the fool, the tipsy monarch, had been sobered by the amazing request of a dancing girl. The swirl of her flimsy skirts, the rhythm of her swaying body, the excitement of the dance, had rushed him into entanglements. Feverishly he had cried, "Ask what you will, and you shall have it, to the half of my kingdom" and now, equally as feverishly, he wished he had been a wiser man.

A KING REMEMBERING

The girl waited; the guests waited; and in a dirty dungeon sat the peaceful prophet of God, the brave John the Baptist whose head the girl had claimed. Every moment seemed endless, but suddenly a sickly smile spread over Herod's debauched face as he gave his command. A little later, when the executioner had presented his gory prize, the dancing girl stumbled out to her sinful mother, and the guests resumed their festivities. Probably alone in the crowd, alone with his nameless fears, Herod knew that for him, at least, the party had ended. Either his pride or his prisoner had to die. The decision could never be rescinded. He had seen the face of the murdered man, and would never forget it. It would haunt him forever. When Herod heard of another prophet, he anxiously asked questions; and then dismissing all other opinions, fearfully said, "This is John the Baptist; he is risen from the dead." And thereafter, each night, he expected a ghost to exact vengeance. It was impossible to escape from his guilty conscience.

A KING REBUKED

With the passing of the months his fear eased, and when Herod had the opportunity to see the new Teacher, his peace of mind was restored immediately. Contemptuously, his lip curled as he heard of new exploits, and ultimately some of his hirelings came to announce that, as Herod had dealt with the first prophet, so also would he deal with the second. Contrary to expectation, the Lord did not run away. Alas, Herod, the fearful murderer, had become Herod the cynic. Assured of temporary safety from any ghostly visitation, he proceeded on another murderous escapade. It is far easier to walk on the path of sin than it is to leave it. All thoughts of the future had been forgotten. Herod was enjoying himself, and nothing else mattered. That his soul might be lost never occurred to him. Jesus said, "Go ye and tell that fox...I shall be perfected."

A KING REJECTED

The months passed by, and Herod came to Jerusalem. He was pleased indeed as he held in his hand a message from Pilate. The Governor would be sending around a prisoner—Jesus. Ah! Jesus, the Healer, Who performed miracles! This would provide great entertainment for the evening. "Officer, bring him in." We cannot tell how long Jesus was required to stay, but His unbroken silence during the time of questioning cries aloud for explanation. His two eyes must have burned as fire into the conscience of the king who taunted Him, and ultimately Herod sent Him back whence He had come. It is tragic that He Who died for sinners should never speak a word to warn this one. Here was a man heading for judgment, and the Lord Jesus Christ made no effort to save him. Soon afterward, Herod toppled from his throne, and before anything could be done, his soul had gone into the darkness. He had sinned away his chances of salvation, for on His soul lay the blood of John the Baptist. God once said, "My spirit shall not always strive with man." There is an end to all things, even the offer of mercy. Herod exchanged his soul for the plaudits of men. It is written "Nevertheless, for the oath's sake, *and them which sat with him at meat*, he commanded John's head to be given her" (Matt. 14:9). It seemed a fair exchange—but he lost on the deal (taken from the author's book, *Bible Cameos*, pp. 89-90).

The Seventh Chapter of Mark

THEME: *The Preaching and Power of the Savior*

OUTLINE:
- I. Christ Rebukes the Denunciators...*Concerning Tradition* (Verses 1-13)
- II. Christ Reassures the Disciples...*Concerning Truth* (Verses 14-23)
- III. Christ Restores a Daughter...*Concerning Trust* (Verses 24-30)
- IV. Christ Returns to Decapolis...*Concerning Testimony* (Verses 31-37)

SECTION ONE

Expository Notes on Christ's Answer to His Critics

Then came together unto Him the Pharisees, and certain of the scribes, which came from Jerusalem. And when they saw some of His disciples eat bread with defiled, that is to say, with unwashen hands, they found fault. For the Pharisees, and all the Jews, except they wash their hands oft, eat not, holding the tradition of the elders. And when they come from the market, except they wash, they eat not. And many other things there be, which they have received to hold, as the washing of cups, and pots, brazen vessels, and of tables. Then the Pharisees and scribes asked Him, Why walk not thy disciples according to the tradition of the elders, but eat bread with unwashen hands? (vv. 1-5)

It is not difficult to imagine the scene described in these verses. If chapter seven is the continuance of the preceding chapter, then at the end of an itinerary, and at the close of a tiring day, the disciples were hungry and ready to partake of a meal. Probably they had worked ceaselessly attending to the needs of others, and as soon as the opportunity presented itself, those hungry men reached for food, and proceeded to enjoy their meal. The Pharisees and scribes, who doubtless had come on a spying trip from Jerusalem, immediately noticed that the disciples had commenced the meal without washing their hands, and since this procedure was contrary to the traditions of the fathers, they began to question the spirituality of the disciples. The incident may be considered under three headings: 1) *The Custom*, 2) *The Complaint*, and 3) *The Cause*.

THE CUSTOM

The Ten Commandments were the foundation upon which the entire framework of Jewish religion rested. God had spoken, and what He said, was considered to be of eternal value. No Jew would have argued with that statement. Yet, the understanding of Jewish laws demanded much more than a cursory acquaintance with the commandments given to Moses on Mount Sinai. There were many other requirements as outlined in the book of Leviticus. Every phase of Jewish life had to be controlled, for it was the Mosaic law which set Israel apart from the Gentile nations among whom the Hebrews had to exist. It was always difficult to cope with the ceremonial laws relating to uncleanness. Therefore, in order to assist Moses, a special panel of Judges was appointed, so that these men could hold local sessions, not only to judge offenders, but to interpret laws to people who could not understand the implications of what had been commanded.

The whole situation was aggravated by the arrival of the scribes, who, a few centuries before Christ, insisted on a more detailed interpretation of everything which had been ordered by Moses. They were ancient fundamentalists, but what they introduced was not fundamental. They were extreme legalists, who, unfortunately, interpreted laws to suit themselves. Consequently, it was not the laws of God which were taught but an insistence upon things the scribes personally desired. Many of the new requirements bore no resemblance whatsoever to the things commanded by Moses. Legalism forged chains which enslaved the souls of men and women. For example, a Gentile was unclean and therefore any food touched by a Gentile became unclean. Thus, whenever a strict Jew returned home from a trip to the market place, he immediately had to bathe himself in order to take away the "unclean" elements from his body. A hollow vase, no matter what size, could become unclean if certain things touched it inside. It then had to be broken in pieces but no unbroken piece could remain large enough to hold oil to anoint the little toe.

In the light of these strange and often bewildering things, it becomes easy to understand the kind of opposition Jesus had to face each time he was confronted by His critical enemies. It has been written that Christ came to set the captives free; but that meant infinitely more than setting souls free from the bondage of sin. Their minds, outlook, and faith had all been blinded to the true light of the Word of God. The commandments of Moses had been hidden by a veritable forest of man-made precepts some of which were without reason.

THE COMPLAINT

"When they saw some of his disciples eat bread with unwashen hands, *they found fault*" (v. 2). Let us not be too harsh in our criticism of those scribes. In some senses, they had inherited their beliefs; they might have been both surprised and sincere. They honestly believed that what they had heard from their predecessors was in accordance with the will of God; it was, therefore, encumbent on all who heard their message, to do what they were supposed to do. Even today, after thousands of years of progress, the same kind of attitude prevails in the Middle East. No Moslem would dare to enter the mosque to worship until he had paused to make his ablutions. Water must be inhaled through the nose, and then spat from the mouth. Hands and feet must be thoroughly washed in water, so that the uncleanness of the street might be washed away. All this may seem strange and unnecessary to the people of Western Civilization, but it might be emphasized that, if Christians practiced the same kind of care in preparing to meet their Heavenly Father, their worship might be more acceptable in God's sight. Alas, many attend the sanctuary, sing the hymns, and bow in prayer, with but little if any thought for the absolute necessity of being clean in the sight of the Almighty. If we saw a man under the influence of drink making mockery of things we hold to be sacred, we would be shocked into making complaints concerning his conduct. That was precisely the case with the misguided scribes who saw the disciples eating with unwashed hands.

THE CAUSE

The disciples were surely aware of what they were doing; possibly they had done this many times earlier, and had never been rebuked by their Master. Did they know they enjoyed His approval and that nothing else mattered? They had found a new kind of freedom and had no intention of abandoning it. This study proves this encounter with the scribes led to the most revolutionary teaching ever to threaten the authority of the fathers. Jesus was introducing new concepts which had never been known. If He were justified, then all the scribes taught was wrong. It was only to be expected that they would challenge His authority in introducing the new doctrine.

He answered and said unto them, Well hath Esaias prophesied of you hypocrites, as it is written, This people honoreth me with their lips, but their heart is far from me. Howbeit in vain do they worship me, teaching for doctrines the commandments of men. For laying aside the commandment of God, ye hold the tradition of men, as the washing of pots and cups: and many other such like things ye do. And He said unto them, Full well ye reject the commandment of God that ye may keep your own tradition (vv. 6-9).

The Lord's indictment was very strong. He quoted Isaiah 29:13, which said, "Wherefore the Lord said, forasmuch as this people draw near me with their mouth, and with their lips do honor me, but have removed their heart far from me, and their fear toward me is taught by the precept of men." The Lord proceeded to call them hypocrites. The word used is *hupokritees*, and this according to Thayer has two root meanings: 1) one who answers; an interpreter, and 2) an actor; a stage-player. He also states that in biblical Greek, the word means a dissembler, a pretender, a hypocrite. When the two interpretations are seen together, we see a man who is speaking, but a man who does not believe what he is saying; rather *he is speaking lines,* that is, *he is acting out a part.* The Lord saw His critics performing on the stage of life; they were professional actors who had learned their lines, and were now expressing something which was basically artificial. They knew about the kingdom of God; they had memorized lines concerning it, but the very essence of true worship was something to which they were complete strangers. Therefore, He questioned their motives as much as they criticized the disciples. They were shams; they were hypocrites; furthermore, they were too blind to recognize God's true laws. They were concerned only with the traditions of men.

It was in this sphere of teaching that Jesus made His greatest impact upon the nation. He saw and proclaimed the difference between formal religion and true worship. He preferred to see tears at the altar, rather than people merely filling the pews in the synagogue. There was nothing so depressing as dead dogma. A broken and a contrite heart was more to be desired than ritualistic sacrifice, and a widow's mite, given in the spirit of love, represented more wealth than the gold placed in the offering plates at a thousand synagogues. Such teachings had never been heard, but the Savior had very much more to say on that day when He aroused the anger of His critics.

> **For Moses said, Honor thy father and thy mother; and, whoso curseth father or mother, let him die the death: but ye say, If a man shall say to his father or mother, It is Corban, that is to say, a gift, by whatsoever thou mightest be profited by me; he shall be free. And ye suffer him no more to do ought for his father or his mother; making the word of God of none effect through your tradition, which ye have delivered: and many such things do ye (vv. 10-13).**

The text quoted by the Lord is found in Exodus 21:17 where a man's duty toward his parents is clearly outlined. Alas, the Jews had found a way of circumventing God's commandments. "If a man shall say to his father or his mother, It is *Corban*. . ." This is a strange word and is not used anywhere else in the New Testament. Explaining its meaning, Gleason L. Archer says, "Under the pious pretext of dedicating his property to the Lord and retaining a life estate in it himself, a man could sidestep his obligation to support his aged parents, alleging that he had no undedicated property from which he could support them. . . The Hebrew word for the same term is *qorban*. . . The *Mishna* states that anything set apart as a *qorban* to the Lord, could never be withdrawn again for secular use, even though the vow was rashly made" (*The Zondervan Pictorial Encyclopedia of the Bible*, Vol. 5, p. 959). Connected with this was some of the most detestable trickery practiced in the nation. Whenever a selfish man desired to escape the obligation to support his parents or even to repay a personal debt, he excused himself by declaring all he possessed was "corban" that is, *Dedicated to the Lord*. Therefore what he had, was not really his. The temple authorities were aware of the practice and were very co-operative in their attitude. The man could give a liberal offering which was considered some kind of a down payment on the rest of his estate. When this had been done, he could not be held responsible for the destitution of his parents. Neither could he be made to sell his property in order to pay his creditors. This was hypocrisy at its very worst. The men who did these things were indeed "actors," pretending to be pious, when in reality, they were utterly ruthless and selfish.

SECTION TWO

Expository Notes on Christ's Explanation of His Sermon

And when He had called all the people unto Him, He said unto them, Hearken unto me every one of you, and understand: There is nothing from without a man, that entering into him can defile him; but the things which come out of him, those are they that defile the man. If any man have ears to hear, let him hear. And when He was entered into the house from the people, His disciples asked Him concerning this parable. And He saith unto them, Are ye so without understanding also? Do ye not perceive that whatsoever thing from without entereth into the man, it cannot defile him. Because it entereth not into his heart, but into the belly, and goeth out into the draught, purging all meats (vv. 14-19).

This sensational announcement demands careful attention, for taken from its context, the verses can be extremely dangerous. At first glance, it would appear that nothing from without can defile a man; that he is therefore free to drink alcohol, swallow drugs, take injections of prohibited materials, and do whatever he pleases in regard to his personal affairs. Obviously that would be in conflict with other parts of the Bible. Paul wrote, "It is good neither to eat flesh, nor to drink wine, nor anything whereby thy brother stumbleth, or is offended, or is made weak" (Romans 14:21). Let us be reminded that Mark wrote what Peter told him to write, and this Gospel does not major on speeches made by the Lord. Matthew—the book-man—also records these statements (Matt. 15:10-20) but this is no cause for amazement as Matthew mentions many speeches. Mark does not do this, and the fact that Simon Peter remembered this particular message indicates the tremendous impression it made upon his soul. He and his colleagues were shocked when they heard the words of Jesus, for they realized this new approach to a debatable topic would arouse the anger of their enemies.

It must be remembered that the Levitical law had much to say about certain types of food forbidden to the Jewish people (see Leviticus 11 and 12). Swineflesh was particularly forbidden to Jews, and that explained Peter's objection when he was told "Arise and eat" (see Acts 10:9-17). God instructed His people to abstain from certain foods because of their connection with idolatry in adjacent countries; because they were harmful to the health of the nation; and because only in this way could He teach the necessity of their being a separate people. The advent of the scribes led to changes which totally destroyed the original purposes outlined in the Scriptures. As the true laws of God and the traditions of the fathers came into conflict, so did the sincere worship of the soul clash with the formalism of the temple services. Strict observance of the law was an absolute essential for every Jewish worshipper. Christ stressed that the law of God written on the heart was far more important than any man-made precept. Certain types of meat might be injurious to physical health, but at least it did not damn a person's soul. A man with an insincere motive did not win the approbation of his Maker simply because his dietary plans pleased the local rabbi. Likewise, a Gentile who ate what Jews despised, was not necessarily displeasing to God. Jesus was emphasizing the simple truth that what a man *was superceded anything he did.* To make His meaning absolutely clear, the Lord proceeded to expound His message.

And He said, That which cometh out of the man, that defileth the man. For from within, out of the heart of men, proceed evil thoughts, adulteries, fornications, murders, thefts, covetousness, wickedness, deceit, lasciviousness, an evil eye, blasphemy, pride, foolishness. All these evil things come from within, and defile the man (vv. 20-23).

Expounding these scriptures, Bishop J. C. Ryle wrote: "There is a deep truth in these words which is frequently overlooked. Our original sinfulness and natural inclination to evil are seldom sufficiently considered. The wickedness of men is often attributed to bad examples, bad company, peculiar temptations, or the snares of the devil. It seems forgotten that every man carries within him a fountain of wickedness. We need no bad company to teach us, and no devil to tempt us, in order to run into sin. We have within us the beginning of every sin under heaven" (J. C. Ryle, *Expository Thoughts on the Gosspels*, p. 142). If any man can read this list and not feel guilty, let him be content; he is acceptable in the sight of God. If on the other hand, he feels ashamed, let him seek forgiveness, for it has been written: "If we confess our sins, He is faithful and just to forgive us our sins, and to cleanse us from all unrighteousness" (1 John 1:9).

SECTION THREE

Expository Notes on Christ's Visit to Tyre and Sidon

And from thence He arose, and went into the borders of Tyre and Sidon, and entered into an house, and would have no man know it; but He

**could not be hid. For a certain woman, whose young daughter had an
unclean spirit, heard of Him, and came and fell at His feet. The woman
was a Greek, a Syrophenician by nation (vv. 24-26).**

The account of Christ's visit to Tyre and Sidon is one of the most
exciting stories in the Gospels. As far as we know, this was His only
visit to the locality, and it would seem that the visit was deliberately
planned. . . . Basically, it was His first penetration into a Gentile world.
Tyre and Sidon were cities of Phoenicea, the coastal land which extended
northward from the borders of Israel. The entire area belonged to Syria,
although it is clear from the records that the cities enjoyed a measure
of independence. Tyre lay approximately fifty miles to the north and
west of Capernaum, and Sidon was between twenty and thirty miles
farther to the north. Both places had wonderful harbors, and their sailors
had explored most of the ancient world. The ruins still visible today
prove that these cities were not only large but important. The wealth
of many nations found its way to Tyre and Sidon and this probably
explains why the cities were subject to many attacks throughout the
centuries. It is interesting to remember that at the time of David and
Solomon, Hiram was the King of Tyre, and that he provided materials
and men for the construction of the temple (see 2 Chronicles 2). He
was also instrumental in helping Solomon to develop trade in the ports
of the Red Sea (see 2 Chronicles 8:17-18). Tyre and Sidon, therefore,
were cities of tremendous importance, and their proximity to Palestine
presented an opportunity for Christ to extend His ministry.

Nevertheless, the Lord's decision to travel fifty miles in that north-
westerly direction surely occasioned surprise for the disciples. First,
the new area was occupied by Gentiles, and if, as they believed, their
own kingdom were to be established, it would only be a waste of time
visiting pagans. Secondly, to reach those cities meant walking fifty to
sixty miles over rough country; they were already tired from unceasing
activities, and to say the least, such a long journey was unnecessary.
Thirdly, their Master had never been in Tyre and Sidon; and, although
Sidonians had attended some of his meetings (Mark 3:8), the disciples
had no real friends in those northern cities. The problems of obtaining
lodging and food could be acute. Fourthly, the meetings in the vicinity
of Capernaum had been attended by many people; the opportunity for
evangelism was immense. Why leave the crowds to seek an audience
among strangers who might have no interest in a Jewish cause?

Somewhere in the area lived a Gentile mother whose inability to attend
meetings was obvious. She had a daughter who required constant

attention. The girl was possessed by an evil spirit, and occasionally, she became totally irresponsible. Since multitudes had heard Jesus speaking, it is probable some of the people had communicated to the woman the news of Christ's ability to deliver demoniacs. Matthew stresses the fact that she was a woman of Canaan, and the unspoken implication is that she, therefore, was a pagan; she was an outcast. When she pretended to be a Jewess, she became the only woman who ever tried to deceive the Lord (see the homily at the end of the chapter). Peter through Mark tells us that after the long journey from the south, the Lord temporarily sought rest in a house. Alas, the news of His arrival spread quickly through the district, and soon the Gentile woman came seeking help for her young daughter. We have not been told who owned the house, but since the giving of hospitality was considered a sacred obligation, the home could have belonged to anyone. The Greek word used for young daughter is *thugatrion* which means a "little daughter". . .she was probably a small child. Modern doctors might be tempted to describe her as suffering from occasional epileptic seizures; but whatever interpretation might be given, it is obvious the child was incapable of controlling her actions. Neighbors believed she was possessed of demons. *The Amplified New Testament* translates the verses as follows: ". . .she came and flung herself down at His feet. . .and kept begging Him to drive the demon out of her little daughter."

But Jesus said unto her, let the children first be filled; for it is not meet to take the children's bread, and to cast it unto the dogs. And she answered and said unto Him, Yes, Lord: yet the dogs under the table eat of the children's crumbs (vv. 27-28).

The same scene described by Matthew is much more graphic (see Matthew 15:21-28). It is difficult to appreciate the finer points of this marvelous study without considering the extra details supplied by Matthew. (*Students are urged again to give careful attention to the homily at the end of this chapter.*) It is interesting to consider the play on words used here by Mark. The Lord said, "It is not meet to take the children's bread and to cast it to dogs"—*kunariois*. The woman replied, "Yes, Lord: yet the puppies (little dogs—*kunaria*) under the table eat of the children's crumb." The scene to be visualized in the descriptions given by Mark was an every day occurrence. Within modern western homes, greasy bones would never be thrown on a carpet. We must remember that more often than not, among the peasants, the ancient homes were often shacks with dirt floors. Wealthy people reclined on couches; but poor people either sat on the floor, or at a wooden table. Dogs were permitted to run into the house, and as always, puppies were especially attractive. The family would eat and then throw their bones to the dogs who waited for their portion. Puppies, which were often too small to fight for their share of the left-overs, slowly salvaged and swallowed anything they could find on the floor beneath the table. Often children would purposely drop tidbits so that the puppy would not go hungry. The woman knew this, and with a shrewdness born of love, introduced that element of pity and love into her repeated requests for assistance. It should be remembered that people did not eat with knives and forks, etc. They ate with their hands, and having done so, wiped those hands on chunks of bread, which were then thrown to the waiting animals. Jesus was not slow to recognize the love behind the woman's plea.

And He said unto her, For this saying go thy way; the devil is gone out of thy daughter. And when she was come to her house, she found the devil gone out, and her daughter laid upon the bed (vv. 29-30).

There is another important element here which should not be ignored. Previously the Lord had preached about what was clean and unclean. Almost expelled from the synagogues, He had gone to the seashore to preach to the assembled crowds. As John wrote, "He came unto His own, and His own received him not" (John 1:11). His mission was to reach a world with His message, and it therefore became understandable that if the Jews would not receive Him, He would go to the Gentiles. It was true that the children, the Jews, should first have a chance to partake of the Bread of Life; but in any case, the Gentile dogs were not excluded from the realm of Grace. The disciples were yet to discover that God's love would encompass the whole world. The events among the Gentiles of Tyre and Sidon were but cameos. "Coming events were already casting their shadows before." It is noteworthy that when Christ had pronounced deliverance, the mother never doubted. Her trust was complete; she returned to her home to see the fruits of her faith. Students attracted to this story might like to consider the following outline.

HER TERRIBLE DISTRESS

Every day this mother's heart ached; each time she saw her daughter, she knew no doctor had the ability to deliver her child. Apparently, the girl was destined to live a lifetime of bondage. Neither rabbi nor physician offered hope, and utterly frustrated and helpless, the woman could only watch as her girl suffered. Would it be too much to suggest that many other people closely resemble that child? Perhaps in her few calm moments, the girl longed to be as other children, but then the bewildering malady overwhelmed her. She longed for something unattainable, and dreamed of a happiness beyond her reach. The daughter and mother had become victims of circumstances over which they had no control. Is it too much to suggest that the enslaving power of sin still produces similar effects in the hearts and lives of people?

HER TIMELY DECISION

When the mother heard that Jesus was in the vicinity, hope began to arise within her breast. She had heard neighbors discussing the powers and miracles of the great Preacher. If He could deliver people elsewhere, He might be willing to do the same thing in Tyre and Sidon. She had nothing to lose. If Jesus refused to help, or even if He could not help, even then things could not be worse than they were before she went to Him. Yes, she would go to Jesus, and beg for His intervention in her daughter's plight. That woman was very wise. She had nothing to lose by coming; she had everything to lose by staying away. All suffering people can learn from her experience. Some folk hear of Christ, and dismiss what they hear as exaggerated fantasy; they do nothing. Others believe help is possible, but are scared to take a chance. They watch from a distance but never draw near to fall at the Savior's feet. Others live to tell that Jesus has never lost His ability to help; He has remained the same throughout the ages.

HER TACTFUL DECLARATION

It should be remembered that this woman was a Gentile, a pagan who knew little if anything about the all-embracing love of God. Probably she worshipped idols as did all others of her race. As the homily will remind you, she set out to deceive the Lord, but was soon caught in a web of her own making. Yet, when she was seemingly rebuffed, her courage and faith did not fail. She referred to herself as a puppy—a small dog. Puppies are not very useful, but they are much loved. This was her confession that in comparison with Jews whom she was trying to emulate, she was not very valuable to the Lord or anyone else, but at least, she hoped He could find a place in His affection for even a worthless Gentile. Surely, it was at that moment that Jesus smiled. Of course, He could love and help her. ''And He said unto her, For this saying go thy way; the devil is gone out of thy daughter'' (v. 29). Our case is never completely hopeless, as long as we remember that God loves us. We also may seem as useless and helpless as a very small puppy, but in some strange and delightful way, that is the kind of soul around whom the Lord loves to place His arms.

HER TREMENDOUS DELIGHT

Doubtless the woman ran all the way to her home, but when she entered the bedroom, her child was peacefully sleeping. She was lying upon her bed. Did the mother awaken the child? Did the tears begin to flow on that woman's face as she realized her daughter was completely delivered? Something had happened; innocence shone in the child's eyes; and although she might have been too young to appreciate all that had taken place, she certainly realized her mother had suddenly become happier than she had ever been. Jesus was never forgotten in that home. As the poet wrote: ''Heaven came down, and glory filled their souls.'' It is so stimulating to know that what He did long ago, He has often done since. Throughout the ages, in every clime and nation, Jesus had demonstrated His power to save. However, it must never be forgotten that, until the woman came to ask for help, the Lord could do nothing for her. And as it was then, so it remains today. Happy are the men and women, who, believing this, hasten to fall at His feet. He said, ''Him that cometh unto me, I will in no wise cast out'' (John 6:37).

> I came to Jesus as I was, weary, and worn, and sad:
> I found in Him a resting place, and He has made me glad.

SECTION FOUR

*Expository Notes on the Man Who Had
an Impediment in His Speech*

And again, departing from the coasts of Tyre and Sidon, He came unto the sea of Galilee, through the midst of the coasts of Decapolis (v. 31).

There is reason to believe that the casual reader of the New Testament will not appreciate the significance of this strange text. Dr. E. Bickersteth in *The Pulpit Commentary* on Mark writes, "According to the most approved authorities, this verse should be read thus: 'And again he went out from the borders of Tyre, and came through Sidon unto the sea of Galilee, through the midst of the borders of Decapolis.' Matthew (15:29) simply says that 'he departed thence, and came nigh unto the sea of Galilee.' But from Mark we learn that He made a circuit, going first northward through Phoenicia, with Galilee on His right, as far as Sidon; and thence, probably over the spurs of Libanus to Damascus, mentioned by Pliny as one of the cities of the Decapolis. This would bring Him probably through Caesarea Philippi to the eastern coast of the sea of Galilee. Here, according to Matthew, He remained for a time in the mountainous district above the plain; choosing the position apparently for the sake of quiet and retirement, and also that, being conspicuous to all from the mountain, He might there await the multitude coming to Him, whether for instruction or for healing."

As we have seen, Sidon was almost thirty miles northeast of Tyre, and if the above paragraph is indeed founded on fact, then one wonders why the necessity for that additional lengthy walk. First, He went North-east; then He turned directly East, and finally went South to the Sea of Galilee. A man journeying from Los Angeles to Chicago, would hardly go via Canada unless he had some reason for so doing! It is thought that the journey to the Sea of Galilee took some eight months. Could it not be that this long journey is the peace before the storm; that is, Christ's long communion with the disciples before the final storm broke?

Much might be written about this detour, but perhaps the most important thing to be remembered is that Jesus needed the quiet time to reflect on what had passed, and to consider what lay ahead. Service is thrilling and necessary, but unless the quality of that service be maintained, it falls short of what is required. Until a man learns to be still before his Lord; he will never know, as he should, the greatness of the power of God.

> Be still, my soul, the Lord is on thy side;
> Bear patiently the cross of grief or pain;
> Leave to thy God to order and provide;
> In every change, He faithful will remain.
> Be still, my soul, thy best, thy heavenly Friend,
> Through thorny ways, leads to a joyful end.
> Katharena von Schlegel (1697)

And they bring unto Him one that was deaf, and had an impediment in his speech; and they beseech Him to put His hand upon him. And He took him aside from the multitude, and put His fingers into his ears, and He spit, and touched his tongue; and looking up to heaven, He sighed, and saith unto him, Ephphatha, that is, Be opened. And straightway his ears were opened, and the string of his tongue was loosed, and he spake plain (vv. 32-35).

It is imperative that we compare Mark 5:19-20 with Mark 7:31-33. Did the testimony of the former demoniac have anything to do with the enthusiastic crowd which awaited the return of Christ to Decapolis?

This story is unique for only Mark mentions the man who had an impediment in his speech. Again we are forced to the conclusion that this incident made a profound impression upon the mind of Simon Peter. When many other people had been forgotten, Peter still saw and remembered the strange man who was brought to the Lord from the cities of Decapolis.

Doubtless the two afflictions mentioned here were inter-related. I know a charming young lady who is completely deaf; she has been so since her childhood, and as a result of her inability to hear sounds of any kind, for many years her speech was inarticulate. I was embarrassed each time she tried to communicate with me for I had no idea what she was trying to say. Modern science, and the unfailing patience of her devoted parents made miraculous changes in the life of that young lady, and today she leads a life which is normal and exceedingly productive. Alas, the man mentioned by Mark did not enjoy such privileges and his friends hardly knew what to do with him. He could not hear what they were saying; and they found it almost impossible to understand what he was trying to express.

Experience teaches that good articulation is dependent upon good hearing. Unless we are able to hear what is taught, it becomes almost impossible to reproduce what is heard. That same law prevails within spiritual realms. A man or woman skilled at listening to God's voice can always be recognized by the manner in which he or she speaks. The testimony is clear, concise, and compelling. An orator may have the most beautiful language; his presentation may be almost theatrical and overwhelming in its effect upon certain listeners, but unless he has drawn upon the resources of Heaven, his speech will be empty and unconvincing. He will be, as Paul said, "a tinkling cymbal." Unless a man walks with God, he had better not talk about Him. True prophets are easily recognized!

It becomes extremely interesting to see how the Lord dealt with this challenging case of need. Let us consider the miracle under the following headings.

SEPARATION. . .How Wise

"And [Jesus] took him aside" (v. 33). Deaf people, and especially those who stammer are easily embarrassed by a crowd. Their inability to speak clearly is often ridiculed by unsympathetic listeners. Their smiles annoy and frustrate nervous people, often making them even worse than they normally would be. On the other hand, within the spiritual realm, it is very difficult to persuade proud people of their own needs. How does one succeed in convincing a man of need when the man is already convinced he knows everything? The Lord took His man aside so that the laughter of onlookers would not embarrass the sufferer and his thoughts could not wander to them. Whatever Jesus had to say, *the man knew it was meant for him.*

SURRENDER. . .How Willing

"And [Jesus] touched his tongue." Surely, before the Lord was able to do this, the man had to cooperate by opening his mouth! I have often said that when I was a boy, my mother could dry-clean my pants without taking them off! I discovered that for the very first time after I had misbehaved in a dentist's chair. Oh, how I disliked that man! He had hurt me on a previous visit, and I had determined he would never do so again. When my mother took me to his office, I had already formulated a plan of action. I sat there with closed mouth. The dentist asked me many times to open my mouth, but I resolutely refused to be trapped. Finally, that fellow became infuriated, and yelling for my mother, told her to "take this young boy home." She did, and "dusted" my pants as well. That the man in our story opened his mouth is clear; otherwise the Lord would have been unable to touch his tongue. We must never limit the ability of God, but surely, He can do even more when we decide to help Him.

SIGHT. . .How Watchful

"And looking up to heaven, [Jesus] sighed" (v. 34). The man could not hear and could only speak poorly, *but at least he could see*, and when the Lord looked toward heaven and sighed, he knew the direction from which help could be forthcoming. He knew that a Man stood before him; but now he realized that Jesus was God's Man, and that through Him God could do the impossible. Thus did the Lord teach the fellow that this was no magic show. God cared about troubled people and would respond to a sincere prayer. Jesus would not always be present to help, but as He had prayed, so the man could pray, then, or at any other time during his life. That day, the Lord preached one of His greatest sermons, and yet He hardly said a word. Sometimes when a person is blind or deaf, other senses become more active. A blind man can often hear what other people miss. Probably this fellow understood more that day than at any other time in his life.

SPEECH . . . How Wonderful

"And . . . his ears were opened, and the string of his tongue was loosed, *and he spake plain*" (v. 35). It is strange that only Simon Peter remembered that tremendous moment. We are glad that he did, and that Mark, at Peter's bidding, recorded for posterity what otherwise might have been lost. "And *they* bring unto him one that was deaf . . ." (v. 32). Who were they? Did they bring a friend because they believed Christ could do the impossible? Did they bring the man because they hoped he might be the first problem too difficult for Christ to solve? In any case, ever afterward, they had much to report to others who had not witnessed the miracle. But what of the man himself? He probably talked "up a storm!" He who had been too embarrassed even to try to communicate with others, now talked endlessly. Why not? He had something worth saying. He had a story to tell, and although many years passed by, the possibility is that he continued to give his testimony until the end of his life. Happy are they who obey the same inclination; happy and wise are they who can say, "Isn't Jesus wonderful!" (see the homily at the end of this chapter).

And He charged them that they should tell no man; but the more He charged them, so much the more a great deal they published it. And were beyond measure astonished, saying, He hath done all things well: He maketh both the deaf to hear, and the dumb to speak (vv. 36-37).

When verse 36 is compared with Mark 5:43, the fact becomes most noticeable that the Lord was still concerned about the danger of insurrection among the people. That He strictly commanded the man and those around him not to broadcast the news of the miracle, indicates the concern within His soul. He had no desire to fan the flames of a false excitement. Any attempt to make Him a king would have been fiercely opposed by the authorities, and as a result, many people would have died. On the other hand, it might have been the Lord was considering the wellbeing of the man himself. Naturally, he would become the center of attraction for a great multitude of people. Their thirst for information would lead to unceasing interrogation, and chased from morning until night, the man might have wished he had never been healed! Such is the high price celebrities pay for fame. Maybe we shall never know all the implications of Christ's insistent demand for silence; but it was all in vain, for greatly astonished, the crowd continued to say, "He hath done all things well. . . ." Solomon, in Ecclesiastes 3:7, said, "There is a time to keep silence, and a time to speak." Wise indeed is the man who knows where and when to exercise both!

HOMILIES

Study No. 13

THE SYROPHENICIAN. . . Who Tried to Deceive Christ

(Matthew 15:22)

How strange it seems that Jesus only went once to certain places; and how suggestive that always the solitary visit led to something supernatural. For example, He arrived in Nain in time to meet a funeral and heal a broken heart. In Tyre and Sidon where apparently His voice had seldom, if ever been heard, He—but let the story speak for itself. Somewhere in the vicinity, a Gentile mother lived with her stricken daughter—one possessed with a devil. Periodically her yearning eyes watched the people going away to the southern towns where the great Healer would be preaching. How she longed to accompany them; but alas, she was needed at home. When the travelers returned, she would ask for news of the meetings, and her eyes would shine with amazement when she heard of the miracles He had performed. "And Jesus," she would ask, "is He a Jew?" "Oh yes," they replied, "and He always works among the people of the chosen race." She remembered the existent racial barriers, and sighing, whispered, "What a pity He is not a Gentile; then perhaps I could have gone to Him."

HOW GREAT THE LORD'S PERCEPTION

When she heard that Jesus was about to visit the district, her desires to see Him became irrepressible, but as she remembered Jewish prejudice, she faced her greatest temptation. She could speak Hebrew, and probably looked like many of the Jewish ladies. He might not detect the deception. Anyhow, it was worth trying, and for her daughter's sake, she went forth with the cry of a Jewess. "O Lord, thou son of David, have mercy on me; my daughter is grievously vexed with a devil. But he answered her not a word." His indifference must have seemed catastrophic to this misguided little mother, for she had yet to learn that all who come to Christ must be honest. Let us be careful to deal kindly with her. She did not know that within the circle of God's fatherly care all racial barriers disappear. She was dishonest; she was playing a part, and the Lord was aware of her indiscretion.

HOW GREAT THE LORD'S PATIENCE

The embarrassed disciples probably found His attitude to be most surprising; it was contradictory of all they had ever known of Him. The crowd also must have been greatly shocked, and finally the disciples whispered, "Send her away, for she crieth after us." He replied, "I am not sent but unto the lost sheep of the house of Israel." The patriots nodded their approval; but desperately, the woman fell at His feet, crying, "Lord, help me." Ah! kindly little soul, you are doing this for the girl's sake; but you are still wrong. You seem to be saying, "If you have come to help the lost sheep of the house of Israel, why not help me?" The Lord patiently waited for her enlightenment to come. He still does when people are difficult.

HOW GREAT HIS POWER

"It is not meet to take the children's bread, and to cast it to dogs" (Mark 7:27). Surely, the warmth of His eyes offset the seeming rebuke of His lips. Momentarily shocked, she could only stare at Him; but ultimately she replied, "Truth, Lord: yet the dogs eat of the crumbs which fall from their master's table — I may be a Gentile, a dog, but is there not a portion for me?" "Of course, little lady, there is a portion for all who come honestly. Listen to the Lord's words, 'O woman, great is thy faith: be it unto thee even as thou wilt' and now hurry home, your little girl is well and waiting for you."

As she went, the Lord Jesus turned, and soon His voice was heard again in the familiar haunts of Galilee. But—and this fact should always be remembered—He had been once at least to Tyre and Sidon. He did not go there in vain. Tonight He might come to us. Let us be ready (taken from the author's book, *Bible Cameos*, pp. 91-92).

HOMILIES
Study No. 14

MR. TALKATIVE... Whose Words Were Somewhat Jumbled

(Mark 7:31-37)

One of the characters introduced by John Bunyan was Mr. Talkative, who joined Christian and Faithful on the road to the celestial city. He was an engaging personality, whose knowledge extended to all matters under the sun. He could quote Scripture or give tips for gamblers; he could chant hymns or utter blasphemies; he was a great talker and was at home in any company. John Bunyan described how, for a while, Faithful was pleasantly surprised by the new companion, but finally, Christian said, "This man is for any company, and for any talk. As he talketh now with you, so will he talk when he is on the ale-bench, and the more drink he hath in his crown, the more of these things he hath in his mouth. Faith hath no place in his heart, or house, or speech; all he hath lieth in his tongue, and his religion is to make a noise therewith." Maybe, Bunyan first found Talkative in Mark's Gospel!

THE STRANGE MAN

"And they bring unto Jesus one that was deaf, and had an impediment in his speech; and they beseech Him to put His hand upon him" (Mark 7:32). This was one of the most remarkable cases ever brought to Jesus. The man was deaf—it was not possible to speak directly to his soul. He was able to talk, but no one was able to understand what he said for there was something wrong with his speech. And these disabilities were inextricably connected. The words of the great Teacher were unheard, and even the greatest sermons left the man unmoved. Truth never reached his soul for his ears were closed. He would never have come to Christ unless other people brought him. His mumblings lacked intelligence. We must excuse John Mark for forgetting to add the man's name. He was Mr. Talkative, whose descendants are still with us. Are there not many people who can as readily converse about spiritual things as about worldly things? Can they not quote Scripture in support of their own unholy practices? Yet they immediately protest when their own spiritual need is mentioned. They never hear the Master's word—they are deaf; they talk—but they have an impediment in their speech!

THE SPECIAL METHODS

"And [Jesus] took him aside from the multitude, and put His fingers into his ears. . ." (Mark 7:33). Slowly, firmly, the Savior held the man's arm, and resolutely led him away from the crowd. The people were still able to see from the distance, but the Savior's action was sufficient to make Mr. Talkative realize Jesus was interested in him personally. Then, as they turned to face each other, Christ placed His fingers into the deaf ears of the strange man, and a remarkable change came over the scene. Mr. Talkative ceased his incoherent mumblings, and became delightfully submissive. Opened ears cleared the way to his soul; he heard the message of Christ and responded. A willingness to cooperate became obvious, for when Christ asked him to open his mouth, he obeyed the command, and was healed of his impediment. Then, side by side, they returned to the crowd, who, "were beyond measure astonished, saying, He hath done all things well: He maketh both the deaf to hear, and the dumb to speak."

THE SUGGESTIVE MIRACLE

This is one of the outstanding miracles of the Lord. It is for that reason, the man may be likened unto John Bunyan's Mr. Talkative. It is a most difficult task to persuade certain people that they need the saving power of Christ. They are truly sincere when they recognize the need of other people, yet strangely unaware of their own predicament. It would appear that the salvation of these folk depend upon the faithful intercession of their spiritual friends. "*And they bring unto Him* one that was deaf and had an impediment in his speech." The power of Christ knows no limitations when He is assisted by the cooperation of His disciples. If Mr. Talkative belongs to my own family, I should find comfort in the fact that prayer can perform the impossible (taken from the author's book, *Bible Pinnacles*, pp. 97-98).

The Eighth Chapter of Mark

THEME: The Compassionate Ministry of Jesus

OUTLINE:
  I. The Inescapable Multitude...*The Special
     Thoughtfulness* (Verses 1-9)
 II. The Inadequate Memories...*The Subtle Temptation*
     (Verses 10-21)
III. The Incomplete Miracle...*The Second Touch*
     (Verses 22-26)
 IV. The Inspired Message...*The Sacred Truth* (Verses
     27-38)

SECTION ONE

Expository Notes on the Feeding of the Four Thousand

**In those days the multitude being very great, and having nothing to
eat, Jesus called His disciples unto Him, and saith unto them, I have
compassion on the multitude, because they have now been with me three
days, and have nothing to eat. And if I send them away fasting to their
own houses, they will faint by the way; for divers of them came from
far (vv. 1-3).**

This scripture is interesting, for it reveals several important facts.
Throughout the centuries, critics of the Bible have affirmed that the
accounts of the feeding of the thousands were in conflict; that one of
the evangelists must have been wrong, for John claimed five thousand
were fed (John 6:10) while Mark says the number was four thousand.
It would appear that the critics were poor readers! Maybe they never
discovered that the Lord fed the multitudes on two separate occasins.
Maybe He did similar things many times, for John wrote, "And there
are also many other things which Jesus did, the which, if they should
be written every one, I suppose that even the world itself, could not
contain the books that should be written" (John 21:25). It is an old and
wise maxim that judgment should never be passed until all the evidence

has been considered. It might be beneficial if we study the verses under three headings.

HIS COMPELLING CHARM

"In those days the multitude being very great...Jesus saith...they have now been with me three days and having nothing to eat" (vv. 1, 2). That simple statement is staggering! Thousands of people had followed along dusty tracks; sat in the sunshine; eaten all their food, and yet they never left Him. Supplies had disappeared; their children must have been begging for food; the entire crowd was beginning to feel extreme tiredness, but they continued to stay. Probably when night arrived they lay on the ground, but sleep was elusive. Let it be remembered that with so many people in close proximity, all kinds of problems would exist. There were the difficulties of sanitation; washing, feeding, drinking. Shops were few if any, and yet the people refused to go home. Reason would have suggested a respite. Why not go home, rest a while and then return to the Carpenter? Did not the men have responsibilities in regard to employment? If they were self-employed, they would still have bills to pay; if they were employed, the employer would surely complain about the irresponsibility which prevented his workmen from attending to waiting jobs. There would be sizeable deductions in their wages at the end of the week. All those men could not have been on vacation at the same time! Then why did the crowd stay for three days? Why did they remain even when they became hungry? Probably they found it impossible to leave.

HIS CONTINUING CONCERN

"I have compassion on the multitude...And if I send them away...they will faint by the way: for many of them came from far" (vv. 2, 3). It has been said that "*the essence of Christianity is to love God and men.*" Here in this text we have an expression of that fact. To love people is to have an irrepressible urge to help them, at any time, in any place. Things have certainly changed, for in today's world the evangelist would probably bid them farewell, and make certain a love-offering was received prior to their departure! With the eyes of a seer, the Lord scanned the distant roads, and foresaw the possibility of women and children falling beside the way; of harassed husbands at wits end, not knowing how to cope with the problem of hunger and weakness. The Savior recognized the importance of reaching men's souls, but at the same time knew the shortest way to a man's heart was sometimes through his stomach! A hungry man is more likely to appreciate the satisfying qualities of the Bread of Life when he has feasted on something more practical! I remember a case in Scotland when a very sophisticated lady offered a beggar the equivalent of ten cents. As she handed over the coin, she stressed the fact: "My man, I am not giving you this because you told me a pack of lies. I did not believe one word you told me. Please understand, I am giving this to you because I am a good woman and it pleases me to help others." Calmly the beggar surveyed the coin, and then asked, "Lady, it pleases you to give this to me?" "Yes, it does." The man's answer was marvelous. He replied, "Lady, make it a half dollar and give yourself a real treat."

HIS CHARACTERISTIC CONFESSION

"*I have compassion on the multitude*" (v. 2). Everybody likes to be loved, and all who came to Christ knew immediately they were not excluded from the love He shared with people.

> A welcome was given by Jesus
> To all who came to His feet,
> And a welcome given by Jesus,
> Was wondrously full and complete.
> There was never a soul who had wondered
> Past the reach of His wonderful love,
> And never one who had fallen
> Too low for the mansions above.

Perhaps this truth is best expressed by the Roman Tribune, Marcellus, who in his defense of Christ before Caesar said, "This Jesus never hurt anyone. He never made people blind, nor lame. He never hurt nor killed anyone, and that's why people love and follow Him." Throughout all history there has never been another comparable with Jesus. He went about doing good. His hands brought healing to sick people; His words brought comfort and help to those without hope; His presence meant life to people who were dying. The Lord never chastised needlessly; and never complained bitterly. He was never slow to accept an opportunity to help a needy soul. Everywhere, the people followed Him, and having listened, they talked about Him for the rest of their lives. Christ loved people who at times appeared to be unlovable, and even when His enemies crucified Him, His last retort was, ''Father, forgive them for they know not what they do.'' Truly, ''never man spake like this man.'' It was this love which anticipated the need of hungry people who would have collapsed returning to their homes. It was this thoughtfulness which inspired and made possible the feeding of that immense multitude. He said, ''I have compassion on the multitude.''

And His disciples answered Him, From whence can a man satisfy these men with bread here in the wilderness? And He asked them, How many loaves have ye? And they said, Seven. And He commanded the people to sit down on the ground: and He took the seven loaves, and gave thanks, and brake, and gave to His disciples to set before them; and they did set them before the people. And they had a few small fishes; and He blessed, and commanded to set them also before them. So they did eat, and were filled; and they took up of the broken meat that was left, seven baskets. And they that had eaten were about four thousand: and He sent them away(vv. 4-9).

There are two words of great interest in this verses. The Greek word translated ''gave thanks'' is *eucharisteesas* and this is used in many places throughout the New Testament. According to Dr. Thayer it not only expresses gratitude, but also praise. Hence the translation, ''. . . And when He had praised God, and given thanks, and asked God to bless them to their use, He ordered that these should be set before them'' (AMPLIFIED). The Lord was intensely grateful for the opportunity of being able to help the multitude, and filled with praise because God had bestowed upon Him the privilege to do so. Gratitude and Praise are twin sisters within the Christian faith. It is interesting to note that the word translated ''basket'' is *spuridas*, and this is a different word from that used in Mark 6:44. There, the word is *kophinos*, and is translated by the *Interlinear Greek Testament* as ''a hand basket.'' At first glance this may not seem to be very important, but a little investigation brings to light interesting details. The Jewish traveler always carried a *kophinos*—a hand basket which was usually hung around the neck. It was smaller at the top than at the bottom, and resembled in shape a vase or pot. It was in such a container that food was carried. Hence, after the first feeding of the multitude, the disciples, possibly using their own bags which they carried, gathered up the fragments that remained and filled all twelve. The word used for basket in the second feeding of the thousands is *spuridas* or *sphuridos* which means "something wound, twisted, or folded together; a reed basket, a plaited basket, a lunch basket or a *hamper*" (Thayer). British people would recognize this as a frail, or a plaited shopping basket with two handles. Acts 9:25 records how the disciples having heard of the plan to assassinate Paul, "took him by night, and let him down by the wall in a basket [*en spuridi*]." Now Paul could hardly have been placed inside a small bottle-like basket slung around the neck of a traveling Jew. It should be remembered that the second feeding of the thousands took place in the midst "of the coast of Decapolis" (Mark 7:31), and that this area of the ten cities was inhabited mostly by Gentiles. Hence the different kind of basket mentioned in Mark's account. The first feeding of the thousands therefore was God's provision for Jews; here we see the Lord providing for Gentiles. Are we justified in interpreting this as symbolical of the greater issues of evangelism? The Gospel is first to the Jews and then to the Gentiles. Students are urged to study again the expository notes of the first feeding of the thousands, and then to compare them with the following.

HELPLESSNESS. . .How Inadequate we are!

Four thousand people were waiting to be fed; and the disciples, possibly with hands on their hips, stood staring at Jesus. This was ridiculous! Where in the wide world could anyone find at such short notice enough food to provide supper for an army? They all signified their approval when one of their number asked, "From whence can a man satisfy these men with bread here in the wilderness?" They were completely helpless and they knew it. But are we not just as helpless as we face the task of feeding a hungry world with the Bread of Life? Our stocks are inadequate; our education too incomplete; our capabilities fall short of what is required. As Charles Haddon Spurgeon, the famous British preacher, once said, "We might as well try to hook an elephant out of a ditch with a toothpick!" It is true the church never had as much money as she possesses today; her buildings were never more imposing, and her organizing abilities exceed anything ever known. But supplies of The Bread of Life are not baked in an oven, nor purchased in a supermarket. We cannot give to others unless we first receive from Him. He alone is able to satisfy the needs of the human heart. Blessed indeed is the church who meets regularly with "the Giver of every good and perfect gift."

HOPEFULNESS...How Fortunate we are!

"...and He gave to his disciples to set before them..." (v. 6). Their resources appeared to be infinitesimal; they had at most, seven small loaves, and a few small sardines. The word *artous* translated "loaves" means "food composed of flour mixed with water and baked." The Israelites made it in the form of an oblong or round cake, as thick as one's thumb, and as large as a plate or platter, hence, "it was not cut but broken" (Thayer). The small fish might have resembled our sardines, and the whole lot put together was probably meant to be a small snack for the disciples as they were walking toward a village. Two hungry men could easily have consumed the total supply. It seemed ludicrous to share this food with thousands of very hungry people. It would be tantamount to asking a modern crowd at a football stadium to share one bag of popcorn! "Little is much when God is in it." The disciples brought what they had, and placed it in the hands of their Master. That was all they could do; that was all He expected them to do. He did the rest. Had they proceeded without His aid, they would have advertised their stupidity. That truth applies to us. In strange and marvelous fashion, the Lord can overshadow our poverty with the riches of His grace. He can still feed the multitude, and do the impossible, but He loves to receive assistance from His followers. What do we possess which could do wonders if placed in His hand?

HAPPINESS...How Privileged we are!

"They set them before the people." The disciples were thrilled when carefully they made their way among the reclining folk to distribute the food. They saw ravenous children, grateful parents, and a great assembly of four thousand delighted participants. Perhaps, if the disciples could speak to us, they would be able to describe what they experienced on that memorable day. Nevertheless, even they would recognize the greater thrills of feeding people with the Bread of Life. To see a sinner making his way back to God; to be able to view his transition passing from death to life; from darkness to light, is something beyond the descriptive powers of man. Many of us have tried to communicate those joys; some have even given lengthy testimonies, but at the conclusion of our speeches we felt inadequate. The joy of winning and feeding precious souls is something indescribable, and if for no other reason, that is why it should be sought by every Christian. The Lord said to Simon Peter, "Feed my sheep," but the same command has been given to us. Blessed are they who, knowing the will of God, do it.

SECTION TWO

Expository Notes on Christ's Discussion With the Disciples

And straightway He entered into a ship with His disciples, and came into the parts of Dalmanutha (v. 10).

This is the only reference to this name in the New Testament, and therefore it has given rise to much discussion. Matthew, in his version of the incident, uses the description, "...the coasts of Magdala" (Matt. 15:39). There was a village in that area, and this has been linked with the ruins north of the modern city of Tiberias on the West shore of the Sea of Galilee. The site may not be very important, but what is obvious is that the Savior was crisscrossing that part of the lake, and as a result, many of His miracles and most of His preaching happened in that vicinity.

And the Pharisees came forth, and began to question with Him, seeking of Him a sign from heaven, tempting Him. And He sighed deeply in His spirit, and saith, Why doth this generation seek after a sign? Verily I say unto you, there shall no sign be given unto this generation. And He left them, and entering into the ship again departed to the other side (vv. 11-13).

A TEMPTING REQUEST

It seems strange that the Pharisees should be seeking a sign when every day the Lord provided irrefutable evidence of His miraculous ministry. Then, and always, the greatest of all signs was the power which transformed men and women. Lepers were being cleansed; the blind made to see; and the hopeless rescued from depths of despondency. What more could any critic desire? There are none so blind as those who have no desire to see! That they were tempting Him indicated their motives were impure. Probably they dismissed the feeding of the thousands as trickery. When they could not deny the authenticity of His deeds, they said His miracles were the result of an alignment with Beelzebub the prince of demons. It would not have mattered what He did or said, they only desired arguments. The fact that it is said, "they came forth" suggests they had been awaiting their chance to pit their wits against His, and Christ's arrival in their district provided the long awaited opportunity to display their cleverness. Jesus could not possibly be a match for their skillful repartee! They probably smiled as they asked their question; they would soon convince the listeners of the fraudulent nature of the Nazarene Preacher! They desired some earth-shattering event; a cataclysmic storm uprooting trees; blackening the heavens; some irrefutable evidence of God-given authority to exercise His ministry. And even if He had acceded to their request, they would have asked for additional evidence. They had no true faith in God; and only desired argument for they were convinced they could offset anything He did or said. The Lord was very wise knowing that no man ever wins an argument. The defeated protagonist only goes away in search of stronger arguments so that he might win the next phase of the verbal battles. Those foolish Pharisees were within inches of the kingdom of God, but they missed it by a mile!

A TROUBLED RESPONSE

"And He sighed deeply in his spirit (v. 12). The Greek word used here is very strong, and means, "*to draw sighs up from the bottom of the breast; to sigh deeply.*" *The Amplified New Testament* translates the passage as "*. . .He groaned and sighed deeply in His spirit.*" We may never know the depth of the grief and disappointment of the Lord as He groaned in His spirit and watched the insolent Pharisees. Imagine, if you can, the revered, scholarly head of a prestigious university, looking at a teen-age boy who apparently knows everything! With all his maturity, knowledge, and compassion he longs to help the youngster, but the silly child begins to criticize his benefactor, and even questions his knowledge and motives. The idea seems ludicrous, but was not that precisely the case when the Pharisees came to tempt the Savior? Jesus was the Lord of Creation; by His power all things had been formed, yet He was being challenged by upstart earthlings who really knew nothing. They were so self-opinionated and arrogant and had no respect for Him whose presence brought benediction to their neighborhood. He had the power to offer eternal salvation, to heal their sick and solve their problems, but they treated Him with disdain and contempt. His love, wisdom, grief, and helplessness were as waves of sorrow meeting in a tumultuous storm deep within His soul, and suddenly He groaned! He *could not* help them; He *would not* punish them, so the only alternative was to leave them. "*And straightway He entered into a ship*" (v. 13).

A TERRIBLE REJECTION

Many years ago when I was a young preacher, my hostess in Ayre, Scotland took me to see a wrecked ship which was high and dry along the shore. She explained the ship had been the pride of a certain Dutch shipping line. One night, the captain, mistaking lights on shore for the lights of the harbor, ran his vessel aground. My friend explained that the accident sent ripples of consternation through the shipping companies of Scotland. Experts were summoned from various parts of the world but the salvage operation was fraught with problems. After several lengthy conferences, plans were formulated by which the salvage operators hoped the vessel could be refloated. With all the costly equipment in readiness, the experts waited for the highest tide of the year, and when this was at its peak, the tugs pulled and every piece of equipment was set in motion in the supreme effort to move the stranded vessel. Alas, everything failed. When I asked what happened afterward, my friend replied, "The salvage people said, 'If the ship would not respond when the tide was at its highest, it will never respond.' Therefore, they removed everything of value from the stricken vessel, and left only the hull as a grim reminder of what can happen to ships when they leave their charted course." Is it too much to suggest that the Pharisees were all stranded human vessels? Was God's tide at its highest peak that day when the Prince of Heaven stood before His critics? When He left them and went back across the lake, were they left stranded forever? We cannot tell, but it certainly behooves every man and woman to think twice before refusing to listen to Jesus.

Now the disciples had forgotten to take bread, neither had they in the ship with them more than one loaf. And He charged them saying, Take heed, beware of the leaven of the Pharisees, and of the leaven of Herod. And they reasoned among themselves, saying, It is because we have no bread. And when Jesus knew it, He saith unto them, Why reason ye, because ye have no bread? perceive ye not yet, neither understand? have ye your heart yet hardened? Having eyes, see ye not? and having ears, hear ye not? and do ye not remember? When I brake the five loaves among five thousand, how many baskets full of fragments took ye up? They say unto Him, Twelve. And when the seven among four thousand, how many baskets full of fragments took ye up? And they said, Seven. And He said unto them, How is it ye do not understand? (vv. 14-21).

Matthew's version of this incident is a little more detailed. He wrote: "How is it that ye do not understand that I spake it not to you concerning bread, that ye should beware of the leaven of the Pharisees and of the Sadducees? Then understood they how that He bade them not beware of the leaven of bread, *but of the doctrine of the Pharisees and of the Sadducees*" (Matt. 16:11-12). It is only possible to understand the full significance of this scripture as we appreciate what leaven meant to an orthodox Jew. Leaven was a piece of dough left from a previous baking. When it began to ferment, it was identified with putrefaction and consequently represented something unclean. For example, Jerome, one of the ancient writers said, "This is the leaven of which the apostle speaks where he says, 'A little leaven leaveneth the whole lump.' Marcion and Valentenus and all heretics have had this kind of leaven, which is on every account to be avoided. Leaven has this property, that, however small it may be in quantity, it spreads influence readily through the mass. And so if only a little spark of heretical doctrine be admitted into the soul, speedily a great flame arises, and envelops the whole man" (*The Pulpit Commentary, Mark*, p. 322).

The boat was slowly making its way across the water; the disciples were pre-occupied as they pulled resolutely on the oars. They had only just crossed the lake, and this unexpected return journey meant strain for their already aching muscles. The Lord sat silently; His thoughts seemed to be far away. Probably there was no sound to break the stillness except for the movement of the oars, and the sighing of the wind as it filled any sail which had been set. Then suddenly the Lord said, "Listen, I want you to be very careful. Beware of the leaven of the Pharisees and of the Sadducees." Momentarily, the men forgot the task in hand and looked toward their Master, and what followed might be summarized in three simple statements. *No Bread! No Blame! No Brains!*

NO BREAD

"They had forgotten to take bread, neither had they any in the ship with them more than one loaf" (v. 14). Let us not be too hasty in our judgment of those disciples. Their departure had been hurried and completely unexpected. Their recent crossing of the lake promised they would be staying at least for a short time among the people of the locality. They had been caught unawares when the Lord suddenly announced His intention to return to the other side of the lake. They had no opportunity to obtain provisions, and their total supply of food amounted to left-overs, one solitary loaf of bread, which in all probability was stale. Leaven suggested bread, and that reminded them soon they would be hungry. Yes, they had forgotten to obtain bread, and seemingly the Master was chiding them for their forgetfulness. It appears to be completely incomprehensible that those men should be worried. They had been witnesses of the most spectacular miracles they had ever seen. The Lord on two occasions had fed thousands of hungry people with the most meager supplies; how then could they be troubled because they only had one loaf? Perhaps they were too tired to think clearly!

NO BLAME

"*And they reasoned among themselves*" (v. 16). The inference seems to be that "they were apportioning blame." There was no bread: why had not someone thought of buying supplies? "Judas, you have the money, and you don't do much else, at least, you could have bought food!" "That's right," said another, "I had to attend to this boat. I have not had a moment to rest all day, so don't look at me. It's not my fault. If you expect me to obtain food for this party, then let someone else take over my duties, and I will buy all the bread you will ever need." And so they reasoned among themselves. Those early disciples, and the rest of us who follow in their footsteps, have much in common. Why is it so easy to blame another? If something goes wrong within the fellowship, *it cannot be my fault*! If discord ever threatens the sanctity of a home, the blame always rests with the other partner. One of the most difficult things in life is to admit, that at least, sometimes, *we might be wrong*! Pride dislikes doing this, but honesty succeeds when pride fails.

NO BRAINS

"And He said unto them, How is it that ye do not understand?" (v. 21). Then He reminded them of the miracles they had witnessed, and the unspoken question behind His remarks was unmistakable. "If I were able to do that on the land, do you not think I can do it in this small boat? If I were able to feed thousands of hungry people, do you think I shall be incapable of feeding twelve fishermen? I speak not of bread, but of that other substance which is supposed to feed your souls. The Pharisees, the Herodians, the Sadducees, have their own brand of teaching, and all claim their words, their leaven alone is true. I say unto you, it is stale; it has been a left-over for a long time; it has already started to ferment. It will ruin your health and poison your minds. Their teaching prevents clear thinking; it endangers progress toward God's kingdom. I say unto you, Beware of the leaven of the Pharisees." "Then understood they how that he bade them not beware of the leaven of bread, but of the doctrine of the Pharisees and of the Sadducees" (Matt. 16:12).

It must always be remembered that He never criticized the laws of Moses which the Pharisees also taught. He condemned their *interpretation* of those laws. The scribes and the Pharisees explained the laws of Moses in a biased way. Let it be candidly admitted, the same things are practiced today by many of the religious cults and sects who claim only their doctrines can be trusted. If the disciples had need to beware of the leaven of the Pharisees, all sincere people today should heed the same message. Love and not law is the overwhelming influence within the kingdom of God. When people or movements continue to find fault with others, it must surely be because they have not taken enough time to examine themselves.

SECTION THREE

Expository Notes on the Blind Man of Bethsaida

And He cometh to Bethsaida; and they bring a blind man unto Him, and besought Him to touch him. And He took the blind man by the hand, and led him out of the town; and when He had spit on his eyes, and put His hands upon him, He asked him if he saw ought. And he looked up, and said, I see men as trees, walking. After that He put his hands again upon his eyes, and made him look up; and he was restored, and saw every man clearly. And He sent him away to his house, saying, Neither go into the town, nor tell it to any in the town (vv. 22-26).

This miracle is unique; only Mark writes about it. Matthew, Luke and John, for reasons unknown, did not mention this man in their gospels. Yet it is a magnificent account and we shall be in Mark's debt eternally for telling us about the Master's Second Touch! I shall never forget the time when this story began to change my outlook upon the Christian life. I was won for Christ through the ministry of a Baptist Church in a Welsh valley. The dominant figure in that church was the manager of the local mine, and he was held in great respect by every person in the community. He had at one time been a notorious drunkard, but the Grace of God had completely changed his life. The desire for alcohol had been overcome, and as a young Christian I was enthralled by this man's example and testimony. His theology became mine; what he said, to me, was irrefutable. He had undergone a sensational experience with Christ, and was very firm in his conviction that every Christian should be able to remember the moment of conversion. He, for example, could point to the time and place of his decision, and in his opinion, all others should be able to do likewise. I accepted the man's word as final; in any case, I also could point to the time and place of my conversion. Whenever I met a person who could not do this, I began immediately to try and win that person for Christ. If he could not remember the time of his conversion; then he had to be lost! Such was my upbringing in that very conservative church in Wales.

Years later, I became a member of a band of traveling preachers and during a visit to a certain English city, I was entertained in the home of a delightful lady. My duties claimed all my time for most of my stay in that community, but toward the end of the week, I had the privilege of sharing experiences with my delightful hostess. I recognized her to be one of the greatest Christians I had ever met, and had looked forward to the time when we could converse together. When I gave my testimony she listened with wrapt attention. Obviously she was thrilled with my story. Then I asked when she had been converted, and was shocked when she replied, "I don't know." My mind was completely ill at ease for I had already discovered she was a far better Christian than I. Slowly she continued, "That's correct. I really do not know when I came to love Christ, for as far back as I can go in thought—even when I was a tiny child—*I always loved Him.*" Then she told me about her Godly parents and the home in which she lived as a child. "Yes" she repeated, "I always loved Him."

Suddenly, I remembered two stories from the Bible. The blind beggar Bartimaeus received his sight instantaneously; the other blind man in Bethsaida received his sight *gradually*, for at first he saw men "as trees walking." That lady in England never knew what she did for me that day. Unfortunately, I never confessed the change that was taking place in my thoughts. As I review the many years of my life, I am unable to remember the time when I was born into this world. Nevertheless, I am quite sure I am alive! Similarly, the proof of one's being born into the family of God is not totally dependent upon the ability to remember the time and place of birth. If I know that I am alive and am sure of my love for Christ, THAT, and THAT ALONE, is all that matters. Readers therefore will understand why the story of the blind man of Bethsaida always attracted me.

THE SIGHTLESS MAN

There are two reasons for the conclusion this man had not been born blind. His blindness was caused either by an accident or disease. The Greek word translated "he was restored" is *apokatestathe* and according to Thayer, means "to restore to its former state." The implication, therefore, is that through the miraculous power of the Savior, the man was restored *to what he had once been*; that is, to the condition of being able to see. Secondly, we are told that after the first touch, the man said, "I see men as trees, walking." Obviously he knew what trees looked like, and although his sight had only been partially restored, he was able to liken men to trees which he had seen earlier in his life. *The Pulpit Commentary* translates the passage: "I see men not much differing in shape and form from trees; but I know they are men, and not trees, for I see them in motion." There is no evidence the man had any faith in Jesus, but the friends who brought him surely were activated by a concern for their blind neighbor, and a strong belief that his condition was not incurable. "They besought Jesus to touch him." Happy and wise are they who never rest until their friends have met Jesus. Had they told the blind man of their intentions, or was this a special surprise for him? Did he stand wondering what was happening as his friends begged the Lord to help?

Professor J. J. Given has written a beautiful paragraph: "We know not whether this blind man had wife or child. It is probable he had, and if so, when he arose in the morning his wife ministered unto him, his children clung to his knees and kissed him while he blessed them. They led him forth to the street or elsewhere out of doors. He could feel them but not behold them. Their smiles, their tears, their bright eyes and sweet faces were to him unknown and by him unseen. All the region round Bethsaida was charming—the glancing waters of the lake; the lovely flowers of the Galilean hills, were a sight worth seeing, but what were all these to this blind man? The district might as well have been dark and dismal, bleak and black; at any rate, a blank, a night without moon or star, midnight with its darkness visible, even, "darkness which might be felt" (*The Pulpit Commentary, Mark*, p. 363).

The Apostle Paul uses strong words in describing the mental state of Israel. Writing to the church at Corinth he said, "And not as Moses, who put a vail over his face, that the children of Israel could not steadfastly look to the end of that which is abolished. But their minds were blinded: *for until this day remaineth the same vail untaken away in the reading of the old testament, which vail is done away in Christ"* (2 Cor. 3:13-14). Unfortunately, the same kind of blindness afflicts Gentiles as well as Jews. They live in the darkness. This should be an evangelistic challenge to all Christians, for if the neighbors in ancient Bethsaida could bring their blind friend to Jesus, surely we should be willing to emulate their example.

THE SPECIAL METHODS

"And He took the blind man by the hand, and led him out of the town; and when He had spit on his eyes, and put His hands upon him, He asked him if he saw ought" (v. 23). This verse suggests several questions. (1) Why did the Lord lead the man out of the town? (2) Why did the Lord spit upon the man's eyes? (3) Why did the Lord ask the man if he were able to see anything? Surely Jesus knew whether or not His touch had been effective. Bethsaida was among the cities known to be hostile to Jesus. Unfortunately, the Lord had to pronounce judgment against the place, for we read in Matthew 11:21, "Woe unto thee, Chorazin! woe unto thee Bethsaida! for if the mighty works, which were done in you, had been done in Tyre and Sidon, they would have repented long ago in sackcloth and ashes." When we remember how the Lord later commanded the man saying, "Neither go into the town, nor tell it to any in the town" (v. 26), we cannot help but wonder if Bethsaida had already lost its opportunity to find peace with God. Was the man told to stay away from the place because his presence there would have led to physical harm? Let us compare this incident with John 12:10. "But the chief priests consulted that *they might put Lazarus also to death; Because that by reason of him, many of the Jews went away, and believed on Jesus."*

Blindness was, and still is, one of the greatest physical scourges in the Middle East. It is still a very common and saddening sight to see beggars and especially small children whose eyes are covered with flies. I have seen eyes from which putrifying matter oozed; eyes that urgently needed cleansing, and yet no one seemed to care. It has been suggested that the Lord spat upon the man's eyes so that the moisture would loosen the eyelids which were already stuck to the cheek. Others draw attention to the fact that all easterners believed in the curative qualities of spittle.

This may seem strange to us, and yet, do we not also place our fingers in our mouths the moment they are pinched or hurt? Finally, did the Lord ask the man to ''look up'' as an indication that he too should be co-operating in the miracle about to be performed. The man was not ''a robot,'' he was a living intelligent being whom Jesus was trying to help. Did the command to look up indicate to the recipient that in all the vicissitudes of life, men ought always to lift their eyes unto the hills from whence cometh help? (see Psalm 121:1).

THE SUGGESTIVE MIRACLE

After that, He put his hands again upon his eyes. . .and he was restored and saw every man clearly'' (v. 25). This is the story of *The Second Touch*! It teaches us that we should never be content with the first touch! God always has much more to give to those who diligently seek Him. There is no sight so depressing as a child apparently unable to grow. Similarly, it is sad to see and hear someone describing an experience with Christ which happened many years earlier, when all the evidence indicates the convert never grew up ''unto the measure of the stature of the fullness of Christ.'' (Eph. 4:13). There is a vast difference between contentedness and complacency. It is thrilling to be content; that is, to be happy in the service of the Lord, but every Christian should desire a continuing passion to do more for Christ; to learn more of Him, and above all else, to be increasingly like Him. Whatever I may know, I have only placed my toes into the water of an unfathomable ocean. Even throughout eternity, our spiritual education will be continued. If Christ has touched us; let us praise Him unceasingly. If we have been thrilled by drinking at the fountain of His soul-satisfying sufficiency, let us come the more often to the fountain head. The Savior's second touch gave much more than the first touch. As it was, so it remains. He has so much more to give. Let us develop the habit of coming often, for the river of the water of life never runs dry. (*See the homily at the end of the chapter.*)

SECTION FOUR

Expository Notes on Peter's Confession and the Sermon Which Followed

And Jesus went out, and His disciples, into the towns of Caesarea Philippi: and by the way He asked His disciples, saying unto them,

Whom do men say that I am? And they answered, John the Baptist; but some say Elias; and others, One of the prophets. And He saith unto them, But whom say ye that I am? And Peter answereth and saith unto Him, Thou art the Christ. And He charged them that they should tell no man of Him (vv. 27-30).

A THOUGHT-PROVOKING OMISSION

When we compare this scripture with the parallel account supplied by Matthew, we cannot fail to notice that Mark only supplied an abbreviated description of what was said that day in Caesarea Philippi. Matthew writes: "When Jesus came into the coasts of Caesarea Philippi, He asked his disciples, saying, Whom do men say that I the Son of man am? And they said, Some say that thou art John the Baptist: some, Elias; and others, Jeremias, or one of the prophets. He saith unto them, But whom say ye that I am? And Simon Peter answered and said, Thou art the Christ, the Son of the living God. *And Jesus answered and said unto him, Blessed art thou, Simon Bar-jona: for flesh and blood hath not revealed it unto thee, but my Father which is in heaven. And I say also unto thee, That thou art Peter, and upon this rock I will build my church; and the gates of hell shall not prevail against it. And I will give unto thee the keys of the kingdom of heaven; and whatsoever thou shalt bind on earth shall be bound in heaven; and whatsoever thou shalt loose on earth shall be loosed in heaven*" (Matt. 16:13-19). It is generally recognized that John Mark was the emanuensis of Simon Peter, and that most of his material was obtained from The Big Fisherman. It is a safe assumption, therefore, that all Mark's material was reviewed by Peter prior to its publication. That Peter either refused to supply the additional material, or that at least he ordered it to be removed from Mark's manuscript, provides food for thought. Surely we are justified in asking why this was done?

Quite obviously Peter had no wish to attract attention to himself; he had no desire to appear to be more important than his brethren. Peter preferred to remain in the background. He did what he could; and never shirked responsibilities, but he shunned anything which would enhance his own reputation. Perhaps he could not forget the time when he had denied his Lord. If Simon Peter could enter the Cathedral bearing his name in The Vatican City today, he would probably have a heart attack. To see many thousands of sincere people kissing his big toe would nauseate him, and his objections might earn an excommunication from the church in which he is so revered.

The short passage of scripture now under consideration will be easily understood if we divide it into four sections.

THE SCENIC COUNTRYSIDE...Caesarea Philippi

This was no ordinary place for it had been the center of idolatry for many generations. George Adam Smith, famous for his geographical writings on Palestine, described, "a deep gorge through which there roars a headlong stream...An old Roman bridge takes you over...through a tangle of trees, brushwood, and fern you break into sight of a high cliff. In the cliff is a cavern. Part of the upper rock has fallen, and from the debris of boulders and shingle below, there bursts and bubbles along a line of thirty feet, a full born river. The place is a very sanctuary of waters...As you stand within the charm of it...you understand why the early Semites adored the Baalim of the subterranean waters even before they raised their gods to heaven and thanked them for the rain. This must have been one of the chief dwellings of the Baalim—perhaps Baal-gad of the Book of Joshua (Joshua 11:17; 12:7; 13:5)." (George A. Smith, *Historical Geography of the Holy Land*, pp. 473-474).

Continuing this quotation, which is taken from *The Zondervan Pictorial Dictionary of the Bible* (p. 682), Professor Blaiklock writes, "When the Greeks came...alert as ever for the deity of the place, they founded a shrine for Pan and called it Paneio...and the district Paneas ...Herod's son, Philip the tetrarch...named it Caesarea Philippi to honor the prince and to distinguish it from his father's similarly named port on the coast of Palestine." Throughout this entire countryside were evidences of the grandeur of former days; everywhere, amidst pomp and ceremony, ancient priests had placated their various gods. Here, amid green fields and towering temples, an uneducated fisherman from Galilee, recognized in a Nazarene Carpenter, the true Son of the Living God; the Maker and Upholder of all things.

A SIMPLE CONVERSATION...
"Whom do men say that I am?" (v. 27)

As the disciples walked with their Master through that picturesque district, Jesus casually asked, "Whom do men say that I am?" The question seemed rather pointless, for surely He knew what the people were saying about Him. He was aware of the approaching storm and was soon to warn His men of the events already showing on his horizons. Why then did He ask about the thoughts of the people in the market places? Surely He had something else in mind, and His question was but a means to an end. It is easy to visualize the scene and to imagine what was said on that memorable occasion. "Master, some people are certain you are John the Baptist risen from the dead. Lord, you look a bit like him and your preaching resembles his. Even Herod is scared each time he thinks about you." Then another said, "Well, Lord, that's not all. Some of the religious leaders quote scriptures that Elias must first come, and they feel sure that you are He." "Ah" said another, "Some have different ideas. They have seen you deep in thought; they know you are grieved by the wickedness of the people, and they remember that Jeremiah had that kind of temperament. Oh, Master, those people in the market place will believe anything."

A STARTLING CONFESSION...
"Thou art the Christ, the Son of the living God" (Matthew 16:16)

"Jesus saith unto them, But whom say ye that I am?" Suddenly the Lord had reached the vital point in the conversation. He was not primarily concerned with the gossip in the market; but He was anxious about the opinions of the men with whom He had been spending His time. He knew the end of His journey was now getting closer; the future of His work rested in the hands of this small company. What would happen after His departure? How would they weather the storms to come? What would they do when faced by the opposition of Rome? Had He made any impression upon those chosen to become His representatives on earth? What did His disciples really think about Him? Here, perhaps as never before, we obtain a glimpse of His soul. He was truly a Man, so strangely like His followers, and yet so infinitely greater than all of them. "Yes, what do you think about me? Who am I?" "And Simon Peter answered and said, *Thou art the Christ, the Son of the living God*" (Matt. 16:16). Maybe the Lord remained silent for a few moments, and then a bewitching smile illuminated His face. So Peter knew! He had not failed in His mission. "Blessed art thou, Simon Bar-jona. Flesh and blood hath not revealed this unto thee, but my Father which is in heaven."

It is significant that this confession was made amidst temples and places where idolatry had abounded. Peter referred to the *LIVING* God. Was he thinking, "Those stupid priests of old worshipped dead gods. Our God alone is the TRUE God; He reigns in the heavens, and Master, YOU ARE HIS SON sent down to help and save us. Yes, Lord, that is what I believe." Maybe the Lord realized Peter was not quite ready to bring the world into God's fold, but at least, his friends knew the message which ultimately would accomplish that miracle.

A STRANGE COMMAND... "And He charged them that they should tell no man of Him" (v. 30)

That was not a command to retire into obscurity; this was not an encouragement to become a hermit! If the world were ever to be evangelized, then Peter and all the others would have to go forth telling the good news of Christ and His salvation. Men were dying every day; the time was short, and the need urgent. Why should the Lord be so reluctant to permit His disciples to testify? The concluding verses in this chapter leave no room for doubt. Peter and his companions might have been ready to preach, but their message needed refining. Israel looked for a Messiah, whose supernatural intervention into the political arena would devastate the Romans and restore Israel to its former grandeur among nations. They had believed military prowess would accomplish this, but centuries of enslavement to other powers had undermined that faith. They recognized their only hope was in God. He could, and would send His representative to annihilate, if necessary, any king or nation standing in His way. If Moses could lift a rod and paralyze the Egyptians, the Messiah would also be able to do this. They had no desire for righteousness and moral reformation. They would live as they pleased, but doing this would be far easier after the Romans had been expelled, and tax paying was no longer mandatory. Had Jesus desired that kind of a kingdom, and had He preached that kind of message, the entire nation would have espoused His cause. Probably even the priests would have become chaplains in His armies! Peter was quite convinced that his Master was the Anointed One the Son of the Living God, but at that time, Simon Peter had not the vaguest idea how Christ intended to establish God's kingdom on earth. That was something still to be learned. Jesus seemed to be introducing a new concept, "Never speak, until you can truly say something." Many years later, Abraham Lincoln had similar thoughts when he said, "Better to remain silent, and be thought a fool, than to speak and remove all doubt!"

And He began to teach them, that the Son of man must suffer many things, and be rejected of the elders, and of the chief priests, and scribes, and be killed, and after three days rise again. And He spake that saying openly. And Peter took Him, and began to rebuke Him. But when He had turned about and looked on His disciples, He rebuked Peter, saying, Get thee behind me, Satan, for thou savourest not the things that be of God, but the things that be of men (vv. 31-33).

"And Peter took Him." The Greek word used here is *proslabomenos* which means "to take hold of: to take to oneself." It would seem that Simon Peter grasped the Master's arm in order to lead Him aside for a private conversation. What Jesus had spoken was so completely incomprehensible and unexpected. Jesus was the Messiah; He was God's Anointed Servant, and therefore no force on earth or in hell could destroy Him. The Master needed to be reassured of this; He must be getting weary! Somebody should remind Him that everything would be wonderful, and Peter thought he was the one to do the job! "Master, Come aside for a moment, there is something I would like to say to you privately!"

The hour had come; there was no longer need to speak in parables. This was the time to speak plainly so that in after days, the disciples might remember what had been said. "*The Son of man will be crucified, and after three days rise again.*" Peter prevented Mark from recording the wonderful things which Jesus said concerning the apostle, but he made sure Mark mentioned this rebuke given by the Master. Here are the hallmarks of a truly great soul. Peter has been called the Big Fisherman; he was also a BIG MAN!

THE STRANGE TEACHING

The Lord now commenced the most important phase in the education of His followers. He wanted them to be aware of coming events. "The Son of man will be crucified." They were not to be surprised when the enemy appeared to prevail. This would be no accident. "The Son of man *MUST* suffer many things" (v. 31). An impelling necessity made the cross inescapable, for only thus could the kingdom of God be established. Any kingdom without citizens is a fantasy; and a king without subjects is a figurehead. The Kingdom of God would be established in righteousness; the King's city would be so holy that "nothing unclean would ever enter therein." Unless a way be found by which unclean people could become qualified for citizenship in that fair country, the King would become an eternal hermit. The disciples were yet to learn that their Master had been the Lamb slain from before the foundation of the world; His sacrifice would atone for sin; His blood would be the antidote for iniquity; His cross the symbol of an empire that would never pass away. His resurrection from the dead would be the irrefutable evidence that what God commenced, He would surely complete. The power of redeeming love would supercede the might of armies; forgiveness would triumph over bitterness, and the simple preachers of those eternal truths would become more illustrious than the political heads of all nations. The Cross of Christ which they would proclaim would become a lighthouse shining to earth's remotest end. People lost in the darkness would see its beam of light and by it, follow the path leading them back to God. Thus would the kingdom be established, and the true nature of God's Messiah be known to all men.

THE SUBTLE TEMPTATION

"And Peter took Him, and began to rebuke Him" (v. 32). Poor Peter, let us be patient with him. How could he have known what Christ was endeavoring to teach? That his wonderful Leader should suffer indignities inflicted by Roman officials was unthinkable. We can almost hear his exclaiming, "Master, over my dead body!" If only Peter, like the rest of us, could have learned to say, "Not my will, but thine be done." He did not know that in actual fact, his good thoughts and kind intentions, were but veneer over something which might have been deadly. Satan had already suggested a way by which the Kingdom of God could have been easily established. He had been thwarted on that occasion, but the evil one never gives up his struggle; Satan never retires from the battle field until he is made to do so. Simon Peter would have been shocked had someone suggested he had become the instrument of evil. Yet it was so, and the Lord had to rebuke him saying, "Get thee behind me, Satan" (v. 33). But was Jesus addressing Peter or Satan? Sometimes, impulsively, unthinkingly, unwisely, we say things to be regretted. Blessed are they who can forgive and love us in spite of any thing we say or do. There are times when our closest friends, without malice or forethought, irritate us, and appear to be Satan's instruments. If we retaliate with sarcasm, bitterness or critical words, we are not following our Lord's example. "We wrestle not against flesh and blood, but against principalities, against powers, against the rulers of darkness" (Eph.

6:12). The Lord's secret of loving men was that He never abandoned
them whatever they did. Sometimes they abandoned Him, but always,
He loved them to the end.

THE SUBLIME TRIUMPH

History has demonstrated the fact that the seed sown that day,
ultimately germinated and produced a great harvest. All that Christ
predicted, and all for which He longed became a reality. He did die;
He was crucified, and thank God, He certainly arose from the dead
to become our Savior. Yet, among His many triumphs, none could have
been more meritable than the way in which He held on to Peter. Much,
much worse was to follow. Peter, who so unwittingly became the
spokesman for Satan, was destined to deny his Lord, and at the same
time cover himself with shame. He would sink to depths of humiliation
beyond his wildest dreams. His cheeks would be wet with tears of guilt
and contrition, and he would consider himself to be a hypocrite; a sham,
a failure and totally unworthy of his Master's friendship. Yet, although
Peter destroyed his happiness, he could never destroy his Master's love.
That he ultimately became the man of Pentecost represents one of the
greatest victories ever won by the persevering grace of God. This teaches
us that we should never lose heart; we must never grow weary in well-
doing. We may lose occasional battles but the loss of one battle does
not signify the end of the campaign. The ultimate triumph rests with
God, and, if we cling to Christ as He clings to us, nothing will be able
to separate us from the love of God which is in Christ Jesus. Paul said,
"For I am persuaded, that neither death, nor life, nor angels, nor
principalities, nor powers, nor things present, nor things to come, Nor
height, nor depth, nor any other creature, shall be able to separate us
from the love of God which is in Christ Jesus our Lord" (Rom. 8:38-39).

**And when He had called the people unto Him with His disciples also,
He said unto them, whosoever will come after me, let him deny himself,
and take up his cross, and follow me. For whosoever will save his life
shall lose it; but whosoever shall lose his life for my sake, and the
gospel's, the same shall save it. For what shall it profit a man, if he
shall gain the whole world, and lose his own soul. Whosoever therefore
shall be ashamed of me, and of my words in this adulterous and sinful
generation; of him also shall the Son of man be ashamed, when he
cometh in the glory of the Father with the holy angels (vv. 34-38).**

We see a profound change in the message now being delivered by Jesus. Formerly, He had drawn vast numbers of listeners and had promised rest to the weary. Now, doubtless, His message would decrease the size of the congregations, for instead of offering rest to the weary, He was beginning to demand more resolution from His listeners. Earlier, the people had been obsessed with what they might lose if they did not attend the services; now they were forced to consider what they might lose *if they came*. Jesus was now offering hardship instead of ease; problems instead of peace; and in some senses, hurt instead of healing. If we might borrow a modern definition; He was about to institute measures which would separate men from boys, women from girls, mature people from the irresponsible, true seekers from spongers! As Gideon of old, He was thinning out His army; He desired only the dependable to walk in His footsteps; He was choosing between persevering saints and persistent humbugs. The icy winds blowing from Calvary's cross were already beginning to chill the enthusiasm of the superficial followers who loved to share His loaves and fishes!

THE CHALLENGE OF DISCIPLESHIP

During the years my wife and I stayed in Southern Africa, we were often made aware of the trickery with which certain traders in the native areas attracted additional customers. The mealie corn used for baking was measured in containers or cans, and the trader who piled the corn highest, attracted the most natives. The extra corn, which never passed unnoticed, was called a bonanza, and it was a delight to see the painted women from the hills rejoicing because they had gotten something for nothing! Alas, seemingly they never discovered that the crafty shopkeeper had placed a false bottom in the container, and that instead of receiving a bonanza, they were being robbed. If the term may be borrowed, let it be stressed that Jesus never attracted His converts by promising something for nothing. The only thing He offered was a cross, and the only demand He made was that His followers should be willing to die on it. He never made capital out of His popularity; He never published sensational reports announcing His phenomenal success. He never exploited people; He preferred to feed them. I have heard stirring sermons in which listeners were promised all kinds of joys in the celestial city, but alas, the fiery preacher forgot to announce that the path leading thereto would often be uphill and thorny. During World War II,

England's great leader, Sir Winston Churchill, made a memorable speech in which he warned of coming perils. He described the advance of the Nazi war machine, and admitted that humanly speaking, the cause was lost. Then he vowed "to fight on the hills; to fight in the valleys; to fight on the rooftops, and to fight in the streets." With profound feeling he declared with a rising lilt in his voice. "We shall neeevah—neeevah surrender." As I listened to that tremendous man, I knew he held the emotions of all British people in his hand. He said he could not promise an easy road to victory; he could only offer blood, sweat and tears. Then he said: "In the end we shall conquooorrr!" We did, and the price paid for our freedom was justified.

THE COST OF DECISION

"For whosoever will save his life shall lose it, but whosoever shall lose his life for my sake and the gospel's, the same shall save it" (v. 35). History attests the simple fact that sooner or later the impact of the Message of Christ is made on the soul of every man and woman. His claims are inescapable, and whether we like it or not, we all do something with Jesus. The Lord's message was very decisive. Either men were for or against Him. Either they open the door to admit Him, or they refuse to do so, and He remains outside. There are people who try to compromise; they neither open the door nor let it remain closed. They unlock the door, but leave on the burglar proof chain! They do not desire to be discourteous, but neither do they leave sufficient space to permit an entrance. The Lord saw such a situation in the church at Laodicea, for He wrote to the members saying, "I know thy works, that thou art neither cold nor hot: I would thou wert cold or hot. So then because thou art lukewarm, and neither cold nor hot, I will spue thee out of my mouth" (Rev. 3:15-16).

It seems to be a simple case of profit-and-loss, and everything depends on what a man most treasures. Some prefer money to the Master; others prefer popularity to the privilege of working for the kingdom of God. Many think only of the NOW; eternity can look after itself when it arrives. Yet there is no man so poor as the one who only possesses money. It was reported of Mike Todd the very popular multi-millionaire, that prior to his ill-fated death in the crash of his airplane, he referred to all his money and said, "There have been times when I would have sacrificed every penny of it just for a moment of happiness." Happy and wise are they who learn how to "lay up treasure in heaven"—there, no thieves are able to steal!

THE CERTAINTY OF DISGRACE

"Whosoever therefore shall be ashamed of me and of my words...of him also shall the Son of man be ashamed, when He cometh in the glory of His Father with the holy angels" (v. 38). We do not have the Hindu caste system in our Western countries, but the lines of demarcation between certain sections of society are clearly visible. The rich and the poor may live in the same town but be separated by much more than distance. The shabby clothing of a very poor woman might hide a heart as big and as wide as the love of God. The elegant very expensive suit or dress of the sophisticated wealthy may hide a soul exceedingly guilty. Eternity alone will reveal the true value of each individual. There, where Christ will be seen in all His radiant splendor, the shabby old lady may be clothed in the finest linen—the righteousness of the saints. There also, the rich earthling will find that his checkbook will be unrecognized; and his elegance, so valued on earth, will be rags. There was once a man who refused to believe this. He probably dismissed it as nonsense. Jesus said, "There was a certain rich man, which was clothed in purple and fine linen, and fared sumptuously every day: And there was a certain beggar named Lazarus, which was laid at his gate, full of sores. And it came to pass that the beggar died...the rich man also died and was buried. And in hell he lifted up his eyes being in torments, and seeth Abraham afar off, and Lazarus in his bosom. And he cried and said, Father Abraham have mercy on me...But Abraham said, Son remember that thou in thy lifetime receivedst thy good things, and likewise Lazarus evil things: but now he is comforted and thou art tormented..." (read Luke 16:19-31). Financiers speak about long-term investments. Christ did the same but in a different way. He said, "Lay not up for yourselves treasures upon earth, where moth and rust doth corrupt, and where thieves break through and steal. But lay up for yourselves treasures in heaven, where neither moth nor rust doth corrupt, and where thieves do not break through nor steal. For where your treasure is, there will your heart be also" (Matt. 6:19-21).

HOMILIES

Study No. 15

THE MAN OF BETHSAIDA ... Who Needed a Second Touch

Chorazin, Bethsaida, and Capernaum were towns situated very near to the northeastern corner of the sea of Galilee, and were probably the first places to feel the impact of the preaching of John the Baptist. Their citizens were among the first to hear the fiery message of the wilderness orator; but during the following months, a startling change took place in their midst. They saw in the coming of the revival crowds, the opportunity of increasing their wealth, and gradually their business instincts overcame their desire for spiritual health. The coming of Jesus increased these possibilities, and it was not a cause for amazement when Christ uttered his message of condemnation. He said "Woe unto thee, Chorazin! woe unto thee, Bethsaida! for if the mighty works which have been done in you, had been done in Tyre and Sidon, they would have repented long ago in sackcloth and ashes ... And thou, Capernaum, which are exalted unto heaven, shall be brought down to hell" (Matt. 11:21-23).

HOW SERIOUS CAN BE HIS ANGER

Every student of the Pauline epistles knows that the first chapters of the letter to the Romans speak of people whose villainy made God give them up. It would appear that Bethsaida and her sister cities had likewise become irretrievably lost. "And He cometh to Bethsaida; and they bring a man unto Him, and besought Him to touch him. And Jesus took the blind man by the hand, *and led him out of the town*" (8:22, 23). And after the Savior had performed the great miracle, He "sent him away to his house, saying *Neither go into the town, nor tell it to any in the town*." We may consider two interpretations of this command. Knowing the evil tendencies of the townspeople, the Lord may have warned His convert against possible persecution. Yet, on the other hand, it seems that He deliberately deprived the people of an opportunity to hear the glad tidings. They had witnessed miracles already, and would only sneer at the man's testimony. When Christ refrains from sending His message to a man or a community, that moment marks the end of spiritual opportunity.

HOW SINCERE CAN BE HIS LOVE

"And He took the blind man by the hand, and led him out of the town; and when He had spit on his eyes, and put His hands upon him, He asked him if he saw ought. And he looked up and said, I see men as trees walking. After that He put His hands again upon his eyes, and made him look up, and he was restored, and saw every man clearly" (vv. 23-25). The Lord Jesus did not command a disciple to lead the blind man; He preferred to do so Himself, and personally superintended every part of the healing process. Many teachers have wondered why Christ did not restore the man's sight immediately. Perhaps He realized that the sudden inrush of brilliant daylight would have occasioned more harm than good, and His omniscience ordained that the transformation should take place gradually. Yet, whatever the reason, Many Christians are glad that it happened thus, for Christ's methods indicate that all experiences are not alike. Some saints can proudly point to the actual moment of their conversion; others cannot, for in their case, sight came gradually. Surely, the pre-eminent thing is that we are able to see, and not the way in which our eyes were opened. Would it not have been stupid if the man of Bethsaida had met Bartimaeus and had argued with him that his eyesight was unorthodox because he had not seen men as trees walking?

HOW STRONG CAN BE HIS POWER

"After that He put His hands again upon his eyes" (v. 25). The Lord Jesus never leaves a task unfinished. Graciously He watches His people, and when it becomes necessary to place His hand upon the needy, He is ready to do so. No case is too difficult, for His power is unlimited. It would seem that He brought a second blessing to His convert from Bethsaida. Yet there is a greater blessing awaiting the children of God. It comes when we take Christ's hand and refuse to let go. Then, there is no need for a second blessing, for we live in the constant enjoyment of an unending experience of companionship. Then, moment by moment, He imparts to us of His own fullness, and together we walk through time into eternity, to remain with Him for ever (taken from the author's book, *Bible Cameos*, pp. 101-102).

The Ninth Chapter of Mark

THEME: *The Majesty and Ministry of the Master*

OUTLINE:
    I. The Surprising Prediction (Verse 1)
    II. The Sublime Portrayal (Verses 2-13)
    III. The Sorrowful Parent (Verses 14-29)
    IV. The Serious Problem (Verses 30-37)
    V. The Strange Preacher (Verses 38-50)

SECTION ONE

Expository Notes on Christ's Strange Prediction

And He said unto them, Verily I say unto you, That there be some of them that stand here, which shall not taste of death, till they have seen the kingdom of God come with power (v. 1).

This prediction was one of the most astonishing ever made by the Savior, and the fact that Matthew, Mark and Luke included it in their writings, is not without significance. Other details of the Lord's ministry might have been forgotten, but they all remembered this one. At the time, it seemed outrageous to the Jews, and their reactions were described by John. "Then said the Jews unto Him, Now we know that thou hast a devil. Abraham is dead, and the prophets; and thou sayest, If a man keep my saying, he shall never taste of death" (John 8:51-52). The way in which the Lord spoke of the "tasting of death" is most interesting, and repays investigation. There are two possible interpretations of this verse. The first is obvious; the second is not so.

To begin, we must be aware of the apparent impossibility of what Christ predicted. Jesus had appeared within the small country of Palestine and had attracted a small band of disciples. His miracles had drawn large crowds of excited onlookers, but many of these would eventually leave Him. The disciples fervently believed their Leader would become the King of Israel, but even they would forsake Him and run for their lives. It must be admitted that a kingdom to be established by Jesus was most unlikely. He would be opposed by the might of Roman arms; His preachers fed to lions, and even the mention of His name would be sufficient cause for persecution and death. Jesus had no army, no weapons, no money, and apparently, no future! Yet, He firmly asserted that some of the hearers that day would not die until they had seen the kingdom of God come with power. We have no means of knowing the ages of the people present on that occasion, but it would be a safe assumption that some were children, and others were teenagers. Some might have been in their early twenties. If they lived another fifty or sixty years, that would have brought them to an age approximating to seventy years. Within that period of time, this new movement would have to become a mighty force sweeping through the world. The insignificant men and women to proclaim the message of Christ, would defy the edicts of Caesar and courageously become martyrs for their cause. Yet in spite of brutal opposition, the cause of Jesus would not only survive, it would become the most dominant movement on earth. It must be remembered that Jesus made this prediction when He was still among His followers. At that time, they were not aware of the crucifixion still to come. Had they known of this early death, they would have been even more amazed.

Who could have thought that within one-half a century, the impossible would become a glorious reality? The death and resurrection of Jesus revolutionized the outlook of the disciples, and the power of the Holy Spirit, flooding their souls, provided the means whereby those untutored men laughed at impossibilities. The advent of Saul of Tarsus gave added impetus; and when Paul became the missionary to the Gentile nations, the Christian movement became a rushing torrent which nothing could stop. The Gospel message spread through Palestine to North Africa; from Jerusalem northward to Syria, and west through Cyprus and Asia to Rome; and thereafter to every part of the Empire. The great Highways, built to facilitate the transportation of armies, became the corridors along which the missionaries traveled, and in spite of terrible persecutions instituted by Rome, there were saints even within Caesar's household. This all happened within fifty or sixty years from the day Jesus said, "There be some...that stand here, which shall not taste of death, till they have seen the kingdom of God come with power." His prediction was literally fulfilled.

There is another interpretation which is not as easily discerned. We must consider two questions. (1) What is meant by "The Kingdom of God"? Is it possible that Jesus was thinking of more than the ever-widening circles of evangelism, and the spread of churches throughout Asia? Luke 9:26-27 seems to indicate a greater thought. "For whosoever shall be ashamed of me and of my words, of him shall the Son of man be ashamed, *when He shall come in His own glory, and in His Father's, and of the holy angels.* But I tell you of a truth, there be some standing here, which shall not taste of death, till they see the kingdom of God." We can hardly associate the spread of the Gospel through Asia and Europe with the coming of Christ in the glory of the Father and the holy angels. The reference suggests that other event at the end of time when Christ will return to establish His kingdom upon this earth; when "He shall inherit the throne of His father David" (see Luke 1:31-33). It is necessary to consider the second question. (2) What did Jesus mean when He spoke about "tasting death"? He said, "There be some standing here which shall not *taste of death* till they have seen the kingdom of God come with power." If the reference indicates eschatological truth, then how could any man living in the time of Christ survive thousands of years to witness the event to take place on the threshold of eternity? Reason dictates that Christ's entire congregation would have been dead and buried within a hundred years of the day when the Lord made His remarkable statement. At this point, it might be beneficial to consider the homily, *The Nastiest Taste In the World*, taken from the author's commentary, *John's Wonderful Gospel*, pp. 194-196.

The term "death" has a three-fold meaning in the Scriptures. (1) Death is the termination of life's journey. It is the experience which, through sickness, accident, or age, eventually overcomes man and removes him from conscious association with fellow beings. (2) Death is used to express the state of unregenerate men. They are said to be dead in trespasses and sins; and by that is inferred the fact that they are unresponsive to the promptings of the Spirit of God. (3) Death is the ultimate tragedy which overwhelms the guilty. When a sinful world appears before the throne of God, each man will be judged according to the facts written in God's records. "And they were judged every man according to their works. And death and hell were cast into the lake of fire. *This is the second death*" (Rev. 20:13-14). There are certain texts of Holy Scripture which can only be understood when they are examined in the light of these facts.

DEATH AND THE CRITICS

And the Lord Jesus said, "Verily, I say unto you, There be some standing here, which shall not taste of death, till they see the Son of man coming in His kingdom'' (Matt. 16:28). This was an outstanding utterance, and can only mean one thing. It will be immediately recognized that neither of the first two interpretations can possibly explain the text. The people to whom Christ referred were hypocrites, and were said to be ''whited sepulchres,'' bigoted zealots who were expert at finding fault in all lives but their own. They were already *dead in sin*. We do not know how long they survived, but it is perfectly safe to say they were buried long ago, while the promise of Christ's coming still awaits fulfillment. It follows that the only possible interpretation of the text is the one which takes our thoughts to the future. Christ recognized the undying hatred of His enemies and predicted that before final doom overtook His critics, they would witness His triumph. And in that one statement He reaffirmed His faith in the survival of the soul. He recognized that physical death was not annihilation but an introduction to a new world. He also declared His belief in the final judgment. ''They shall not taste of death *till* they see the Son of man coming in the kingdom.''

DEATH AND THE CHRIST

''But we see Jesus, who was made a little lower than the angels for the suffering of death, crowned with glory and honor: that He by the grace of God should *taste death for every man*'' (Heb. 2:9). The Lord Jesus was never dead in sin, for ''. . .he was in all points tempted like as we are, yet without sin'' (Heb. 4:15). It is also extremely difficult to understand how His succumbing to physical weakness could materially affect every man. Unless there be spiritual truth connected with His sacrifice, then a death two thousand years ago could hardly change modern people. The *second death* means separation from God, a state of inexpressible remorse, the outcome of lost opportunities, the inevitable reward of sin. ''Christ tasted death for every man.'' He took our sins and went into the darkness. When the three hours of impenetrable blackness gave place to the new dawn, Christ uttered a cry of glad relief. He said, ''My God, my God, why didst thou forsake me?'' The aorist tense of the verb is used in this verse, indicating something completely accomplished in the past. The work was finished, the struggle had ended. Christ had been in the dark, so that we could remain in the light for ever.

DEATH AND THE CHRISTIAN

''Then said the Jews unto Him, Now we know thou hast a devil. Abraham is dead, and the prophets; and thou sayest, If a man keep my saying, he shall never taste of death" (John 8:52). It is not difficult to appreciate the problems of those Jewish listeners. It seemed fantastic that this Carpenter should speak apparent absurdities. Yet as Paul afterward declared, "These things are spiritually discerned." Jesus said unto Martha, "I am the resurrection, and the life: he that believeth in me, though he were dead, yet shall he live; and whosoever liveth and believeth in me, shall never die" (John 11:25-26). Once again, two interpretations are instantly ruled out. We were born in sin and shapen in iniquity, and since countless thousands of saints have already passed through the valley of the shadow of death, the text can only mean one thing. The Christian can never know the anguish of eternal condemnation, because, in Christ, he has been pardoned. The Lord Jesus said, "They shall not come into condemnation" (John 5:24). We shall never taste of the bitterness of eternal death, because He tasted it for us.

SECTION TWO

Expository Notes on the Transfiguration of the Lord

And after six days, Jesus taketh Peter, and James, and John, and leadeth them up into a high mountain apart by themselves; and He was transfigured before them. And His raiment became shining, exceeding white as snow; so as no fuller on earth can white them (vv. 2-3).

About a week after the Lord had delivered His message concerning the people of that generation witnessing the coming of God's kingdom, He took three of His special disciples into a high mountain to let them see intimately what they had never before witnessed. Mark says six days had elapsed; Luke says eight days; but their different records are of little consequence. This would be tantamount to our saying, "About a week later." *The Pulpit Commentary* is very informative on the location of that high mountain. "A tradition from the time of Jerome identifies this mountain with Tabor i Galilee. There are two weighty objections to this view. (1) Our Lord was at this time in the neighborhood of Caesarea Philippi, a considerable distance from Tabor, and (2) there is a strong reason for believing that Tabor had at this time a fortress on its summit. It must be remembered that Caesarea Philippi was at the foot of Libanus; and the spurs of Libanus would present several eminences answering to the description, 'a high mountain.' The Mount of Transfiguration was in all probability Hermon, a position of extreme grandeur and beauty, its snowy peaks overlooking the whole extent of

Palestine. 'High up' says Dean Stanley, 'on its southern slopes, there must be many a point where the disciples could be taken *apart by themselves.* Even the transient splendor of the snow, where alone it could be seen in Palestine, should not, perhaps, be wholly overlooked. At any rate, the remote heights above the sources of the Jordan, witnessed the moment when, His work being ended, He set His face for the last time to go up to Jerusalem.'''

It may be of importance to remember the identity of the three disciples who shared this amazing experience, and to inquire why they were taken and not the others. Peter, the preacher, was destined to become one of the spearheads of the Christian advance toward the outer world. He would be the messenger to make the first impact on the multitudes, for when people attended the feast of Pentecost, Simon would be the man to make the initial presentation of the Gospel. James, the brother of John, would be the first of the twelve to become a martyr and seal the testimony with his blood. John, the visionary, was the one who would write, "In the beginning was the Word, and the Word was with God, and the Word was God" (John 1:1). John alone was the writer who had the greater vision of his Lord; John alone recognized Jesus to be the One Who upheld all things by the word of His power; the One by Whom everything was made. Peter never forgot what he saw in the mountain, for many years later he wrote, "... we were eyewitnesses of his majesty. For He received from God the Father honor and glory, when there came a voice to Him from the excellent glory, This is my beloved Son, in whom I am well pleased. And this voice which came from heaven we heard, *when we were with Him in the holy mount"* (2 Peter 1:16-18). James, maybe, was the most privileged of all, for having enjoyed a brief preview of the glory of Christ, he was transported to Heaven to see the eternal magnificence of his Savior. Peter, James and John were chosen by the Lord to view a very special scene for a very important reason. They were privileged men.

The Living Bible translates the verses: "Suddenly, His face began to shine with glory, and His clothing became dazzling white, far more glorious than any earthly process could ever make it." Matthew said, "... and His face did shine as the sun, and His raiment was white as the light" (Matt. 17:2). *Phillips Modern English Translation of the Bible* translates the text: "His whole appearance changed before their eyes, while His clothes became white, dazzling white, whiter than any earthly bleaching could make them." When the disciples awakened from their sleep, the sight awaiting them beggared description. Their Master's face

was radiant; His clothing was resplendent with something the like of
which they had never seen. He was dressed in garments of glistening
splendor, and they were astonished. There should never be a cause for
amazement in this text. The Lord Jesus Christ had come from Heaven.
He deliberately laid aside the garments of majesty, and had become
"bone of our bone and flesh of our flesh." He came to live as a man,
and not as God, but that could never change His true identity. What
He became could not change the eternal characteristics of His person.
He was still the everlasting One, but His glory had been temporarily
hidden by a veneer of humanity. There were times when His flesh was
unable to prevent the outshining of what was within, and that was the
reason for the change in His appearance in the mountain. He was indeed
God manifest in the flesh; He was indeed EMMANUEL — God with us!

**And there appeared unto them Elias with Moses: and they were talking
with Jesus. And Peter answered and said to Jesus, Master, it is good
for us to be here; and let us make three tabernacles: one for Thee, and
one for Moses, and one for Elias. For he wist not what to say; for they
were so afraid (vv. 4-6).**

Momentarily, Peter and his companions had forgotten the people who
lived in the valley. Their needs did not exist! The disciples had never
been so close to heaven; and in those glorious moments of excitement,
they believed there was no need to look for a kingdom: thank God,
it had arrived! The King of all kings had already been crowned with
majestic splendor, and if this were heaven, Peter had no desire to go
elsewhere. We cannot blame him. When all is said and done, who would
desire to live in a smog-filled valley when the clear mountain air was
so fresh and attractive?

Luke tells us these visitors from outer space ". . . appeared in glory,
and spake of His decease which He should accomplish at Jerusalem"
(Luke 9:31). It is quite obvious, therefore, that the Old Testament saints
were aware of Christ's purpose in coming to earth. It is hardly likely
that they were *instructing* Jesus, for He knew all He needed to know
about God's plan of salvation. Possibly they were there to encourage
Him, for they knew the difficulties of the path He had elected to walk.
Moses representing the law, and Elias, the greatest of all the prophets,
combined in themselves all that God had ever said to man. Previously,
they had witnessed of Him via the prophetic word; now they were doing
so face to face. They agreed when God said: "This is my beloved Son,
in whom, I am well pleased."

1. *"There is life beyond the grave.* Critics have said that the transfiguration was a dream or a nightmare which troubled the sleep of weary men, but the independence of the various narratives outlaws the suggestion. . . Moses the man who had died, and Elijah the man who had been caught up into the clouds, were present with the Lord in glory. This surely was a type of that other great event described by Paul in 1 Thessalonians 4:16-17, 'For the Lord himself shall descend from heaven with a shout, with the voice of the archangel, and with the trump of God; and *the dead in Christ* shall rise first: Then *we which are alive* and remain shall *be caught up together with them in the clouds to meet the Lord in the air*: and so shall we ever be with the Lord.' . . . 2. *There is intelligent life beyond the grave.* These visitors from the other world were able to speak, to move, to converse with Christ concerning the future. The word translated "accomplished" reveals that the death to take place in Jerusalem was not to be a succumbing to natural weakness; the result of any accident or unexpected catastrophy. This was a part of the plans of God; *this was something to be done* . . . 3. *There is glorious life beyond the grave.* It is true that Moses had died and had been buried by God (Deut. 34:6), but on the Mount of Transfiguration, he appeared in glory; that is, his mortal had put on the garments of immortality. Elijah had been carried to Heaven in a chariot of splendor. Possibly he had been changed in a moment, in the twinkling of an eye, but he, too, was living in the power of an endless life . . . 4. *There is useful life beyond the grave.* Moses and Elijah were ministering to the Lord. The old idea of saints playing harps throughout eternity has long been discarded. The eternal world will be a place of progress, and although at present, our finite minds may be unable to conceive of what might transpire in the hereafter, we may be sure our interests will revolve around the Person of Christ, without Whom we would never be there" (condensed from the author's commentary, *Luke's Thrilling Gospel,* pp. 228-229).

And there was a cloud that overshadowed them: and a voice came out of the cloud, saying, This is my beloved Son: hear Him. And suddenly, when they had looked round about, they saw no man anymore, save Jesus only with themselves. And as they came down from the mountain, He charged them that they should tell no man what things they had seen, till the Son of man were risen from the dead. And they kept that saying with themselves, questioning one with another what the rising from the dead should mean (vv. 7-10).

These verses represent four sections each suggesting a simple question. Let us consider them systematically.

THE CLOUD. . . Where?

"And there was a cloud *which overshadowed them*" (v. 7). The word translated "overshadowed" is the Greek word *episkiazousa*, and, to say the least, it has interesting connotations. Primarily, it means "to throw a shadow upon, to envelop in shadow, to overshadow." Throughout the Old Testament, the presence of the cloud over the Tabernacle indicated that God was within His sanctuary. Thus when the cloud hovered above the disciples and Christ, it indicated that the God of Heaven was just as present on that hilltop as He ever was within the Most Holy part of the Tabernacle. But the same word is used in connection with the birth of the Lord (Luke 1:35). Dr. J. H. Thayer, the eminent Greek scholar, says, "It is used of the Holy Spirit exerting creative energy upon the womb of the virgin Mary and impregnating it, (a use of the word which seems to have been drawn from the familiar Old Testament idea of a cloud as symbolizing the immediate presence and power of God)" (*The Greek-English Lexicon of the New Testament*, p. 242). Associated with Mary, the cloud suggests the presence of God *to impart life*. The cloud hovering above the disciples indicated the presence of God, *to impart wisdom*. Hence, the command, "Hear Him" (Mark 9:7).

THE CHRIST. . . When?

". . .And suddenly, . . .they saw no man any more" (v. 8). God had departed. Moses and Elijah had withdrawn. For the time being at least, Heaven had no more to say; the law and the prophets had nothing further to announce — only Jesus was left, but He was sufficient. All they needed, God had provided; all they required to hear, God had already uttered. "*Hear Him.*" Of course, God could have preached for an unlimited period and the libraries of the world would now be filled with whatever He might have said. God was declaring, "I have no need whatsoever to tell you anything else. Listen to Jesus, and you will discover all you need to know." His withdrawal announced: "When all else seems to fail; when I appear to be silent; when Moses and Elijah are unavailable for counsel, remember Jesus will still be there. Look for Him; listen to Him; do whatever He tells you to do, and all will be well."

THE COMMAND . . . Why?

" . . . tell no man . . . till the Son of man be risen from the dead" (v. 9). Again and again throughout the Gospel, Mark reminds readers of Christ's forbidding the disciples to announce certain things. This time, a limit was placed on the period of frustrating silence. They were only to remain silent, until the Son of man had risen from the dead. It is not difficult to detect the wisdom within the command. What they had witnessed was so unbelievable; that, had they broadcast the news of what had transpired on the mountain, their hearers would have considered them to be insane. Rather than enhancing the message, they would have invited criticism and brought discredit upon the work they had been commissioned to do. When the resurrection became a bright and glorious reality, the story of the transfiguration almost faded into insignificance. Instead of ridiculing its details, hearers were enthralled by its message, and saw in it one of the infallible reasons why the grave could never hold Jesus. The immortality of the Savior, the glory which had been evident on the hilltop, would easily shine through and shatter the power of death. The disciples, however, had little desire to proclaim what they had seen. They were frustrated, not by His command to remain silent, but because their minds could not understand the content of His message. That their Master should even contemplate death was terrible. They firmly believed the kingdom would come by force of arms, and were thrilled by their belief that when the time for insurrection arrived, thousands of their countrymen would follow their Messiah, and Rome would be vanquished. They had much to learn, but thank God, they succeeded; and blessed are they who profit from their example.

THE CONCERN . . . What?

" . . . they questioned one with another what the rising from the dead should mean" (v. 10). The full significance of God's command, "Hear Him" now becomes clear. The disciples were as little children trying to understand the intricate problems of higher education. Their minds were still dominated by preconceived notions, and what their Master had suggested seemed preposterous! Yet, to remember once again the meaning of the overshadowing cloud, God, Who had impregnated Mary's womb with life, was now to impregnate their minds with truth. They were to learn that the Cross, and the Cross alone, would provide the eternal foundations upon which the kingdom of God would rest.

Love, not military prowess would conquer the nations. Redemption made possible by the death of Christ would not expel the Romans, but it would embrace, cleanse, and bring them into a kingdom in which all men could be brothers. This glad tidings of God's grace would become the most revolutionary message ever preached; it would undermine pagan empires, and then rebuild them in righteousness. It would bring hope to the hopeless, help to the helpless; and always upon its banner would be, not the ensignias of aristocratic families, but a simple Cross, the evidence of God's unfailing love for sinners. All this was incomprehensible to the untutored minds of the disciples; and as they came down from that memorable scene on the mountain, they could only discuss among themselves the strange words their Leader had spoken. Time changes things, and this was very evident when Peter, many years later, wrote: "For we have not followed cunningly devised fables, when we made known unto you the power and coming of our Lord Jesus Christ, but were eyewitnesses of His majesty...We have also a more sure word of prophecy; whereunto ye do well, that ye take heed, as unto a light that shineth in a dark place, until the day dawn, and the daystar arise in your hearts" (2 Peter 1:16-19). Peter had learned great lessons. Blessed are they who emulate his example.

And they asked Him saying, Why say the scribes that Elias must first come? And He answered and told them, Elias verily cometh first and restoreth all things; and how it is written of the Son of man, that He must suffer many things, and be set at nought. But I say unto you, That Elias is indeed come, and they have done unto him whatsoever they listed, as it is written of him (vv. 11-13).

Bishop J. C. Ryle says: "The coming of Elias, which was the topic of conversation between our Lord and His disciples in the latter part of this passage, was a deep and mysterious subject. According to one class of interpreters, the ministry of John the Baptist, represented the coming of Elias. They teach from Malachi 4:5-6 that Elijah the prophet or John was sent before the great and dreadful day of the Lord, and no other coming of Elias is to be expected. According to another class of interpreters, a literal coming of Elias is yet to take place. They consider that John the Baptist only went before our Lord in the "*spirit and power of Elias*! (Luke 1:17), and that the words of Malachi are yet to be fulfilled. This is the view maintained by nearly all the Fathers, by the great majority of Roman Catholic commentators, and by not a few modern Protestant divines, both English and Continental at the present time.

"If I must express an opinion...I must honestly confess that I decidedly incline to the second of the two interpretations given. I believe that a literal appearing of Elijah the Prophet before the second coming of Christ may be expected...Any other view seems to do violence to the plain meaning of the words of Malachi 4:5-6, Matthew 17:11, and John 1:21. There seems to be no reason why there should not be a double "coming of Elias." The first, in spirit and power, when John the Baptist preached; the second, "literal and in person" when he shall come at the end of the world, immediately before the great and dreadful day of the Lord...I see much fewer difficulties in the way of the interpretation to which I lean, than in the way of the other. I hold with Augustine, Jerome, Chrysostom, Hilary, Jansenius, Brentius, Gresswell, Alford, and Stier that Malachi 4:5-6 is not yet completely fulfilled, and that Elijah the Prophet will yet come" (J. C. Ryle, *Expository Thoughts on the Gospels, Mark*, pp. 178-180).

The preceding paragraph possibly says all that needs to be said, but one detail might be added. John, in the Book of Revelation, describes two witnesses who will preach to Israel during the days of the tribulation yet to come upon the earth. His account of these men is found in chapter eleven. The following paragraph is reproduced from the author's book, *What In the World Will Happen Next?* pp. 96-99. "Paul said, 'Wherefore, as by one man sin entered into the world, and death by sin; *and so death passed upon all men*, for that all have sinned' (Rom. 5:12, italics mine). 'For as in Adam, *all die*, even so in Christ shall all be made alive' (1 Cor. 15:22). Strictly speaking, *as of this moment*, these verses are untrue, for in spite of the fact that almost all the descendants of Adam died, *two did not*. 'And Enoch walked with God; and he was not, for God took him' (Gen. 5:24). 'And it came to pass, as they [Elijah and Elisha] still went on, and talked, that, behold, there appeared a chariot of fire, and horses of fire, and parted them both asunder; and Elijah went up by a whirlwind into heaven' (2 Kings 2:11). Enoch and Elijah were the only two men who escaped the sentence of death passed upon all people when Adam sinned. How can it be said that death passed upon *all men*, when two did not die? If the witnesses to appear in the end times be Enoch and Elijah, then the accuracy of the Scriptures will be proved once more. The Antichrist will make war with these servants of God and overcome them. It is said that their dead bodies will remain unburied in the streets, until they are resurrected and received into heaven" (see the homily *The Face of Jesus* at the end of the chapter).

Section Three

Expository Notes on the Healing of the Boy With the Dumb Spirit

And when He came to his disciples, He saw a great multitude about them, and the scribes questioning with them. And straightway all the people, when they beheld Him, were greatly amazed, and running to Him saluted Him. And He asked the scribes, What question ye with them? And one of the multitude answered and said, I have brought unto thee my son, which hath a dumb spirit; and wheresoever he taketh him, he teareth him; and he foameth, and gnasheth with his teeth, and pineth away; and I spake to thy disciples that they should cast him out; and they could not (vv. 14-18).

This is an interesting passage of scripture, and may be divided into three sections. While the Lord was in the mountain, the nine disciples remaining in the valley had encountered problems and opposition. Their inability to help a troubled parent had provided an opportunity for the critical scribes to launch a verbal attack against the followers of Jesus. The Lord arrived in time to rescue the disciples from further embarrassment.

A TREMENDOUS ASTONISHMENT

"...all the people, when they beheld Jesus, were greatly amazed..." (v. 15). The word translated "were greatly amazed" is *exethambeethee*, and this, according to Thayer, means "to be astonished, to be amazed, to be frightened." Why were the people astonished even to the point of being frightened? Had they been surprised or even delighted, the text would present no problems. Probably they had seen the Lord on many occasions, and, in such a small country, would have been aware of the locality in which He could be found. To see Jesus was no cause for astonishment, and therefore we must seek elsewhere for an explanation of the verse. *The Amplified New Testament* provides an interesting translation. It reads, "And immediately all the crowd, when they saw Jesus returning from the holy mount, *His face and person yet glistening*, were greatly amazed, and ran to Him and greeted Him." That one suggestion introduces us to a new world of meaning. We are told that when Moses returned from the holy mount, the skin of his face shone, although he himself was unaware of the change in his appearance (see Exodus 34:29-34). The glory of God shining upon

Moses had caused what might be described as a heavenly sunburn! It was the stamp of the approval and nearness of God, *but the shining came from without!* When Jesus came down from the mountain, His face also must have been shining; His entire being still carried testimony to the fact that He also had been with God. Yet in His case, *the glory came from within.* A glow, a radiance emanated from His soul, and the waiting, watching crowd recognized something strange had happened. Hence, they were astonished and fearful.

A TROUBLESOME ARGUMENT

The crowd was in turmoil, voices were raised, and accusations were being uttered. The scribes were very belligerent, and standing in the midst were the disciples, silent, helpless, and embarrassed. Recognizing that something was wrong, the Lord asked, "What question ye among yourselves?" Then one of the men explained how he had brought an afflicted child to the disciples seeking help; but his coming had been in vain, as the nine disciples had been unable to provide assistance. The scribes had been delighted by the impotence of the followers of Jesus, and, seizing their opportunity, loudly criticized the frustrated disciples. One thing led to another, and finally there was danger of a brawl. It has ever been thus. The world expects so much of a powerless church, and when faced with a situation comparable with the one described in the text, the critics are loud in their condemnation. The scribes had witnessed many marvelous miracles, but instead of rejoicing, had attributed the miracles to an association with Beelzebub. Now that a failure was obvious, they forgot the real miracles, and concentrating on the solitary disappointment, proceeded to denounce everything connected with the Lord. Nearly two thousand years have passed since those days in Galilee, but alas, the world has not changed.

A TERRIBLE ANGUISH

"...Master, I have brought unto thee my son, which hath a dumb spirit; and wheresoever [the spirit] taketh him, he teareth him: and he foameth, and gnasheth with his teeth, and pineth away...And [Jesus] asked,...How long is it since this came unto him? And he said, Of a child" (vv. 17-21). Mark graphically describes in a few words the anguish of a lifetime. It would appear that the child suffered from some kind of epilepsy, and that as far as the people were concerned, the malady was attributed to the presence and power of indwelling demons. The father continued his heart rending story: "And oftimes the evil spirit hath cast him into the fire, and into the waters, to destroy him; but if thou canst do anything, have compassion on us, and help us" (v. 22). That disappointed, harassed parent did not reiterate all the condemnatory remarks concerning the helpless disciples; he did not elaborate on the disappointing results of his earlier request. He brought his problem child to Jesus. Other people in a similar situation might have remained at home allowing their molehill of disappointment to become a mountain of bitterness. This man seemed to have practiced the old adage, "If at first you don't succeed, try, try again." He ceased looking at the helpless disciples, and focused his attention on the Lord. Our world today would be a happier place if people emulated the example given by that wise father.

> **Jesus answered him and saith, O faithless generation, how long shall I be with you? how long shall I suffer you? bring him to me. And they brought him unto Him; and when He saw him, straightway the spirit tare him; and he fell on the ground, and wallowed foaming. And He asked his father, How long is it since this came unto him? And he said, Of a child...Jesus said unto him, If thou canst believe, all things are possible to him that believeth. And straightway, the father of the child cried out, and said with tears, Lord, I believe; help thou mine unbelief. When Jesus saw that the people came running together, He rebuked the foul spirit, saying unto him, Thou dumb and deaf spirit, I charge thee, come out of him, and enter no more into him. And the spirit cried and rent him so, and came out of him; and [the boy] was as one dead; insomuch that many said, he is dead. But Jesus took him by the hand, and lifted him up; and he arose (vv. 19-27).**

THE SUDDEN CHALLENGE

The scene described in these verses constitutes one of the saddest sights of the New Testament. The boy was rolling on the ground; his face contorted with indescribable horror; he was foaming at the mouth, and completely irresponsible. He represented what evil can do to destroy a human being. The Prince of Peace stood watching, and the people who were present were destined to see one of the Lord's greatest miracles. The demon lost no time ISSUING HIS CHALLENGE. "If this be the Son of God, let us see what He can do in this situation." Was this the last desperate fling of a devil who knew his domination of the boy was about to end? It is stimulating to remember that Jesus never knew defeat throughout His ministry. He stilled the storm, raised the dead, expelled demons, gave sight to the blind, and healed the sick. His triumph resulted from face to face contact with the evil powers threatening mankind. Unbelief alone was the greatest challenge to His ministry. Foolish people never seemed able to recognize their moment of opportunity; sin had become cataracts on human eyes and hearts. Yet Jesus never capitulated. Determined to find a way into the hidden depths of the human spirit, Christ went all the way to His cross, so that the power of His redeeming love would enable men to open, from within, the door that was locked.

THE SIMPLE CONDITION

"Jesus said unto him, If thou canst believe, all things are possible..." (v. 23). That one simple statement was the way into God's ever-widening world of possibility. No burden would be too heavy, no problem too difficult, no task too hard — if only men would believe! That Jesus was introducing a new way to live was apparently lost on that watching crowd. The law emphasized the importance of doing things. It was necessary to observe all the requirements of the Mosaic teaching; it was important to obey all the instructions of the scribes, to fast regularly, and to give alms to the poor. Jesus never denied the importance of those precepts; but when He said, "ONLY BELIEVE," He made possible to men and women something beyond all they had ever known.

Today, people are urged to do many things. Some are advised to go on lengthy pilgrimages to important shrines. Alas, many are unable to make the journey. Some are told to keep the law, but the more they try, the more they realize their inability to do so. Others are aware of their lack of faith, and sinking in despair, cease to struggle. Jesus believed faith made up for the lack of all other qualities. If our faith seems small, then the Bible tells us of the man who said, "Lord I do believe," but somehow, my faith seems inadequate — "Help Thou mine unbelief."

THE SUBLIME CLIMAX

Faith Requesting. Faith without works is dead! Faith within the man's heart would have been insufficient unless it had motivated speech. Because he believed, he requested help. *Faith Receiving.* Jesus said, "Thou dumb and deaf spirit, I charge thee, come out of him, *and enter no more into him"* (v. 25). Life seems marred by unexpected events. Men triumph temporarily, but then in some unfortunate manner, slip back into the ditch from which apparently they had been lifted, and "the end of that man is worse than the beginning." *Faith Rejoicing.* When the Lord expelled this demon, He gave an added bonus. He not only provided for immediate deliverance, but made certain the boy's future should be safeguarded. ". . .enter no more into him."

> I cannot read His future plans, but this I know:
> I have the smiling of His face,
> And all the refuge of His grace while here below.
> Enough! this covers all my wants, and so I rest.
> For what I cannot, He can see
> And in His care I saved shall be, forever blest.

And when He was come into the house, His disciples asked Him privately, Why could not we cast him out? And He said unto them, This kind can come forth by nothing, but by prayer and fasting (vv. 28-29).

These are verses in which we see startling contrasts. The mountain top is compared with the valley, fasting with the feasts, which the nine disciples had possibly enjoyed in the homes of unmentioned friends. Here we see Christ communing with His Father, and the disciples eagerly, animatedly speaking with anybody but the Father. Here we sense the followers inhaling the smoke in the valley, opposed to the Lord's breathing the pure air of the mountain top. Here we see the snowy heights of Mount Hermon compared with the dirty streets of Caesarea Philippi. We see the two ends of a motionless seesaw. The Lord was exalted in the power of God; the disciples were low, very low on the floor of frustration and failure. "Lord" they seemed to say, "We went through the motions, we uttered the same words, we had the correct approach and used the same formula, but nothing happened. Why Lord?"

THE PLACE OF PRAYER

Dr. Graham Scroggie wrote: "It is easier to organize than agonize;" and, if I might enlarge his statement, let me say, "It is far easier to attend a party in the home of delightful friends, than to climb a mountain and stay there throughout the night.'' Those in the mountain enjoy very select company — if they stay awake! Those in the valley are generally busy doing nothing! Prayer has always been the reason for the success of God's servants. With its power they prevailed even in weakness; without it, they were defeated even when they appeared to be invincible. The busiest of God's successful servants still make time to pray. Are we among that number?

THE PRICE OF POWER

Pardon from God is a gift; *Power from God* is not a gift; it has to be bought, and sometimes the price is high. The Lord spoke about fasting, but for the most part this has been associated with refraining from eating food. That is good, and many doctors say Americans in particular would be healthier if they ate less. The text surely means much more than going without meals in order to pray. A man might fast regularly but unless he masters the art of refraining from sin, his going without food is a waste of time. The lusts of the flesh; the secret enjoyment, even mentally, of prohibited pleasures negates any results of prolonged abstinence from meals. Blessed is the man who regularly springcleans his soul! Prayers from a cleansed life will accomplish far more than any observance of man-made laws.

THE PROBLEM OF PREACHING

"*Why could not we cast him out?*" (v. 28). This question echoes the sentiments of every preacher and pastor throughout the world. The minister who has not known defeat is a rare orchid in a cold world. Whatever realm of Christian service is explored, we encounter difficulties. Despondency is the child of defeat. Even the Sunday school class can become a place of torment, if scholars are unresponsive. A church service may become a place to be feared, if the audience continues to be critical. Failure is apt to become a dense fog in which a vision of the holy mountain is an impossibility. Excellent organization may create the machinery of the church, and ardent study produce marvelous sermons; but it is prevailing prayer which supplies power both for the church and its pastor. Unless we make the time to do our own type of *prayer and fasting*, we shall never overcome the problems besetting our work.

SECTION FOUR

Expository Notes on the Argument on the Highway

And they departed thence, and passed through Galilee; and He would not that any man should know it. For He taught His disciples, and said unto them, The Son of man is delivered into the hands of sinful men, and they shall kill Him; and after that He is killed, He shall rise the third day. But they understood not that saying, and were afraid to ask Him (vv. 30-32).

It would be a mistake to pass these verses quickly; they may be divided into four sections, and each has much to teach.

HIS CONSIDERABLE APPREHENSION

At this time, the Lord had deliberately left the "safe" area in the northern territory and was now making His way toward Jerusalem. He was fully aware of the dangers ahead, but even greater problems apparently weighed on His mind. He had no illusions about the events to terminate His ministry. He was aware of His approaching death, and of the triumphant resurrection to follow, but His greatest concern was for His followers. These were the men in whose hands the future of God's kingdom would rest; these were to be the preachers to explain the meaning of redemption. Alas, at that time, they had no idea of what the death of Christ would mean; they were confused, and utterly unequal to the important task awaiting them. The Lord knew this, and decided it was necessary to concentrate on preparing His messengers for the future tasks. The education of His men could not be postponed.

HIS CLEAR ANNOUNCEMENT

"The Son of man is delivered into the hands of sinful men, and they shall kill Him..." (v. 31). Expounding the meaning of the word *paradidotai*, translated, "is delivered," Dr. Thayer says it means: "to give into the hands of another, to give over into ones power or use, to deliver up to be burned, to be judged, condemned, punished, scourged, tormented, put to death." The interesting thing about the text is that, in the mind of Jesus, this seemed as though it was already happening. He did not say, "The Son of man will be delivered." He said, "the Son of man *is* delivered." The Lord appeared to be living already in the reality of what was coming. He was aware of the betrayal to come; He knew of the treacherous plot already forming in the perverted mind of Judas. This only increased the urgency of making His disciples knowledgeable of the events looming on the horizon. It would not be safe, nor wise, for them to be caught unawares. Even though they might not fully understand the implications of all He would say, it was necessary for them to hear the truth, so that in after days they might remember what had been predicted.

HIS CALM ASSURANCE

"...and after that He is killed, He shall rise the third day." The Lord knew precisely what was to take place. Writing to the Hebrews, the author of that epistle said, "looking unto Jesus the author and finisher of our faith; *who for the joy that was set before Him, endured the cross, despising the shame, and is set down at the right hand of the throne of God*" (Heb. 12:2). The Lord never made unwise movements, and never uttered stupid thoughts. He knew what He wanted to do, and nothing was ever permitted to turn Him from His ordained path. This control of life produced a serenity unmatched in the history of men. Alas, it was difficult to share His peace; when He spoke of the coming crucifixion, the disciples shuddered. Their Master was the King of Israel, how then could wicked men prevail against Him? The Lord was a marvelous Teacher; His patience equalled His mercy. Although His students did not graduate immediately, at least they studied the lessons taught, and the Lord was perfectly satisfied. He knew that ultimately the seeds of truth sown in their minds would germinate and produce a glorious harvest.

HIS CONFUSED ASSISTANTS

"But they understood not that saying, and were afraid to ask Him" (v. 32). Let us not be critical of their lack of understanding. After two thousand years of Church history, we look back and find it easy to understand what Christ said. The disciples were immature students entering realms of higher education; they were kindergarten students entering God's university! They remind us of people who having heard bad news, say, "That is enough! I do not wish to hear any more." They did not like His insinuations, and were scared that if they asked questions, He might tell them something they did not wish to hear. Is it not a cause for amazement that these untutored men were destined to become the first great leaders of the Church, the instruments used by God to challenge the might of tradition and military power? Paul was correct when he wrote: "But God hath chosen the foolish things of the world to confound the wise, and God hath chosen the weak things of the world to confound the things which are mighty. And base things of the world, and things which are despised, hath God chosen, yea, and things which are not, to bring to nought things that are: *That no flesh should glory in his presence*" (1 Cor. 1:27-29).

And He came to Capernaum, and being in the house He asked them, What was it that ye disputed among yourselves by the way? But they held their peace: for by the way they had disputed among themselves, who should be the greatest. And He sat down and called the twelve, and saith unto them, If any man desire to be first, the same shall be last of all, and servant of all. And He took a child, and set him in the midst of them; and when He had taken him in His arms, He said unto them, Whosoever shall receive one of such children in my name, receiveth me; and whosoever shall receive me, receiveth not me, but Him that sent me (vv. 33-37).

THE UNFORTUNATE TENSION

"They had disputed among themselves, who should be the greatest" (v. 34). We may never be sure how the argument commenced, but we know how it ended. The Lord had been speaking about His impending death, and His words had left the disciples somber and confused. Perhaps one of them said, "Well, whatever happens, I will be there to help Him" and instantly another said, "And I shall help Him more than any of you." Then one thing led to another resulting in a damaging clash of personalities. It is not too difficult to imagine Simon Peter with his face set in rigid lines, insisting that with his dominant strength, he would be worth six of Matthew's type! And Matthew might retort, "Peter, you excel in words, but when it comes to brains, you have none!" Did John, nick-named *the son of thunder*, say, "Ah fellows, you make me tired. My brother James and I would slay a regiment while you were making your plans!" Who knows how any argument begins? One match can create a prairie fire; one spark can destroy a community. Our homes and churches would be safer and happier places, if each member learned to control himself before he ever thought of controlling others.

THE UNSURPASSED TENDERNESS

Jesus did not scold them. He knew that their nerves were raw, their spirits apprehensive, and their motives were good, even if their words were unwise. He asked, "What were you speaking about during the journey?" How did He know they had talked about anything? He knew everything! "Listen!" He said, "If you wish to be great, you must learn to be small; if you wish to climb a ladder of success, you must begin at the bottom. Here, let me show you what I mean." "And He took a child and set him in the midst of them, and when He had taken the boy in His arms, He said unto them, Whosoever shall receive one of such children in my name, receiveth me..." (v. 36, 37). Who was that little boy? Did he remember in the years which followed the moment when the arms of Jesus had encircled him? Was his name Isaac, or Benjamin, or Joseph, or Simon? We have not been given that information, and perhaps for good reasons. If we know how to become childlike, we might be justified in placing our name there. Even though we may be adults, His arms are still able to enfold us.

THE UNIQUE TRUTH

When I was a student, a Salvation Army officer of great renown came to the lecture hall to address the student body. Alas, I have long since forgotten most of what he said, but one statement will never be forgotten. That great man looked at us and said, "Gentlemen, remember that each time you place a hand on a child's head, you touch a mother's heart." I think that saintly officer had been studying at the feet of Jesus. Jesus seemed to say, "Each time you welcome a little child, you are welcoming your heavenly Father." That child must have been small, for he was lifted to sit on the Savior's knee. Small children are always attractive; alas, sometimes, older children are not. Older children can be arrogant, selfish, naughty and rude. Small children are helpless; they have no strength, and are dependent on others. They are ignorant, knowing very little about anything. They respond — especially to loving outstretched arms. They are lovable and irresistible. The Lord possibly reminded His disciples of all these characteristics, and then shocked them with His suggestion that they should be as little children. "But Lord, how can we become as that child?" Did the Master smile and say, "Never feel that you know everything. Never feel so strong that you can do without each other. Never be so arrogant that you will cease to be loved.

Never lose the chance to accept the invitation when God stretches His arms in your direction.'' All those men desired to be great in the estimation of their Leader, but for a while at least, they were not quite sure that His ideas would work in their selfish world.

SECTION FIVE

*Expository Notes on the Disciples' Objections
to the Strange Preacher*

And John answered Him saying, We saw one casting out devils in thy name, and he followeth not us: and we forbad him, because he followed not us. But Jesus said, Forbid him not; for there is no man which shall do a miracle in my name, that can lightly speak evil of me. For he that is not against us is on our part (vv. 38-40).

The concluding verses of this chapter bring to us things not easily understood, and problems which no theologian has been able to solve satisfactorily. The passage may be divided into three sections, and it behooves us to advance cautiously. The first section comprises verses 38-40 and introduces us to:

THE OTHER BROTHER

"Master we saw one casting out devils in thy name . . . and we forbad him . . ." (v. 38). There are at least two explanations of this episode. The unknown exorcist might have been a genuine believer in Christ, and although he was not an actual follower of the Lord, nevertheless, loved Him. There were disciples who left all to become itinerant preachers in the company of Jesus; there might have been others, equally sincere, who exercised a more local and limited ministry. Perhaps this man belonged to that number. On the other hand, he might have been one of the professional exorcists of his time. There were many of these who practiced their art in order to earn a living. It was commonly believed that mental illness was attributable to demon possessions, and the unfailing way to expel a demon was to solicit the aid of a stronger demon. Perhaps the unknown brother had witnessed the deeds of Jesus, and had become convinced that Jesus WAS STRONGER THAN ANY OTHER DEMON. Therefore, he called upon the power of the Lord to frighten and possibly expel the weaker spirit dominating the life of the sufferer. The Lord's words concerning this man seem to indicate that the first explanation would be true. If the exorcist were merely using the Lord's name in a superstitious, professional manner, Jesus could hardly have referred to "doing a miracle in his name."

The scene presented by the texts is extremely interesting. Somewhere along the highway, the disciples had been attracted to a crowd. Amazed they watched and listened as a stranger, probably unaware of their presence, proceeded to speak about the name of Jesus. With absolute confidence, he placed his hands upon a mentally retarded person, and commanded an evil spirit to leave the sufferer. The eyes of the disciples opened widely in wonderment, when they witnessed what followed. They were utterly dumbfounded, and turning one to another asked, "Who is he?" They probably saw the people thanking and praising their benefactor, and suddenly the anger of the disciples was stirred. They pushed their way through the crowd, and accosting the stranger said, "You have no right to use our Master's name. You are not a follower of Jesus, so stop meddling in that which is not your concern. . . ." Their prominent jaws added emphasis to their commands; they were disturbed and ready to defend their monopoly on the art of exorcism. Perhaps they were still remembering their inability to deliver the demoniac who was brought by his father to the foot of the Mount of Transfiguration. We are not told whether the man obeyed the command of the disciples, but we do know the reaction of the Lord when He was informed of the incident. "But Jesus said, Forbid him not: for there is no man which shall do a miracle in my name, that can lightly speak evil of me" (v. 39).

Thus did Jesus teach the value of tolerance. If He were here today in person, He would find it necessary to repeat His words. The cause of Christ is infinitely greater than any man who represents it, and neither man nor movement has a monopoly on the privilege of witnessing for Jesus. Exponents of the Gospel may not think exactly as others think, but since the essence of Christianity is found in a heart of love more than in a theological mind, we should examine motives rather than denominational connections. The words ". . .he followeth not with us. . ." seem to have modern overtones. Invariably, the church which claims to be the only authentic church, is totally wrong. The preacher who thinks he knows everything, has not even commenced to learn. When we meet a man who loves Christ, we should be ready to fellowship with him, and not wait until we have explored his every point of doctrine. The Bible speaks of the oneness of the Body of Christ; alas some professing Christians try to be surgeons; they carve it to pieces.

For whosoever shall give you a cup of water to drink in my name, because ye belong to Christ, verily I say unto you, he shall not lose his reward. And whosoever shall offend one of these little ones that believe in me, it is better for him that a millstone were hanged about his neck, and he were cast into the sea (vv. 41-42).

THE ODD BEHAVIOR

The words translated "a millstone" are *lithos mulikos*. This combination of words is interesting. *Lithos* means a "stone"; *mulikos* means, as does the Latin *mola* and English, "meal." "A large mill consisting of two stones, an upper and an under one; the 'nether' one was stationary, but the upper one was turned by an ass" (Thayer). It seems fitting that this statement should follow the account of the strange preacher. If he were one of "God's little ones" then it behooved the disciples to refrain from unjust criticism. The scripture also teaches that nothing done for Christ can ever pass undetected. Obviously there will be rewards for faithful service and since God must have "a time sheet," we cannot afford to waste precious moments.

And if thy hand offend thee, cut it off: it is better for thee to enter into life maimed, than having two hands to go into hell, into the fire that never shall be quenched, where their worm dieth not, and the fire is not quenched. And if thy foot offend thee, cut it off: it is better for thee to enter halt into life, than having two feet to be cast into hell, into the fire that never shall be quenched, where their worm dieth not, and the fire is not quenched. And if thine eye offend thee, pluck it out; it is better for thee to enter into the kingdom of God with one eye, than having two eyes to be cast into hell fire, where their worm dieth not, and the fire is not quenched (vv. 43-48).

To understand all the implications of this scripture, it is necessary to know something about the location of Israel's valley of Hinnom. "It is first referred to in Joshua 15:8 and 18:16 as marking the boundaries between the tribe of Judah and Benjamin. In recent times, until the Arab-Israeli war in 1967, it was divided in two by the border between Israel and Jordan. During the reigns of Ahaz and Manasseh, at Topheth in the valley of Hinnom, human sacrifices were offered to the heathen god, Molech. Josiah, in his reforms, "defiled" Topheth, and prevented any further use of the valley for that purpose (see 2 Kings 23:10). Jeremiah (7:30-33) announced that the name of the valley will be changed to the "Valley of Slaughter," because when the Lord judges Judah for her sins, the number of dead would be so great, that they would be thrown into the valley to lie there without burial. In later times the valley seems to have been used for burning refuse, and also the bodies of criminals'' (*The Zondervan Pictorial Encyclopedia of the Bible*, Vol. 5, p. 671).

Every person knew about Israel's garbage dump; all people associated this terrible place with the ultimate doom of the unrepentant. Knowing this fact, the Lord used the place as an illustration to make clear to His hearers some of the most important things He ever uttered. He drew attention to (1) the hand, (2) the foot, and (3) the eye, and explained that all three could be associated with evil practices. These words were not meant to be taken literally. Had that been so, every listener would have needed the attention of a surgeon, and every hospital would have become overcrowded. He was not advising people to mutilate their bodies. He was trying to explain to them that whatever stood between their being true to the principles of holiness, should be sacrificed in order to remove temptation. If someone is prone to sexual misbehavior, he should cease reading evil books; he should destroy them, so that his eyes would never again endanger the sanctity of his soul. That would produce the same results as if he had removed his eye! The Lord applied the same truths to the use of the hand and the foot. He stressed repeatedly the necessity of removing all temptations. He emphasized that it would be better to enter into life without certain things, than to retain them and lose one's soul. For example, money can be one of the most useful commodities, but if the acquisition of wealth overrides and overrules the laws of decency and honesty, then the desire for increasing riches might be an indication of spiritual bankruptcy. All the money in the world will not purchase peace if the millionaire be in Hell. This was very pointed preaching and was never meant to please congregations. A deep-rooted cancer requires much more than a band-aid. It is not judgment which makes the surgeon grasp the scalpel; it is mercy endeavoring to save a man's life. The Lord never sacrificed truth on the altar of popularity. He came to save mankind, and sometimes to do that, He had to hurt them. If sometimes we think He is cutting us, it is wise to remember that love holds the scalpel.

For every one shall be salted with fire, and every sacrifice shall be salted with salt. Salt is good; but if the salt has lost its saltness, wherewith will ye season it? Have salt in yourselves, and have peace one with another (vv. 49-50).

THE OVERCOMING BELIEVER

It is somewhat difficult to explain why the statements of verses 49-50 are found at the end of this chapter, for at first glance, it appears they have little if any connection with the preceding verses. Some commentators believe these were utterances made at different occasions, and the fact they all mention salt, accounts for their staying in the thoughts of Simon Peter whose influence can be detected throughout Mark's Gospel. That may be the case, but all who believe the Holy Spirit influenced even the compilation of the various messages, will expect to find some truth in what was written. We have already considered the relevance of the hand, the foot, and the eyes in regard to hindrances to effective service for Christ. The Lord had already spoken of the need for the removal of all hindrances, so that the soul may escape "gehenna." Surely then, the inclusion of the verses at this point suggests the salt has something to do with effective service for Christ. It is with that thought in mind that we should pursue our studies.

SALT WAS THE SEAL OF A COVENANT

"And every oblation of thy meat offering shalt thou season with salt; neither shalt thou suffer the salt of the covenant of thy God to be lacking from thy meat offering: with all thine offerings thou shalt offer salt" (Lev. 2:13). "...it is a covenant of salt for ever before the Lord unto thee, and to thy seed with thee..." (Num. 18:19). Abijah speaking to Jeroboam and all Israel said, "Ought ye not to know that the Lord God of Israel gave the kingdom over Israel to David for ever, even to him and to his sons *by a covenant of salt*" (2 Chron. 13:5). Salt was the sign and seal of a covenant, not only between God and His people but also between the nation and Jehovah. To add salt was the recognition that eternal vows had been made between both parties. Therefore, when Jesus said, "For every one shall be salted with fire, and every sacrifice shall be salted with salt," He was reminding His hearers of an eternal bond which had been forged between Heaven and earth, and it directly concerned them. Like marriage, "it was not to be entered into lightly, but discreetly, reverently, advisedly, soberly, and in the fear of God."

SALT WAS THE SIGN OF CONSECRATION

Throughout the world, then and now, salt has been used as a

preservative; a preventative of corruption. Both salt and fire were means of purification; it was by a process of heating that dross was removed from gold; it was by the addition of salt, that meat was preserved and prevented from becoming obnoxious. Paul applying this truth to Christian conduct said, "Let your speech be always with grace, *seasoned with salt*, that ye may know how ye ought to answer every man" (Col. 4:6). If all the followers of the Savior practiced these things and honored the Lord's commands, many unnecessary, and sometimes defiling, words would be eliminated from our vocabularies. The theme of the earlier verses deals with what should be done as we "enter into life" and "into the kingdom of God." The addition of this message about the value of salt may have been deliberately planned by the Holy Spirit. The Lord said it would be profitable to cut off a hand, a foot, and even to pluck out an eye in order to be satisfactory in God's sight. Perhaps He was also thinking about sections of man's vocabulary where the Lord's name is so often used in vain. No human should ever utter the words "Oh God" unless they are to be followed by a prayer.

SALT — GOOD SALT WAS THE EVIDENCE OF CAREFULNESS

Enlarging upon the same text, Luke wrote: "Salt is good; but if the salt has lost its savour, wherewith shall it be seasoned? It is neither fit for the land, not yet for the dunghill; but men cast it out. He that hath ears to hear, let him hear" (Luke 14:35). "Salt, by exposure to sun or rain may lose its pungency and virtue, in spite of the fact that it retains its appearance. Most of the world's commercial salt is produced by steam or direct heating of rock salt. The salt is first dissolved in water which is forced through pipes into the salt bed. The brine is afterward pumped to the surface through another pipe. When rid of all clay impurities, the solution is evaporated to precipitate any present, and is then evaporated again to precipitate the salt" (*Funk and Wagnells Encyclopedia*, p. 7781). Great care has to be exercised both in the production of salt and also in its own preservation. If the salt is to perform its very important task in purifying other commodities, it must itself be free from impurities. These facts become very important when we recall how Jesus said to His disciples, "Ye are the salt of the earth" (Matt. 5:13). If we are to combat the corruption around us, then we ourselves must be pure. "He that hath ears to hear, let him hear."

HOMILIES

Study No. 16

THE FOUR FACES OF JESUS

If I were an artist, I would paint a portrait of the Lord, but I am sure I would have difficulties painting His face. It has often been said that a man's face is the window of his soul. Sorrow never begets laughter, and intense mirth is never accompanied by sobs. How can any painter harmonize pity, pain, and pleasure in one picture? If I were an artist I would have to paint four pictures of the Lord, but they would hang together in one special gallery.

THE SHINING FACE

The first painting would be based on what happened on the Mount of Transfiguration, where the Lord's face shone as the sun (Matt. 17:2). The shining face seems to be a characteristic of all who live in the immediate presence of God. Evidence of this may be found in the experiences of Moses and Daniel, and elsewhere in the Scriptures. We are told that, at the resurrection of Christ, two angels appeared in white and testified that Christ had risen from the dead. *Phillip's* translation says, "Their faces were dazzling!" *The New English Bible* says, "they shone!" Yet, these incidents differ from what we are privileged to see on the Mount of Transfiguration. With men and angels, the glory resembled a holy sunburn; it was something which came from without, stamping its mark upon those present. With Christ, the radiance came from within. The glory which Christ had known from the beginning; the majesty of His inner self, broke through the frail barrier of human flesh, and the heavenly sunshine shone out for all to see. The question concerning His true identity was answered in the mountain. But what artist could effectively paint that scene?

THE SUFFERING FACE

Isaiah (52:14) predicted that "...his visage was so marred more than any man." This has been translated as being so marred as to be *unrecognizable*. That the Lord's face should be twisted by agony and bruised by punches, makes all wise men shudder. Christ had been mercilessly scourged, until the flesh on His back was lacerated and broken; He had been forced to carry His cross, until even the soldiers recognized He could carry it no more. He had been nailed to a cross, which in turn had been lifted and dropped into the prepared hole in the ground. Then the entire weight of His body had cruelly sagged on the nails. He had suffered anguish beyond measure, and as a result, His face had become distorted through pain. It seemed a very long way from the shining face to the suffering face, and we should remember the distance was only bridged by His unfailing redeeming love for men and women.

THE SOLEMN FACE

"...and every bondman, and every free man, hid themselves in the dens and in the rocks of the mountains; and said to the mountain and rocks, fall on us, and hide us from the face of Him that sitteth on the throne, and from the wrath of the Lamb. For the great day of His wrath is come; and who shall be able to stand?" (Rev. 6:15-17). "It is appointed unto men once to die, and after death, the judgment" (Heb. 9:27). For many people, this subject has become the forgotten or ignored part of Bible teaching. Knowledge begets responsibility, and all who have heard the Gospel must account to God and His Son for the reception given to that message. The Lord Jesus died to make forgiveness possible, but if people ignore or reject what God has done and said, there "remains a certain fearful looking for judgment...He that despised Moses law died without mercy under two or three witnesses: Of how much sorer punishment, suppose ye, shall he be thought worthy, who hath trodden under foot the Son of God, and hath counted the blood of the covenant, wherewith he was sanctified, an unholy thing, and hath done despite unto the Spirit of grace?" (Heb. 10:27-29).

THE SERENE FACE

The fourth in the collection of paintings would be based on Revelation 22:4. "And they shall see His face; and His name shall be in their foreheads." Probably there will be many thrilling and wonderful sights in the hereafter, but there is reason to believe the face of Jesus will outshine them all. The closing chapters of the Bible describe many beautiful things. The redeemed saints will see the river of the water of life, the New Jerusalem and all the marvelous things provided by

God, in a realm where sickness and pain and limitations of every kind will be unknown. There will be a choir in which will sing "ten thousand times ten thousand and thousands of thousands." There will be no hospitals, no cemeteries, no funeral parlors, no hovels, no dirt and nothing to displease. But amidst the galaxies of shining stars, none will shine more than the face of Him Who made all this possible for redeemed sinners. "And they shall see His face." Blessed is the man; happy is the woman able to say with assurance,

> And I shall see Him face to face,
> And tell the story, saved by grace.

The Tenth Chapter of Mark

THEME: *Jesus Encounters Problems of Many Kinds*

OUTLINE:

SECTION ONE

Expository Notes on the Problems of Divorce

And He arose from thence, and cometh into the coasts of Judea by the farther side of Jordan: and the people resort unto Him again; and, as He was wont, He taught them again. And the Pharisees came to Him, and asked Him, Is it lawful for a man to put away his wife? tempting Him (vv. 1-2).

The problems connected with divorce have troubled the church from its inception. We might be justified in saying it has troubled mankind almost from the beginning of time. Continuing debates have ruined good friendships; and even ministers have been critical of each other, because their interpretation of biblical laws differed. There are church leaders who say divorce is evil viewed from any angle; that under no circumstances should it be tolerated within the assembly. Marriage vows are for ever, and any abrogation of the ancient commandments must be avoided at any cost. Others are more liberal in their attitude, believing that under certain circumstances, divorce is permissible, and that ministers are justified in marrying divorcees. This is particularly so when the one to be married was innocent in the tragedy which caused the earlier divorce proceedings. Unfortunately, these divisions will continue until the end of time. However, it is essential that we understand what was meant by divorce when the Lord was questioned concerning the subject. No interpreter is justified in taking a verse out of its context, and trying to make it mean something never intended in the first place.

DIVORCE ACCORDING TO THE SCRIBES

History tells us that about sixty years before Christ, a man of Babylon known for his poverty and his desire for knowledge, came to Jerusalem to study law. His name was Hillel, and eventually he established a law school in Jerusalem. One of his students named Shammai disagreed with his master, and later, commenced a rival school, also in Jerusalem. Hillel was liberal both in theology and manner of living. Shammai was the exact opposite. He was extremely orthodox, a little harsh, dogmatic and unyielding. The two schools opposed each other on many topics, but the most important concerned divorce. The followers of Shammai taught that divorce could only be permitted in cases of adultery. There could not be any other grounds to justify the termination of a marriage. They believed that when a man or a woman committed adultery, the marriage vows no longer existed. Therefore, when a man divorced his wife, he was free to remarry. The earlier school of Hillel strongly disagreed with this interpretation of the law, and stated that matters concerning divorce applied only to men. They could divorce women but women could not divorce men. This seems unreasonable to us, but it should be remembered that throughout the eastern world, a woman was treated as a thing! Her only value was in childbearing, cooking, housework, and being the slave of her husband in whatever he desired. Even today, in the countries of the Middle East, it is a common sight to see a man riding a donkey, while his wife walks behind carrying packages. A woman was of little value, and litigation concerning her rested with her husband. She had no legal rights whatsoever as she was totally at the disposal of the male head of the family. Though a man could divorce his wife on many grounds, the woman only had a few motives for divorcing her husband. Among these were if her husband became a leper or if he falsely accused her of pre-nuptial sin.

It is essential that we understand the background to the question asked by the Pharisees. Some of the questioners might have been sincere, wondering which of the two viewpoints was in accordance with the will of God. Yet the fact that Mark says "*they were tempting him*" indicates an evil intent. Matthew describing the incident gives a little more information. He wrote: "The Pharisees also came unto Him, tempting Him, and saying unto Him, Is it lawful for a man to put away his wife *for every cause*?" (19:3). As we have seen, Matthew was the Book-Man and it is certain that his version is closer to the truth. The men who asked the question knew of many reasons for requesting a divorce, and for some, the question could have been very important. The entire debate about the subject centered on the statement in Deuteronomy 24:1-2. "When a man hath taken a woman, and married her, and it come to pass that she find no favour in his eyes, *because he hath found some uncleanness in her*: then let him write her a bill of divorcement, and give it into her hand, and send her out of his house. And when she is departed out of his house, *she may go and be another man's wife*." Everything rested upon the statement, "*because he hath found some uncleanness in her*." The theologians of Christ's day argued as to what might be considered unclean in a woman, and this certainly embittered the discussions. The followers of Shammai were adamant in their statement that uncleanness meant only adultery. The supporters of Hillel went to extremes interpreting the passage as liberally as possible. For example, they affirmed that if a wife talked to a strange man, spoke disrespectfully of her husband in his presence, or did something that caused the food to spoil, she could be considered unclean. Thus divorce was granted for whatever trivial reason.

It is against this background the reply of the Lord must be considered. He knew what was taking place in Jerusalem and was aware of the thoughts of His questioners. Obviously divorce was not justified *for every cause*, but He carefully refrained from saying so, at least, at that moment. "The object of this artful question was to entrap our Lord and to bring Him into collision with one or other of these two opposing parties. For if He had said it was not lawful for a man to put away his wife, He would have exposed Himself to the hostility of many of the wealthy classes, who put away their wives for any cause. But if He had allowed the lawfulness of divorce at all, they would have found fault with His doctrine as imperfect and carnal, although He professed to be a spiritual Teacher of a perfect system, sent down from heaven" (Dr. E. Bickersteth in *The Pulpit Commentary, Mark,* p. 59). It should also be remembered that the entire nation knew Herod had put away his wife, and any unwise answer from the Lord would have increased the repercussions resulting from His reply. The Savior was aware of these possibilities, and with patience and skill, answered their question with one of His own.

DIVORCE ACCORDING TO THE SAVIOR

And He answered and said unto them, What did Moses command you? And they said, Moses suffered to write a bill of divorcement, and to

put her away. And Jesus answered and said unto them, for the hardness of your heart he wrote this precept. But from the beginning of the creation God made them male and female. For this cause shall a man leave his father and his mother, and cleave to his wife; and they twain shall be one flesh: so then they are no more twain, but one flesh. What therefore God hath joined together, let not man put asunder (vv. 3-9).

Obviously the Lord recognized the validity of the statement made by Moses in Deuteronomy 24:1-2, but His statement infers that what was said on that occasion could hardly be considered the final word on divorce. Moses spoke *because of a certain situation.* "For the hardness of your hearts he wrote you this precept." Had the hearts of the people been more responsive to God and His word, such a commandment would not have been given. At best, anything resulting from obedience to the word of Moses could only be considered as *second-best.* There was a relationship to be more desired, and in order to draw attention to that fact, Christ went further back in time to speak of events in the garden of Eden. He stated that God had joined Adam and Eve together making them one entity. To break that unity, was to undermine the act of God and destroy what He had planned. God considered marriage to be something sacred, a bond in which either would find security, happiness, and productivity in the other. Both Adam and Eve needed a partner in whom to find fellowship, love, and usefulness that would last for eternity. No person would ever be justified in breaking, or in helping to break, that holy union made by God. Christ reminded His questioners of that which God desired, but did not deny the wisdom of the commandment given by Moses. In any case, Moses was only the channel through which God was addressing the children of Israel. Seeing a situation which was continually deteriorating, God gave guidance regarding the procedure to be followed when Eden's bliss became impossible. If a man committed sin, and unjustly put away his wife, she was free to become the wife of another man.

And in the house His disciples asked Him again of the same matter. And He saith unto them, whosoever shall put away his wife, and marry another, committeth adultery against her. And if a woman shall put away her husband, and be married to another, she committeth adultery (vv. 10-12).

The disciples, understandably so, were confused by the Lord's remarks, and as soon as the opportunity presented itself, asked for an explanation of what had been stated. They knew, as we should know

THAT UNDER LAW *it was not possible to marry a divorcee*. If a man or woman were found guilty of adultery, the penalty was *death by stoning* (see Leviticus 20:10). It would hardly be possible to marry someone *who was already dead*! The Lord was focusing attention on that one act of flagrant sin, and at the same time was exposing the utter superficiality of the many other reasons for desiring divorce.

Attention must also be given to Matthew's rendering of the same text. "And I say unto you, Whosoever shall put away his wife *EXCEPT IT BE FOR FORNICATION*, and shall marry another, committeth adultery: and whoso marrieth her which is put away doth commit adultery" (Matt. 19:9).

DIVORCE ACCORDING TO THE SCRIPTURE

It should be remembered that the laws of God regarding divorce were meant *to protect* a woman, and not *to punish* her for something she never did. The attitude of some sections of the church has been hard, unrelenting, and unforgiving. If a woman or a man for that matter, is a divorcee, the ecclesiastical edict prevents that person from remarrying; that is, the discarded partner is condemned to a life of continuing loneliness, and is sometimes deprived of the blessings of the church in which he or she has served for years. To say the least, this is unfair and not in keeping with the love of God.

Unfortunately, we live in an age of profligacy where divorce can be obtained for the flimsiest of reasons. It is appalling to read of people who enter into marriage only because they are assured of an easy exit should the marriage not live up to expectations. Lust has been substituted for love; carnal pleasures for the responsibility of promoting a healthy family relationship in which children are introduced to the joys of living. The Roman Catholic Church and very many Protestant ministers are adamant in their interpretation of the biblical verses. They outlaw divorce in any shape or form. The Eastern Churches do not agree with this interpretation, and so in the final analysis, each individual must weigh the pros and cons of the matter and seek his own individual guidance from God.

SHOULD THE CHURCH MARRY ANYONE
WHO HAS BEEN DIVORCED?

It is common knowledge that this is one of the most perplexing problems in the world today. Even the Church is divided, for certain bishops are arguing that drastic reforms be made in church policy. Arguments have taken place behind the scenes in every denomination, but in most cases ministers have to decide their own course of action. I would like to emphasize that I am only expressing my own opinion, when I confess I do not agree with the attitude of those who refuse under any consideration to marry divorcees. The Scriptures declare that to marry someone guilty of adultery is to become guilty oneself. But I am not convinced this applies to the innocent party in a divorce action. To penalize an innocent person for the rest of her life is something not in keeping with fair play, and as far as I am concerned not in keeping with the kindness of God. I knew a young man who returned from the battle front to discover that his wife was an utterly faithless person. She had deserted their baby and had gone to live with another man. That brave young husband did his utmost to win her back, but ultimately it became evident to all that his wife was a bad woman. In due course they were divorced, and with rare devotion and courage, the young man became both father and mother to his child. I was ministering in the church where he fell in love with a charming young Christian. She returned his affection, and there was every prospect that a lovely new home was about to come into being. Alas, the minister refused to perform the ceremony, and bringing pressure to bear on the woman, he caused a great deal of pain and ultimately separated the couple. Had I been asked to marry this man and woman, I would have done so. The dictatorial, high-handed action of certain church leaders is apt to cause increasing pain in a world already torn by discord. I do not agree, as many others do not agree, with the unyielding practice of condemning innocent people to a lifetime of loneliness. I am fully aware that many readers may disagree with my viewpoint, so just to be provocative, I add one other detail. According to Jeremiah 31:34, the grace of God is sufficient to *forget* my sin. "...for I will forgive their iniquity, *and I will remember their sin no more.*" A man may be very guilty, but when in true penitence he yields his life to God, his sins are instantly cancelled *and forgotten by God for ever.* Never, never again will God even think of them. By what standards, then, am I justified in resurrecting what God has eternally buried? By whose authority do I remember another's sin, and even hold it against him in preventing his following a path that leads to happiness? I have a conviction that if God dealt with us as we often deal with others, few, if any would want to appear in public" (reproduced from the author's book, *This I believe,* pp. 219-220).

SECTION TWO

Expository Notes on Christ's Attitude Toward Children

And they brought young children to Him, that He should touch them: and His disciples rebuked those that brought them. But when Jesus saw it, He was much displeased, and said unto them, Suffer the little children to come unto me, and forbid them not; for of such is the kingdom of God. Verily I say unto you, Whosoever shall not receive the kingdom of God as a little child, he shall not enter therein. And He took them up in His arms, put His hands upon them, and blessed them (vv. 13-16).

THE MOTHER'S DESIRE

Matthew says in his gospel, ''. . .there were brought unto Him little children, that He might put His hands on them *and pray*. . .'' (Matt. 19:13). Mark is content to say ''. . .that He should touch them.'' Luke adds, ''And they brought unto Him infants'' (Luke 18:15). The word used means newly-born babies. All this was in accord with Jewish practice. Every Jewish mother desired her child to be blessed by any distinguished rabbi, but it is interesting to note that Matthew suggests they requested Christ to ask God's blessing on their children. This often happened on the first birthday of the child, and might be likened to the dedication services for children practiced in churches today. Happy are the mothers who recognize their babies to be gifts from God. Wise are they who thank Him and seek His blessing.

THE MEN'S DEMAND

We cannot be sure of the reason for the rebuke of the disciples. Perhaps they were trying to prevent harassment of their tired Master. They had been walking through the country; people had crowded around them; the Lord was weary. The insistent cries of emotional women could be a nuisance! Maybe the disciples were a little irritable, for they also had experienced a difficult day. ''And the disciples rebuked those that brought them.'' It is easy to imagine what might have been said. ''Ladies, the Master is tired, please go away and take your children. Come back tomorrow, and Jesus will listen to you.'' If some of those babies were screaming, the rebuke might have been stronger, for tired people seldom appreciate crying infants! When we are about to rebuke anyone, it is wiser to remain silent until we are sure our actions will please the Lord.

THE MASTER'S DISPLEASURE

"But when Jesus saw it, *He was much displeased*" (v. 14). A literal translation of the verse would be, "He was very indignant." However tired the Savior may have been, He was never too tired to listen to the cries of anxious people, and never too weary to welcome children to His arms. Perhaps He saw in the helpless babes a purity missing in adults. Knowing that He was already on His way to Calvary, the sight of the babes encouraged Him, reminding Him that what He was about to accomplish would mean an infinitely better world in which children would enjoy real happiness. He said, "Let the little children come unto me, and forbid them not: for of such is the kingdom of God." We do well when we remember:

> Jesus loves the little children:
> All the children of the world.
> Red and yellow; black and white,
> All are precious in His sight.
> Jesus loves the little children of the world.

THE MARVELOUS DECLARATION

". . . of such is the kingdom of God. Verily I say unto you, Whosoever shall not receive the kingdom of God as a little child, he shall not enter therein" (vv. 15, 16). One commentator thinks this statement means that children who die in infancy are always before the throne of God, because by virtue of the redeeming blood of Christ, they are assured of a place in the eternal kingdom. "Take heed that ye despise not one of these little ones; for I say unto you, That in heaven their angels do always behold the face of my Father which is in heaven" (Matt. 18:10). Upon this verse is based the teaching that the baptizing and receiving of infants into the church is justified. It is difficult to accept this premise, for what Jesus said had nothing to do with baptism, either by sprinkling or immersion. The key to the passage is found in Matthew 18:2-3. "And Jesus called a little child unto Him, and set him in the midst of them, and said, Verily I say unto you, *Except ye be converted, and become as little children*, ye shall not enter into the kingdom of heaven." The Revised version of the Bible renders this as "except ye turn and become as little children." Conversion, the result of an exercising of personal faith, has little if anything to do with a newborn babe. The passage, therefore, must refer to childlikeness; the innocence, trust, and sincerity of a baby responding to the outstretched arms of God. This, and not the works of righteousness, is the key that unlocks heaven's treasures.

THE MOVING DISPLAY

"And He took them up in His arms, put His hands upon them, and blessed them" (v. 16). First, the Lord held out His arms to welcome them; then He enfolded them by putting His arms around them; and finally, He lifted one hand to place it on the child's head in blessing. Thus would He teach adults the steps of salvation. First, He calls and welcomes us. Secondly, He lifts and holds us safely. Thirdly, He anoints us with the blessing of the Almighty. The Lord, indisputably, was a tremendous Preacher, but some of His greatest sermons were expressed in deeds not words. "Whosoever shall not receive the kingdom of God as a little child, *he shall not enter therein.*" There is no other way into God's kingdom. Unless we enter by that door, we shall forever be excluded.

SECTION THREE

Expository Notes on Christ's Encounter With the Rich Young Ruler

And when He was gone forth into the way, there came one running, and kneeled to Him, and asked Him, Good Master, what shall I do that I may inherit eternal life? (v. 17).

This incident probably happened as Jesus was leaving the home in which He had been resting. A crowd would be filling the street, for the presence of Jesus in any district was sufficient to attract onlookers. Suddenly, a man came running down the street, and pushing human obstacles aside, the newcomer flung himself at the feet of Jesus to ask his question. That was an electrifying moment and from it comes three things worthy of consideration. (1) *His enthusiasm.* It is said that he came *running.* He was determined not to miss this opportunity of interviewing the great Teacher. Something, somewhere, had stirred this young man's soul. He had either heard Jesus speaking about eternal life, or had listened as others spoke about the subject. He could not suppress his emotions; if there were such a thing as eternal life, he desired to know more about it. (2) *His humility.* "...he kneeled to Him..." Possibly that rich young ruler had never kneeled to any person throughout his entire lifetime. He was wealthy and maybe employed many people.

He was master in his own domain; a man accustomed to being respected and honored. People kneeled before him, but he never kneeled to anyone. When he respectfully knelt before a Teacher known to be hated by the religious leaders, a Man soon to be condemned and crucified, the people stared in amazement. It was evident he considered Jesus to be greater than he. (3) *His request.* "Good Master, what shall I do that I may inherit eternal life?" (v. 17). The ruler already possessed everything his world offered. He had wealth, position, prestige, his future was secure; he had need of nothing! Every person in the listening crowd would have gladly exchanged places in life with him. He had everything; they had little. At that moment, the rich young ruler possessed nothing comparable to what he most desired — eternal life. Maybe he had already given much thought to the subject, and had reached the conclusion that Jesus could answer his question. The presence of the Savior in the locality provided the opportunity to seek additional information, and nothing would prevent him from discovering what he wanted to know. *"He came running."*

And Jesus said unto him, Why callest thou me good? there is none good but one, that is God (v. 18).

A TERM OF RESPECT

Did the young man utter the words, "Good Master," merely because he saw character and integrity in Jesus? Would he have addressed any other distinguished rabbi in the same way? Was this the beginning and the end of his opinions concerning the Savior? We may never know the answers to these questions, but the fact that Jesus restrained the young man's emotions is thought-provoking.

A TIME FOR REFLECTION

"There is none good but one, that is God." "Young man, you are asking about eternal life. Anything eternal emanates from God. Do you realize that only God is good? All other people are sinful — and that includes you. Do you understand?" It was as though the Lord said, "Young man, I am not saying that you are wrong to address me as 'Good Master.' Since only God is GOOD, is it possible that you address me thus, because you are beginning to believe I might be more than a mere man? Are you beginning to think that I might be God, and for that reason, have come to enquire about something that only God can give?'' ''Why callest thou *ME* good?''

A TEST OF RECOGNITION

Within the few moments of questioning the Lord probably did more for that man than all the rabbis could have done in a lifetime. On another occasion the Lord said, ''. . .I am the way, the truth, and the life: no man cometh unto the Father, but by me. If ye had known me, ye should have known my Father also: and from henceforth ye know Him, *and have seen Him*'' (John 14:6-7). What is God like? The answer is ''Jesus.'' What does God say? The answer is ''Listen to Jesus and you will know.''

Thou knowest the commandments, Do not commit adultery, Do not kill, Do not steal, Do not bear false witness, Defraud not, Honor thy father and mother. And he answered and said unto Him, Master, all these have I observed from my youth. Then Jesus beholding him loved him, and said unto him, One thing thou lackest: go thy way, sell whatsoever thou hast, and give to the poor, and thou shalt have treasure in heaven: and come, take up the cross, and follow me. And he was sad at that saying, and went away grieved: for he had great possessions (vv. 19-22).

THE MAN'S CONFESSION. . .Good works alone, are insufficient

The man's confession was clear, concise, and very commendable. He had lived an exemplary life, and recognizing this, the Lord loved him. There was neither conceit nor pride in the ruler's testimony; his confession was a statement of fact; to the best of his ability he had endeavored to lead a good life. Yet, in spite of his being a very worthy citizen, he remained aware of a terrible emptiness in his soul. His goodness could only take him as far as a grave. What lay beyond the tomb remained a mystery. If there were such a thing as eternal life, he had no assurance of it. If it were possible to acquire it, he wanted to know what good deeds merited it. Nowhere else in Scripture is the truth more clearly stated that mere respectability is insufficient in the sight of God to guarantee a place in heaven.

THE MAN'S CHALLENGE. . .
''Whatsoever thou hast. . .give to the poor'' (v. 21)

Many years ago, I heard Dr. Frank Boreham, that very great author and preacher say, ''If you possess something you cannot live without, give it away." The degree to which a man desires spiritual wealth can be measured by the price he is willing to pay for it. Things which are easily obtained, are often considered inconsequential. When Christ directed the man's attention to the possibility of losing his wealth, the desire for life-everlasting began to abate. Obviously his whole life was centered in his possessions. Without them, he would be nothing, and the thought of becoming an itinerant preacher was appalling. He preferred sleeping in a comfortable bed rather than beneath a tree. He loved to dine sumptuously, and the idea of having to beg bread appeared ludicrous. "Master, is there no other way?" "No Son, not for you." "And he went away grieved."

Probably had the rich young man consented to do as the Lord suggested, he would have been sent home with a benediction. The only condition for obtaining eternal life is that Christ must be first in the recipient's life. Actually, the test revealed the man's unwillingness *to dethrone wealth in order to enthrone Christ.* Unless a man crowns Christ Lord of all, he does not crown Him Lord at all.

THE MAN'S COLLAPSE...He...went away (v. 22)

One wonders which had the greater grief — the rich young ruler, or the Lord! He had great possessions! Actually, they possessed him! When anything is so important that it controls a man's actions, then he is not ruler in his own life. He does as he is bidden by a desire for illegitimate and often unwise things. Had the rich young man died that night he would have had a very expensive funeral, but would have gone into eternity penniless. The fellow had cataracts upon his eyes; his vision had been seriously impaired. He saw only life without his money; just beyond the range of his failing eyesight stood the city foresquare where "moth nor rust doth not corrupt and where thieves do not break through nor steal" (Matt. 6:19-21). The ruler saw the corruptible things which perished with him; he forgot the imperishable treasures which were almost within his grasp. Unfortunately, he permitted them to slip away.

And Jesus looked round about, and saith unto His disciples, How hardly shall they that have riches enter into the kingdom of God. And the disciples were astonished at His words. But Jesus answereth again, and saith unto them, Children, how hard is it for them that trust in riches to enter into the kingdom of God. It is easier for a camel to go through the eye of a needle, than for a rich man to enter into the kingdom of God. And they were astonished out of measure, saying among

themselves, Who then can be saved? And Jesus looking upon them saith, With men it is impossible, but not with God: for with God all things are possible (vv. 23-27).

"The reference to the camel passing through the needle's eye was well known. Alongside the main gates of a city, was a smaller gate used only by pedestrians. This served a two-fold purpose. When at sunset, or on the sabbath, the large gates were closed to keep out the cameliers with their animals, ordinary people could still enter or leave by the smaller door. This entrance was said to be only about three or four feet high, and was called the needle's eye. There were occasions when an angry camelier literally tried to get his camel through the eye of a needle — that is, the small gate. This was possible, but nevertheless it was exceedingly difficult. There were three pre-requisites. The animal had to be small; the load had to be taken from its back, and the camel, somehow, had to go forward on its knees. It could be done, but it was difficult. It was also possible for wealthy men to get into the kingdom of God, but the same three conditions applied. Those who desired admittance had to be small in their own estimation; they had to offload anything that would hinder progress; they had to kneel, and thus seek entrance into the kingdom of God. Another interpretation comes from the fact that two Greek words are very similar. *Kameelos* means "camel," but *kamilos*, an unusual word, meant a "ship's cable," that is a rope. It will be easily understood that one word could be mistaken for the other; that the tone of a man's voice; his accent; his emphasis on either word might have made it sound as though he had uttered the other. Therefore, some teachers think the Lord was referring to the impossible task of threading a needle with a piece of rope. This, I believe is not the correct interpretation. To do this would be *impossible* whereas it was possible to get a wealthy man into the kingdom of God. From every angle the former interpretation seems to be the more reasonable. The question asked by the disciples indicated the strange wonder filling their souls, but the answer forthcoming from their Leader was destined to give courage to saints in every age" (reproduced from the author's book, *Luke's Thrilling Gospel*, pp. 385-365).

Then Peter began to say unto Him, Lo, we have left all, and have followed thee. And Jesus answered and said, Verily I say unto you, There is no man that hath left house, or brethren, or sisters, or father, or mother, or wife, or children, or lands, for my sake, and the gospel's, but he shall receive an hundredfold now in this time, houses, and brethren, and sisters, and mothers, and children, and lands, with persecutions; and in the world to come eternal life. But many that are first shall be last; and the last first (vv. 28-31).

A GREAT REASONING. . .It is impossible to out-give God

Peter watched as a wealthy young man chose to leave Christ, and had heard his Master's words concerning the difficulties of entering the kingdom of God. Instinctively he had compared himself with the foolish ruler. He and his companions had been wiser; they had indeed left all to become disciples. Peter did not ask about the possibilities of being rewarded, but thought it could do no harm to remind the Lord how privileged He was to have such devoted followers! Simon was indeed very lovable, for although he often said foolish things, he only expressed what would have been in the thoughts of us all. It was then that Jesus indicated the impossibility of out-giving God. God has a unique way of paying debts, and eventually, anyone who has sacrificed anything will receive "an hundredfold. . .now in this world, . . .and in the world to come." The first section of His prediction was gloriously fulfilled in the lives of the disciples. Having forsaken their families, each disciple had been initiated into the fellowship of the church. Each became a member of a far greater family in which he found innumerable brothers and sisters, whose loyalty and love often exceed that of blood relations. Every Christian home throughout the world would be a haven of rest and refuge; the disciple having nothing, would possess everything. Jesus emphasized this would take place even in this world, but He had more to promise.

A GREAT REWARD. . . "Ye shall sit on thrones"

It is perhaps thought-provoking that of the three Gospel writers, only Matthew records the unique promise made by Jesus. The Lord said, ". . .Verily I say unto you, That ye which have followed me, in the regeneration when the Son of man shall sit on the throne of his glory, *ye also shall sit upon twelve thrones, judging the twelve tribes of Israel*" (Matt. 19:28). It should be remembered that primarily Matthew was writing for Jews, and therefore any mention of the twelve tribes of Israel would be of particular significance to his readers. The disciples were Jews, and to occupy such a position would be the highest reward possible. Jesus seemed to say, "Do not be boastful concerning sacrifices you have made. Whatever you give or do, you will always be indebted to your heavenly Father."

A GREAT REVELATION. . . The first shall be last; the last first

This was the Lord's way of saying, "Never count your chickens before they are hatched." Many who might expect great recompense will be disappointed; many who expect nothing will be immensely surprised. It is not possible to predict what may take place when God assesses the worth of a man's sacrifice. God has His own way of detecting merit and rewarding it. A man may appear to be very great; his name may head the list of donors to a worthy cause; he might be the greatest in importance in every realm he enters, yet he might be motivated by a desire to be popular. Even the man himself would be shocked if someone suggested he sought only self-glory. On the contrary, the widow woman who placed two mites in the offering at the temple would have been surprised had God told her she had given more than any other.

It is worthy of note that Jesus included "persecution" among the possible rewards. At first glance, and to express it in modern terms, the Lord was saying "You will receive thousands of dollars and some counterfeit money." Peter was a good student with an excellent memory, for long afterward he wrote: "If ye be reproached for the name of Christ, happy are ye. . . " Sometimes very great treasures are wrapped in brown paper! Occasionally Heaven's gifts are wrapped in swaddling clothes! (See homily "Two Men Who Asked the Same Questions," in the author's book, *Luke's Thrilling Gospel*, p. 387.)

SECTION FOUR

Expository Notes on Christ's Prediction of His Approaching Death and Resurrection

And they were in the way going up to Jerusalem; and Jesus went before them: and they were amazed; and as they followed Him, they were afraid. And He took again the twelve, and began to tell them what things should happen unto Him, Saying, Behold, we go up to Jerusalem; and the Son of man shall be delivered unto the chief priests, and unto the scribes, and they shall condemn Him to death, and shall deliver Him to the Gentiles: and they shall mock Him, and shall scourge Him, and shall spit upon Him, and shall kill Him: and the third day He shall rise again (vv. 32-34).

To read these verses is to feel we are upon holy ground. "And Jesus went before them!" He was awfully alone. The shadow of the cross was already falling across His heart; He saw clearly what lay ahead.

Uncomprehending, the disciples were behind Him, wondering what was to happen next. Their hope for the establishing of a kingdom had received a setback; things were not going according to their pre-conceived ideas. Alone with His thoughts, the Lord walked ahead. Experience has taught the church that He always leads His flock as a shepherd leads the sheep. If there be danger ahead, He stands to guard us; if we need spiritual food, He leads into green pastures and beside still waters.

"And He took again the twelve and began to tell them what things should happen to Him" (v. 32). Perhaps it is unnecessary to seek the source of His knowledge, for He knew everything. During a later walk to Emmaus (Luke 24:25-27) the Lord said to two of His disciples, "O fools, and slow of heart to believe all that the prophets have spoken: Ought not Christ to have suffered these things, and to enter into His glory? *And beginning at Moses and all the prophets, He expounded unto them in all the scriptures the things concerning Himself.*" Understanding completely all the Scriptures said of the Messiah, He knew each detail of the events soon to take place, and was able to instruct His despondent followers. This was the third occasion for Him so to do. First, He had announced His rejection (Mark 8:31). Secondly, He announced His betrayal (Mark 9:31), and finally, He gave additional details and indicated He would die and rise again (Mark 10:33-34). Three things are worthy of consideration.

HIS GRACIOUS CONCERN

He was about to suffer as no man had ever suffered. He would endure excruciating agony, and this alone was sufficient to trouble His soul. Yet, in the midst of His problems, He still made time to instruct His followers; He still cared for them and was anxious to do everything possible to prevent overwhelming grief. He knew they had not fully comprehended what had been said on earlier occasions. Perhaps He was a little apprehensive about their reactions when they would see their world disintegrating. Love always thinks of others.

HIS GREAT COURAGE

He recognized the ferocity of the hatred awaiting Him in Jerusalem; He knew all that would befall Him, but He never turned back! He had said on one occasion, "No man, having put his hand to the plough, and looking back, is fit for the kingdom of God" (Luke 9:62). He practiced what He preached. In the light of this great fact, we do well to heed the advice offered in Hebrews 12:1-2: "Wherefore seeing we are encompassed about with so great a cloud of witnesses, let us lay aside every weight, and the sin which doth so easily beset us, and let us run with patience the race that is set before us, looking unto Jesus the author and finisher of our faith; who for the joy that was set before him, *endured the cross, despising the shame, and is set down at the right hand of the throne of God.*"

HIS GLORIOUS CONFIDENCE

"And they shall mock Him, and scourge Him . . . and shall kill Him: *and the third day He shall rise again*" (v. 34). As far as the Lord was concerned, the end was never in doubt. Perhaps He often recalled to mind what had happened to Joseph. Men placed the patriarch in the prison, but eventually the king brought him out and exalted him to his own right hand. Thus it would be with Jesus. Men and their sin would place the Lord in the darkness of the prison, but God, the King Eternal, would bring Him out and exalt Him to the right hand of the Majesty on High. He would be made a Prince and a Savior. The resurrection would shatter the power of death, enabling all true believers to say, "O death, where is thy sting? O grave, where is thy victory?" (1 Cor. 15:55).

SECTION FIVE

Expository Notes on the Strange Request of James and John

And James and John, the sons of Zebedee, come unto Him, saying, Master, we would that thou shouldest do for us whatsoever we shall desire. And He said unto them, What would ye that I should do for you? They said unto Him, Grant unto us that we may sit, one on thy right hand, and the other on thy left hand, in thy glory (vv. 35-37).

The Bible accounts of this statement contain two very important features. Matthew says: "Then came to Him the mother of Zebedee's children *with her sons*, worshipping Him, and desiring a certain thing of Him" (Matt. 20:20). Mark does not mention the mother. There is no contradiction in the varying versions. We are not told in whose mind the thought originated; maybe the woman desired the best for her sons and tried to obtain it. On the other hand, the ambitious sons might have been a little reluctant and asked the mother to make their request. Already James and John were recognized as being among the leading disciples; and since they had come from a well-to-do family in Galilee, they and their mother might have considered themselves to be worthy of promotion.

The other interesting feature concerns the time when the request was made. The Lord had just spoken of His forthcoming death and resurrection, and according to Matthew, had promised that His followers should sit on twelve thrones judging the tribes of Israel (Matt. 19:28). Were the disciples still thinking of His expelling the Romans in order to establish a kingdom? Had the Lord's words about His impending death fallen on deaf ears? On the other hand, had they heard and understood all that was predicted, and with rare faith were reassured by the fact that He would rise again and establish a better kingdom resplendent with the glory of God? The text suggests they were ambitious men trying to gain pre-eminence over others in their party. Their request was ill advised.

But Jesus said unto them, Ye know not what ye ask: can ye drink of the cup that I drink of? and be baptized with the baptism that I am baptized with? And they said unto Him, We can. And Jesus said unto them, Ye shall indeed drink of the cup that I drink of; and with the baptism that I am baptized withal shall ye be baptized; but to sit on my right hand and on my left hand is not mine to give; but it shall be given to them for whom it is prepared (vv. 38-40).

A REASONABLE REPLY

"Ye know not what ye ask. Can ye drink of the cup that I drink of?" (v. 38). "The figure is derived from the ancient custom, by which the ruler of the feast, tempered the wine according to his own will, and appointed to each guest his own portion, which was his duty to drink. Our Lord then proceeds to describe His own passion, which he had already spoken of as His cup; as His baptism. He uses this image because He would be totally buried, immersed, so to speak, in His own passion" (*The Pulpit Commentary*, Mark, p. 64). The term "the cup" means the experience which God permits, or "hands out," to men and women. The Psalmist in Psalm 75:8 says, "For in the hand of the Lord there is a cup." This illustrates the fate soon to befall the wicked, and those who resisted the will of God. When the Lord spoke of "His cup," He was referring to that experience which God would "hand out" to Him as He went to the appointed crucifixion. He was asking His followers if they could suffer as He would suffer; would they be able to die as He would die?

A READY RESPONSE

"And they said unto Him, We can" (v. 39). Was that an impetuous answer, or was it the expression of a determination never to leave their Lord? James truly proved that he was speaking the truth for he literally laid down his life for the Lord (see Acts 12:1-2). John also suffered many things, but he never turned back; he was faithful to the end. There seemed to be an outstanding enthusiasm about these men, and, although at times their remarks were not wise, none can ever doubt that James and John loved their Master immeasurably. Had James been permitted to live longer, his testimony would have thrilled the churches. Yet his courage in dying might have been more eloquent than any sermons he ever preached. John and James "drank of the Lord's cup" in different ways. John by living and James by death. Doubtless they both earned the commendation of their Lord. Nevertheless, the Savior emphasized that honor within the kingdom would depend upon the quality of service rendered in this life. Later He said, "Be thou faithful unto death, and I will give thee a crown of life" (Rev. 2:10).

A ROYAL REWARD

"It shall be given to them *for whom it is prepared*" (v. 40). The word-picture behind "the cup" suggested a wedding or feast to which many guests would be invited. The King would sit in splendor to survey those gathered with Him. "And many of them that sleep in the dust of the earth shall awake, some to everlasting life, and some to shame and everlasting contempt. And they that be wise shall shine as the brightness of the firmament; and they that turn many to righteousness as the stars for ever and ever" (Dan. 12:2-3). The Bible teaches that entrance into the kingdom depends upon faith in Christ; our status within the kingdom is something yet to be decided. The Lord said to the church at Philadelphia, "Behold, I come quickly; hold that fast which thou hast, *that no man take thy crown*" (Rev. 3:11).

And when the ten heard it, they began to be much displeased with James and John. But Jesus called them to Him, and saith unto them, Ye know

that they which are accounted to rule over the Gentiles exercise lordship over them; and their great ones exercise authority upon them. But so shall it not be among you: but whosoever will be great among you, shall be your minister; and whosoever of you will be the chiefest, shall be servant of all. For even the Son of man came not to be ministered unto, but to minister, and to give His life a ransom for many (vv. 41-45).

A DANGEROUS SITUATION

"And the ten. . . began to be much displeased with James and John" (v. 41). The Greek word translated displeased is *aganaktein*, and according to Thayer has two root meanings. (1) To feel pain, and (2) to be indignant. When the Lord perceived the trouble brewing among the disciples, He was hurt; there was pain deep within Him, and that distress begat acute disappointment. The men into whose hands He was entrusting the future of His cause were quarreling among themselves. How could they bring peace to a troubled world when they were incapable of knowing peace within their own fellowship? Something had to be done immediately for a small spark of fiery dissension might lead to a disastrous conflagration. The dominant James and John could become belligerent, and would defend what they had done, even though they knew they were wrong. If Simon Peter's temper were aroused, he might even lift his hands in anger. The outlook was bleak and very stormy; the future was at stake; and as He contemplated the possibilities of a terrible quarrel among His followers, the Lord felt pain within His soul. Had they been with Him so long and learned nothing? Had they heard so much and yet remained ignorant? There was danger of a bushfire; He had to extinguish the blaze before things got out of hand.

A DISCERNING SAVIOR

". . .they which. . .rule over the Gentiles exercise lordship. . .But so shall it not be among you" (vv. 42, 43). In every age, men sought power. Hitler became a despot because he desired international dominance. Stalin and the Russians planned world conquest, because they coveted superiority, and were willing to sacrifice anything to get it. Politicians promise many things to constituents because votes can bring prestige and a seat in congress. Alas, so often, the promises are quickly forgotten. Money begets greed for more money; power begets desire for more power, and even decent men may become despots in their efforts to increase their authority. A man without ambition is often a bore, but a man controlled ruthlessly by his lust for importance becomes a menace. There is no harm in an employee wishing to become a director of his firm, but if he resorts to criminal acts to further his cause, he destroys all that is best in human nature. "It shall not be so among you."

A DELIGHTFUL SERMON

"Whosoever shall be great among you, shall be your minister" (v. 43). The Lord seemed to say "If you wish to control the firm, learn to understand the problems of the office boy! If you wish to become a millionaire, learn the value of a few cents! If you wish to build skyscrapers, first learn how to lay bricks! The man who knows everything has lived too long! If you wish to become great, practice, in spirit at least, how to be content being nothing! "For even the Son of man came not to be ministered unto, but to minister. I have not asked you to wash my feet; I have washed your feet. I have not insisted on your preparing my meals; I have blessed the loaves and fishes and fed you and the multitudes. There is joy in serving others. If you wish people to respect and think highly of you, then make them feel you love them. The way up is the way that first goes down, and a man is never taller than when he is on his knees. As I have been, you must be, for I have come to minister and to give my life a ransom for many." "This is the first distinct utterance, we may note, of the plan and method of His work. He had spoken before of 'saving' the lost (Matt. 18:11); now He declares that the work of 'salvation' was to be also one of 'redemption.' It could only be accomplished by the payment of a price, and that price was His own life" (Plumptre).

Throughout the existence of the church men have asked foolish questions regarding the identity of the one to whom the ransom price was paid. We know that man "was sold under sin;" we know that man needed redemption. Within the universe of God are important laws known to, and honored by angels. God is just and holy, and sin of any kind is an abomination in His eyes. Man violated the laws of God and was thereby condemned. When the Lord took our sins to the Cross, He bared His soul to the outpouring of judgment which should have been ours. Thus He demonstrated before all witnesses, both in this world, and the one to come, that the price of redemption had been paid. The resultant offer of salvation to sinners was not primarily based on the mercy of God, great as that was, but rather on the righteousness of God. Even God could not withhold salvation from anyone who came believing in the Redeemer. Therefore, as Jesus was willing to sacrifice Himself for the benefit of even the most undeserving sinners, the disciples should count it an inestimable privilege to do any kind of service for any kind of person. That was to be the basic law of God's kingdom, and the tone of His voice and the manner in which He spoke, made the disciples understand, He meant exactly what He said. We should listen and learn very carefully.

SECTION SIX

Expository Notes on Christ's Meeting With Blind Bartimaeus

And they came to Jericho; and as they went out of Jericho with His disciples and a great number of people, blind Bartimaeus, the son of Timaeus, sat by the highway begging. And when he heard that it was Jesus of Nazareth, he began to cry out, and say, Jesus, thou Son of David, have mercy on me. And many charged him that he should hold his peace; but he cried the more a great deal, Thou Son of David, have mercy on me (vv. 46-48).

"The upland pastures of Peraea were now behind them, and the road led down through the sunken channel of the Jordan, and the 'divine' district of Jericho. This small but rich plain was the most luxuriant spot in Palestine. Sloping gently upwards from the level of the Dead Sea . . . it had the climate of lower Egypt, and displayed the vegetation of the tropics. Its fig trees were pre-eminently famous; it was unique in its growth of palms of many kinds; its crops of dates were a proverb. The balsam plant furnished a costly perfume, and was in great repute for healing wounds. Maize yielded a double harvest, wheat ripened a whole month earlier than in Galilee, and innumerable bees found a paradise in its many aromatic flowers and plants. . . Rising like an amphitheatre from amidst this luxuriant scene lay Jericho, the chief place east of Jerusalem, seven or eight miles distant from the Jordan. . . Once the stronghold of the Canaanites, it was still, in the days of Christ, surrounded by towers and castles. A great stone acqueduct of eleven arches brought a copious supply of water . . ., and the Roman military road ran through the city" (condensed from Dr. Geikie's, *The Life of Christ*, Vol. II, p. 384).

A great number of priests lived in this beautiful city, and whenever they were not on duty in the Temple, they enjoyed the balmy weather and resplendent surroundings of the elegant city. At the time of Christ's visit, vast crowds would have been thronging the area, for, according to the Mosaic law, every person able to attend the Passover was obligated to do so. Those who were unable to obey the command, seized the opportunity to gather in the streets to watch pilgrims passing through on their journey. When Jesus passed through Jericho, He would have been recognized and afforded the same welcome given to any distinguished rabbi.

A comparison of the Gospel accounts of this visit provides problems which theologians have been unable to solve. Matthew 20:29-34 indicates that *two beggars* met Him as He was *leaving* the city. Luke 18:35 suggests that *one beggar* met Him as He was *entering* the place. Mark 10:46 tells us that one man, Bartimaeus, met Him as He was *leaving* Jericho. All three writers of the Gospels agree the man or men sat alongside the highway; that was logical, for beggars would sit where travelers would see them. Were Matthew, Mark, and Luke thinking of a special place from which measurements were taken? Today we think of a central point in a community; when we are entering, we come to it; when we are exiting, we leave it? If that were the case, all three accounts could be descriptions of what happened within a few yards of entering and leaving Jericho. Was there a kind of circular route by which travelers could avoid the narrow streets and the jostling crowds of merchants anxious to sell their wares? If so, there might have been an entrance gate half way around the wall where people could enter the city at some special point. This was certainly the case in Jerusalem where there were many gates. We are not told if this were the case in Jericho, but *if it were*, no problem would arise from the apparently conflicting records of the three Gospels. It is not quite so easy to reconcile the accounts in regard to the number of beggars to whom Christ gave sight. It is, however, interesting that a similar situation may be found in regard to the demoniacs who were delivered when Christ visited the land of the Gadarenes. Compare the one man of Luke 8:27 with the two men of Matthew 8:28. That they used the same approach, ''Thou Son of David'' occasions no difficulty. If indeed there were two men, one could have heard the other asking for help, and, emulating his example, could have made an identical appeal. Probably there is not a great deal of importance in the different renderings for Matthew, the book-man, might have been exact in his description, whereas Mark and Luke were content just to mention the one beggar. Furthermore, who can tell whether or not the Lord allowed this seeming contradiction in the narratives. Maybe He meant us to consider that He is able to help one or two or three or even a thousand beggars, if they have enough wisdom to solicit His aid.

It is interesting to recognize that although the beggar was told, "Jesus of Nazareth" was passing by, he addressed Him as "Jesus, thou Son of David." There was great difference between the two titles. The Lord's enemies spoke with disdain and derision when they referred to Jesus as "The Nazarene." They believed that no good thing could come out of Nazareth. The title, "The Son of David" enshrined everything of value among the traditions of the nation. It spoke of royalty and respect, and suggested the Messiah had come!

The Amplified New Testament renders the parallel passage from Luke 18:39, "They told him, Jesus of Nazareth is passing by. And he shouted saying, Jesus, Son of David, take pity and have mercy on me. But those that were in the front, reproved him, telling him to keep quiet; yet he screamed and shrieked so much the more, Son of David, take pity, and have mercy on me." "This translation rests upon the fact that Luke uses two different words. *Eboeesen*, translated "shout" or "he cried," means "to lift up one's voice and cry aloud." *Ekrazen*, the word used in verse 39, and translated "he cried so much the more" is a much stronger word. Thayer says it means "to cry out; to cry aloud, to vociferate particularly of inarticulate cries." It is also used to express "a croak," hence "a scream" or "desperate screech." It suggests "the croak of a frog." The first cry of the blind beggar was born of intense desire; the second by deepening despair. The first was produced by a longing for help; the second by the fear that he might be too late to get what he wanted" (condensed from the author's commentary, *Luke's Thrilling Gospel*, p. 391).

And Jesus stood still, and commanded him to be called. And they call the blind man, saying unto him, Be of good comfort, rise; He calleth thee. And he, casting away his garment, rose and came to Jesus. And Jesus answered and said unto him, What wilt thou that I shall do unto thee? The blind man said unto Him, Lord, that I might receive my sight. And Jesus said unto him, Go thy way; thy faith hath made thee whole. And immediately he received his sight, and followed Jesus in the way (vv. 49-52).

A COMPLETE ATTENTION

"And Jesus stood still" (v. 49). That day was perhaps the most exciting one in the history of Jericho. Many pilgrims were passing through on their way to Jerusalem. Hawkers would be shouting to attract possible buyers for their wares. Others were arguing in an attempt to get traders to lower their prices. Any rabbi or learned man on the journey would be teaching as he walked, and the noise was continuous. Jesus also was teaching; disciples and others were asking questions, when suddenly, abruptly, the Lord stopped. They watched as He turned and were amazed when He said, "Tell him to come." They could be excused if they had asked, "Master, whom do you wish called?" Probably most of the people close to Christ were not even aware of the appeal for help. Yet Jesus heard it, and the beggar's cry brought Him to a halt. There is reason to believe that even if Christ were creating another world, the cry of a needy soul would cause a temporary postponement in the operation. A similar thing had happened with the woman who touched the hem of Christ's garment. It is thrilling to remember that He is never too busy to listen to the appeal of a suppliant.

A CROWD'S ASSISTANCE

"And many charged him that he should hold his peace" (v. 48). It does not say they *all* did so. However hostile the company may appear; however difficult the circumstances may seem, there are always people ready to help. Elijah despondently said, "I, only I am left" yet his conclusions were wrong. God told him there were still thousands of friends left in Israel. Crowds may be noisy, but the adage declares, "Empty barrels make the most sound. Always, not very far away, are strangers waiting to become the messengers of the Lord. The man standing in the darkness heard voices saying, "Be of good comfort, rise; He calleth thee." We may not possess the power to heal broken hearts, but at least, we can be instruments by which others may be brought to Christ. The Lord can do all kinds of marvelous things when we decide to help Him.

A CURIOUS ABANDONMENT

"And he, casting away his garment, rose, and came to Jesus" (v. 50). The word translated "garment" is *himation* and this signifies "a cloak; an outer garment; something thrown over a tunic." Beggars were generally so poor that the only clothing they possessed had been found in a refuse area. Why then did the beggar throw away something which to him at least was an article of value? Probably he never saw that garment again; other beggars claimed it. The blind man recognized that in this particular matter, his cloak could become a hindrance; it might trip him as he hurried toward his Benefactor. He had no wish to fall flat on his face, so with rare abandon he made absolutely sure the hindrance was removed before it had the chance to do damage. He had some sight after all, but it emanated from his soul and not his eyes. There was another man, a very rich man, whose cloak was made of riches; alas, he did not throw it away, and it became such a hindrance that, seemingly, he remained in his darkness for ever. What is the cloak which might be hindering our progress?

A CHARMING ANSWER

"Go thy way; thy faith hath made thee whole. And immediately he received his sight, and followed Jesus in the way" (v. 50). Peter never forgot that thrilling incident, and it is not surprising that when he saw John Mark writing notes concerning Jesus, the great apostle said, "Son, put this into your story." Christ always responds to the cry of faith, but alas, some recipients of His grace refrain from becoming disciples. The Lord had much more to give to the suppliant, but not even Jesus could have shared the additional blessings had the beggar decided to stay away. The man might have gone anywhere: to his home, to meet his family, to see his friends, to buy another cloak! No! He was very wise. He had discovered a goldmine, and had no wish to pick daisies! The tragedy of modern evangelism seems to be that everybody wants something for nothing; but very few live to render real service to Him from Whom they received so much.

The man in this story had rare eyesight, even before he met Jesus. (1) He saw that his greatest need was to meet Christ. (2) When he heard that Jesus of Nazareth was passing by, he saw that his greatest opportunity had arrived. (3) When the people standing by told him to be quiet, he saw that he could not afford to remain silent. This could be his last opportunity — and it was. Christ was on His way to Jerusalem, and He never returned to Jericho. (4) When Christ told him to "go thy way" he refused to obey, choosing rather to follow Jesus *in His way*. Christ's way is always better than ours (condensed from "The Man Who Could See Without Eyes, the author's commentary, *Luke's Thrilling Gospel*, pp. 392-394).

The Eleventh Chapter of Mark

THEME: *Jesus Comes to Jerusalem*

OUTLINE:
  I. Christ and the Docile Colt (Verses 1-10)
  II. Christ and His Deadly Curse (Verses 11-14, 20-22)
  III. Christ and His Dramatic Cleansing (Verses 15-19)
  IV. Christ and His Disturbing Comments (Verses 22-26)
  V. Christ and His Deliberate Carefulness (Verses 27-33)

SECTION ONE

Expository Notes on Christ's Entry Into Jerusalem

And when they came nigh to Jerusalem, unto Bethphage and Bethany, at the mount of Olives, He sendeth forth two of His disciples, and saith unto them, Go your way into the village over against you; and as soon as ye be entered into it, ye shall find a colt tied, whereon never man sat; loose him, and bring him. And if any man say unto you, Why do ye this? say ye that the Lord hath need of him; and straightway he will send him hither (vv. 1-3).

It would appear from Mark's Gospel that this was the Savior's first visit to Jerusalem, but that is not true. To obtain a complete understanding of the story, it is necessary to read and compare all the accounts in the synoptic Gospels. Jesus left the main body of pilgrims somewhere along the Jericho road, and as they proceeded to Jerusalem, He and His disciples went to Bethany to stay overnight. During that short visit, He had supper in the house of Simon the leper, and the following day, proceeded toward Jerusalem. ''The site of Bethany is well known, but the place and importance of Bethphage are obscure. It has been said that Bethphage was a suburb of Jerusalem; that it was a convenient extension to the sacred precincts of the city; an extension made necessary by the ever-increasing number of pilgrims who came to the feasts. There were legal requirements which demanded that worshippers should be housed within the camp — the city, but when this became an impossibility, something had to be done to remedy the situation. The priests therefore, or so it has been claimed, *sanctified* that portion of land which stretched out from the city walls toward the Mount of Olives. This was known as Bethphage. Bethany itself was only two miles from Jerusalem, and therefore it should be easily understood why the two places appear together in the sacred record'' (quoted from the author's commentary, *Luke's Thrilling Gospel*, p. 406). It has been estimated from ancient records that the number of people attending this feast would have been in excess of three million, and Jerusalem was unable to accommodate that number. Hence, many of the pilgrims would need accommodation outside the immediate city, and it was for that reason, the priests *sanctified* the additional territory.

To appreciate the full significance of Christ's entry into the city, it is necessary to visualize what was taking place. Many pilgrims were already there, and every street was crowded to capacity. People had traveled great distances, and probably had heard strange and wonderful stories about the new Prophet. Naturally, they would wish to see Him, if that were possible. The city itself had put on its finery; shopkeepers were eager for trade, and possibly flags were flying everywhere. This had always been the greatest event in the year, and the present feast promised to surpass anything ever known. It was common knowledge that the Scribes and Pharisees were determined to accuse the Prophet, and at least imprison Him. It was freely said in the market place, that plans had been made whereby He might even be crucified. To say the least, the future promised to be exciting!

THE STRANGE COMMAND. . .Preparing

'' . . .ye shall find a colt tied, whereon never man sat; loose him, and bring him'' (v. 2). Dr. William Barclay thinks this had been prearranged by the Lord during an earlier visit to the city. The Lord had many friends in the neighborhood, and if Barclay's suggestion is correct, then Jesus had privately warned one of them of what eventually would take place. The man was willing to help in any way possible, but to prevent his animal from being stolen, had arranged a password by which the identity of the men to be sent, would be recognized. ''The Lord hath need of him,'' the words quoted in all the synoptic versions, must have been prearranged between Jesus and that unknown friend. Matthew states there were two animals, an ass and her colt (Matt. 21:2). Luke apparently agrees with Mark mentioning only one. There is no real conflict here as it would be perfectly normal for the mother to be accompanied by her offspring; furthermore the presence of the donkey would help to calm the colt which had never been tamed.

The fact that Jesus wished to ride the colt, in itself, was suggestive. Throughout His entire ministry the Lord had walked from place to place; this was the first occasion when He rode, and the privilege of carrying Him was given to a donkey.

THE DONKEY'S TESTIMONY

When fishes flew and forests walked
and figs grew upon thorn;
Some moment when the moon was blood,
Then surely I was born.

With monstrous head and sickening cry
And ears like errant wings,
The devil's walking parody
Of all four-footed things.

The tattered outlaw of the earth
Of ancient crooked will;
Starve, scourge, deride me, I am dumb
I keep my secret still.

Fools! For I also had my hour,
One far fierce hour and sweet;
There was a shout about my ears,
And palms before my feet.

G. K. Chesterton

The fact that He rode upon the young donkey was interesting. Formerly He had given strict instructions that testimony concerning His greatness and exploits should be suppressed. He had forbidden disciples and others to spread news which might incite rebellion. Now the Lord had changed. His choosing to ride upon the ass was the fulfillment of the Messianic prediction in Zechariah 9:9. "Rejoice greatly, O daughter of Zion; shout, O daughter of Jerusalem: behold, *THY KING COMETH UNTO THEE:* He is just and having salvation; lowly, *and riding upon an ass*, and upon a colt, the foal of an ass.'' There was no more need for silence; for all who had ears to hear and eyes to see, this was a deliberate declaration of His Kingship. He was the Messiah; the fulfillment of all the prophets had spoken. When kings went into battle, *they rode upon horses*! Men of peace rode upon white asses (see Judges 5:10, 10:4, and 12:14). It was being made perfectly clear that THIS KING OF ISRAEL was not going to war; He was riding in peace, hoping to bring harmony to a troubled world. Outside Jerusalem was a city of tents where pilgrims had made temporary homes. When the news arrived announcing the nearness of Jesus, an immense throng went out to meet Him. Eagerness was upon each face; excitement filled every heart. This was a day to be remembered!

THE SUBDUED COLT. . .Permitting

"A colt tied, whereon never man sat!'' (v. 2). There appears to be something strange and mysterious about this statement. Its type of message may be found throughout the Scriptures. The command enunciated in Numbers 19:2 said, '' . . . Speak unto the children of Israel, that they bring thee a red heifer without spot, wherein is no blemish, and upon which *never came yoke*.'' This instruction was reiterated in Deuteronomy 21:3. Furthermore, when David contemplated returning the ark to its place in Jerusalem, he was told, "Now therefore make a new cart, and take two milch kine [cows], *on which there hath come no yoke*, and tie the kine to the cart, and bring their calves home from them: . . .'' Articles used in the service of God had to be set apart; they had to be free from defilement of any kind. Yet there is more in the text. An unbroken colt can become a nightmare to any rider. Its arching back, twisting rebellious body, and kicking feet can present problems hard to solve. An inexperienced rider is likely to land in the dust! Skilled in the art of breaking and training animals, cowboys can tame such beasts, but even they have to conquer their unruly steeds. It is significant that this lowly donkey never rebelled; he never put up a fight. Compare that with the strange command already quoted from 1 Samuel 6:7, and the subject becomes exceedingly interesting. When calves are first taken from their mothers, they create a great commotion, and may be heard all over the area. When a calf cries, instinctively the mother cow responds by going to its aid. Yet this never happened with those drawing David's cart. "And the kine took the straight way to the way of Bethshemesh, and went along the highway, lowing as they went, and turned not aside to the right hand nor to the left. . . '' Even the pitiful cries of their calves could not turn them from the important task of serving the Most High God. When we also consider how Balaam's ass rebuked its master, we are compelled to believe that sometimes animals have more brains than their owners!

And they went their way, and found the colt tied by the door without in a place where two ways met; and they loosed him. And certain of them that stood there said unto them, What do ye, loosing the colt? And they said unto them even as Jesus had commanded; and they let them go. And they brought the colt to Jesus, and cast their garments on him; and He sat upon him. And many spread their garments in the way; and others cut down branches off the trees, and strewed them in the way. And they that went before, and they that followed, cried saying, Hosanna; Blessed is He that cometh in the name of the Lord: Blessed be the kingdom of our father David, that cometh in the name of the Lord: Hosanna in the highest (vv. 4-10).

The Greek word translated "where two ways met" is *amphodou* and means "a road around anything; a street" (Thayer). The instructions were clear and concise. The young animal would be tethered to a door, or near to the door of a corner house. There would be two streets, and the animal would be seen as they were about to go around the corner into the next street. The text suggests this arrangement had been made earlier when the Lord spoke with the owner of the donkey. The Lord also knew that men would be conversing near the spot, and so gave explicit instructions what should be said if the bystanders questioned the actions of the disciples. Even though Jesus had arranged for the use of the donkey, He also knew a group of men would be there to witness the act.

THE SHOUTING CROWD. . .Praying

The situation seemed on the verge of becoming uncontrollable. People were pressing from all sides, and the disciples were experiencing difficulty protecting their Master. Yet they were thrilled also, for with so many ardent supporters, anything could happen. The Kingdom was at hand! From thousands of throats the cry arose: "Hosanna. . .Blessed be the kingdom of our father David." It cannot be stressed too much that the term *Hosanna* does not mean what many people think it does. This was an appeal for deliverance. Hosanna means "Save us." The people, overwhelmed by their enthusiasm, cheered lustily for their new Champion, and shouted their prayer, "Save us now." They fully expected God to intervene in some extraordinary way; to rend the heavens, so to speak, and descend in mighty power to annihilate the Romans. If this Jesus were the Messiah, then He would be the Captain of the Hosts of God. Their dreams were about to come true; their deliverance was at hand. "Hosanna, Hosanna, Hosanna." Thus did they shout, and their cry echoed throughout the city. Poor, stupid, misguided people! Had their desires been granted, by nightfall their bodies would have been in the city morgues. When Jesus heard their appeal and looked over the city, the sight broke His heart — He wept (see the homily at the end of Chapter Nine, *The Faces of Jesus*).

SECTION TWO

Expository Notes on the Cursing of the Fig Tree

And Jesus entered into Jerusalem, and into the temple; and when He had looked round about upon all things, and now the eventide was come, He went out unto Bethany with the twelve. And on the morrow when they were come from Bethany, He was hungry. And seeing a fig tree afar off having leaves, He came, if haply He might find anything thereon; and when He came to it, He found nothing but leaves; for the time of figs was not yet. And Jesus answered and said unto it, No man eat fruit of thee hereafter forever. And His disciples heard it (vv. 11-14).

The Lord was very calm, methodical and deliberate as He entered both the city and the temple. Aware of the conflict to commence the next day, He was surveying the battle-ground. Things were happening within the temple area which were an insult to the name of God. Jesus knew He would be obliged to take action against those who were responsible for the evil deeds. Having looked at the despicable scene, He returned to the vicinity of Bethany, but apparently chose not to stay with His friends. Some expositors think He stayed two days, and that during this time, He not only visited Martha, Mary, and Lazarus, but also enjoyed a supper in the home of Simon the leper. If this were so, He would have had sufficient time in which to do this. However, it appears that at least for the final night, Jesus did not sleep in the home of His friends. Probably He spent those hours in prayer and fasting, gleaning the strength which would be necessary to challenge the religious authorities within the temple. It is written that "He was hungry." Obviously, Martha had not supplied breakfast that morning!

AN UNWARRANTED ASSUMPTION

We are now to consider, what to many people is the most complex, the most difficult of all the Bible stories. The following morning as the Lord walked toward Jerusalem, He saw a fig tree alongside the road, and expecting to find figs, drew near in search of food. When He discovered that the tree only had leaves, the Lord placed a curse on it, and immediately the tree began to die. Some critics accused the Lord of being impatient; moody to the point of being embittered, and completely unfair in the cursing of the fig tree. This, they affirm, is obvious, for it has been written, "the time of figs was not yet." That means, so they say, the Lord was expecting figs out of season; at a time when it was impossible for the tree to be bearing its fruit. That interpretation is false, misleading and inexcusable. Let us explore the facts related to this strange story.

"In the East the fig tree produces two definite crops of figs per season. The normal winter figs ripen in May and June, and the summer figs in August and September. Sometimes the crops overlap. The baby fig buds are generally seen in February before the leaves appear in April each year. It is possible to pick figs over nine or ten months of the year in Israel. . .Our Lord condemned the fig tree at Passover time (April). This tree should have borne early, ripe figs. The Lord would have known whether the tree should have been cropping. Moses had said that fruit on trees by the wayside could be picked by passers by. A fig tree produces masses of large green leaves and gives ample welcome shade in a hot country" (W. E. Shewell-Cooper, *The Zondervan Pictorial Encyclopedia of the Bible*, Volume two, p. 534).

"This fig tree had leaves, but no fruit, for it was not the season of fruit. Other trees would be bare at this early season, but the fig trees would be putting forth their broad green leaves. It is possible that this tree, standing by itself as it would seem, was more forward than the other trees around. It was seen from afar and therefore it must have had the full benefit of the sun. . .But then it is peculiar to the fig tree that its fruit begins to appear before its leaves. It was therefore a natural supposition that on this tree, with its leaves fully developed, there might be found at least some ripened fruit. . .The leaves of this fig tree deceived the passer by, who, from seeing them, would naturally expect the fruit. And so the fig tree was cursed, not for being barren, but for being false" (*The Pulpit Commentary, Mark*, p. 121). The statement "for the time

of figs was not yet" can only mean "for the time of fruit gathering
or the time of harvest, was not yet." It will be seen, therefore, that
criticism of this incident was unjust and uninformed.

AN UNPARALLELED ANNOUNCEMENT

"And Jesus answered and said, unto it, No man eat fruit of thee
hereafter for ever" (v. 14). The possibility exists that this fig tree was
wild, growing alongside the road, and that it had been neglected. It
professed to be able to feed people, but in reality, it could not do so.
Let it be remembered this incident took place between the evening visit
to the temple, and the subsequent driving out of the money changers
(see Matt. 21:12-14). Within the temple courts, Christ had seen a false
profession; the place in which souls were supposed to be fed had become
a center in which they were robbed. Instead of a sweet-smelling savour
ascending before the Mercy Seat, there was the stench of animals'
excrement. The sanctuary had become the very opposite of what God
intended, and this realization deeply disturbed the Savior. Had He not
been sorrowfully indignant, Heaven would have been shamed. What
He had seen in the temple, He was seeing again in the fig tree; something
which could have been invaluable had become worthless. His words
to the tree indicated what He planned to say and do in the House of
God. "Coming events were casting their shadows before."

AN UNEXPECTED ASSERTION

**And in the morning as they passed by, they saw the fig tree dried up
from the roots. And Peter calling to remembrance saith unto Him,
Master, behold, the fig tree which thou cursedst is withered away. And
Jesus answering sayeth unto them, Have faith in God. For verily I say
unto you, That whosoever shall say unto this mountain, Be thou removed, and be thou cast into the sea; and shall not doubt in his heart,
but shall believe that those things which he saith shall come to pass;
he shall have whatever he saith. Therefore I say unto you, What things
soever ye desire, when ye pray, believe that ye receive them, and ye
shall have them (vv. 20-24).**

The Lord cursed the fig tree the day after His triumphant entry into
Jerusalem. Then He entered into the temple precincts to drive out the
money changers, and that evening He returned to Bethany. The following

morning as He went back to Jerusalem, the disciples were able to see what had happened to the tree. With increasing interest and amazement, they looked at the sad sight, but they were even more surprised when the Lord spoke about the invincibility of faith. They were standing on the Mount of Olives when He mentioned the possibility of moving the mountain into the sea. If there be any difficulty in this scripture, it is not with His cursing the fig tree but rather in His message concerning the omnipotent power of prayer. No one has ever prayed and then watched a real mountain miraculously moving! When men need to shift mountains, they use bulldozers! What then was Christ trying to teach? His discourse about prayer may be divided into three sections.

CONFIDENCE

"Have faith in God...believe...do not doubt in your heart" (vv. 22, 23). The Lord was aware of the events soon to shatter the happiness of His followers; He knew their souls would reel from the heavy blows circumstances were about to deal. His death would shatter their preconceived notions and leave them utterly desolate. They would need real faith during the trying days about to come. Their fear, doubt, and helplessness, would outweigh a thousand mountains. There would never be need to remove Olivet, but the removing of their own individual mountain of problems would soon be a necessity. Jesus was stressing the advisability of having faith in God. This would bring them safely through the difficult storms about to break upon their souls.

COURAGE

"Whatever things ye desire, when ye pray, believe, believe, believe" (v. 24). Keep on keeping on, for sometimes God's answer may appear to be late in arriving. "Verily I say unto you that whosoever...shall not doubt in his heart." Did the disciples understand the motive for His speaking these words? We may never know, but He saw clearly the severe testings which would lead to the tragedy expressed later in Mark's gospel, "And they all forsook Him and fled." To believe that God has ceased to care for us; that He may never forgive what we have done, is the prelude to continuing disaster. Perhaps the poet captured the sentiments of the Lord when he wrote:

> Never a trial that He is not there
> Never a burden that He doth not bear,
> Never a sorrow that He doth not share,
> Moment by moment I'm under His care.
>
> Never a heart ache, and never a groan,
> Never a tear drop and never a moan,
> Never a danger, but there on the throne,
> Moment by moment, He thinks of His own.

To remember these precious truths is to have an immovable anchor in every storm of life. Have courage!

CLEANLINESS

Although there is evidence that some of these verses do not belong chronologically to this story, their place in the record is at least understandable. As we have considered, certain statements made by the Lord remained in Peter's mind, and occasionally, something would revive his memories. This usually led to additions in Mark's manuscript. On the other hand, the Lord could have uttered His words at the time indicated, for in thinking of an unclean temple, it would be easy to think also of an unclean heart. To harbor an unforgiving spirit would defeat the entire purpose of praying. The instructions given in Matthew 5:23-24 were very explicit. No man can truly approach the Mercy Seat unless he too is merciful. No suppliant has a right to expect forgiveness unless he is willing to dispense it. The Lord cleansed the temple in Jerusalem; it is our duty to cleanse the sanctuary within our own souls.

SECTION THREE

Expository Notes on the Cleansing of the Temple

And they come to Jerusalem: and Jesus went into the temple, and began to cast out them that sold and bought in the temple, and overthrew the tables of the money changers, and the seats of them that sold doves; and would not suffer that any man should carry any vessel through the temple. And He taught saying unto them, Is it not written, My house shall be called of all nations, the house of prayer? but ye have made it a den of thieves. And the scribes and chief priests heard it, and sought how they might destroy Him: for they feared Him, because all the people were astonished at His doctrine (vv. 15-18).

A SERIOUS CONDITION

To understand this scripture, and to appreciate the indignation of the Lord, it is essential to know what was taking place within the temple courtyards. At the beginning of His ministry, Jesus cleansed the temple, but apparently the lesson taught then had been forgotten (see John 2:13-17). The men who had been expelled, soon returned to exploit worshippers who needed to change money. Unfortunately the part known as the court of the Gentiles had become a market. The rabbinical records refer to "the booths of the son of Hanan or Annas." The High Priest possessed a very lucrative business, and in his employ were many "temple inspectors" who ruthlessly cheated customers. For example, the law of Moses insisted that offerings be brought to the sanctuary, and these varied in value. Wealthy people such as land owners could bring a bullock; less wealthy folk could offer a lamb, and the poor could offer turtledoves. All these offerings could be purchased outside the city at a fraction of what they cost within the temple precincts. Let's use American currency to illustrate. A pair of doves could have been purchased in the city for five cents. However, the offerings would have been rejected by the inspector who always declared them to be imperfect. The doves would then be confiscated, and sold to another customer for four dollars, or 80 times the original cost. This was outrageous, but when we remember this only applied to the selling of doves, it is easy to understand the extortion practiced by men who were supposed to be the servants of the Most High God. Some of the ill-gotten gains were used for varying purposes, such as the repair of temple roads, the upkeep of the buildings, etc.; but when all costs had been paid, the High Priest made millions of dollars for himself. Every man, according to the law, was required to present one half shekel of silver as "atonement money." The priests insisted that this be paid near to Passover time.

The money could be paid in booths which were set up in the villages about a month before. After a certain date, however, it could be paid only in the temple itself. As the majority of the pilgrims came from other countries, they were able to pay the tax in certain currencies that were equally accepted in Palestine. It could not, however, be paid in ingots of silver but only stamped currency, nor could it be paid in coins of inferior alloy, but only of high quality silver. It could be paid in shekels of the sanctuary, in Galilean half-shekels, and especially Tyrian currency which was of a high standard. The duty of the moneychangers was to exchange unsuitable currencies into the correct ones. All this was very proper and appeared to be justified, but the moneychangers charged exorbitant prices for their services. If they had to give change, they doubled their fee, and as a result, the offering of the Lord became obnoxious to all who visited the temple. History speaks of a certain Rabbi Simon ben Gamaliel who denounced these practices and became famous because "he insisted that doves be sold for silver coins instead of gold coins."

Conditions within the temple courts had deteriorated to such an extent that almost every priest had become a trader. Passover time was anticipated with great delight, not because it offered the opportunity for fellowship and worship, but rather for the exploitation of thousands of worshippers. Tethered to the walls of the courtyard were animals whose odor defiled the sanctuary. People argued about prices; the noise was continuous, and the whole scene sufficient to make a sincere worshipper sick in his soul. It was to such a place that Jesus came, and the fact that indignation filled His soul was not surprising. Jerome, the ancient writer said, "A fiery splendor flashed from His eyes, and the Majesty of Deity shone in His countenance." Again let it be remembered that this was the second occasion on which He had cleansed the temple. He cleansed it, but afterward it was the duty of the priests to keep it clean. They had failed in their task. Paul emphasized that we are the temple of God and that the Holy Spirit dwells within us (see 1 Cor. 3:16). Christ made us clean, but it remains our duty to maintain the purity of His sanctuary.

A SHORT CUT

"And He would not suffer that any man should carry any vessel through the temple" (v. 16). The court of the Gentiles was long and awkward for any person who wished to travel from the sheep market into the upper part of the city. There was a much shorter route, but it went through this court and out through Solomon's porch. The priests permitted pedestrians to take this short cut, especially if they were carrying heavy parcels. At first, this seemed wise and beneficial, but the permission had encouraged people to make the route a thoroughfare along which went all kinds of traffic. The sanctity of the area had been completely ruined, and the short cut resembled a road to a stadium. That Jesus restrained people; that He pushed them back, is thought-provoking. How could He accomplish this feat when there were so many people involved? Maybe "the flashing eyes, and majestic countenance," mentioned by Jerome, supplies the answer. The incident begets a question. Are there not others who make the church a short cut to riches, popularity, political gain, and many other things? I knew an Undertaker in Britain who attended the largest church in his area, because business was likely to be better there than in a smaller church. I have known politicians who were ardent church-attenders prior to an election, but in some strange fashion they soon became too busy to attend any service. I knew a Bank Manager who was transferred to a new area. The local people were thrilled because in their small assembly the addition of that man to the membership roll could be of significant importance. Alas, he joined the largest church in the city. At least he was honest, for he admitted he needed the prestige of belonging to an important church in the community. He used his new religion as a short cut to the place of eminence he so much desired.

A SUBLIME CONFESSION

"And He taught, saying unto them, Is it not written, My house shall be called the house of prayer for all nations?" (v. 17). Perhaps there is significance in the fact that these words were spoken in the court of the Gentiles. The temple authorities had very strict rules governing the conduct of Gentiles within the sacred area. They were only permitted to go so far; if they went further, the penalty was death. The temple was one of the outstanding sights to be seen anywhere in the world, and all tourists wanted to see its architectural beauty. Gentiles were watched every moment, for ecclesiastical laws had no elasticity. The literal translation of the text says it was a House of Prayer for *all nations* — not merely for Jews. Why then had the custodians of the place erected barriers to exclude others whom God loved? The love of God knows no racial barriers. It was not the pigmentation of the skin, nor the pride of race that pleased God. The sacrifices most appreciated by the Almighty were a broken heart and a contrite spirit. When the Lord added, "Ye have made it a den of thieves," He was doubtless referring to the message given by Jeremiah. "And come and stand before me in this house, which is called by my name, and say, We are delivered to do all these abominations. Is this house which is called by my name, become a den of robbers in your eyes? Behold, even I have seen it, saith the Lord" (Jer. 7:10-11). Isaiah had written: "Even them will I bring to my holy mountain, and make them joyful in my house of prayer. . . for mine house shall be called a house of prayer *for all people*" (Isa. 56:7).

There are two interesting words used in the Greek Testament, and both have a bearing on the subject of robbers. The first is *kleptees* which means "an embezzler" or "a pilferer." The second is *leestees* which means "a robber; a plunderer; a freebooter; a brigand." Both words are seen together in John 10:1. "...He that entereth not by the door into the sheepfold, but climbeth up some other way, the same is a thief [*kleptees*] and a robber [*leestees*]. The difference is subtle but obvious. The thief who embezzles does so by stealth; his deed may be covered by a veneer of respectability; he may not easily be recognized as a robber. The other type is a brigand, whose foul deeds may be accompanied by force. This is the word (*leestais*) used in Luke 10:30 where the verse reads: "...A certain man went down from Jerusalem to Jericho, and fell among thieves [*leestais*], which stripped him of his raiment, *and wounded him*, and departed leaving him *half dead*." The Lord's indictment of the priests in the temple was very strong. He charged them with having turned the House of Prayer into a den of brigands (*leestees*). He said they were worse than the outlaws who operated along the Jericho road. They were thieves of the worst kind. The priests were not only robbers, they were hypocrites, since they did these things under the guise of religion.

A SENSELESS CONDEMNATION

"...And sought how they might destroy Him: for they feared Him, because all the people were astonished at His doctrine" (v. 18). To hear the truth is often painful; to resist it is always fatal. Truth cannot be ignored. Having heard it, the listener either respects and obeys its injunctions, or he rejects it and follows his own course of action, irrespective of the consequences to come. When we compare this statement with Acts 6:7, the subject suggests questions. Luke wrote, "And the word of God increased, and the number of the disciples multiplied in Jerusalem greatly, *and a great company of the priests were obedient to the faith*." It becomes clear from the Scriptures the preaching of the Gospel can never be totally in vain. Even from the most unlikely hearers, there can be a miraculous response. Happy and wise are the preachers who never grow weary in well doing. It takes time for an acorn to become an oak tree; for a seed to become a beautiful flower. Similarly, it takes time for the seed of the Gospel to germinate within the hearts of men and women; to grow and develop, until the sinner becomes a saint. Nevertheless this cannot happen unless, initially, the soul receiving the seed be receptive and co-operative. Alas, many of the priests who heard the words of Jesus resented His message and resisted His efforts to bring them into alignment with the will of God. They, and all of their kind, were condemned then; they are to be condemned now, and alas, they will be condemned eternally when they stand before God.

SECTION FOUR

Expository Notes on Christ's Carefulness in Answering Questions

And they come again to Jerusalem; and as He was walking in the temple, there come to Him the chief priests, and the scribes, and the elders, and say unto Him, By what authority doest thou these things? and who gave thee this authority to do these things? And Jesus answered and said unto them, I will also ask of you one question, and answer me, and I will tell you by what authority I do these things. The baptism of John, was it from heaven or of men? answer me. And they reasoned with themselves, saying, if we shall say, From heaven; He will say, Why then did ye not believe him? But if we shall say, Of men; they feared the people: for all men counted John, that he was a prophet indeed. And they answered and said unto Jesus, We cannot tell. And Jesus answering saith unto them, Neither do I tell you by what authority I do these things (vv. 27-33).

THE WALKING PLACE

Christ taught in the cloistures of the Temple. On the east side was Solomon's Porch and on the south side was the Court of the Gentiles. The Porch was a large arcade made by Corinthian columns 35 feet high. The arcade on the south side was even more splendid as it was formed by four rows of white marble columns, each six feet in diameter and 30 feet high. The rabbis customarily strolled through the 162 columns, which protected them from the sun, rain and wind, and they taught as they made their way through the arcade.

THE WILELY PRIESTS

Mark has already described the evil intent of the Lord's enemies (11:18), but now the Sanhedrin had convened a special meeting. The leaders of the nation had debated the possibilities of arresting Jesus, but were aware of the danger of adopting this measure without legal proof to vindicate their action. They thought it was advisable, somehow, to trap Him into making prejudicial statements. Probably after much discussion, one of the legal experts suggested a plan which promised success. The Sanhedrin then appointed an official deputation to act on behalf of the entire body. To make it fully representative, they included members from each of the three sections of the National Council. The Chief Priests represented the ecclesiastical heads of the nation; the scribes were the official interpreters of the law, and the elders were those representing the leading families; the aristocrats of the Jewish people. The deputation would express fully the sentiments of the entire Sanhedrin; and should blame be apportioned for anything done, no party could accuse the others.

Their plan of action had probably been suggested by a lawyer. "They say unto Him, By what authority doest thou these things? and who gave thee this authority to do these things?" Let it be remembered that He had already ridden triumphantly into the city, and had been ecstatically welcomed by an enormous crowd. He had severely reprimanded the moneychangers and had expelled them from the sacred precincts. No one knew what to expect next. The deputation had to proceed with extreme caution. They had probably discussed the pros and cons of any, or every, answer He might give, and were prepared to wait and see what would be said. If Jesus asserted Himself saying there was no need for any bestowed authority; that His will alone was all that mattered, they would have grounds upon which to accuse Him of blasphemy. He would be assuming responsibility for cleansing His own House; that is, He would have been making Himself equal with God. If on the other hand, He claimed to have been authorized by the Almighty, they would have considered Him to be mentally deficient; a man overwhelmed by a false sense of His own importance; a menace to the religious stability of the nation. They would have consigned Him to a mental institution.

THE WISE PREACHER

"And Jesus answered and said unto them, I will also ask of you one question, and answer me, and I will tell you by what authority I do these things. The baptism of John, was it from heaven, or of men? answer me" (vv. 29, 30). There are times in warfare when the best defense is to attack! Jesus knew that a war was threatening; that the enemies were trying to corner Him. Suddenly, and with great wisdom, He returned their question and they were soon on the horns of a dilemma. How stupid can people become? Mortal men were challenging Him who created the universe. They were troubled when they heard His question and realized they were in deep trouble. One of the number whispered, "Be careful: If we say John's ministry was of God, He will ask us why we did not heed his message and become disciples. If we say, he had nothing to do with God; that he was just another fanatical preacher, we shall be scorned by the people, for they consider John to be a national hero. Be careful brethren: Jesus is very clever. Wait and let Him make the mistake." It was obvious they were debating what answer to give, but suddenly, one acting as spokesman for the others said, "We cannot tell." That statement in itself was tremendous, for the scribes were the final authority in interpreting the law. Even if they did not say so, they at least believed *they knew everything*! Calm and completely unperturbed, the Lord looked at them and said, "Neither do I tell you by what authority I do these things." They had failed once again; they had thrown a boomerang which returned to damage their pride.

The Twelfth Chapter of Mark

THEME: *The Preaching and Teaching of Jesus*

SECTION ONE

Expository Notes on the Tragedy in the Vineyard

And He began to speak unto them by parables. A certain man planted a vineyard, and set an hedge about it, and digged a place for the winefat, and built a tower, and let it out to husbandmen, and went into a far country. And at the season, he sent unto the husbandmen a servant, that he might receive from the husbandmen of the fruit of the vineyard (vv. 1-2).

There appears to be a four-fold division in this introductory passage of scripture. Verse 12 of this chapter indicates the people to whom the parable was spoken understood perfectly that Jesus was speaking directly to them. "...they knew that He had spoken the parable against them." Obviously, the planter of the vineyard was God; the vineyard itself was Israel, that special nation in which He hoped to find fruit. The husbandmen in charge of the vineyard can only be the rulers of the nation; the people entrusted by God with the responsibility of continuing the work during the absence of the owner. With these thoughts in mind we are able to proceed with the study.

GOD'S BOUNTIFUL PROVISION

Doubtless the Lord remembered the words of Isaiah when He told this story. The prophet had said, "For the vineyard of the Lord of Hosts is the house of Israel, and the men of Judah His pleasant plant" (read Isaiah 5:1-7). It is imperative that all students of this parable read first the message given by the prophet. Consider verse 4 of Isaiah, chapter 5. "What could have been done more to my vineyard, that I have not done in it? wherefore, when I looked that it should bring forth grapes, brought it forth wild grapes?" Isaiah's message was probably the setting for the Lord's parable, but it will be seen instantly that Jesus was more deliberate in apportioning blame. The prophet said God would punish the offenders, but Jesus explained in more detail why the custodians of the vineyard deserved their punishment. This account reminds us of the other garden made by God. The Garden of Eden was the most lovely place in the world; the stamp of perfection was upon every detail; it was the best that God could create. The same details may be attributed to the vineyard planted by God; Israel was very special and different from all others.

GOD'S BOUNDLESS PROTECTION

"...and set an hedge about it, and digged a place for the winefat, and built a tower" (v. 16). The owner of the vineyard provided everything needed for the welfare of his workmen. All who heard Christ's parable could easily visualize the scene, for such places could be found all over their land. The *hedge* was made of prickly cacti plants. This was indeed a formidable barrier against which dogs could not prevail, and even men had problems getting into a vineyard unlawfully. The *place for the winefat* was a hole dug in the ground. It had a sloping base leading to a deeper hole. Sometimes this was carved out of the rock, but at least the upper section had to be paved, for as workmen trampled grapes beneath their feet, the juice ran into the receptacle at the lower level. All visitors to Jerusalem can see this kind of thing near to the Garden Tomb.

The *Tower* was built of stones and stood about "ten cubits high and four cubits square." The rabbis said it was to be "a high place, where the vine dresser stands to overlook the vineyard.'' I have often seen such places in the vine-growing areas of Israel. During the Lord's lifetime, thieves were very numerous in Palestine, and measures had to be taken to safeguard the crop and the workmen. The tower was sometimes used as a residence. It was always a look-out place, and in extreme emergencies became a fortress. Thus did the owner of the vineyard foresee the needs of his servants. Obviously, as Isaiah described in his writings, God similarly did all that was possible for the happiness and protection of His people. He was therefore justified in asking, ''What more could have been done to my vineyard that was not done?''

GOD'S BESTOWED PRIVILEGE

''...and let it out to husbandmen'' (v. 1c). The Lord always sought the cooperation of His people. The Bible mentions numerous incidents in which the Lord used angels to do His bidding; but in every major crisis, the privilege of assisting the Almighty was given to men and women. It is not too much to suggest that He could have found other laborers for His vineyard, but for some inscrutable reason, He chose these workmen. Although they failed in their mission, their privilege was of incalculable worth. Israel was set apart as God's chosen people. Surrounded by enemies who were determined to hinder the fulfillment of eternal purposes, God's servants might have been the channel through which eternal blessing flowed to other nations. Alas, this was seldom the case, for instead of exalting the true God, Israel emulated the example of the heathens and made false gods. The nation that was meant to be the greatest of all became an object of derision, and ultimately was carried captive to Babylon. It was this kind of situation which made Joshua say, ''Choose you this day whom ye will serve...but as for me and mine house, we will serve the Lord'' (Josh. 24:15). This truth applies to believers in every age. The Savior reminded His followers that even a cup of cold water given in His name would not pass unnoticed. It appears to be inconceivable that humans would ever be reluctant to offer their talents and time for the service of the Lord. Alas, our world is filled with people who make time for anything except the things of eternal value.

GOD'S BENEFICIAL PURPOSE

''And at the season he sent to the husbandmen a servant...that he might receive...the fruit of the vineyard'' (v. 2). The people hearing

Christ's parable understood perfectly the type of arrangement made between owners and workmen. It was not always necessary for the landowners to vacation in foreign countries; sometimes they lived in a city, whereas their property was at the other end of the nation. Those men did not see their vines for long periods of time, but regularly they enquired as to the size and value of the crop. Harvest was a time of celebration. The owner arranged a feast at which his workmen were suitably rewarded. All shared in the celebrations. The lord of the vineyard rejoiced in his prosperity, and his workmen appreciated his generosity. Stingy employers never attracted the best workmen. When they rejoiced together, all were satisfied and happy. These facts were expressed in the parable of the vineyard.

It is a startling thought that God's happiness is always linked with His people. In some mysterious way, the life and emotions of the Almighty have always been associated with man. Does He know any joys apart from fellowship with humans? We know little of the eternal realm, but the Bible makes it clear that God's interests are associated with us. It is said that there is joy in the presence of the angels of God, but even that is dependent upon the repentance of prodigal sinners. God's pleasures are inevitably linked with men and women. It follows therefore, that at harvest time in God's Vineyard, the happiness of heaven and earth will be inseparable.

And they caught him, and beat him, and sent him away empty. And again he sent unto them another servant; and at him they cast stones, and wounded him in the head, and sent him away shamefully handled. And again he sent another; and him they killed, and many others; beating some, and killing some (vv. 3-5).

Let it be remembered that even as Jesus was speaking, His hearers realized "He had spoken the parable against them." As they listened, mentally they reviewed the history of their nation, and identification with the persecution of the prophets was obvious. They detested what they heard, but they were defenseless against the indictment being made by Jesus. Three things must be considered.

HOW INIQUITOUS THE POSITION OF MAN

Throughout the ages, God sent many prophets to preach against the increasing sin of His people. Describing the fate of these men, the writer to the Hebrews said, "And others had trials of cruel mockings and scourgings, yea, moreover of bonds and imprisonment: They were stoned, they were sawn asunder, were tempted, were slain with the sword: they wandered about in sheepskins and goatskins; being destitute, afflicted, tormented (of whom the world was not worthy) they wandered in deserts, and in mountains, and in dens and caves of the earth" (Heb. 11:36-38). It was inconceivable that men should inflict such punishment upon God's servants, but that was exactly what they did. Sinners were angry whenever their sin was exposed!

HOW INSCRUTABLE THE PATIENCE OF GOD

"He sent a servant. . .and again he sent another servant. . .*and many others*. . ." (v. 4). We do not know how many times the prophets tried to turn Israel from evil practices; neither do we know how God continued to be so patient with His undeserving people. It appears to be incomprehensible that God should continue to plead with Israel when omniscience made Him aware of the rejection awaiting every prophet. Was He not wasting His time? To finite minds this seems to be the case; but we must remember, it was incumbent that He act as He did. When the day of judgment arrives, no man nor nation will be able to accuse God of impatience; no one will be able to say, "If you had only tried once more." God never gives up until it is useless to continue.

HOW INFORMED THE PREACHING OF JESUS

No other preacher could have expressed so much in such few words; no other expositor could have traveled so far in such a short time. Jesus put thousands of years of history into one short story, and furthermore, He did it in such a way that His presentation was never forgotten. He not only interpreted the past, He predicted the future; for when He spoke of the assassination of the owner's son, He was obviously aware of what was about to take place. He was never taken by surprise; He saw clearly the path ahead, and with dignified deliberation walked the appointed way. Somewhere within the city was a cross upon which He would soon die; in one of the blacksmith's shops were spikes soon to pierce His body. He was aware of all these things, but if this were to be the price of redemption, He would never rest until it had been paid. His description of the events in the vineyard revealed clearly what He anticipated.

Having yet therefore one son, his well-beloved, he sent him also last unto them, saying, They will reverence my son. But those husbandmen

said among themselves, This is the heir; come, let us kill him, and the inheritance shall be ours. And they took him, and killed him, and cast him out of the vineyard. What shall therefore the Lord of the vineyard do? he will come and destroy the husbandmen, and will give the vineyard unto others (vv. 6-9).

"There were many landowners who rented their acres to tenants while they vacationed elsewhere. The rent was seldom paid in cash; the husbandman preferred to give an agreed portion of the harvest to the landowner. At the proper season, an emissary was dispatched to collect these dues, and for the most part, everybody was satisfied. Occasionally there was some trouble, and therefore this parable was easily understood by the Lord's audience. Nevertheless, even as they listened, they were able to discern deeper trends of truth. This was a story with an appliation; this was a parable with a very obvious meaning" (quoted from the author's commentary, *Luke's Thrilling Gospel*, pp. 414-415).

THE FINAL ATTEMPT

"Having yet therefore one son, his well-beloved, he sent him saying. . . They will reverence my son" (v. 6). This was the final effort made by the landowner to gain what was rightfully his. The true meaning behind this part of the story was easy to discern. Jesus of Nazareth was claiming to be the beloved, the only begotten Son of God, and that His mission to earth had been planned in Heaven, from whence He came. If they rejected Him, they were rejecting God; if they refused to listen to His entreaty, there remained only judgment. There is nothing confusing nor misleading about His claim. Either He was what He claimed to be, or He was the most abominable liar that ever lived! These are the issues which must be considered by all who would answer the question, "What think ye of Christ?"

THE FINAL ATTACK

"And they took him, and killed him, and cast him out of the vineyard" (v. 8). The Lord knew exactly what would happen in the days ahead, but He also predicted the stone rejected by the builders would eventually become the head stone in the edifice. It is thought-provoking to note that in Luke's version of this incident, he quotes the enemies as saying, "May it never be." They were more concerned with what might happen to the vineyard than they were with the murder of the owner's son.

Read Luke 20:16 and remember that in the Greek New Testament, the word "God" is missing. When Jesus spoke of the vineyard being given to another, they were horrified and replied, "May it never be."

THE FINAL ASSIZE

"What shall therefore the lord of the vineyard do? He will come and destroy the husbandmen, and will give the vineyard unto others" (v. 9). Had those listeners been able to see what lay ahead, they would have shuddered in fear. During the year 70 A.D. their beloved city fell before the Roman onslaught; thousands of their people were nailed to crosses, and a river of blood flowed through every gate. The cry uttered at the trial of Jesus, "His blood be on us and on our children" has echoed throughout the ages. Alas, "the wheels of God's judgment grind slowly, but they grind exceeding small." The Bible warns that people reap what they sow, and all students of history know that, especially among the Jewish people, those words were very true.

And have ye not read this scripture; The stone which the builders rejected is become the head of the corner: This was the Lord's doing and it is marvelous in our eyes? And they sought to lay hands on Him, but feared the people: for they knew that He had spoken this parable against them; and they left Him and went their way (vv. 10-12).

The message concerning the rejected stone is a quotation from Psalm 118:22. It became one of the favorite utterances of the early church, and is quoted in several places in the New Testament. "The meaning is plainly this, that the chief priests and scribes, as the builders of Jewish church, rejected Christ from the building as a useless stone; yea, more — they condemned and crucified Him. They rejected Him. The Greek word is *apedokimasan* and this implies that the stone was first examined, and then deliberately refused. But this stone, thus disallowed and set at nought by the builders, was made the head of the corner. The image used here is different from that used in the epistles where Christ is spoken of as the chief Cornerstone in the foundation. Here He is represented as the Cornerstone in the cornice. In real truth He is both. He is the tried foundation stone, but He is also the head of the corner. In the great spiritual building He is 'all and in all', uniting and binding together all in one" (E. Bickersteth in *The Pulpit Commentary, Mark,* p. 154).

CHRIST'S TREMENDOUS CONFIDENCE

It should never be forgotten that the Lord remembered and uttered the words of this passage of Scripture only days before His death. He had no illusions concerning His immediate future. He knew He was to be rejected of men, and nailed to a cross, but never for a single moment did He waver in His determination to complete what had been commenced. He saw the end, and not merely the beginning. He rejoiced in the salvation that would be brought to sinful man, and He was not deterred by the sufferings to be endured ere the work was finished. He was absolutely certain that His body would never see corruption (Ps. 16:10).

CHRIST'S TERRIBLE CRUCIFIXION

"The stone which the builders rejected..." (v. 10b). Predicting this event, Isaiah had written, "...when we shall see him, there is no beauty that we should desire him. He is despised and rejected of men; a man of sorrows, and acquainted with grief..." (Isa. 53:2-3). The builders examined Him, and found no beauty in Him. They had cataracts on their eyes! Michael Angelo, the great sculptor, was walking past a yard one day when he saw an ugly block of discarded marble. Its owner confessed it was so filled with flaws that it was without value. Looking at the block, Michael Angelo said, "I see an angel in it." He took the marble and began to chisel, and today, his masterpiece is one of the greatest attractions in Italy. His stone, which also had been rejected, became one of the greatest of his works.

CHRIST'S TRIUMPHANT CORONATION

"...is become the head of the corner" (v. 10c). Probably only eternity will reveal how true this will be. He will bring together living stones from the ends of the earth, and these will be built into an imperishable edifice. Innumerable voices will sing His praise, and throughout eternity, He Who once was the rejected of men, will be the light, the life, and the joy of redeemed people. "And every creature which is in heaven and on the earth...heard I saying, Blessing, and honor, and glory, and power, be unto Him that sitteth upon the throne, and unto the Lamb for ever and ever..." (Rev. 5:13). Perhaps, as we see the glories of Christ and His kingdom, we shall say as never before, "This was the Lord's doing, and it is marvelous in our eyes."

The fact that the listening crowd could hear and see so much and then forsake Him to "go their way," indicates three vital things. Their fear, folly and fate. It is possible to be within inches of the kingdom of God and yet to miss it by a mile!

SECTION TWO

Expository Notes on the Question Concerning Caesar's Coin

And they send unto Him certain of the Pharisees and of the Herodians, to catch Him in His words. And when they were come, they say unto Him, Master we know that thou art true, and carest for no man; for thou regardest not the person of men, but teachest the way of God in truth: Is it lawful to give tribute to Caesar or not? Shall we give, or shall we not give? But He, knowing their hypocrisy, said unto them, Why tempt ye me? bring me a penny, that I may see it. And they brought it. And He saith unto them, Whose is this image and superscription? And they said unto Him, Caesar's. And Jesus answering said unto them, Render to Caesar the things that are Caesar's, and to God the things that are God's. And they marvelled at Him (vv. 13-17).

During these days the Roman provinces, that were at peace and required no troops, were governed by the Senate and ruled by the pro-consuls. Those provinces which required troops because of some troubled situation, were under the rule of the Emperor and governed by the procurators. Southern Palestine was in this second category and thus subject to the Emperor. The governor, Cyrenius, decided to take a census in order to make way for a fair taxation and general administration. Though this was accepted by the majority of the people, Judas the Gaudonite, led an opposition against it. His cry was that "taxation was no better than an introduction to slavery." He argued that God would be for them, only if the people reacted violently against the governor's ruling. To him, as a Jew, God was the only ruler and thus the people should be willing to die, if need be, rather than call any man, Lord. Though the Romans had to deal with him, the fanatical Jews continued their battle cry of "No tribute to the Romans."

Three taxes were imposed upon the people. The "Ground Tax" consisted of one-tenth of all the grain and one-fifth of the wine and fruit produced. This tax was paid for partly in kind and partly in money. The "Income Tax" amounted to one percent of a person's income. The "Poll Tax" of one dinarius, which had to be paid just for the privilege of existing, was levied upon all men from fourteen to sixty-five years of age and upon all women from twelve to sixty-five.

A CONSPICUOUS ALLIANCE

"And they send unto Him, certain of the Pharisees and of the Herodians, to catch Him in his words" (v. 13). To say the least, it is interesting that two rival groups should unite their forces in an effort to discredit Jesus. "These Herodians were a sect of the Jews who supported the House of Herod, and were in favor of giving tribute to the Roman Caesar. They were so called at first from Herod the Great who was a loyal supporter of Caesar. Tertullian, Jerome, and others say that these Herodians thought Herod was the promised Messiah, because they saw that in him, the scepter had departed from Judah (see Genesis 49:10). Herod encouraged these flatterers and so put to death the infants at Bethlehem, that he might thus get rid of Christ, lest any other than himself be regarded as Christ. They said it was on this account that he rebuilt the temple with such magnificence. The Pharisees, of course, took the other side, and stood forward as the supporters of the Law of Moses and of their national freedom. So, in order that they might ensnare Jesus, they sent to Him their disciples, with the Herodians, and in the most artful manner, proposed to Him, apparently in good faith, a question, which, answer as He may, would throw Him upon the horns of a dilemma" (Bickersteth, *The Pulpit Commentary, Mark*, p. 154).

A CONTINUING ANIMOSITY

The fires of undying hatred were now burning within their breasts. It mattered not what He said or did, they were intent on defeating His every purpose, and if at all possible, to discredit Him before His listeners. Their principles, beliefs, and traditions were to be sacrificed upon the altar of expediency. If they could entangle Him in His words, so much the better, but if they could not, they were willing for their enemies to enjoy that honor. Nothing mattered except the downfall of the Carpenter whose life and words were contrary to everything they believed. We can only imagine how the Herodians and Pharisees met to plan their strategy. What one leader could not say, others could, and would, say. Their common hatred of Jesus united them in one of the most dastardly attacks ever made upon the Savior. When men sink to such low levels of morality, it is extremely doubtful if even God can do anything to save them from further degradation.

A CUNNING ATTEMPT

"Is it lawful to give tribute to Caesar, or not?" (v. 14b). Their hypocritical, flattering approach to the question did not pass unnoticed. As modern commentators would say, "they were setting Him up" for the main attack. Their smiles were meant to hide the cynicism of their hearts. To them, the trap being set was inescapable. If He favored paying tribute to the Romans, the Pharisees and all the patriots throughout the nation would denounce His decision. On the other hand, if He advised against the payment of taxes, they could inform the authorities and suggest the agitator Jesus should be arrested for incitement to rebellion. The fact that the Sadducees were not included in this incident, may or may not, have been planned. As we shall see later, they also were to have their day! Those critics might have been better employed. They could have been bringing their sick to Christ; they might have been sitting at His feet to learn eternal truth. Alas, their eyes and hearts were closed to the light; they preferred to walk in darkness.

A CAREFUL ANSWER

"But He, knowing their hypocrisy, said unto them, Why tempt ye me? bring me a denarius [a penny]" (v. 15). It is thought-provoking that He had to ask for a penny; apparently He did not possess one. This was the only occasion when Jesus appealed for money, and after using the coin, doubtless He gave it back to the owner. When He asked about the inscription clearly to be seen upon the denarius, He was drawing attention to the indisputable fact that the coin was indeed the property of Caesar. It was not lawful for anyone to mint coins anywhere within the empire. Caesar alone did this. The same law applies throughout the world of today. Men who counterfeit money, when caught, are imprisoned. Southern Palestine was a trouble center of the empire; there, Caesar reigned, and taxes were paid directly into the coffers of Rome. The Emperor supplied the currency for public circulation, but the fact that his likeness was stamped upon every coin was a reminder that all belonged to the reigning monarch. Around the edge of each coin was an inscription which read "Tiberias Caesar, the divine Augustus, son of Augustus." The fiery Jewish Zealots detested the inscription, because it proclaimed the divinity of the Emperor; and this was contrary to the precepts taught by Moses. God alone was worthy of such a title, and therefore each and every Roman coin was blasphemous! Nevertheless, whatever they thought or taught on the subject, no one could deny the coin was the property of Caesar.

Jesus took the coin; looked at it, and then asked, "Whose is this image and superscription? And they said unto Him, Caesar's. And Jesus answering said unto them, Render to Caesar the things that are Caesar's, and to God the things that are God's. And they marvelled at Him" (vv. 16, 17). It was in this remarkable way that Jesus drew the line of demarcation separating the Church and State. They are two different worlds, yet in some ways are interrelated, depending one on the other. When a man enjoys the facilities offered by a country, it is just that he should pay for the privilege. When water is piped into his home; when electrical power helps to make life a little easier; when a man uses the highways and demands protection from the civil authorities, he should be willing to pay his share of the imposed taxes which make these amenities possible. If a man enjoys the blessings and privileges of the church, the service of its ministers, and the many other blessings connected with worship, he should be generous in supporting the continuing work of God's kingdom. Yet, if ever State and God be in apparent opposition, if a man's conscience be torn between the two, the duty of the Christian is clearly expressed. Jesus said, "No man can serve two masters: for either he will hate the one, and love the other; or else he will hold to the one, and despise the other. Ye cannot serve God and mammon" (Matt. 6:24).

Nevertheless, it is imperative to remember that Jesus was speaking about the advisability of giving taxes to Caesar, and not the deliberate destruction of human life with all its potential. There are people who refuse all kinds of assistance because they believe these interfere with religious freedom. This matter of a coin had nothing to do with sacrificing a life. If a man does not wish to receive, for example, medical assistance to overcome a physical problem or even to prolong his life, that is his responsibility. If he chooses to die rather than betray his faith, perhaps he is to be commended for integrity. But if that man willfully tries to impose his will on others, then he is violating one of the most sacred things in life. If, for example, he is willing to sacrifice the life of another in order that he remains faithful to his creed, he is to be condemned, for in the sight of God, he might even be guilty of murder. There is prevailing sanity about all God's commands. When actions suggest stupidity, a man's words should be heard with extreme caution.

SECTION THREE

Expository Notes on the Sadducees' Question Regarding Survival

Then came unto Him the Sadducees, which say there is no resurrection; and they asked Him, saying, Master, Moses wrote unto us, If a man's brother die, and leave his wife behind him, and leave no children, that his brother should take his wife, and raise up seed unto his brother. Now there were seven brethren: and the first took a wife, and dying left no seed; and the second took her, and died, neither left he any seed; and the third likewise. And the seven had her, and left no seed; last of all the woman died also. In the resurrection therefore, when they shall rise, whose wife shall she be of them? for the seven had her to wife (vv. 18-23).

Josephus, the ancient writer, informs us that during the days of Judas Maccabaeus there were three sects of Jews: Pharisees, Sadducees, and Essenes. The first two types often came into touch with the Lord, but little has been written about the third class. We know they produced the manuscripts known as "The Dead Sea Scrolls" found in the caves alongside the Dead Sea. They were doubtless very hard working, scholarly men who preferred solitude to public life. The Pharisees and Sadducees were different in that they did not agree on what was, and what was not, the revealed word of God. The Sadducees were both educated and wealthy, they occupied very important positions in Israel, but they accepted only the five books of Moses as the true word of Jehovah. The Pharisees revered both the law and the prophets, and also accepted the traditions of the fathers. Both sides based their teaching on what they read, and, consequently, the difference of opinion was widespread. The Pharisees believed in a life beyond the grave; the Sadducees did not. The former class believed in spirits and angels, and cited these as evidence of life after death; the latter class denied the existence of both. Probably, the Sadducees had been delighted when the Pharisees lost their verbal battle with Jesus, but considering that they were superior to both the Pharisees and the Herodians, did not shrink from asking their question. They had often expressed the same kind of argument, and had never met anyone able to refute their teachings.

THE UNYIELDING SADDUCEES

They had watched, listened, and smiled as with ease, Jesus offset the attack of the Pharisees. They recognized the skill of the Preacher, but it was inconceivable to them that He or anyone else could supply an answer to their oft-asked question. They were aware of the words of Moses written in Deuteronomy 25:5-10, and possibly could quote them from memory.

> If brethren dwell together, and one of them die, and have no child, the wife of the dead shall not marry without unto a stranger: her husband's brother shall go in unto her, and take her to him to wife, and perform the duty of an husband's brother unto her. And it shall be, that the first born which she beareth, shall succeed in the name of his brother which is dead, that his name be not put out of Israel. And if the man like not to take his brother's wife, then let his brother's wife go up to the gate unto the elders, and say, My husband's brother refuseth to raise up unto his brother a name in Israel, he will not perform the duty of my husband's brother. Then the elders of his city shall call him, and speak unto him: and if he stand to it, and say, I like not to take her; then shall his brother's wife come unto him in the presence of the elders, and loose his shoe from off his foot, and spit in his face, and shall answer and say, So shall it be done unto that man that will not build up his brother's house. And his name shall be called in Israel, The house of him that hath his shoe loosed.

The Sadducees believed only the message found in the five books of the law, but since Moses had spoken these words, the case of the Solitary Wife was not only acceptable; it was interesting. It should be noted that they only quoted a part of what Moses commanded. The likelihood of seven brothers meeting in the hereafter was of course only fantasy, as they did not believe in the resurrection. Yet, even had they believed in survival, the chances of this taking place were nil.

THE UNLIKELY SITUATION

If *seven brothers lived together*, the description suggested a commune, or at least, a family which had never been separated. The hypothetical brother who took a wife, did not move out of the household to establish his own home, but decided to continue as he had always been. It would have taken years for all seven men to die, and for sufficient time to have elapsed between each death, for the next in line to perform, or refuse to perform, the duties of a husband. Unless some hereditary disease struck them down, it would be improbable that one wife would outlive seven husbands. Furthermore, the Sadducees made no mention of the additional provision made for a rejected woman. This idea of trouble in a future world was something they had conceived, and their question reflected their pride and stupidity in asking such a question.

THE UNKNOWN SCRIPTURES

The Sadducees only accepted the books which did not contradict their own brand of teaching. Affirming there was nothing in the writings of Moses to support the doctrine of survival, they said, life ended at death. They were not disturbed by the words of other ancient writings, for these, so they said, were not the words of God. Job said, "For I know that my redeemer liveth, and that he shall stand at the latter day upon the earth. And though. . .*worms destroy this body*, yet in my flesh shall I see God" (Job 19:25-26). Isaiah said, "The dead men shall live, together with my dead body shall they arise. Awake and sing ye that dwell in dust" (Isa. 26:19). Daniel said, "And many of them that sleep in the dust of the earth shall awake, some to everlasting life, and some to shame and everlasting contempt" (Dan. 12:2). The Sadducees apparently did not know of these predictions, but even if they did, they only believed what was acceptable in their sight. There are none so deaf as those who have no desire to hear; none so blind as they who have no wish to see; and none so foolish as the people who think they know everything.

And Jesus answering said unto them, Do ye not therefore err, because ye know not the scriptures, neither the power of God? For when they shall rise from the dead, they neither marry, nor are given in marriage; but are as the angels which are in heaven. And as touching the dead that they rise; have ye not read in the book of Moses, how in the bush God spake unto him, saying, I am the God of Abraham, and the God of Isaac, and the God of Jacob? He is not the God of the dead, but the God of the living; ye do therefore greatly err (vv. 24-27).

THE GREATNESS OF LEARNING

Knowledge is something to be acquired. A newly born baby is not a mechanical genius; a very young child is not a superb engineer. Wisdom is something to be gained. The possibilities for obtaining knowledge may be inherent, but the only way to grow mentally is to watch, to listen, and when possible, to study the textbooks written by a master. The source of truth is God, but since He does not stand in a lecture hall to teach, it becomes necessary to study the textbook which

He wrote. That book is the Bible. All He wishes to teach is expressed in His Word. Jesus accused the Sadducees of being ignorant. They had neglected God's textbook; they had concentrated on the first few chapters, and had deliberately rejected the rest of the volume. He insinuated that they were not only poor students; they were exceedingly foolish. Furthermore, the power of imparting knowledge had been given to one great Teacher, the Holy Spirit, but the Sadducees had boycotted His classes! Content with what they had learned in the kindergarten, they had despised the opportunity of furthering their studies in God's university. The result of their stupidity was seen clearly in that they knew not the scriptures, nor the power to interpret what God's textbook contained. They were very eloquent in their statements, but exceedingly shallow in their thoughts. Their religion was a sham; their outlook, a reflection of warped, preconceived ideas.

THE GLORY OF LOVING

"For when they shall rise from the dead, they neither marry, nor are given in marriage; but are as angels . . ." (v.25). Marriage on earth became a necessity when man sinned. With sin came death, and unless God had permitted the birth of children, the human race would have ceased to exist. There was need for replacements and therefore God blessed and sanctified marriage. The eternal state will be different. There will be neither sin nor death. Graveyards, funeral parlors, and hospitals will belong to earth's history. Tears will never be shed, and bereavement will never devastate families. The need for replacements will be unknown, and therefore marriage, as we now understand it, will not be necessary. The redeemed will be as angels, seeing and serving and praising God. God's eternal kingdom will not be a place of indolence; we shall not remain motionless, nor play musical instruments for ever. As the angels in every age served God, and carried out assignments allocated to them; so shall the saints of future ages serve God and perhaps seek to extend the eternal kingdom as He may direct. We do not know the details of what God has provided, but we may be assured that we shall be a part of a world of progress the like of which has never been known. To see the Lamb with the nailprints still in His hands, will be sufficient to make us sing His praises, and serve with undying devotion. Here, love is centered on some other person who gains our attention, stirs the emotions, and creates the desire for loving fellowship. To share life with that other person becomes the motivating power in every word and deed. Doubtless, saints will enjoy the presence of each other when they reach God's country, but the center of all attraction will be "the Lamb upon the throne." Saints will love each other, but all will love the Lord. Thus did Jesus draw the fine lines of demarcation between the preconceived conceptions of His critics, and the ennobling truths of God's infallible Word.

THE GOD OF THE LIVING

It is stimulating to remember that although Christ was acquainted with all the Scriptures (see Luke 24:27), He chose to quote only from the writings of Moses; the books which the Sadducees accepted as authentic. Quoting from Exodus 3:6, He stressed the fact that God is not the God of the dead, but of the living. He did not say that God *was*, or *had been*, the God of the patriarchs. GOD IS STILL THEIR GOD. The Almighty was not the supreme Monarch of graveyards; He was not a connoisseur of bones! A king cannot be a king unless he has subjects over whom to reign. A man can hardly be a headmaster of a school if there be no children within a thousand miles. Jesus stressed the fact that God could hardly be the God of Abraham, Isaac, and Jacob, if these people had long since ceased to exist. "*. . .ye therefore do greatly err*" (v. 27b). They were wrong because they rejected the greater part of what God had announced; they were wrong in that they refrained from listening to the Teacher Whom God had supplied; and they were unforgivably stupid in that they valued their own ideas more than the precepts being taught by the Lord.

There are many areas in life where men can afford to make mistakes. Financial mistakes may impoverish speculators, but there is always a chance later to learn from a costly error. Athletes may fail at important times during a contest, but there is always the possibility that in another game, the same man might be acclaimed as a hero. There are occasions when this law applies within the religious world. Someone, such as Simon Peter, may stumble and disgrace himself, but with true penitence, that man may recover and become a leader in his church. However, let it be noted that in this instance the Lord was speaking of eternity. He had been questioned about hypothetical situations which might arise in the hereafter. The emphasis was not on time, but eternity. Within this realm, no person can afford to be wrong. The biggest mistake the Sadducees were making was that they were gambling, *with their souls as the stake!* The Lord knew this, and said so.

SECTION FOUR

Expository Notes on the Sincere Scribe and His Question

And one of the scribes came, and having heard them reasoning together, and perceiving that He had answered them well, asked Him, Which is the first commandment of all? And Jesus answered him, The first of all the commandments is, Hear, O Israel; The Lord our God is one Lord: And thou shalt love the Lord thy God with all thy heart, and with all thy soul, and with all thy mind, and with all thy strength: this is the first commandment. And the second is like, namely this, Thou shalt love thy neighbour as thyself. There is none other commandment greater than these (vv. 28-31).

It is interesting to compare the accounts of this incident given by Matthew and Mark. Matthew writes: "But when the Pharisees had heard that He had put the Sadducees to silence, they were gathered together. Then one of them which was a lawyer, asked Him a question, *tempting Him*..." (Matt. 22:34-35). Mark, on the other hand, infers the lawyer had listened to the conversation of the Sadducees, and was somewhat elated by the discomfiture of the questioners. Probably they were both correct. Pharisees and Sadducees could have been in close proximity when the Lord spoke about the problem of the lonely widow. Noticing the frustration of their opponents, the Pharisees might have discussed what had taken place, and from among their number came the scribe, to "tempt" Jesus. The word used in Matthew's gospel is *peirazon*, which according to Thayer means, "to try, to attempt, to endeavor for the purpose of ascertaining what one thinks, or how he will behave himself." The word should, therefore, be translated, "...a lawyer asked him a question, testing him; to ascertain what he thought on the subject under discussion."

AN IMPORTANT REQUEST

Jesus did something which had seldom been done. He took two of the most important precepts of the Old Testament and joined them together. The entire Jewish theology rested upon one great statement found in Deuteronomy 6:4, "Hear, O Israel; the Lord our God is one Lord." Moses continued saying: "And thou shalt love the Lord thy God with all thine heart, and with all thy soul, and with all thy might." The second precept was found in Leviticus 19:18: "Thou shalt not avenge, nor bear any grudge against the children of thy people, but thou shalt love thy neighbour as thyself: I am the Lord.'' It must be remembered that when Moses uttered these words, they were spoken to Israel *about other Israelites*. The neighbors were always Jews. Contact and fellowship with Gentiles were not permitted. A Jew was not allowed to bear a grudge against a fellow Jew, *but he could hate a Gentile as much as he desired*. Jesus destroyed all the man-made fences which divided people, and insisted that all men should be brothers. This was a concept never before considered by the Jewish people. They had thousands of laws, and were constantly adding new ones to the long list. The leaders often discussed the relative values of edicts, and the debates were sometimes long and damaging. The lawyer who come to question Jesus could have been sincere. Possibly he had grown weary of the emphasis placed on religious protocol, and, recognizing Jesus to be an impartial Teacher of God's Truth, desired to know the Lord's opinion about a very controversial subject.

AN INSPIRED RESPONSE

The answer given by the Savior was not only spontaneous; it was in harmony with the Scriptures. As He looked at the temple precincts, He was aware of the insistence made on the fulfillment of the requirements of Mosaic and oral laws. A man could be condemned if his offering were not up to required standards, and an impoverished man might not be able to supply even the inexpensive turtle doves. He knew also that some of His hearers were waiting to criticize anything He might say. His answer was precise and fundamental, in that He uttered words easily understood and compatible with the dictates of Moses. The joining of the two ancient commandments surely occasioned surprise, and perhaps at first, some of the listeners were amazed. Jesus seemed to be initiating a new theology. True religion not only reached the heart of God, it also reached out to the needs of men and women. At a much later date, John was to write: "But whoso hath this world's goods, and seeth his brother have need, and shutteth up his bowels of compassion from him, how dwelleth the love of God in him? My little children, let us not love in word; but in deed and in truth" (1 John 3:17-18). God has always been concerned about people; He desires to help in every time of need. The essence of true faith is that all who worship Him share this desire. Jesus said, "Come unto me, . . .and I will give you rest" (Matt. 11:28). He also said, "Go ye therefore, and teach all nations'' (Matt. 28:19). True disciples never become hermits! Those who kneel at Christ's feet receive a commission to help the people of all nations. A man cannot be a true Christian if he remains uninterested in those for whom Christ died.

AN INSTANT RECOGNITION

''And the scribe said unto Him, Well, thou hast said the truth. . . . To love God . . . and one's neighbour is more than all whole burnt offerings and sacrifices'' (vv. 32-33). The Scribes had to be very exact in their writing the laws and traditions; the lawyers had to be cautious in sifting and examining evidence. Propagation of false data could lead to acute embarrassment. Obviously this lawyer had already decided about the relative values of penitence and the observance of certain legal practices. He knew where to find reality. A false but wealthy worshipper could offer innumerable offerings and remain a hypocrite. A poor widow might be unable to offer anything but a contrite heart, and the astute lawyer realized which, in the sight of God, would be the more acceptable. Very few, if any, of his associates would support his ideas and some might criticize His new kind of liberalism. Yet, the lawyer was convinced old interpretations left much to be desired, and, in search of confirmation of his thoughts, approached Jesus. He must have been delighted with what he heard; here was a Man after his own heart! The Pharisaical insistence on certain practices had become nauseating; religion was not a thing to be exploited, but it is something to be enjoyed in fellowship with the Almighty. It was never meant to be a scourge, threatening people with all kinds of nameless disasters, but an oasis in a worldly desert where weary, thirsty, and tired souls found refreshment. ''Master, Thou hast well said. Nobody seems to believe me, but I have believed these things for a long time. Thank You.''

AN INTERESTING REMARK

''And when Jesus saw that he answered discreetly, He said unto him, Thou art not far from the kingdom of God. And no man after that durst ask Him any question'' (v. 34). It would be nice to know just how far that scribe was from the kingdom of God. It would be thrilling if we could be sure the lawyer ultimately became a disciple. Yet, these things have not been revealed to us, and perhaps even that omission was planned by God. It is possible to be within inches of an open door and yet never to enter. Luke mentioned men of this type. He described how one enthusiastically exclaimed, "Lord, I will follow thee whithersoever thou goest", but apparently never took one step in carrying out what had been promised. Another man expressed a similar willingness, but sought permission to remain at home until after the death of his father. Still another said, "Lord, I will come, but it would be so nice if I could have a short vacation in order to say farewell to my family and relatives." The Lord never traveled more than a few days' journey from any place within the country, and therefore the man in question could easily have seen relatives at any time. He was not being sent as a missionary to a distant country; he would always be within a few miles of his home. His testimony was shallow, unreal, and misleading. They and many others were within a step of the kingdom of God, but alas, they took their eyes from the Lord, and saw only the temporal pleasures of earth. "Actions speak louder than words." A man is more likely to be remembered by his deeds than by his sermons! It is unfortunate that some orators are never heard, because their lives overshadow the words they utter. Even the most eloquent orations become meaningless whispers when the actions of the speakers are not in harmony with their message. The scribe who questioned Jesus was very discreet; probably he was utterly sincere, but unfortunately these qualities could not obtain an entrance into the kingdom of God. He certainly believed what Jesus said, but we do not know if he did anything afterward. Since faith without works is dead, maybe the lawyer died within sight of the ultimate goal. We cannot be sure about his destiny, but we can and must be certain of our own.

SECTION FIVE

Expository Notes About Christ's Message in the Temple

And Jesus answered and said, while He taught in the temple, How say the scribes that Christ is the Son of David? For David himself said by the Holy Ghost, The Lord said to my Lord, Sit thou on my right hand, till I make thine enemies thy footstool. David therefore himself calleth Him Lord; and whence is He then his son? and the common people heard Him gladly (vv. 35-37).

The Lord was a Master Preacher; He not only knew the Scriptures, He knew how to apply God's Word to His listeners. The scribes were experts at quoting many things, but when they had finished speaking, the people seldom understood what had been said. Jesus was completely different. He directed attention to the important issues, and asked questions impossible to answer without embarrassment to His opponents. The passage now under consideration is a classic example of that truth.

HIS MESSAGE...He believed in the Inspiration of the Scriptures

"...David himself said by the Holy Ghost" (v. 36a). This utterance was most significant, for he was surrounded by Sadducees who only accepted the Pentateuch — the first five books of the Bible. David lived centuries after the death of the Patriarch, and yet Christ affirmed that he had been impelled by the Holy Spirit to deliver his message. Throughout His ministry, the Lord often referred to the law and the prophets, and it became obvious to listeners that the Scriptures were "His source book." As others criticized it, the Lord preached it, and that was the secret of His thrilling ministry. It has always been far better to preach the message than to talk about it! There is a vast difference between the two styles of preaching. Charles Haddon Spurgeon once said, "There is no need to defend a lion; let it out of the cage and it will defend itself." Similarly, there is no need to defend the Bible; preach its message and it will do its own work.

HIS MAJESTY...Jesus claimed to be David's Lord

"And Jesus answered and said, ...How say the scribes that Christ is the son of David? For David himself said, *by the Holy Ghost*, The Lord said to my Lord, Sit thou on my right hand..." (vv. 35,36). This quotation comes from Psalm 110:1, and, furthermore, it became one of the best loved and most used of all the Old Testament writings. Let it be considered that *there are two Lords in the text*. David's Lord was obviously the Messiah. Another Lord, *THE* Lord spoke to David's Lord inviting Him to occupy a place of supreme honor until all opposition had been quelled. Every Hebrew knew that to sit on the right hand of a king was the highest honor the monarch could bestow. It signified pleasure, approval, admiration, reward and love. That a Carpenter from Nazareth could aspire to such exaltation was amazing; it was unbelievable, and this mystified and angered some of the audience. David was their great father, and yet he bowed reverently before his Lord. Either Jesus was mentally deranged, or *He was what He claimed to be*. That fact is as obvious today as it was the day Christ uttered the words.

HIS MISSION...He was sure about His ultimate triumph

"Sit thou on my right hand, *till I make thine enemies thy footstool*" (see Acts 2:34-35). The Lord was one with the Father; they shared an affinity of life and purpose. The Savior came to earth to complete only one phase of what had been planned. Having done what He was meant to do, He retired to the Right Hand of the Majesty on High absolutely assured that what He had commenced, His Father would complete. The Cross would not sound a death knell for hopes of world dominion; it would become the foundation upon which the imperishable kingdom would be erected. It was this glorious realization which took Him triumphantly to His crucifixion. The writer to the Hebrews wrote, "...Looking unto Jesus the author and finisher of our faith; who for the joy that was set before him, endured the cross, despising the shame, and is set down at the right hand of God" (Heb. 12:2). Jesus knew that although His immediate path in life led through the valley of the shadow of death, it was in reality but a tunnel through which He would reach the land of eternal day. This was the source of His strength, for when the disciples were on the edge of panic, Jesus calmly said, "My peace I give unto you...Let not your heart be troubled."

HIS METHODS...He knew how to present truth

"David therefore himself calleth Him Lord; whence is He then his son?" (v. 37). This question was truly devastating, for the scribes taught this Psalm of David was Messianic in its implications. With profound respect they taught a father was always greater than the son to whom he gave life. Although Joseph became the great benefactor of the ancient Hebrews, the twelve sons of Jacob, including Joseph, bowed respectfully before their aged father. This was understood throughout the entire nation. Therefore the idea of David addressing "his son" as *Lord* appeared to be ludicrous. The simple question, "How can David's son be David's Lord?" presented problems too great to solve. The fact that the common people heard Him gladly suggests they were delighted that finally, someone had arrived who could dumbfound the arrogant scribes who thought they knew everything! The audience was silent; the critics were embarrassed and could only wait to see what would happen next. Their waiting time was very brief.

And He said unto them in His doctrine, Beware of the scribes, which love to go in long clothing and love salutations in the market places,

and the chief seats in the synagogues, and the uppermost rooms at feasts: Which devour widows' houses, and for a pretense make long prayers: these shall receive greater damnation (vv. 38-40).

Luke supplies a little more information concerning the time and method of this message. He writes, "Then in the audience of all the people He said unto His disciples, Beware of the scribes . . ." (20:45). It is easy to visualize the scene. Surrounded by a large crowd of enthusiastic people, and not far from the irate but silent enemies, Jesus, turning to His disciples, began to issue warnings. His denunciation of the religious leaders was possibly the most deliberate ever made. With calculated precision He proceeded to mention six things, in the practice of which, all the scribes were to be condemned.

". . . they love to go in long clothing"

This is an interesting statement, which possibly has connections with the commandment found in Numbers 15:38-39. The children of Israel were commanded to wear "fringes of blue on the borders of their garments." These resembled tassels and were to be daily reminders of the commandments of God. Matthew writing of the scribes said, "they make broad their phylacteries, and enlarge the borders of their garments." Even today in the countries of the Middle East, most of the men wear long, flowing garments. However, for the most part, these are inexpensive and are made of very thin materials. The long majestic robes mentioned in these verses indicated men of wealth and leisure, leaders who were obsessed with the idea of attracting attention to themselves. They did not "enlarge the borders of their garments" as a reminder of God's commandments; they did so to advertise their own importance.

". . . and love salutations in the marketplaces"

To be secretly admired was insufficient to satisfy the vain ambitions of these opinionated men. They loved to hear publicly the praises of other citizens. Each time a pedestrian bowed in respect and uttered ostentatious terms of praise, the smiles of the Rabbi indicated extreme pleasure. The term *Rabbi* means "My Great One" — Master — Lord. The Pharisees believed they were superior to others, but desired the fact to be acknowledged publicly. They were self made gods who worshipped at their own shrines.

"...and the chief seats in the synagogues"

Within the ruins of the synagogue at Capernaum, is the seat of the elders which perfectly illustrates this text. It was set apart from all other benches, and occupied a place of importance at right angles to the rest of the seats in the sanctuary. To sit there was not only an honor in itself; it was a privilege all could see. People in every service would have been able to recognize the important men of the synagogue. That was precisely what the leaders desired. It was also one of the reasons why they detested the teaching of Jesus. He taught that those who aspired to greatness should be willing to serve. *"He that is great among you, let him be the least."*

"...and the uppermost rooms at feasts"

The word translated "uppermost rooms" is *protoklisias* and means "the first reclining place; the chief place at the banquet table or couch." This is but an expansion of the earlier things mentioned by the Lord. Places of honor at a king's banquet were allocated by the Host. His chief friend usually occupied the place next to the right hand of the king. The second in importance sat on the other side of the ruler. Thereafter, distinguished guests, in order, sat right and left of the throne. The prevailing idea in all these indictments was that the scribes sought the honors bestowed by men, and ignored honors bestowed by God.

"...which devour widow's houses and for a pretense make long prayers"

Perhaps this may be regarded as the strongest indictment of all. Unfortunately women, and especially widows, have always been easy prey for human vultures. Widows, having lost their husbands, and sometimes lacking good counsel, have been victimized by confidence men in every age. It has been said that fools and their money are easily parted. It might also be said that among the most unwise victims are women who are easily swayed by eloquence and promises which appear to be heaven-sent. The scribes with their long prayers, mesmerized the widows who paid exorbitant prices for the temporary pleasure derived from the scoundrels who exploited them.

"...and these shall receive greater damnation"

The twenty-third chapter of Matthew's gospel is probably among the most forthright of all the utterances of Jesus. For example, Matthew records Jesus as saying, "Woe unto you scribes, and Pharisees, hypocrites! for ye compass sea and land to make one proselyte, and when he is made, ye make him two-fold more the child of hell than yourselves." Mark writes of the "greater damnation." Obviously, Jesus believed there would come a day of judgment, when the hypocritical leaders of the people would answer to God for their evil practices. However much people may argue, the fact remains that Jesus of Nazareth not only believed in the reality of hell; He preached about it, and emulating the example set by John the Baptist, warned men to flee from the wrath to come. All the preachers who dilute or deny that message advertise their stupidity.

SECTION SIX

Expository Notes on Christ's Evaluation of the Widow's Offering

And Jesus sat over against the treasury, and beheld how people cast money into the treasury; and many that were rich cast in much. And there came a certain poor widow, and she threw in two mites, which make a farthing. And He called unto Him His disciples, and saith unto them, Verily, I say unto you, That this poor widow hath cast in more than all they which have cast into the treasury: For all they did cast in of their abundance; but she of her want did cast in all that she had, even all her living (vv. 41-44).

THE WIDOW'S GRIEF

This is one of the most beautiful stories in the Bible; it supplies a picture of love and self-sacrifice seldom found among people. Possibly the Lord had retired from the argumentative crowds, and was resting in that part of the Temple known as the Treasury. Ancient writers tell us there were numerous collection boxes known as "The Trumpets" because they resembled that kind of instrument. The wide mouth made it easy for givers to throw in their coins, and the narrow neck going down into the large box made it impossible for any coin to be reclaimed after it had been deposited. The same idea is to be found at bridges where tolls have to be paid to the authorities. Motorists with correct change can throw their money into the receptacle, and then proceed on their way. History also informs us that the varying trumpet boxes were labeled, so that people knew to what worthy cause they were contributing. To say the least, it is thought-provoking that this woman who had lost her husband was anxious to give to God. We may never know the anguish she had suffered, but obviously she had no grudge against the Almighty. Bereavement had drawn her closer to the Lord, and His Temple had become her chief attraction. Many others in her situation made bereavement a cause for complaint, and an excuse to abstain from attending any worship services.

THE WIDOW'S GRATITUDE

The Pulpit Commentary says, "It is a touching picture, this of the lonely woman, who had lost her husband, and whose heart was sad, whose means were scanty, and whose life was obscure and cheerless. But she had found strength and consolation in waiting upon God. And the temple, the appointed place for worship, with its services so helpful to devotion... was dear to her heart." We may never know how often she had attended services; we are unaware of the times when she had poured out her soul before the Lord. Had her eyes been focused on unpleasant circumstances, she might have become embittered. She was a very wise lady; she knew "...that all things work together for good to them that love God, to them who are the called according to His purpose." She was intensely grateful to God, and her actions amplified the love in her soul.

THE WIDOW'S GIFT

"She threw in two mites, which make a farthing" (v. 42). The coins were the smallest in use; they were called a *lepton* which literally means "a thin one." One *lepton*, so we have been informed, equalled one sixteenth of a penny. Two of them equalled an English farthing, which was so worthless, its production was discontinued in Britain. The whole point of the passage is that the woman could not have given less; her love forbad retaining one *lepton* for herself. Neither could she have given more, for this was all she possessed. We can only imagine her quietly apologizing to God for the poverty-stricken offering. She did not know that God, at that moment, was seated only a few yards away watching her every action. It seemed surprising that He knew exactly what she was giving. The small coins would have been hidden in her hand. She would be ashamed for anyone to know how little she was giving, and yet He knew. He was fully aware of her gift; He knew every detail of the sacrifice behind her offering. He probably knew also that she who would give her last coin, would also be willing to give her last breath for the Lord and His house. We cannot help but wonder how we compare with this woman of a bygone age.

THE WIDOW'S GLORY

Jesus said, "This poor widow hath cast in more than all they which have cast into the treasury." Thus did an insignificant woman gain admittance to God's Hall of Fame. It might be said of her as was said of another wonderful lady, "...Wheresoever this gospel shall be preached throughout the whole world, this also that she hath done shall be spoken of as a memorial of her" (Mark 14:9). The true value of a gift, whether it be in money or service, is only measured by the sacrifice it occasions. The affluent gave of their surplus, and never missed a penny; the widow gave her all, and wished she could have given more. There still remained more in the woman's empty purse than the wealthy ever possessed. Let us be honest and admit we know little of the joy of such sacrificial giving.

HOMILIES

Study No. 17

THE ART OF GIVING TO CHRIST

It is suggested that all preachers compare and contrast the following gifts and their givers.

1. Giving Gladly... *The Boy who gave his lunch* (John 6:9)
2. Giving Gloriously... *The Widow who gave all her money* (Mark 12:44)
3. Giving Grudgingly... *The Church Members who only gave a part* (Acts 5:2)
4. Giving Gratefully... *Joseph who gave his tomb* (Matthew 29:59-60)
5. Giving Graciously... *The Men who gave their donkey* (Luke 19:33)

Suggested song: What Shall I Give Thee, Master?

The Thirteenth Chapter of Mark

THEME: *Jesus Predicts the Future. Key Word... Watch (Verse 37)*

OUTLINE:

SECTION ONE

Expository Notes on the Destruction of the Temple

And as He went out of the temple, one of His disciples saith unto Him, Master, see what manner of stones and what buildings are here! And Jesus answering said unto him, Seest thou these great buildings? there shall not be left one stone upon another, that shall not be thrown down. And as He sat upon the Mount of Olives over against the temple, Peter and James and John and Andrew asked Him privately, Tell us, when shall these things be? and what shall be the sign when all these things shall be fulfilled? (vv. 1-4).

It is impossible to understand fully the magnificence of Herod's temple unless we are informed of the details of its construction. Flavius Josephus, the famous historian, in *the Complete Works of Josephus*, Book XV, Chapter XI, pp.334-336, supplies in much detail the historical facts related to one of the greatest architectural wonders the world has ever known. He describes how Herod was aware of the reluctance of the people to embark upon his project, and in hope of gaining support, made a great speech before their assembly. He reminded them of the importance of the Jewish Nation, and how after the Babylonian captivity, their ancestors erected a temple which was inferior to the one built by Solomon. This, he stated, was something which had to be corrected. Recognizing their fear that he might start something which would never be completed, he promised that before he commenced dismantling the old temple, everything would be in readiness for the erection of its successor. Furthermore, he emphasized he was a wealthy man and would pay for the construction. This, he said, was not an attempt to win praise for himself, but a sincere expression of gratitude to God for kindness received at His hand. Herod also stated that Caesar favored the project, and there would be no opposition from the Roman authorities.

Josephus continues: "But while they were in this disposition, the king encouraged them, and told them he would not pull down their temple till all things were gotten ready for building it up entirely again. And as he promised them this beforehand, so he did not break his word with them, but got ready a thousand wagons, that were to bring stones for the building, and chose out ten thousand of the most skillful workmen, and bought a thousand sacerdotal garments for as many of the priests, and had some of them taught the arts of stonecutters, and others of carpenters, and then began to build; but this not till everything was well prepared for the work. . ." (p. 334). Having described the details of construction and the numerous cloisters, Josephus continued, "However, he took care of the cloisters and the outer enclosures; and these he built in eight years. But the temple itself was built by the priests in a year and six months, — upon which all the people were full of joy" (p. 336).

The temple which Herod built was one of the wonders of the world, begun in 20-19 B.C., and built on the top of Mount Moriah. Josephus describes how, instead of levelling off the summit of the mountain, a kind of vast platform had been formed by raising up walls of massive masonry and so enclosing the whole area. On these walls a platform was laid, strengthened by piers which distributed the weight of the superstructure. Josephus tells us that some of these stones were forty feet long, by twelve feet high, by eighteen feet wide. The most magnificent entrance of the temple was at the southwest angle. Here between the city and the Temple hill there stretched the Tyropoeon Valley over which was a marvelous bridge. Each arch was forty-one and one-half feet, and there were stones used in the building of it which measured twenty-four feet long. The valley was no less than two hundred and twenty-five feet below. The breadth of the cleft which the bridge spanned was three hundred and fifty-four feet, and the bridge itself was fifty-four feet in breadth. The bridge led straight into the Royal Porch. The Porch consisted of a double row of Corinthian pillars, all thirty-seven and one-half feet high, and each one of them cut out of a solid block of marble. Josephus writes, "Now the outward face of the temple in its front wanted nothing that was likely to surprise men's minds or their eyes, for it was covered all over with plates of gold of great weight, and, at the first rising of the sun, reflected back a very fiery splendour, and made them who forced themselves to look upon it, to turn their eyes away, just as they would have done at the sun's own rays. But this temple appeared to strangers, when they were at a distance, like a mountain covered with snow, for, as to those parts which were not gilt, they were exceeding white. . . Of its stones, some of them were forty-five cubits in length, five in height and six in breadth" (*Complete Works of Josephus*, p. 555). A cubit is eighteen inches.

Walking amidst such magnificence, it was understandable why the disciples drew the Lord's attention to the grandeur of the temple. It was the kind of thing any ordinary tourist would have done. We can imagine the astonishment of the disciples when the Lord said, "Seest thou these great buildings? there shall not be left one stone upon another, that shall not be thrown down." It was customary for people in those days to view the temple with increasing awe; they believed it to be indestructible. The idea of it being destroyed was preposterous! Only the world's greatest earthquake could accomplish what Jesus had just predicted. Unfortunately, within forty years, His words, at least in part, were fulfilled.

The historian describes the terrible famine that killed many thousands of Jews; the devouring fires set by the Roman invaders, and the utter destruction of what had been the greatest city on earth. When the Romans finally entered Jerusalem, the sights were sickening to behold. Piles of dead, charred corpses were piled high in the streets; the stench from rotting bodies was nauseating, and the noise so deafening that when military commands were shouted the general's voice could not be heard. The Lord's prediction had been fulfilled in all but one detail. He had prophesied that not one stone would be left upon another, and this did not happen. Another report from antiquity describes how the Romans in their lust for gold, were frustrated because the stones of the temple were too hot to be touched. Days passed before the temple walls sufficiently cooled to permit the approach of treasure hunters. Then, so we have been told, the soldiers, with rare patience, dismantled the temple stone by stone, seeking molten gold which might have entered cracks in the buildings. They removed the stones one by one, searching in every crevice, hole and crack. Their task was not finished until they examined even the foundations of the ruined temple. However, it appears that one part of the temple was untouched. For centuries that sole surviving relic of the Temple was known as "The Wailing Wall", where Jews went regularly to pray and to weep over the dispersion of Israel. The Israelis still pray daily in the same location, but the wall is now called "The Great West Wall." It was never dismantled, and this suggests a question. Those who believe the Bible's message stress the fact that Jesus predicted not one stone would be left upon another. If there is to be a literal fulfillment of the Lord's prediction, then at some future time, the West Wall will be dismantled. Only then will the veracity of the Bible be completely vindicated. It is now believed that one of the foremost aspirations in modern Israel is the rebuilding of the temple. The late Ben Gurion said, "We are not a religious people, but we need our temple to bind us all together." Even to those Jews who have no religious interests, all the stones in that wall are sacred. They remind of ancestors whose love of liberty outshone their fear of death. When modern Israel rebuilds the temple, the West Wall will be carefully dismantled and every stone used in the new construction. So will come to pass what Jesus predicted two thousand years ago.

It is interesting that four of the disciples asked Jesus privately when these things would take place. Were they more thoughtful than others in the party? Had the rest of the company dismissed the prediction as fantasy? We may never know. It seems obvious that Jesus did not wish His disciples to be caught unawares by the coming catastrophe. They had need to know in order to prepare for the approaching storm. The same truth applies today. There is reason to believe the final act of fulfillment is drawing near. Wise indeed are they who remain awake when there is need to watch.

SECTION TWO

*Expository Notes on Christ's Prediction
Regarding International Tension*

And Jesus answering them began to say, Take heed lest any man deceive you: For many shall come in my name, saying, I am Christ; and shall deceive many. And when ye shall hear of wars and rumours of wars, be ye not troubled; for such things must needs be; but the end shall

not be yet. For nation shall rise against nation, and kingdom against kingdom: and there shall be earthquakes in diverse places, and there shall be famines and troubles: these are the beginnings of sorrows (vv. 5-8).

The Lord and His followers had now left the temple, and probably, on the way to Bethany, paused for a while on the Mount of Olives. As they looked back at the temple, the scene beggared description. Dean Farrar describing the picture, said, "They stopped to cast upon it one last lingering gaze, and one of them was eager to call His attention to its goodly stones and splendid offerings — those nine gates overlaid with gold and silver, and the one of solid Corinthian brass yet more precious; those graceful and towering porches; those bevelled blocks of marble, forty cubits long and ten cubits high; those double cloisters and stately pillars; that lavish adornment of sculpture and arabesque; those alternate blocks of red and white marble, recalling the crest and hollow of the sea-waves; those vast clusters of golden grapes; each cluster as large as a man, which twined their splendid luxuriance over the golden doors. They would have Him gaze with them on the rising terraces of Courts; the Court of the Gentiles with its monolithic columns and rich mosaic. Above this the flight of fourteen steps which led to the Court of the Priests; then once more, the twelve steps which led to the final platform crowned by the actual holy place, and holy of holies, which the rabbis fondly compared for its shape to a crouching lion, and which, with its marbled whiteness and gilded roofs looked like a glorious mountain whose snowy summit was gilded by the sun."

Farrar's description is breath-taking, but to be there with Jesus surveying that scene of splendor must have exceeded anything imaginable. "Master", said the disciples, "You tell us all this will pass away. When shall this be?" At that moment, the Lord not only saw the destruction of the temple, He saw and described things to happen throughout future ages. It should be recognized that when Jesus spoke of His return to earth, He advised caution, saying, "*but the end shall not be yet.*" Obviously Jesus believed there would be an end to time, and this fact should never be forgotten. We know that most of the catastrophies predicted happened during the next fifty years, but others still await fulfillment.

False prophets did arise (see Acts 5:36 and 8:9-10). Other self-proclaimed Messiahs have appeared throughout the entire history of the church, and unfortunately, many people were swayed by their eloquence. There have been wars and rumors of wars, and today, peace is the most elusive thing in the world. Within a generation of the Lord's prediction, a terrible earthquake devastated Laodicea, and in the year 79 A.D. Mount Vesuvius erupted to bury Pompeii with red hot ashes. Earthquakes have continued, at intervals, to the present time, and alas, famines have killed millions of people. The Lord clearly foresaw the coming of these catastrophies and plainly warned His disciples that these were but *the beginning of sorrows*. The Greek word used here is *odinon*; it refers to the pains of childbirth. The Lord was warning that the earth would be as a woman in grievous travail; struggling to bring forth something new, but almost dying in the process of delivery. No intelligent person would deny the accuracy of predictions already fulfilled; why then should any man question what still awaits fulfillment? Obviously, Jesus knew what He was saying. Having forewarned His followers, He urged them to be patient. What they had commenced, they should continue. A world of lost sinners needed evangelism. If the disciples, having put their hand to the plough turned back, they would be unworthy to enter the kingdom about which they had been commissioned to preach.

SECTION THREE

Expository Notes on the Inescapable Difficulties Awaiting the Disciples

But take heed to yourselves: for they shall deliver you up to councils; and in the synagogues ye shall be beaten; and ye shall be brought before rulers and kings for my sake, for a testimony against them. And the gospel must first be published among all nations. But when they shall lead you, and deliver you up, take no thought beforehand what ye shall speak, neither do ye premeditate; but whatsoever shall be given you in that hour, that speak ye; for it is not ye that speak, but the Holy Ghost. Now the brother shall betray the brother to death, and the father the son; and children shall rise up against their parents, and shall cause them to be put to death. And ye shall be hated of all men for my name's sake: but he that shall endure unto the end, the same shall be saved (vv. 9-13).

We become aware of a change of emphasis in the Lord's message. Having stressed the severity of events to come, Jesus now speaks of what this would mean to His followers. He is no longer speaking about approaching storms; His thoughts are directed toward the boat of faith which alone could carry them through the approaching tempest. The verses may be better understood if we divide them into four categories.

CONTINUING PERSECUTION

"But take heed to yourselves: for they shall deliver you up to councils; and in the synagogues ye shall be beaten. . ." (v. 9). The Savior was very much aware that for three centuries after His death, the Roman Empire would do its utmost to destroy the church; that innumerable Christians would be killed, and that only the courageous would succeed in being faithful unto death. It is worthy of attention that the Lord never increased the number of His followers by promising great rewards. He never misled those who listened to His words. Jesus spoke of trials, persecutions, torture, and death. He never attracted people with false promises, for above all else, He desired them to be genuine believers. If they became as chaff, the winds of persecution would quickly drive them away. He had said, "Whosoever will come after me, let him deny himself, and take up his cross, and follow me" (Mark 8:34). He believed, as all wise men believe, that quality is better than quantity!

COMMISSIONED PREACHING

"And the gospel must be first published among all nations" (v. 10). There are two ways of interpreting this scripture. It is a fact that within fifty years of the death and resurrection of Christ, the known world had heard the Message of redemption. Paul writes in Romans 10:17-18, "So then faith cometh by hearing, and hearing by the word of God. But I say, Have they not heard? Yes verily, their sound went *into all the earth, and their words unto the end of the world."* Writing to the church of the Colossians, Paul said, ". . .the word of the truth of the gospel; which is come unto you, *as it is in all the world. . ."* (1:5, 6). Within fifty years of the inception of the Christian church, assemblies had been formed in all parts of the Roman Empire, and this was accomplished through the continuing preaching of "those who were scattered abroad" through persecution.

However, it is imperative that we remember the world of Caesar's time was vastly smaller than the one we know. Frontiers have been pushed back; explorers have gone into remote corners of our planet, and today, there are very few, if any, large territories unexplored by man. Furthermore, it must be remembered that through the miracle of short wave radio broadcasts, the message of the gospel has been beamed to every inhabited part of the world. Missionaries have penetrated into the unevangelized areas of both jungle and desert, and even the most remote people have in one way or another become aware of the message of Jesus. It is very difficult to avoid the conclusion that since all this has been accomplished, the end of time must be approaching.

CONSECRATED PREPARATION

"But when they shall . . . deliver you up, take no thought beforehand what ye shall speak, neither do ye premeditate: but whatsoever shall be given you in that hour, that speak ye: for it is not ye that speak, but the Holy Ghost" (v. 11). Unfortunately, this text has been made to mean something that was never in the Savior's mind. It is an indisputable fact that God honors preparation. A lazy pastor is sure to produce a critical audience. As Dr. Jowett once said, "A pastor's study should be an upper room and not a lounge." A preacher who neglects the study of his Bible is sure to become a shadow boxer; he might be very active throwing punches but will succeed in hitting nothing! I once heard a minister say, "I have no need to prepare my sermons, for as God promised, I have only to open my mouth and He will fill it." I was never quite sure whether he had too large a mouth or too small a brain! It cannot be overstressed that when Jesus made this statement, He was encouraging believers not to be dismayed because of their having to stand before tribunals. They would be questioned by expert lawyers; their defenses would be woefully inadequate; their knowledge dismally poor, but they were to remember they would never stand alone. The Holy Spirit would never leave them, and all His infinite resources would be at their disposal. They would be unaware of the charges brought against them; they would be unable to prepare intellectually to meet the onslaughts of pagan educationalists. There was no need to be alarmed. What they would need would be given to them at the right moment. They could not prepare their minds, but it was very necessary that they prepare their souls. The lines of communication between their inmost being and the Divine Spirit had to be kept open. They were not to be pre-occupied with other matters. At the appropriate time, Heaven's voice would come through on their built-in telephone line, and they would know what they had to say to questioners and judges.

COURAGEOUS PERSEVERANCE

"Now the brother shall betray the brother to death . . . And ye shall be hated of all men for my name's sake, but he that shall endure unto the end, the same shall be saved" (vv. 12,13). The people who lived through the Nazi occupation of Europe, had real evidence of the horrors predicted by Jesus. The "Informer" became one of the most feared of all people, and unfortunately, even children betrayed their parents because their minds had been polluted by the teaching of Hitler. The same kind of betrayal was often seen in the realms of Caesar, for even the best of emperors feared the practice of Christianity would alarm and anger the gods of Rome. To gain favor with the authorities, men and women informed on their neighbors, and as a result, innocent people became martyrs.

The Greek word translated "endure" is *hupomeinas*, and means, "to remain; to persevere; to endure; to bear bravely and calmly." Jesus declared that if His followers did this to the end, they would be saved. This cannot mean the salvation obtained through faith in the Lord Jesus Christ. Forgiveness is the free gift of God made possible through the sacrificial death of the Lamb of God. The salvation which is the reward for faithful service is something more important. It embodies the greater aspect of salvation destined to make us like Christ. John wrote, "Beloved, now are we the sons of God, and it doth not yet appear what we shall be: but we know that, when He shall appear, we shall be like Him; for we shall see Him as He is" (1 John 3:2). The Lord said to the church at Smyrna, " . . . ye shall have tribulation . . . be thou faithful unto death, and I will give thee a crown of life" (Rev. 2:10).

SECTION FOUR

Expository Notes on Christ's Prediction of the End Times

But when ye shall see the abomination of desolation, spoken of by Daniel the prophet, standing where it ought not, (Let him that readeth understand,) then let them that be in Judea flee to the mountains: And let him that is on the housetop not go down into the house, neither enter therein, to take anything out of his house: And let him that is in the field not turn back again for to take up his garment (vv. 14-16)

These words are among the most discussed statements in the Bible. It is clear that Jesus was speaking of the times to precede His return to earth, but His quotation of prophecies made by Daniel demands consideration. Speaking of "a Prince that should come," the prophet said, "...he shall cause the sacrifice and the oblation to cease...he shall make it desolate" (Dan. 9:27). Then in 9:31, Daniel further says, "And arms shall stand on his part, and they shall pollute the sanctuary of strength, and shall take away the daily sacrifice, and they shall place the abomination that maketh desolate." Finally, in 12:11, the prophet says, "And from the time that the daily sacrifice shall be taken away, and the abomination that maketh desolate set up, shall be a thousand two hundred and ninety days." The fact that the Lord made this statement establishes a very important rule of biblical interpretation. Jesus indicated "the abomination which maketh desolate" was something *still to be fulfilled.* This was important because there had already been a partial fulfillment of Daniel's prediction. The first book of Maccabees 1:54, describes how in the year B.C. 168, Antiochus Epiphanes set up "the abomination of desolation upon the altar." He did this by placing a statue of Jupiter on the great altar of burnt sacrifice in repudiation and defiance of all that was believed and taught by the Jews. When Jesus said the fulfillment of Daniel's prophecy was still to come, it became clear that what happened prior to Christ's birth was only a forerunner of a greater tragedy to follow. There are teachers who affirm Daniel's prediction was fulfilled by Antiochus and therefore, what was said has no bearing upon today's events. Their conclusions are wrong.

The second episode to be considered concerns the destruction of the temple in 70 A.D. Josephus in his "Wars of the Jews", Book 4, Chapter 6, (*The Complete Works of Josephus*, pp. 535-537), describes what happened when fanatical zealots were permitted to enter the temple. They became savages who killed their own people, plundered the treasures found in the sacred house, and turned a sanctuary into a scene of unprecedented horror. They ransacked the Holy Place, and their insane butchery brought upon them an outpouring of the wrath of God. There is ample evidence that Jesus was thinking of this sad event when He uttered warnings to the disciples. The famine which brought destruction to thousands of people within the city, and the fires which burned uncontrolled for many days, almost destroyed the nation. Continuing disaster fell upon the citizens, and often, there was no way to escape. Jesus had said, "When ye see the abomination of desolation...flee to the mountains" (v. 14). Unfortunately, forgetting this advice, the people sought refuge within the city, and their action was fatal.

Houses, for the most part, had flat roofs, and were built close together. It would seem that Jesus was advising hearers to go from housetop to housetop until they could find a safe place to descend and run toward the distant hills. Workers usually left their outer garment or cloak at home, or on the edge of the field so that they could work more freely. These were told not to reclaim their garments but to flee immediately for refuge. The danger would be so great and the opportunity to escape so limited, nothing should be permitted to prevent their immediate run for safety. It would be better to lose a garment, than to die.

Finally, we have to consider another scripture. Doubtless Paul was aware of what Daniel and the Lord had spoken, but he believed the final fulfillment of those important predictions would only take place in the end times. Writing to the Thessalonians, the apostle Paul said, "Let no man deceive you by any means: for that day [the day of Christ's coming] shall not come, except there come a falling away first, and that man of sin be revealed, the son of perdition; Who opposeth and exalteth himself above all that is called God, so that he as God sitteth in the temple of God, shewing himself that he is God" (2 Thess. 2:3-4). The Bible teaches that in the last days, the Anti-christ will arise, and possessed by Satan, will endeavor to destroy religion. He will go to Jerusalem and demand that the sacrifices and oblation cease; that he alone be worshipped as God. The Jewish people will refuse to cooperate, and their action will precipitate World War III. This is called the Battle of Armageddon (Rev. 16:16). It will be more horrible and deadly than any war known to man. When Jerusalem is encompassed by armies, those able to flee for refuge, should do so immediately.

But woe to them that are with child, and to them that give suck in those days. And pray ye that your flight be not in winter. For in those days shall be affliction, such as was not from the beginning of the creation which God created unto this time, neither shall be. And except that the Lord had shortened those days, no flesh should be saved; but for the elect's sake, whom He hath chosen, He hath shortened the days. And then if any man shall say unto you, Lo, here is Christ; or, lo, He is there; believe him not. For false Christs and false prophets shall rise, and shall shew signs and wonders, to seduce, if it were possible, even the elect. But take ye heed: behold, I have foretold you all things (vv. 17-23).

Three thoughts appear to be expressed in this group of verses. Each has its own distinctive message. (1) *The Special Consideration*. Expectant mothers would need to exercise great care, for a desperate journey into the wilderness could present problems; their lives could be threatened by hazardous circumstances. Should the journey be made during the winter season, travel conditions would be extremely unpleasant. Snow and ice in the mountains might place them in increasing jeopardy. (2) *The Superb Care*. The severity of the approaching time of trouble would beggar description, for it would surpass anything known in the history of man. The Scriptures described many outpourings of judgment, but none of them could compare with those still to come. The flood in Noah's generation, the destruction of Sodom and Gomorrah, and the destruction of Jericho, would be insignificant when compared with the destruction of the temple and the holocaust to be known in the end times. And yet, in that extremely dark sky, one brilliant star would continue to shine. Severe as the judgments might be, they would be limited and restricted. For the elect's sake God would shorten the time. There could never be a moment when God's children would be forgotten. He would give His angels charge over them to keep them in all their ways. Inevitably, there would be Christians inside the city of Jerusalem; circumstances beyond control might have prevented escape; God would therefore guarantee their safety. In strange and mysterious ways, He would, so to speak, chain the dog that might bite them! The enemy might denounce but never destroy them. This was literally fulfilled during the siege of Jerusalem, and one of the reasons for the mercy shown toward the Jews, was the friendship existing between the ruler Titus and Josephus, the Jewish historian. It would appear that the same truth is to be known during the final holocaust to devastate Israel. "And when the dragon saw that he was cast unto the earth, he persecuted the woman [Israel] that brought forth the man child [Jesus]. And to the woman were given two wings of a great eagle [*maybe* the American Air Force] that she might fly into the wilderness, into her place, where she is nourished for a time, and times, and half a time [three and a half years], from the face of the serpent" (Rev. 12:13-14).

> God is still on the throne,
> He never forsaketh His own.

Finally, we must consider the third section, *The Seditious Claims*. "...false Christs and false prophets shall rise, and shall shew signs and wonders, to seduce, if it were possible, even the elect" (v. 22). We know that false prophets arose during the first century after Christ; others are operating today, and many more will appear as we approach the end of this age. Apparent miracles are not always the evidence of credibility. The proof of divine ordination is to be found in holiness and not in miraculous manifestations of healing power, which might, or might not, be genuine. Some of the most successful prophets have been charlatans, skilled in the dubious art of forming new sects, and "feathering their own nests!"

> **But in those days, after that tribulation, the sun shall be darkened, and the moon shall not give her light, and the stars of heaven shall fall, and the powers that are in heaven shall be shaken. And then shall they see the Son of man coming in the clouds with great power and glory. And then shall He send His angels, and shall gather together His elect from the four winds, from the uttermost part of the earth to the uttermost part of heaven (vv. 24-27).**

Here is all the evidence needed to prove the Lord was speaking primarily of His return to earth, when He delivered the discourse about the destruction of the temple. Whatever happened during the years preceding His coming and prior to the siege of Jerusalem, there were no celestial calamities, and angels were not dispatched to summon God's people from every corner of the earth. Three important features are mentioned in these verses.

THE DISTURBANCE IN THE SKY

"...the sun shall be darkened, and the moon shall not give her light, and the stars of heaven shall fall, and the powers that are in heaven shall fall" (vv. 24, 25). First, it must be considered that this utterance of Jesus was a reiteration of things predicted by the prophets. Isaiah (30:26) wrote: "Moreover the light of the moon shall be as the light of the sun, and the light of the sun shall be sevenfold, as the light of seven days, *in the day that the Lord bindeth up the breach of his people, and healeth the stroke of their wound.*" Joel wrote: "The earth shall quake before them; the heavens shall tremble: the sun and the moon shall be dark, and the stars shall withdraw their shining...The sun shall be turned into darkness, and the moon into blood, before *the great and the terrible day of the Lord come*" (2:10, 31). Matthew's version of the same discourse mentioned by Mark is very graphic. He writes: "Immediately after the tribulation of those days shall the sun be darkened, and the moon shall not give her light, and the stars shall fall from heaven, and the powers of the heavens shall be shaken: And then shall appear the sign of the Son of man in heaven: and then shall all the tribes of the earth mourn, and they shall see the Son of man coming in the clouds of heaven with power and great glory. And He shall send His angels with a great sound of a trumpet, and they shall gather together His elect from the four winds, from one end of heaven to the other'' (24:29-31). It will be noted that all these events are linked with the time of tribulation, which Christ predicted would come prior to His return to earth.

During the year 1974, two scientists published a book in which they forecast imminent changes in heavenly bodies, and predicted earthquakes and other disasters for certain prominent cities. Their computations were based on what they claimed would be an unusual line up of the planets. Their predictions caused intense discussions throughout the world. Some scientists agreed with the findings of the two men, but others did not. In the ongoing debates, the outstanding predictions of other internationally-known scholars were quoted, and as doomsday approached, millions of people became increasingly apprehensive of the fate which they thought would soon overtake them. We know the expected catastrophe did not occur, and some scientists were embarrassed. One admitted he had been mistaken in his calculations.

It's an ill wind that blows no good! Out of the debates came interesting facts. Attention was drawn to the possibility that the sun (a small planet in the back alleys of space) would eventually undergo ''a nova.'' The untrained, uninitiated into the mysteries of astronomy, were told that when a star novas, it shines with tremendous intensity for a period of eight to fourteen days, and then becomes dead. Bible students were interested in these revelations, realizing Isaiah had described perfectly the novaring of a star. He said *the sun would be as the light of seven days, and that the moon would shine as the sun.* Joel said the sun would cease to shine. To say the least, although we cannot be sure when these scriptures will finally be fulfilled, we know *how it will happen* whenever the time arrives. The Book of Revelation gives even more details of the catastrophic events to come.

THE DESCENT OF THE SAVIOR

''And then shall they see the Son of man coming in the clouds with great power and glory'' (v. 26). It is very difficult to understand how people who profess to believe the Bible, reject the teaching concerning the personal return of Christ to earth. God promised through His servants that Messiah would come to Israel to establish an imperishable kingdom (see Daniel 2:44 and 7:13-14). The Lord not only quoted those prophecies, He used them as a basis for His own preaching. If there is any meaning in the scripture; if God meant what He said, then someday, the Son of God must return to establish that earthly kingdom. The day will come when men and women will see the Savior descending from Heaven. John described that event when he wrote, "And I saw heaven opened, and behold, a white horse; and he that sat upon him was called Faithful and True, and in righteousness he doth judge and make war. His eyes were as a flame of fire, and on his head were many crowns...And He was clothed with a vesture dipped in blood: and His name is called, The Word of God... And He hath on His vesture and on His thigh a name written, KING OF KINGS AND LORD OF LORDS" (Rev. 19:11-16). John later exclaimed, "Even so, come, Lord Jesus." Happy are they who share his sentiments.

THE DESTINATION OF THE SAINTS

"And then shall He send His angels, and shall gather together His elect from the four winds, from the uttermost part of the earth to the uttermost part of heaven" (v. 27). It should be understood this ingathering has nothing to do with any harvest of souls to be reaped "at the end of the world." This is a bringing together of the elect at the return of Christ to earth. Many evangelical teachers connect this with Paul's statement in 1 Thessalonians 4:16-18 where the apostle speaks of the dead being raised, and the living saints caught up together to meet the Lord in the air. It is very difficult to accept that interpretation, for when Christ returns at the end of the tribulation, He will come to end a terrible war and establish an eternal kingdom. The people who believe in the Rapture of the Church can hardly link this scripture with the one from Mark's gospel. There are teachers who say no person will gain acceptance with God during the time of Jacob's Trouble, because, so they teach, the Holy Spirit will have been withdrawn before the appearance of the Man of Sin (2 Thess. 2:7-8). This is wrong (see Revelation 20:4 and notice that the resurrected saints who reign with Christ will have died because they refused to cooperate with the Antichrist). If they are *to reign with Christ*, they must be acceptable in the sight of God. Many people will become martyrs rather than submit to something known to be wrong; there will be others who will survive in the nations where Antichrist will be unable to enforce his rule. Literally, in those days of terror, "they who endure to the end, shall be saved." The most feasible interpretation of the text seems to be that when Christ returns to destroy His adversaries, the saints in Heaven will accompany Him, and the saints on earth will be gathered, so that the entire family of the faithful will be present to share in the Lord's coronation at Jerusalem.

SECTION FIVE

Expository Notes on the Parable of the Fig Tree

Now learn a parable of the fig tree; When her branch is yet tender, and putteth forth leaves, ye know that summer is near: So in like manner, when ye shall see these things come to pass, know that it is nigh, even at the doors. Verily I say unto you, that this generation shall not pass, till all these things be done. Heaven and earth shall pass away: but my words shall not pass away. But of that day and that hour knoweth no man, no, not the angels which are in heaven, neither the Son, but the Father (vv. 28-32).

WATCH AND WAIT

The most obvious lessons to be learned from this passage of Scripture are (1) Christ promised that He would return to earth, and (2) no person knows when this event will occur. People who set times and dates for the return of the Savior are unquestionably stupid, for Jesus admitted that this is a secret known only to God. The most that anyone can predict concerning this important event is its nearness. The Lord, having specified certain events to take place prior to His return, said, "...When ye shall see these things come to pass, know that it is nigh, even at the doors" (v. 29). As evidence of this He spoke of the fig tree. Fig trees in the Middle East require a great amount of warmth in order to produce leaves and fruit practically at the same time. As with most trees, the presence of new shoots indicates the winter is ending and summer is approaching. A man did not need a great amount of education to recognize signs of approaching summer; similarly, a man does not need to be an expert theologian to understand the signs of the times. The Lord spoke of the bushes and trees of time beginning to show signs of life after being dormant for a very long winter. He said certain things would inevitably come to pass, and when these became evident, His long awaited coming would be imminent.

It is interesting to note that He said "...this generation shall not pass, till all these things be done." The word translated "generation" is *genea* which means, "a begetting; a birth; men of the same stock; a family; a natural descent." The same word in Philippians 2:15 has been translated "nation." Although there has been much debate as to the correct interpretation of the statement, it seems the Lord said, "this race of Jews will not pass away until all these things have been fulfilled." Had He been speaking exclusively concerning the destruction of the temple, His words would have been literally fulfilled. However, it must be recognized the theme of this passage is His personal return to earth, and this did not happen during the onslaught made against Jerusalem. Let it also be considered that Jesus said, "MY WORDS shall not pass away" (v. 31). He might have said, "*God's words* shall not pass away." This was yet another claim to deity. Even the world with its planets might eventually be destroyed but the words He uttered would abide eternally. Had He been only a man, His statement would have been outrageous and worthy of condemnation.

WATCH AND WORK

"No man. . .knoweth. . .neither the Son, but the Father" (v. 32). It is a little difficult to recognize here the fine line of demarcation between the humanity and divinity of the Lord. As God, He obviously knew everything. As man, to some extent at least, He was aware of limitation. Was this some special secret unrevealed to Christ, or was He drawing attention to the fact that mankind would have to await the moment when the will of the Father would be revealed? Let us be honest and admit that we do not know the answer. The only matter of real importance is that we never lose our sense of expectancy; that until He comes, we work unceasingly to extend and strengthen His kingdom.

Take ye heed, watch and pray; for ye know not when the time is. For the Son of man is as a man taking a far journey, who left his house, and gave authority to his servants, and to every man his work, and commanded the porter to watch. Watch ye therefore for ye know not when the master of the house cometh, at evening, or at midnight, or at the cockcrowing, or in the morning: Lest coming suddenly he find you sleeping. And what I say unto you I say unto all, Watch (vv. 33-37).

The word-picture supplied by the Lord was easily understood. Work was apportioned by the vacationing master, and the trusted servants were expected to fulfill their responsibilities until he returned to reward them. Similarly, the Lord was about to return whence He had come, but He was expecting the disciples to be faithful during His absence. Much work had to be done; a lost world had to be evangelized, and He was giving that task to His servants. We are reminded of another parable mentioned by Luke. "A certain nobleman went into a far country to receive for himself a kingdom, and to return. And he called his ten servants, and delivered them ten pounds, and said unto them, Occupy till I come" (Luke 19:12-13). We are informed that Jesus spake this parable because the hearers "thought that the kingdom of God should immediately appear." The Lord realized that as the nobleman, He too was going into a far country where He would be crowned with glory and honour (Heb. 2:9). He was, therefore, emphasizing that the disciples had much to do; they should never become weary in well-doing. They had need to watch for His return, and "to do with all their might what their hand found to do."

WATCH AND WITNESS

It is interesting that Jesus mentioned four periods of time in which His return was possible. "...at even, or at midnight, or at the cockcrowing, or in the morning" (v. 35). Porters could not be expected to watch every minute of every day and night. Even they had need to sleep. The Lord realized this and was certainly not advocating His servants refrain from resting. He was stressing that His servants should maintain a constant state of readiness. If He came at any time, there should never be need for last minute preparation; they should be able instantly to rise and say, "Lord, we have been waiting for you. Welcome!" Unfortunately, if He arrived at some inconvenient moment, many Christians might need a few hours in which to springclean their temples. He might find cobwebs around the altar! This constant state of readiness means that by life and lip Christians should be performing their allotted tasks.

HOMILIES

Study No. 18

HOW TO STAY OUT OF TROUBLE!

Prior to a recent election, a commentator on national television compared two of the candidates. He said the one was an expert at getting into trouble when everything was going well. The other was an expert getting out of trouble when everything was going wrong. Most folk know the first is easy; the second presents problems. Happy is the Christian who avoids falling into ditches! It is easier to fall in, than to climb out. At the beginning of this chapter, an outline of its contents was suggested. All five of the headings may be illustrated from incidents mentioned in the Bible.

WATCH AND PREPARE...Don't get robbed! (Matthew 24:43)

The Lord, when speaking about the advisability of being prepared for His return, said, "Watch therefore: for ye know not what hour your Lord doth come. But know this that if the goodman of the house, had known in what watch the thief would come, he would have watched, and would not have suffered his house to be broken up." The Lord also said, "And because iniquity shall abound the love of many shall wax cold" (Matt. 24:12). Speaking to the church at Philadelphia, He said, "Behold I come quickly; hold that fast which thou hast, *that no man take thy crown*" (Rev. 3:11). There was a man who went down from Jerusalem to Jericho, and alas, he fell among thieves. Dr. Parker used to say, "He asked for it! No man could go from Jerusalem to Jericho without first *turning his back on the altar*. Yes, he asked for it!" So shall we if we emulate his example.

WATCH AND PREACH...Don't get blamed! (Ezekiel 33:6)

The prophet said, "But if the watchman see the sword come, and blow not the trumpet, and the people be not warned; if the sword come, and take away any person from among them, he is taken away in his iniquity; *but his blood will I require at the watchman's hands.*" People who are unaware of danger cannot be expected to guard against it, but if a blind man be permitted to walk over a precipice when a seeing person could prevent the accident, the man with sight is to be blamed. God reminds us of the responsibility of witnessing to those who do not know the danger of being lost eternally. It is our task to make them aware of what lies ahead. If they reject our testimony, at least we shall not be blamed for having failed in our mission. Yet if we refrain from witnessing, God may hold us responsible for the loss of those precious souls.

WATCH AND PREVAIL...Don't get vanquished. (Exodus 17:11-12)

"So Joshua did as Moses had said to him, and fought with Amalek: and Moses, Aaron and Hur went up to the top of the hill. And it came to pass, when Moses held up his hand, that Israel prevailed: and when he let down his hand, Amalek prevailed. But Moses' hands were heavy; and they took a stone, and put it under him, and he sat thereon; and Aaron and Hur stayed up his hands, the one on the one side, and the other on the other side; and his hands were steady until the going down of the sun. And Joshua discomfited Amelek. . . ." It is easy to visualize that ancient scene. From their vantage point on the hilltop, it was possible to see the progress of the battle. When Moses' hands were not lifted toward heaven, somehow the power of Joshua appeared to be waning; when Moses lifted his hands, Israel remained invincible. Aaron and Hur were quick to notice things; alas, there are times when we are too busy to lift our hands in prayer, and this always leads to defeat. Jesus said, "Men ought always to pray."

WATCH AND PERCEIVE. . Don't get starved to death! (2 Kings 4:9-10)
"And the Shunammite said unto her husband, Behold, now, I perceive that this is an holy man of God, which passeth by us continually. Let us make a little chamber. . .and it shall be, when he cometh to us, that he shall turn in thither." That woman's eyesight saved her life. God knows how to pay His debts, and when later a famine devastated the land, the prophet was sent to warn the lady to leave the country. Furthermore, although her vacation lasted seven years, she never lost a penny (see 2 Kings 8:1-6). Long before the text was uttered, she proved that when a person seeks first the kingdom of God and His righteousness, all other things are added. Alas, we are often too selfish and seldom witness the miracles God is able to perform.

WATCH AND PRAY. . .Don't get drowsy! (Luke 22:45-46)
"And when Jesus rose up from prayer, and was come to His disciples, He found them sleeping for sorrow, And said unto them, Why sleep ye? rise and pray, lest ye enter into temptation." The New Testament describes various events which happened in the Garden of Gethsemane, but how much more would we know if the disciples had remained awake on that eventful night? They slept through the most important moments of Christ's life, and their loss was immeasurable. Alas, the same thing happened on the Mount of Transfiguration. Many things may cause spiritual drowsiness. To guard against them should be our constant task. Unfortunately, when we sleep we do nothing for the Lord! Surely Jesus had this in mind when He said, "I must work the works of Him that sent me, while it is day; the night cometh when no man can work" (John 9:4).

The Fourteenth Chapter of Mark

THEME: *Jesus Approaches the End of His Life*

OUTLINE:

SECTION ONE

Expository Notes on the Priests' Desire to Kill Jesus

After two days was the feast of the passover, and of unleavened bread; and the chief priests and the scribes sought how they might take Him by craft, and put Him to death. But they said, Not on the feast day, lest there be an uproar of the people (vv. 1-2).

THE IMMENSE CROWDS... *Waiting!*

Passover is still the greatest event in the Jewish year, but during the days when the Lord was upon earth, this feast brought the enthusiasm of the people to its greatest height. Our studies indicate that the Feast of the Passover fell on the 14th of Nisan, that is, about the 14th of April, followed by a seven-day Feast of Unleavened Bread. The Passover was a major feast and was kept like a Sabbath. The Feast of Unleavened Bread was called a minor festival. Although no work could be begun during this time, such work as was necessary for public interest, or to provide against private loss, was permitted. The Passover Day, of course, was the great day.

Most of our information concerning the events of the first century comes to us through the works of Flavius Josephus. He described in great detail many interesting things, and not the least among them was a request made by the Governor of Palestine to the High Priest, asking that a census or record be kept of the number of lambs sacrificed at the Feast of Passover. This man whose name was Cestius, had difficulty in persuading Nero that the Jewish nation with its feasts and festivals was worthy of increasing attention. The Emperor had been indifferent to all that was taking place, and the frustrated Cestius hoped statistics would prevail where persuasion had failed. The ensuing census, according to Josephus, revealed that about 256,500 lambs were slain during Passover. That in itself is a staggering number, but another detail must be considered. Jewish law insisted that for each lamb, there had to be a *minimum* of ten worshippers. Passover was based on the ancient story of how Israel was protected during a night of fear and death in Egypt. Their safety lay in the sprinkling of the blood of sacrifice on the entrance to their homes, and a special provision allowed *impoverished families to share one offering* (see Exodus 12:4). Possibly the law, insisting there be ten persons per lamb, was based upon the ancient example. Josephus supplies the figures which enable us to know that there could have been between two and a half to three million people present in Jerusalem at that time.

This commentary is being written in the year 1984, and this part is being completed just before the commencement of the Olympic Games in Los Angeles, California. Every citizen of the State is acutely aware of the intense preparations being made for the great event. Special signs are being erected along the highways; the Olympic Torch has passed through the entire country, East to West, and is about to be taken into the Stadium; special villages have been erected to accommodate the athletes, and there are innumerable citizens who consider this to be the most exciting time of their lives. It is easy, therefore, to appreciate the excitement which preceded the Feast of Passover. Weeks before its commencement, the story of the deliverance from Egypt was expounded in the synagogues; special signs were erected directing pilgrims on their journey, and security of a different type prevailed everywhere. Historians remind us of the whitewashing teams dispersed along the highways. When travelers died during a journey, their bodies were often buried alongside the highway; they were buried where they died. But since contact with the dead was considered a defilement, any traveler who inadvertently touched one of those tombs was prohibited from enjoying the feast. Therefore, warnings had to be issued, and this was done by whitening the grave markers. In addition to pilgrims who journeyed many miles to be at the Passover, every male person who lived within fifteen miles of Jerusalem was obliged to attend whether he wanted to or not. His presence was mandatory. All Jews considered attendance to be the greatest of all privileges, and representatives would be there from almost every nation in the world.

It was impossible to accommodate three million people within the city, but people were permitted to seek lodging in the nearby villages such as Bethphage and Bethany. There was also a very large "tent city" which stretched in all directions outside the walls of Jerusalem.

THE INSIDIOUS CONSPIRACY. . . Working!

". . . The chief priests and the scribes sought how they might take Him by craft, and put Him to death" (v. 1). Matthew supplies a little more information. He includes the elders of the people, who were representative of the most aristocratic families in the nation. Matthew also states that the special meeting was held in "the palace of the high priest, who was called Caiaphas" (Matt. 26:3). Behind the closed doors of that palace, the leaders of the nation met and "consulted that they might take Jesus by subtlety, and kill Him. . ." (Matt. 26:4). They had attempted to entangle Jesus in His words; they sent officers to arrest Him; they had tried to throw Him from a high cliff; their efforts had completely failed. Alas, they would not quit; they were determined to silence His voice, and no stone would be left unturned until their objective had been gained. It would appear that, like Pharaoh of old, they hardened their hearts, until even God could do nothing for them. The word translated "craft" comes from the Greek word *dolos* which means "to catch with a bait, to lure, to snare, hence, it is sometimes translated, "craft, deceit, guile." They were very deliberate in their acts. As a fisherman with great care baits his hook, or a trapper secretly hides his snare, these detestable people baited their hooks and placed snares, in the hope that Jesus would be captured. They were determined at any cost to kill Him.

THE ILLUMINATING CONCLUSION. . . Wondering!

"But they said, Not on the feast day, lest there be an uproar of the people" (v. 2). The immense crowd thronging the streets of Jerusalem contained at least three types of people. (1) The overwhelming majority came as sightseers not only to worship but to enjoy a vacation in the city of their fathers. They were very excited, and naturally, wanted to see the Prophet about Whom so much had been heard. (2) There were those who had received blessing through the ministry of Jesus, and among these would be some who had been healed of disease. Their testimony added fuel to the fires of excitement, and no speaker with such a story lacked an audience. (3) The Zealots would be there in record numbers. They were always ready to take advantage of any incident or circumstance likely to embarrass the Romans. With a little encouragement, they were ready to incite rebellion, and this probably was the greatest threat known during the feast. Disturbances during Passover had to be avoided at all costs; the high priest would be adamant about that decision. The sale of a quarter of a million lambs, plus the income derived from the sales of other offerings, meant a profit of many millions of shekels. A very large part of this money eventually went into the priest's coffers, for he had created a system by which his inspectors defrauded worshippers. An outbreak of violence would disrupt the economic process operating within the temple, and to lose this money was almost as distasteful as losing Jesus. His philosophy was quite simple. "Let us make sure of our income, and afterward, we might even use some of the money to bribe informers against the Nazarene." Poor man! He was on the verge of bankruptcy and did not know it.

SECTION TWO

Expository Notes About Mary's Gift of Ointment

And being in Bethany in the house of Simon the leper as He sat at meat, there came a woman having an alabaster box of ointment of spikenard very precious; and she brake the box, and poured it on His head. And there were some that had indignation within themselves, and said, why was this waste of ointment made? For it might have been sold for more

than three hundred pence, and have been given to the poor. And they murmured against her (vv. 3-5).

A PERSONAL GRATITUDE FOR DELIVERANCE

It is exceedingly interesting to read that Jesus attended a supper in the house of *Simon the leper*! Under ordinary circumstances that would have been unwise and illegal, for no clean person was ever permitted to run the risk of contamination by fellowship with a leper. Obviously, the host at that meal was no longer unclean. At sometime in his life he had been cleansed by Jesus of Nazareth.

"If this were the case, the home of the former leper might have been impoverished, and the aid offered by Martha in preparing a supper, would have been gladly welcomed by the man who greatly desired to express his appreciation to the Master. Four very simple but thought-provoking features seem to be closely associated with this man: (1) *He had been fearful.* Leprosy was a dreaded disease necessitating separation from family and friends. Unless a miracle was performed, the sufferer knew he would remain an outcast until death released him from agony. Through every day and night of existence, the leper would hardly be free of the mental anguish which constantly affirmed his case was hopeless. (2) *He had been found.* There had been a day when the impossible happened; somewhere, somehow he had come in contact with Christ. Divine grace had been manifest and eternal love overflowed to reach a man in his misery. The impossible had taken place; the leper had found new life. (3) *He was fervent.* Unlike others mentioned by Luke (17:12-19) this man constantly remembered the grace which rescued him. Gratitude filled his heart, and when the opportunity came to do something for his Savior, he did what was possible. (4) *He desired fellowship.* There had been a time when he came because he wanted *to receive* something; now he is present because he desires *to give* something. Formerly he desired salvation; now he yearns to sit with the Master, to listen to His voice, to rejoice in His presence, to learn at His feet. Simon the leper set an example which all men should follow" (reprinted from the author's commentary on *John's Wonderful Gospel*, pp. 256-257).

A PRECIOUS GIFT OF DEVOTION

"There came a woman having an alabaster box of ointment of spikenard very precious; and she brake the box, and poured it on His head'' (v. 3). Dr. Rice states that this expensive perfume ''was made from the stem of a plant of the valerian family, probably *Nardostachys Jatamansi*, found in India. The finished product was very precious, and the assessment of its worth by Judas further indicates its value in the markets of that day.'' It would be interesting if we knew how such a treasure became the property of Mary. Did she belong to a wealthy family, and did she have sufficient money to purchase this herself? Was it a birthday gift from her brother and sister? Did some would-be suitor give it to her? We may never know the answer to that question, but we may be sure it represented the most treasured of all her possessions. She had reached the conclusion that Jesus merited the best gift possible. Her decision was doubtless the climax of fellowship enjoyed in His presence. She had welcomed Him to her home; had listened when He taught, and as day succeeded day, her love for Him deepened. Mary appreciated Simon's desire to entertain the Lord, and accepted gladly the invitation to be at the supper.

She listened as the Lord quietly spoke to the audience, but with intuition inherent in women, saw the lines etching His face, and read aright the problems reflected in His eyes. An inner sense told her the disciples were wrong in expecting a kingdom. The Master meant what He had uttered. He was going to Jerusalem to be crucified. She could not understand this; the whole idea seemed terrible, but nevertheless it was true. Mary had no desire to wait and give floral tributes at His funeral. What she had to give should be given immediately. There was no time to be lost. Asking to be excused for a few moments, she ran up the cobbled street; and into her bedroom, and soon had the costly gift in her hand. She wanted the Lord to know she adored Him, and the best way to make that confession was in surrendering the best of her possessions. When the Lord was anointed with her precious ointment, the broken box or empty flask revealed the overflowing love of this woman's heart. The escaping fragrance not only filled the house, it entered the street, filled the town, and in ever-widening circles of blessedness, proceeded to fill the world.

A PERSISTENT GROWL OF DISPLEASURE

''And there were some that had indignation within themselves'' (v. 4). The Greek word translated ''indignation'' is *aganaktountes* and this is very expressive. Dr. Thayer says it means ''to feel pain; to grieve; to become indignant.'' It will, therefore, be understandable why one authority translates the text "they growled with displeasure," while another says, "they ached with vexation." John 12:4 informs us that Judas was the actual spokesman, but a comparison of the Gospels indicates identical thoughts were in the minds of others in attendance at the supper. John further adds that Mary's treasure weighed one pound, and with Mark, agrees that it might have been sold for three hundred pence. Since a man who worked in the vineyards for a twelve hour day only received a penny in wages, it becomes evident Mary's gift was indeed valuable. Men were not permitted to work on the Sabbath, therefore a man would need to work twelve hours a day, six days a week for almost one year in order to get enough money to purchase a similar gift. But another factor must be considered. Out of his wages, sufficient money would need to be deducted to pay for food and other expenses connected with his home and family. Probably he would find it difficult to save any of his income for luxuries. Hence, if he were indeed an ordinary workman, the task of saving 300 pence would be almost impossible. If we might be permitted to express these figures in modern American values, then it might be that Mary's gift was worth at least five thousand dollars, and probably even more. This was no ordinary gift; it was her greatest treasure.

The disciples who saw what appeared to be a regrettable waste of much needed money, began silently to question the wisdom of her act. When Judas expressed disapproval, their growls of displeasure announced agreement with his objection. Actually in the sight of God, Mary retained what she sacrificed; the critics lost what they withheld. Unfortunately, only people with spiritual discernment would be able to explain this strange mathematical reasoning.

And Jesus said, Let her alone; why trouble ye her? she hath wrought a good work on me. For ye have the poor with you always, and whensoever ye will ye may do them good: but me ye have not always. She hath done what she could: she is come aforehand to anoint my body to the burying. Verily I say unto you, wheresoever this gospel shall be preached throughout the whole world, this also that she hath done, shall be spoken of for a memorial of her (vv. 6-9).

A GREAT CONTRAST

It should not be forgotten that a little earlier in his manuscript, Mark had written of the widow who cast two mites into the treasury (Mark 12:42-44). Now he mentions this very expensive gift brought by Mary.

His gospel unites two extremes; it brings together two widely separated women and makes them sisters. The widow possibly lived alone; she had no dependents; and was utterly impoverished. Mary had relations who might resent her giving away such a valuable item. Yet both women only thought of their Lord, and anything less than the best was considered unworthy to present to Him. The widow concealed her gift in the palm of her hand; possibly she was too ashamed for others to know how small was her offering. Mary openly anointed the Lord caring not what anyone said. The Lord who saw the actions of both women probably thought of them as twin sisters in the family of faith. They possessed an identical quality — overflowing love for God. If we had to decide which was the greater woman, it would be exceedingly difficult to choose. If we had to decide whether or not we resemble either of them, there would be no need to think!

A GRACIOUS CONSIDERATION

"*Let her alone*" (v. 6). Was Mary embarrassed by the looks and words of the disciples? Was she ashamed of her action, and hurt by the insinuations of her critics? The Lord sympathized and hastened to comfort and reassure her. His testimony, "She hath done what she could," indicated it would have been impossible to give more. He linked her deed with His forthcoming death, and by doing this, left us with a question, "Did she know that He was going to die?" Many of us think so, but it is necessary to consider another possibility. It was a Jewish custom to anoint a dead body prior to burial. This happened with the body and burial of the Lord (see John 19:39-40). Is it possible that the Holy Spirit constrained her to act as she did, so that in after years, the entire church would look back and realize this was no accident; every detail was planned in Heaven? Jesus, the Son of God, had been the Lamb slain from before the foundation of the world? It is wonderful to recognize the speed with which Jesus went to the aid of a discomforted lady. Her action has since won the acclaim of the entire world; it was unfortunate that those who witnessed the incident could only criticize. Probably Judas, the treasurer, was a little envious. He could have used that money for all kinds of things. John 12:6 says, "This Judas said, not that he cared for the poor; *but because he was a thief*, and had the bag, and bare what was put therein."

SECTION THREE

Expository Notes on the Treachery of Judas

And Judas Iscariot, one of the twelve, went unto the chief priests, to betray Him unto them: And when they heard it, they were glad, and promised to give him money. And he sought how he might conveniently betray Him (vv. 10-11).

We are living in times when liberal theologians and zealous film producers are strenuously trying to minimize the guilt of Judas. It has been suggested that the betrayor intended to use ill-gotten gains to purchase a pardon for his Master; that he has been misrepresented by preachers in all ages; that basically he was a good man who desired the best for his country! It is strange how these men strain at a gnat and swallow a camel in an endeavor to please their audiences. Judas was a thief; an unfaithful follower of Jesus, who finally thought more of himself than he did of the greatest Person who ever lived. Speaking to His disciples, the Lord said, "One of you is a devil" (John 6:70). No amount of bleaching can turn mud into snow and no amount of dexterity can turn a traitor into a hero! Judas was a betrayer who lost his soul. Jesus said so (see John 17:12).

A DELIBERATE COMMITMENT

"And Judas. . .went unto the chief priests, to betray Jesus unto them" (v. 10). This was a deliberate act, possibly preconceived and brought to its climax by the apparent waste of money in the sacrifice of Mary's box of ointment. Judas had become increasingly apprehensive about the future. He had hoped for a place of eminence in the kingdom of the Messiah, but now he was not sure there would be a kingdom. His leader seemed determined to die. Instead of handling vast amounts of money, Judas would soon be unemployed. When he saw Jesus condoning Mary's wastefulness, his feelings erupted, and this was "the final straw that broke the camel's back!" He had to make the best of a bad job; it was necessary to get out of his predicament while the opportunity lasted. His perverted thoughts suggested salvaging anything of value. Even thirty pieces of silver were better than nothing! Poor Judas; his ill-gotten gains were destined to trouble him forever. As the Prophet Haggai suggested, he was placing his wages into a bag with holes (see Haggai 1:6).

A DELIGHTED COMPANY

When Judas offered help to the frustrated Jewish leaders, the officials could hardly believe their eyes and ears. Their astonishment gave place to joy, for at last, a way had been found by which the hated Nazarene could be trapped. At that moment, Judas could have asked any reward, but when they saw the anxiety of the traitor, their shrewd minds suggested bargaining, and finally they agreed on a fixed price of thirty pieces of silver. Any one of them would have paid more for a slave in the market. Unfortunately, Judas was not a good business man; he was swindled, and he paid with his soul. Probably the counselors failed to sleep that night; they were ecstatic; their problems had been solved; Jesus was as good as dead already! Perhaps we are able to see here the difference between happiness and joy. The former depends upon circumstances; events can change abruptly; and when this happens, the temporal surge of elated feelings can disappear in moments. Joy is something infinitely deeper and greater. It abides in the soul, and although tempests beat upon it, true joy remains. Anchored in the knowledge of God, it is indestructible. The Jews could afford thirty pieces of silver, but could not afford to lose their souls.

A PREMEDITATED PLAN

"He sought how he might *conveniently* betray Him" (v. 11). The Greek word *eukairos* means "to seek a convenient opportunity; a suitable time or place." There was no particular hurry: the feast was not to be disrupted; business had to proceed as usual; they could afford to wait. Did Judas sit counseling with them? Did they discuss plans by which Jesus could be ensnared? Did the traitor say: "Gentlemen! Do not be anxious. I know His every movement. I could find Him when others failed. The best time would be at night when most of His supporters will be in bed. Let the soldiers be ready at my bidding, and afterward when the people seek Him, He will be in jail. Yes, I am the man for the job, but I would like to be paid in advance. This could be tricky business, you should know how elusive Jesus can be. You need to be smart to take him, and since I alone can meet those requirements, let us make the deal now. Give me my money." They did, and doubtless to money-hungry Judas, the payment shone with desirable splendor. Alas, the coins soon lost their luster and the traitor threw them away. That was the prelude to his self-inflicted execution (see Matthew 27:3-10) (see special instructions for homily at the end of this chapter).

A GLORIOUS COMMENDATION

"Wheresoever this gospel shall be preached throughout the whole world, this also that she hath done, shall be spoken of for a memorial of her" (v. 9). His statement was thrilling; in spite of the threats made against His life, the Lord knew the Gospel would be preached throughout the world. His promise, that the woman's deed would never be forgotten, has already been proved true. Thus did He teach that anything done in His Name would not be overlooked; that in the day when saints appear before the judgment seat of Christ, even a cup of cold water given to the Lord will bring its reward. The widow who gave two mites would have been scared by notoriety, and Mary, in all probability, would shrink from the fame gained by her act of devotion. Yet Christ unmistakably indicated that as we give, so shall it be given to us "shaken together, pressed down, and running over," (see Luke 6:38). "Then shall the king say unto them on his right hand, Come, ye blessed of my Father, inherit the kingdom prepared for you from the foundation of the world: For I was an hungered, and ye gave me meat: I was thirsty, and ye gave me drink: I was a stranger, and ye took me in: Naked, and ye clothed me: I was sick, and ye visited me: I was in prison, and ye came unto me. Then shall the righteous answer him, saying, Lord, When saw we thee an hungered, and fed thee? or thirsty, and gave thee drink? When saw we thee a stranger, and took thee in? or naked, and clothed thee? Or when saw we thee sick, or in prison, and came unto thee? And the king shall answer and say unto them, Verily, I say unto you, Inasmuch as ye have done it unto one of the least of these my brethren, YE HAVE DONE IT UNTO ME" (Matt. 25:34-40) (see suggestion for a special homily at the end of the chapter).

SECTION FOUR

Expository Notes on the Man Who Owned a Large Upper Room

And the first day of unleavened bread, when they killed the passover, His disciples said unto Him, Where wilt thou that we go and prepare that thou mayest eat the passover? And He sendeth forth two of His disciples, and saith unto them, Go ye into the city, and there shall meet you a man bearing a pitcher of water: follow him. And wheresoever he shall go in, say ye to the goodman of the house, The Master saith, Where is the guestchamber, where I shall eat the passover with my disciples? And he will shew you a large upper room furnished and

prepared: there make ready for us. And His disciples went forth, and came into the city, and found as He had said unto them: and they made ready the passover (vv. 12-16).

THE SIMPLE REQUEST

"Where wilt thou . . . that we prepare the passover?" (v. 12). The request made by the disciples appears to indicate they had no idea where they would celebrate Passover. Had they known, they would not have asked their question. Yet it is obvious that Jesus had already made preparation for this necessity; the unknown householder within the city was expecting his guests, and had prepared accommodation. One wonders how the Lord had found time for these matters of business, but it is understandable that He never left anything for last minute preparation. The owner of the house must have been a man of means and possibly a disciple of Jesus. It has been suggested that he was the father of John Mark, and that this home became famous during the early history of the Church (see Acts 12:12). There was a time, somewhere during the later ministry of the Lord, when Jesus made arrangements with this friend; that is, He made reservations by which the large upper room would be ready for use at the appointed time. Did He deliberately withhold this information from His followers, lest inadvertently they should speak of it, and so inform the enemies where He might be found? Perhaps He did not tell them, so that the arrangement would be as a nice surprise!

THE STRANGE REVELATION

"Go ye into the city, and there shall meet you *a man bearing a pitcher of water*" (v. 13). Either this was an arranged signal, or we are again provided with evidence of omniscience. In any case, either would testify of undisputed wisdom. Then and now, *women* carry the waterpitchers; more often than not, on their heads. It was considered beneath the dignity of men to be engaged in such mundane tasks. A man carrying a container of water on his shoulder would have been visible even in the midst of the largest crowd; he would "have stuck out like a sore thumb!" We cannot be absolutely sure whether or not this was a pre-arranged sign by which the disciples would be directed to the correct guide, but one other detail deserves attention. Since the disciples met the water carrier at an unspecified time, the Lord surely had some idea when the man would be on the street. The water-carrier could hardly have been walking around for hours!

THE SURPRISING RESPONSE

"Follow him. And wheresoever he shall go in, say ye to the goodman of the house, The Master saith, Where is the guestchamber, where I shall eat the passover with my disciples? And he will shew you a large upper room furnished and prepared" (vv. 14, 15). The two disciples commissioned for this important task were Peter and John (see Luke 22:8). As far as we know, they never spoke with the guide; they merely followed him to his place of employment. There they met the owner of the home, and following instructions, asked their question. The man was obviously expecting them, for already the large upper room had been prepared to receive Jesus and His followers.

Today, in Jerusalem, tourists are taken to see what is claimed to be "the upper room." There exists the possibility that the claim to authenticity is false; the appearance of the building is far too modern to be identified with something two thousand years old! However, visitors can at least get an idea of what once was customary in ancient Palestine. Many homes were little more than hovels, but those belonging to the more affluent citizens were recognized by a small room built on the top of the main dwelling. It resembled an old fashioned loaf of bread, with a smaller loaf on top of the larger one. Access to the upstairs room was gained by an outside stairway. The upper section was the most useful part of the dwelling.

The room was often used for storage; it was a splendid place for seclusion, rest and meditation, and when the necessity arose, it could be used for instructional classes taught by an elder, or a visiting rabbi. Believing it to be a suitable place in which to celebrate Passover, Jesus engaged it for that purpose. Did He pay for the use of the room? We can be sure that He offered, but if the unknown host were a true disciple, payment would have been refused. This might have been a gift to his Lord; an expression of enduring love. To give anything to the Savior was a privilege of inestimable worth. If the room had been used to store commodities, the goods would have been removed and couches from downstairs brought to furnish the upper section. At least thirteen people would need something on which to recline. The householder had been a very busy man!

THE SPECIAL RESPONSIBILITY

"...there, make ready for us...And His disciples...found as He had said unto them: and they made ready the passover" (vv. 15, 16). Peter and John had much to do, for the requirements of the law were exacting. Precise preparations had to be made for the Passover. The first ceremony was the ceremonial search for leaven which took place the day before the Passover. The master of the house took a lighted candle and ceremonially searched the house for leaven. Then every particle of leaven had to be removed in order to show how the first Passover in Egypt (Exod. 12) had been eaten with unleavened bread. Unleavened bread was not really bread at all but rather like a water biscuit which could be baked more quickly than a loaf baked with leaven. You will recall that, during the escape from Egypt, the Passover had been eaten in haste as everyone had to be ready for the journey. Leaven is fermented dough and, as the Jews identified fermentation with putrefaction, thus leaven stood for rottenness and corruption.

Next on the list of requirements was the lamb to be slain. This had to be as near to perfection as possible; the lamb had to be without blemish. The purchaser, or head of the family, was required to take the animal to the temple and slay it before the officiating priests. The lamb's throat was cut, and the blood drained into a bowl. This was ceremonially passed hand to hand along a line of waiting priests, until the man at the end of the line smashed the bowl on the altar, scattering blood in every direction. The animal was then skinned; the entrails, part of the sacrifice, was removed; and the carcase was then returned to the worshipper, so that he could roast it on a spit over an open fire. The spit had to be made of pomegranate wood. Peter and John had also to provide bitter herbs to remind participants of the bitterness of the bondage, from which they had been redeemed in the days of Moses.

I shall never forget the occasion when I was a privileged guest in a Bedouin encampment. Earlier in the day, my friends and I had been invited to see the primitive home of these nomads, but later when I returned alone, I had the great honor of being entertained by the men of the family who had been away during the morning hour. A wonderful old fellow offered me a cup of the most bitter coffee I ever tasted. To say the least it was terrible, and I confess with shame that, as soon as my host turned his back, I hastily poured the concoction into the desert sand. However, another cup of coffee was soon forthcoming. It was as sweet as honey. I was informed that the bitter coffee was indicative of the hardship of trying to eke a living out of the wilderness; the second to remind of the sweetness of family life. Something of that kind of procedure prevailed at the Passover. Every worshipper was reminded by the bitter herbs of the terrible anguish known by their forefathers. This they were never permitted to forget. The possibility exists that the owner of the homestead assisted the two disciples in preparing the necessary commodities.

SECTION FIVE

Expository Notes on the Observance of the Passover Feast

And in the evening He cometh with the twelve. And as they sat and did eat, Jesus said, Verily, I say unto you, One of you that eateth with me shall betray me. And they began to be sorrowful, and to say unto Him one by one, Is it I? and another said, Is it I? (vv. 17-19).

THE SPECIAL TIME

A Jewish day always began at 6 P.M., and since the Passover feast was celebrated in the evening, it would have been necessary to attend to the details of preparation during the afternoon. The lamb would have been presented to the priest; the other necessary functions would have been fulfilled; and finally, when all was in readiness, Peter and John rejoined the disciple band. The information that everything was in readiness was relayed to the Lord, "And in the evening, He cometh with the twelve" (v. 17). Thousands of other visitors to Jerusalem would, at that same time, be celebrating their own feast of the Passover, but there is reason to believe Heaven's attention was focused on but one group. The Lamb of God was indeed about to be slain, but only Heaven seemed aware of that fact.

THE SAD TRUTH

"One of you...shall betray me" (v. 18). The Lord was sad; probably an Old Testament text was in His thoughts: "Yea, mine own familiar friend, in whom I trusted, which did eat of my bread, hath lifted up his heel against me" (Ps. 41:9). Peter and John had removed all leaven from the room; alas, there was another kind of defilement of which they were unaware. The heart and mind of Judas had become corrupted and his presence brought sadness to Jesus. It was difficult to believe that one so near could be so far away. That Judas should contemplate treachery was unthinkable; but the fact was undeniable; there was uncleanness within the camp. With the case of Achan (Josh. 7), the uncleanness had been removed by stoning the offender; with Judas, that was not permitted; Jesus could only love him.

THE SICKENING TREACHERY

"The Son of man goeth as it is written of Him: but woe unto that man by whom the Son of man is betrayed! It had been good for that man if he had not been born. Then Judas, which betrayed Him, answered and said, Master, is it I? Jesus said unto him, Thou hast said" (Matt. 26:24-25). Judas surely suspected that Jesus was aware of what had been arranged, but he failed to recognize the love and pity in his Master's eyes. Alas, he was a human fly caught in a web of his own weaving. Each time he moved, he became increasingly entangled in circumstances preventing an escape. That he carried through his obnoxious plan to its climax; that he chose a kiss as a sign of identification for the enemy, branded him the most detestable man that ever walked the earth. And yet it cannot be denied — Christ loved him. It is easy to blame Judas, but if we sacrifice the same Lord for any personal gain, are we not emulating the example given to us by the traitor?

THE SUBLIME TESTIMONY

Perhaps the most thought-provoking detail of the entire story is the inability of the disciples to identify the betrayer. Even John asked, "Is it I?" Probably they all looked around trying to detect the criminal in their midst. But apparently no one suspected Judas. During three and a half years, never, by deed nor word, had Jesus revealed the identity of the enemy. Let us be truthful and admit that this is beyond our comprehension. Had we been the leader of that band of men, our looks and attitude toward Judas would have been frigid. Everyone would have been aware of the displeasure we felt toward the traitor.

And He answered and said unto them, It is one of the twelve, that dippeth with me in the dish. The Son of man indeed goeth, as it is written

of Him: but woe to that man by whom the Son of man is betrayed! good
were it for that man if he had never been born (vv. 20-21).

JUDAS THE DISCIPLE. . .Deciding. What possibilities!

There was a day when Judas met Jesus for the first time. We wonder
what were his reactions. Did he feel any response within his soul when
he heard the Lord's message? Was there enthusiasm within his heart
as he contemplated following the Savior? Day after day he enjoyed a
privilege which every believer envied. Not everyone had the honor of
sitting at the Lord's feet, listening to His teaching, and basking in the
sunshine of His love. Yet Judas had that inestimable privilege. During
three and one-half years a new world was opening before him, and the
possibilities of spiritual accomplishment were unlimited.

JUDAS THE EVANGELIST. . .Declaring. What privileges!

When the Lord sent out His disciples, first the twelve, and afterward
the seventy, Judas was included in the number. During the first
evangelistic effort, he was the traveling companion of one other disciple.
We have been told that when they returned to report to the Lord, they
said, "Even the devils were subject unto us in thy name." When at
a later date, the number of evangelists increased, Judas once again went
from village to village announcing the glad tidings of the Gospel. Was
he a fiery preacher announcing to congregations the need to repent of
sins and to prepare for the coming kingdom? Did he ever sit to counsel
with enquirers? Was he ever proud of what he had done? At those
moments, every angel in heaven would have gladly changed places with
him. Alas, so we have been informed, when the day of final judgment
arrives, many will say, "Lord, we have preached in Thy Name. And
Jesus will answer, "I never knew you."

JUDAS THE BUSINESS MAN. . .Demanding. What perversion!

Judas believed in cutting his losses. Confronted by problems, he
believed in taking the easy way out of his difficulties, and would have
said that half an apple was better than no apple. He had planned what
to do when he became rich; but when his dreams proved to be unreal,
he thought he was brilliantly clever in salvaging thirty pieces of silver.
The other disciples did not get a penny, but that was their fault! This
astute business man had information to sell, but wished to be sure he

could make something on the deal. "How much is it worth to have me on your side?" he asked, and when he felt the coins in his hand, a sense of achievement thrilled his perverted soul. Some people say, "It's a long way from heaven to hell." Apparently Judas found a short cut!

JUDAS THE SUICIDE...Dying. What poverty!

"Then Judas,...when he saw that he was condemned, repented himself, and brought again the thirty pieces of silver to the chief priests and elders, Saying, I have sinned...and they said, What is that to us? see thou to that. And he cast down the pieces of silver in the temple, and departed, and went and hanged himself" (Matt. 27:3-5). Somebody found his body dangling at the end of a rope. The authorities cut that rope and buried the one-time preacher in a pauper's grave. No one mourned his death, except perhaps, the One whom he had betrayed. No one attended the funeral; no relatives were present; no rabbi read a committal service; no one sent flowers. Judas died without having a friend. He had been so near to the kingdom of God, but somehow lost his way in the darkness. What a pity he was unable to read the words of the hymn:

> Have you counted the cost if your soul should be lost
> Tho' you gain the whole world for your own?
> Even now it may be that the line you have crossed.
> Have you counted, have you counted the cost?

And as they did eat, Jesus took bread, and blessed, and brake it, and gave to them, and said, Take, eat: this is my body. And He took the cup, and when He had given thanks, He gave it to them; and they all drank of it. And He said unto them, This is my blood of the new testament, which is shed for many. Verily I say unto you, I will drink no more of the fruit of the vine, until that day when I drink it new in the kingdom of God. And when they had sung a hymn, they went out into the mount of Olives (vv. 22-26).

A TRUTH COMMEMORATED

This group of verses, together with the parallel passages in the other Gospels, are, in some sense, among the most important sections of the New Testament. We cannot over-emphasize the fact, until the death of Jesus, the Feast of the Passover was indisputably the greatest event in the disciples' year. With great anticipation they prepared for the occasion, and there is reason to believe they enjoyed every moment of it. Yet after the death and resurrection of their Lord, the Passover feast had neither attraction nor importance for the followers of Christ. Apart from the Epistle to the Hebrews, where the meaning of the true Passover is expounded, there is no mention of the feast in the New Testament, and there is no record of the disciples observing it. As far as they were concerned, Passover had fulfilled its purpose in pointing to the true Lamb of God, and there remained no obligation even to remember it. A new covenant had taken the place of the old; new ideas were expressed in new ways, and even the importance of the Sabbath was less than they had always believed. Throughout the history of the early church, Christians did not observe the seventh day; they preferred to meet together on the first day of the week (Acts 20:7). They only went to the synagogues on the Sabbath because, by doing so, they were able to witness to congregations gathered for the customary services. To express it bluntly, the Sabbath, the laws of Moses, and the once all-important Passover had no meaning for the early church. The transition from the old to the new began in the final Passover attended by Jesus. Somewhere in that observance, the Lord directed the attention of His followers to the new course they would be expected to follow.

Passover was the commemoration of the deliverance from the bondage of Egypt. Part of the ceremonial proceedings included a recital of the events outlined in Exodus 12, and provision was made whereby even the children would be taught the importance of the slain lamb. It is not necessary within the scope of this commentary to inform readers of the entire program followed at a Passover feast. It is sufficient to say there were numerous washings of hands; there were at least four occasions when wine was drunk, several prayers were recited, and numerous psalms sung by the entire company. Since Peter and John had prepared very carefully for the observance of the Passover ritual, we are safe in assuming the Lord proceeded step by step through the entire program. Then at *one special point in the service*, He took certain parts of the ritual and deliberately imparted to them a new meaning. It is to that act and words of transition we must devote our attention.

The end of the Passover was always celebrated by a feast, when those present participated in eating the roasted lamb. It was probably at this point Jesus instituted the Memorial of the Last Supper. It was as though He had said, "This feast is ending in more senses than one; Behold, I now institute another feast which will last forever." "*And as they did eat*, Jesus took bread. . .and He took the cup, and when He had given thanks, He gave it to them: and they all drank of it'' (vv. 22,23).

A THRILLING COVENANT

"This is my blood of the new testament [covenant]'' (v. 24). A covenant was understood by all Jews. Each person in the nation was reminded daily of the obligation to keep and honor the covenant made by God and Israel in the days of Moses (read Exodus 24:3-8). The covenant was an agreement of mutual consent based on law. God would be true to Israel, if Israel remained true to God. If they were faithful, He would bless them; if they were not, He would curse them. Hence every Jew was reminded of the need to observe the law and thereby indicate, before God and man, faithfulness to Jehovah. Alas, their profession was meaningless, for they were unable to keep their promises. If the observance of the law brought salvation, then unfortunately, Israel was condemned forever as they were unable to complete their side of the covenant. When Christ referred to His blood being shed for them, it became clear He was dying to bring them out of a more grievous bondage. This deliverance from the enslaving power of sin should be commemorated forever. They were instructed to meet together — not once a year, as they had done with the Passover feast, but "as oft as ye do it in remembrance of me.'' At first, the disciples could not understand this, but when the Holy Spirit came at Pentecost to illumine their minds and refresh their memories, suddenly the true significance of the Passover became clear, and from that moment onward, the Jewish feast had no attraction for them. Jesus had instituted something new; something extremely wonderful.

A TREMENDOUS CLAIM

"I will drink no more of the fruit of the vine, *until that day that I drink it new in the kingdom of God*" (v. 25). The Lord knew He was about to die, but in spite of the impending crucifixion, remained sure that His kingdom would be established, and that crowned with splendor, He would be there to "drink the cup of thanksgiving.'' The Lord knew His death would be followed by resurrection; He would not die in vain. "Except a corn of wheat fall into the ground and die, it abideth alone: but if it die, it bringeth forth much fruit. . .And I, if I be lifted up from the earth, will draw all men unto me'' (John 12:24-32). We can understand how difficult it was for those disciples to understand the immensity of what was being said. He was teaching advanced theology; alas, they were only kindergarten students! Unperturbed, He knew that soon they would not only understand His message; they would preach it throughout the world.

A TRIUMPHANT CONCLUSION

"And when they had sung a hymn, they went out into the Mount of Olives" (v. 26). It seems unbelievable that in the midst of impending sorrow and suffering, the Lord was able to sing! Others might have been weeping. Probably He pitched the tune, and then encouraged the disciples to sing the hymn of praise. It is possible the hymn sung was Psalm 136, which is still known as The Great Hallel. "O give thanks unto the Lord; for He is good: for His mercy endureth for ever." We should note that there are twenty-six verses in the Psalm, and each one ends with the words: "FOR HIS MERCY ENDURETH FOR EVER." Surely, the Psalmist was trying to tell us something! Imagine, if you can, how the Lord presided at that inaugural supper, and then bow your head and worship at His feet.

> Oh to grace, how great a debtor,
> Daily I'm constrained to be.

SECTION SIX

Expository Notes on Christ's Warning to the Disciples

And Jesus saith unto them, All ye shall be offended because of me this night: for it is written, I will smite the shepherd, and the sheep shall be scattered. But after that I am risen, I will go before you into Galilee. But Peter said unto Him, Although all shall be offended, yet will not I. And Jesus saith unto him, Verily I say unto thee, That this day, even in this night, before the cock crow twice, thou shalt deny me thrice. But he spake the more vehemently, If I should die with thee, I will not deny thee in any wise. Likewise also said they all (vv. 27-31).

A SAD PREDICTION

The disciples had become exceedingly apprehensive; with each moment their hopes for a kingdom were abating. They looked at the

Lord and knew He was troubled. What had gone wrong with their carefully laid plans? They were puzzled; He had already demonstrated His ability to handle the enemy, yet He was doing nothing. Had they been the leader with His power, the kingdom would already have been established! Then suddenly He was speaking: "All ye shall be offended because of me this night: for it is written, I will smite the shepherd, and the sheep shall be scattered" (v. 27). This was a quotation from Zechariah 13:7. It was interesting that each time the Lord quoted Scriptures from the Old Testament, He affirmed they were prophecies relating to Himself. This was not surprising, for basically He was the Author of the Book! By His Spirit He had suggested the subject matter for each prophet, and had even inspired their books. The Greek word translated "offended" is *skandalistheesesthe*; it came from the verb *skandalizo*. Another closely related word was *skandalon*. There was no doubt about the meaning of the first word. It signified "a stumbling block; something placed in one's way; an impediment." The second word, according to Thayer was a biblical word, used in the Greek translation of the Old and New Testaments. It had a different shade of meaning, signifying "the trigger of a trap, a trap-stick, a snare, something placed in the way to cause stumbling or entrapment." These words have caused lengthy discussions. If both translations be combined, then Jesus was trying to warn the disciples that snares would be in their pathway; there was need to proceed with caution, for what was to happen that night would lead to confusion, possible entrapment, and certain disappointment. A night of terror and trial awaited them; they had need to watch and pray.

A SERIOUS PRESUMPTION

"But Peter said unto Him, Although all shall be offended, yet will not I" (v. 29). Peter's impetuosity was understandable, but inexcusable. He apparently looked with disdain upon his colleagues. Yes, they were capable of failing in emergencies; but Simon Peter would never be as they — never! That spark of self-confident boasting could have started a bush fire! Had the others present been less startled by the Lord's prediction, they might have launched a very devastating verbal attack against their boastful brother. Peter would have been a wiser man had he considered the words of the prophet Micah, (6:8). "He hath shewed thee, O man, what is good; and what doth the Lord require of thee, but to do justly, and to love mercy, and *to walk humbly with thy God*".

Humility was not exactly Peter's greatest asset. He was only tall when he was kneeling!

A STUPID PERSISTENCE

"And Jesus saith unto him, Verily I say unto thee, That this day, even in this night, before the cock crow twice, thou shalt deny me thrice. But [Peter] spoke *the more vehemently*, If I should die with thee, I will not deny thee in any wise. Likewise also said they all" (vv. 30,31). Peter was beginning to get angry; his emotions were getting out of control! Actually he was questioning and condemning the Lord's words. Anger usually blinds a man to the realities of life; it is an exposure of personal weakness. Peter considered the Lord's remarks to be an insinuation of unreliability. Simon Peter was as good as anybody, and the Lord needed to be reminded of that fact! A flash of indignation came to Peter's eyes; his jaw protruded a little more than was usual; he was in a fighting mood! He was about to explode, but suddenly his colleagues came to the rescue. Their voices were raised as they firmly assured the Lord He was mistaken. They were stupid and short-sighted, and it is not surprising to read in Mark 14:50, "And they all forsook Him and fled."

SECTION SEVEN

Expository Notes on the Events in the Garden of Gethsemane

And they came to a place which is named Gethsemane: and He saith to His disciples, Sit ye here while I shall pray. And He taketh with Him Peter and James and John, and began to be sore amazed, and to be very heavy; And saith unto them, My soul is exceeding sorrowful unto death: tarry ye here and watch. And He went forward a little, and fell on the ground, and prayed that, if it were possible, the hour might pass from Him. And He said, Abba Father, all things are possible unto thee; take away this cup from me: nevertheless not what I will, but what thou wilt (vv. 32-36).

A PRIVATE RETREAT

"When Jesus had spoken these words, He went forth with His disciples over the brook Cedron, *where was a garden*, into the which He entered, and His disciples" (John 18:1). "And they came to a place which was named Gethsemane: and He saith to His disciples, Sit ye here, while I shall pray'' (v. 32). We've read that Jerusalem had no gardens as the city was too overcrowded. There was a law that stated that the city's sacred soil should not be polluted with manure for the gardens. Josephus tells us that many of the rich citizens owned gardens on the Mount of Olives, and the probability exists that some wealthy friend had given the Lord permission to use his garden at any time of the day or night. John says (18:2) ''And Judas also, which betrayed Him, knew the place: *for Jesus ofttimes resorted thither with His disciples.*'' It was fitting therefore that when Jesus needed privacy, He should go, as He had often done, to the seclusion of the garden on the Mount of Olives. He took with Him three disciples, but even these were left behind, when He proceeded to speak with God. Friends are very wonderful, but when the soul desperately needs to be alone with God, even they may be intruders.

We are now obliged to consider a problem. The narrative we are to consider describes sleeping disciples. ''. . . for their eyes were heavy.'' If they slept, then who saw what happened, and later described those events to the writers of the Gospels? There are four possibilities. (1) Did the disciples remain awake long enough to see some of the events taking place? They went to sleep at least on three occasions, but during intervals, did they see such vivid scenes that long afterward, they were still able to describe those unforgettable details? (2) If they slept almost continually, did one of the other disciples left outside, quietly enter the garden to discover what was taking place? Did he pass his slumbering brethren, and see the agony of the Lord? Did this unknown man later confess what he had done, and did he become the source of information for the most intimate moments in the experiences of Jesus? (3) If the disciples within the garden slept, and if there were no eavesdropper, then what happened that night must have been revealed by the Holy Spirit at a later date. (4) There is a fourth possibility and it concerns John Mark. This will be considered later in this commentary.

A PRAYER REPEATED

''And [He] saith unto them, My soul is exceeding sorrowful unto death. . .'' (v. 34). *The Amplified New Testament* says: ''He began to be struck with terror and amazement, and deeply troubled and depressed.'' It is necessary to try and understand the depth of meaning expressed by the original words used by Mark. The two words in Greek are very significant: *ekthambeisthai* means "to be thrown into amazement or terror, to alarm thoroughly, to terrify." The word *adeemonein* which has been translated "to be very heavy," has a strange connotation. Primarily, it means: "not to be at home, to be distressed." If we consider these phases of meaning, the text could easily read: Jesus "began to be exceedingly terrified; His spirit was in danger 'of not being at home' and he was greatly distressed." The Amplified version of verse Mark 14:34 is indicative of these facts. "And he said to them, My soul is exceedingly sad — overwhelmed with grief — so that it almost kills Me!" There was indeed danger that "He would not be at home much longer" (see Thayer's comments in *The Greek-English Lexicon of the New Testament,* pp. 11 and 195). This is also expressed in Hebrews 5:7. "Who in the days of His flesh, when He had offered up prayers and supplications with strong [agonized] crying and tears unto Him that was able to save Him from death, and *was heard in that He feared.*" The Lord was deeply stirred with anguish when He prayed; it is noteworthy that His petition was repeated several times.

Special consideration must now be given to the prayer itself. The Lord prayed asking that the cup should pass from Him. "Probably there is very much more in the text than would at first appear. What was this cup to which the Lord referred? It was unthinkable that He should be seeking a way to avoid the death of the cross. It was for that specific cause He came into the world, and Hebrews 12:1-2 makes it perfectly clear that when He contemplated going to the Cross, He did so with great joy. He never shirked His responsibilities; He never tried to avoid what He had helped plan in the earliest of all ages. Therefore *the cup* could not have meant the cross.

"Hebrews 5:7 makes an important contribution to our consideration. 'Who in the days of His flesh, when He had offered up prayers and supplications with strong crying and tears unto Him that was ABLE TO SAVE HIM FROM DEATH, and was heard in that *He feared.*' First, let it be clearly understood that *Christ's prayer was answered.* The cup DID pass from Him. This is something we need to comprehend. The Lord never prayed any prayer but what it was answered; He always prayed in the will of God. This is the first thing we must remember. The Savior's petition *was granted* while a deadly fear gripped His soul. It was not the fear of death, but rather the fear that *He might die too soon.* Reconciliation was to be made through the blood of the Cross; there, the forces of evil would be put to flight. Even Satan believed this, and knowing the time was short, the hosts of evil attacked the Son of God. This was the greatest attempt ever made upon the Lord's life. The onslaught was so intense that blood began to ooze from the Savior's temples. When His life seemed to be in jeopardy, the thought occurred —'Am I to die within sight of my goal?' The cup was the experience of physical weakness, and the Lord's desperate cry for help was answered when the angel came to assist Him. The imparted strength enabled Jesus to vanquish the forces besieging His soul and to proceed calmly toward the realization of His greatest ambition. The Savior's submissiveness was never in doubt. Although He desired to redeem sinners, His yieldedness to His Father was obvious when He said, 'Not my will but thine be done.' He yearned to save a lost world, but longed even more to please His Father. Only thus could He prove His fitness to become our Redeemer. IT WAS THE WILL OF GOD TO SAVE HIM; and in answer to the Son's prayer, the angel came to do what was necessary'' (see Luke 22:41-43) (reprinted from the author's commentary, *Luke's Thrilling Gospel*, p. 460.)

A POWER RECEIVED

As we have just read, an angel arrived from Heaven to dispense strength to the Lord. How this was accomplished, we can only conjecture. The ground upon which we are treading seems too holy for us to remain unnecessarily. Nevertheless, we retire with one pre-eminent thought. God is able to meet our every need. James said, "Every good gift and every perfect gift is from above, and cometh down from the Father...with whom there is no variableness, neither shadow of turning" (James 1:17). However, the same writer also said, "Ye ask and receive not, because ye ask amiss..." (James 4:3).

And He cometh and findeth them sleeping, and saith unto Peter, Simon, sleepest thou? couldest not thou watch one hour? Watch ye and pray, lest ye enter into temptation. The spirit truly is ready, but the flesh is weak. And again He went away and prayed, and spake the same words. And when He returned He found them asleep again, (for their eyes were heavy) neither wist they what to answer Him. And He cometh the third time, and saith unto them, Sleep on now, and take your rest: it is enough, the hour is come; behold, the Son of man is betrayed into the hands of sinners. Rise up, let us go; lo, he that betrayeth me is at hand (vv. 37-42).

Much of this passage of Scripture has already been expounded in the earlier section; however, there are a few additional areas awaiting exploration. The word *apechei* translated "it is enough" has caused much debate. Apparently it admits of two interpretations. It could mean as indicated. Jesus said, "Sleep on now, and take your rest," but it is difficult to understand how immediately, the Lord said, "Rise up, let us go." How could the disciples continue their sleep when He was asking them to follow Him? The other interpretation of the text seems more understandable. Thayer indicates the word means "to be away, to be absent, to be distant." Therefore, the Lord might have been saying, "You can continue your sleep, for he who betrays me is still a little distance away." Dr. E. Bickersteth writes: "There is a tone of reproach in His final permission, 'Sleep on now.' Now that the glimmering of torches is seen through the olive boughs as their bearers cross the deep ravine; now that the step of the traitor falls upon the ear of the betrayed. A sad reminder of 'the irreparable past;' an everlasting expostulation, again and again in coming years, to ring in the ear of each slumberous, unsympathetic disciple, and rouse to diligence, to watchfulness, to prayer." There is, for all of us, abounding comfort in the words: "...having loved His own, He loved them unto the end." Disciples may fail; Simon Peter would deny; and even John, with the rest of his colleagues might run for life, but as Paul wrote: "...neither death nor life; nor angels, nor principalities; nor powers, nor things present, nor things to come, Nor height nor depth, nor any other creature, shall be able to separate us from the love of God, which is in Christ Jesus our Lord" (Rom. 8:37-39).

> **And immediately, while he yet spake, cometh Judas, one of the twelve, and with him a great multitude with swords and staves, from the chief priests and the scribes and the elders. And he that betrayed Him had given them a token, saying, Whomsoever I shall kiss, that same is He; take Him and lead Him away safely. And as soon as he was come, he goeth straightway to Him, and saith, Master, Master; and kissed Him. And they laid their hands on Him, and took Him (vv. 43-46).**

A FINAL LOOK

The silence of the garden would soon be shattered. Standing with His disciples among the olive trees, the Lord was able to look up at the walls of the city. As the crowd surged through the gateway and started to descend the hill to the foot of the Mount of Olives, their lanterns and torches would be clearly visible to the disciples. John (18:3) says, "Judas then, having received a band of men and officers...cometh thither . . ." The Greek word translated "band" is *Speiran*, and means the "tenth part of a legion," that is about six hundred men. This was a military operation and not a casual arrest by an officer of the law. When we take into consideration that there would be representatives of the Pharisees, scribes, and elders, and that in addition there would be a host of sightseers hoping to see something sensational, it becomes clear that at least a thousand soldiers and civilians would be making a real commotion as they marched to make their arrest. Below in the valley, the Lord calmly awaited their arrival. As indicated by John 18:6, He could have destroyed the whole party in one moment. However, He had not come to kill people, but to save them. That night He looked for the last time upon a city which He loved, and perhaps from His heart arose the expression of sorrow: "O Jerusalem, Jerusalem, thou that killest the prophets, and stonest them which are sent unto thee, how often would I have gathered thy children together, even as a hen gathereth her chickens under her wings, and ye would not? Behold your house is left unto you desolate" (Matt. 23:37-38).

A FEARED LOSS

"Whomsoever I shall kiss, that same is He; take Him and lead Him away safely" (v. 44). It was as though Judas said, "Stay close to me and do not make any mistake. Once I identify your man, seize Him; make sure He does not escape. Do not underestimate His powers; He might try to escape, so hold Him tightly, and guard Him well." Judas was aware that thirty pieces of silver might be at stake; he had already abandoned hope of becoming the Minister of Finance in God's kingdom, but he was safeguarding his precious coins. It is very difficult to understand how a man who had been so prominent in the service of Jesus could become such a detestable traitor. To exchange his soul for silver revealed him to be a senseless fool. Never again would he be able to fellowship with his colleagues; they would hate him, and feel contaminated by his presence. Wherever he went, people would call him the greatest of traitors. He would be without home, friends, peace; he would be a lost soul wandering in unending darkness — and all for thirty pieces of silver!

A FAITHLESS LOVER

"And as soon as he was come, he goeth straightway to Jesus, and saith, Master, Master, and kissed Him" (v. 45). *The Amplified New*

Testament translates the verse: ''. . .he went up to Jesus immediately, and said, Master! *Master,* and embraced Him, and *kissed Him fervently.*'' Let us note a very important variation of words in this narrative. Apparently, Judas felt that they needed definite guidance concerning the one they were to arrest. The flare of the torches only dimly lit the darkness of the trees of the garden. Thus he chose to give a kiss. It was customary to greet a Rabbi with a kiss. It was a sign of respect and affection for a well-loved teacher. Let us notice this terrible thing here. When Judas says, ''Whom I shall kiss, that is He,'' he used the word *philein*, which is the ordinary word. But when it is said that he came forward and kissed Jesus, the word is *kataphilein*. Now the *kata* is intensive and *kataphilein* is the word for to kiss as *a lover kisses his beloved.* Judas' sign of the betrayal, rather than being a mere formal kiss of respectful greeting, was *a lover's kiss.* Do you agree this is the grimmest and most terrible thing in all the gospel story?

We have already seen in the earlier studies that the word for hypocrite means ''an actor.'' Judas was indeed a dramatic actor in the garden; he played the part of an impassioned disciple as he embraced the Lord and fervently kissed Him. Unfortunately, the darkness within his soul was more intense than the darkness enveloping Jerusalem. Within a few hours, the sun arose in splendor over that ill-fated city, but there was never another sunrise for Judas. It is written that ''he went out, *and it was night* (John 13:30). Unfortunately, for that desperate sinner, it is still night!

And one of them that stood by drew a sword, and smote a servant of the high priest, and cut off his ear. And Jesus answered and said unto them, Are ye come out as against a thief, with swords and with staves to take me? I was daily with you in the temple teaching, and ye took me not; but the Scriptures must be fulfilled. And they all forsook Him and fled. And there followed Him a certain young man, having a lined cloth cast about his naked body; and the young men laid hold on him. And he left the linen cloth, and fled from them naked (vv. 47-52).

IMPULSIVENESS. . . The Act of the Liberator!

The flames of defiance were still burning within Peter's soul. He could not understand all that was taking place around him, but at least, the moment for resistance had come! These interfering enemies had said and done enough; the time for action had arrived, and Peter took his sword from its scabbard. The first blow for the liberation of Israel would announce the beginning of the revolution. Within a matter of seconds, blood was flowing from the side of a victim's head; a man was moaning with pain, but Peter's flashing eyes testified eloquently to the determination filling his soul. If these wretches were to attack the Master, then they would pay for their folly. Peter was ready to take on the whole of Caesar's army! He had already told the Master that he would be willing to die for Him, but obviously the time had come for actions not words! Luke informs us that the victim was a servant of the high priest and that the man's ear was severed. John gives us the name of the servant. "Then Simon Peter having a sword drew it, and smote the high priest's servant, and cut off his right ear. The servant's name was Malchus. Then said Jesus unto Peter, Put up thy sword into the sheath: the cup which my Father hath given me, shall I not drink it?" (John 18:10-11). Matthew supplies a little more information. "Then said Jesus unto Peter, Put up again thy sword into his place: for all they that take the sword shall perish with the sword. Thinkest thou that I cannot now pray to my Father, and he shall presently give me more than twelve legions of angels? But how then shall the Scriptures be fulfilled, that thus it must be?" (Matt. 26:52-54). Luke, the medical doctor, found excitement in this account, for he carefully includes the thrilling climax of the account. "And one of them smote the servant of the high priest, and cut off his right ear. And Jesus answered and said, Suffer ye thus far. *And He touched his ear and healed him*" (Luke 22:50-51). Thus did the overwhelming love of the Lord bring a possible insurrection to an abrupt end. The disciples' lives at that moment were hanging as it were by a thread; the soldiers had already drawn their swords and lifted their spears. Had not Jesus acted immediately, the garden of Gethsemane would have been stained with the blood of every disciple.

INDITEMENT. . . The Announcement of the Lord

"Are ye come out, as against a thief with swords and with staves to take me? I was daily with you in the temple. . .and ye took me not" (vv. 48,49). It was as though the Lord asked, "What has changed? I was with you publicly in daylight; I was teaching in the temple; why did you not take Me then? Were you afraid that the people might resist your action? Were you afraid of unpleasant publicity? Or perhaps those who sent you thought the operation would have a better chance to succeed if all My friends were in bed! Why do you come with weapons of war;

are you afraid of Me? Look around and see how many of My followers are present. There are twelve of us — yes, there were thirteen, but one of My men deserted to your side. But look at us. Are we a threat to your safety, that you must cloak your actions with the shadows of the night?'' Then with dramatic suddenness an indescribable glory emanated from His being: He said, ''I am'' and in a moment of blinding confusion, they were swept from their feet (see John 18:5-8 and compare the text with Exodus 3:13-14).

IGNOMINY. . . The Absconding of the Listeners

''And they all forsook Him and fled'' (v. 50). The disciples were utterly bewildered; their Master did not intend to fight. Obviously He had the capability of resisting; had He not knocked them flat? But He was surrendering on the condition that they be permitted to escape. His words, ''Let these go their way'' were the most ominous they had ever heard. Those pesky Romans would have their pound of flesh! They would never permit anyone to escape! Suddenly, one of the disciples whispered, ''Let's go,'' and within moments the eleven disciples were running for their lives. Circumstances are said to alter cases. Peter had promised never to be unfaithful to his Lord, and even as he uttered his words, the brethren, in chorus, said, ''Peter, we agree. We shall never be offended in the Master.'' ''So said they all.'' Let us not be harsh in our condemnation of those frightened men. It had been so easy to promise to die for Christ when death seemed to be a million miles away. They were now looking into the face of the threatening monster, and the terrible prospect of becoming martyrs petrified them. They ran, and possibly, had we been present that night, we might have outrun them all!

IDENTIFICATION. . . The Anonymity of the Lad

''And there followed Him a certain young man. . .'' (v. 51). Let it be considered that the young man was attracted to Jesus; that he may have been present before the arrival of the soldiers. Somewhere he had heard of Christ and had probably seen Him. There was, for the boy, an impelling attraction about that wonderful Jesus. It seems strange that he should have been naked, with only a bed sheet wrapped around his youthful body. The consensus of theological thought is that the boy was none other than the author of this Gospel. The home of John Mark was the outstanding Christian home in Jerusalem; the place to which the disciples went to pray (see Acts 12:12). Probably the Lord had visited that home on several occasions; some scholars identify the family as the owners of the donkey loaned to Jesus for the triumphant entry into the city. If this were indeed the case, then young Mark would have been aware of all that was taking place. Then one night, after he had retired to bed, he probably overheard his parents speaking of the tragic events about to happen, and fearing for the safety of his Friend, John Mark slipped out of bed. Wrapping a cloth around his body, he ran into the darkness. Maybe, and I repeat, *MAYBE*, he found the Lord in the garden of Gethsemane, and if that were the case, could have witnessed and overheard all that was spoken. If, as has been suggested in early notes, the disciples slept through the time of the Lord's agony, Mark might have been the only eye-witness. Later, when opportunity permitted, he was able to describe what took place. Seeing this half-naked youngster standing near, the youths in the crowd, intent on having fun, grabbed the boy, but releasing his hold on the covering sheet, John Mark escaped with his immortal story (see special instructions for homily at the end of this chapter).

SECTION EIGHT

Expository Notes on the Lord's Appearance Before the High Priest

And they led Jesus away to the high priest; and with Him were assembled all the chief priests and the elders and the scribes. And Peter followed Him afar off, even into the palace of the high priest; and he sat with the servants, and warmed himself at the fire. And the chief priests and all the council sought for witness against Jesus to put Him to death and found none. For many bare false witness against Him, but their witness agreed not together. And there rose certain, and bare false witness against Him saying, We heard Him say, I will destroy this temple made with hands, and within three days I will build another made without hands. But neither so did their witness agree together (vv. 53-59).

The Lord knew the storm was about to break. He permitted His captors to lead Him away into the night, but it will forever be a source of amazement that, although He had the power to destroy His enemies, He never did so. Probably the angels were astonished when they saw the King of Heaven fettered!

THE UNLAWFUL ASSEMBLY

The *Mishnah* gives some very interesting information about the Sanhedrin. This was the supreme court of the Jews, being composed of seventy-one members. The Sadducees, the priestly classes all belonged to this group — the Pharisees and the Scribes, the experts in the law, and other respected men who were the elders were the members of the Sanhedrins. The court was presided over by the High Priest and the members sat in a semi-circle so any member could see others. The students of the Rabbis like to sit facing the members. They were allowed to speak on behalf of the person on trial but not speak against him. The official meetings took place in the Hall of Hewn Stone which was within the Temple precincts. The Sanhedrin could not make any valid decisions unless they met at this place, and the court could not meet at night nor during any of the great feasts. The witnesses had to be examined separately and every evidence had to agree on every detail. Each member of the court would then have to give his verdict separately, beginning with the youngest and going to the eldest. Any death verdict could not be carried out until a night had elapsed, in case the court wanted to change its mind and pronounce a more lenient decision. The Sanhedrin, however, kept breaking its own rules: as many times it did not meet in the proper place, meetings were held at night, nor were there individually-given verdicts. Thus when the Jewish authorities wanted to eliminate Jesus, they did not hesitate to break their own laws.

THE UNASHAMED ACCUSERS

The hastily convened meeting was held in the palace of the High Priest. Ordinarily most of the rulers would have been in bed at that late hour, but sleep would have been impossible. The tramp of soldiers through the streets; the excited shouts of the crowd; and, above all, the loud clamor of disturbed consciences were making this a night of unprecedented infamy. Utter confusion reigned within the palace, as prosecutors tried in vain to formulate a case against Jesus. As soon as they found a man with what appeared to be a valid testimony, another witness appeared to contradict and deny what the other had spoken. Finally, even the lawyers realized they were exhibiting stupidity. None of the evidence would be permissible within a court of law. The desperate hunt for new witnesses continued. It was at this point in the story, that Mark probably looked at Peter who was describing the events, to ask:

"Peter, what were you doing during all this?" The apostle paused for a moment and then replied: "Son, I had followed at a distance, but finally had gained admittance to the Palace. I was embarrassed standing alone, so I went up to a fire and warmed myself. Yes, Son, I know now that was the greatest mistake of my life, but let us finish this part of your book, and afterward, I will describe what happened to me."

THE UNTRUE ACCUSATIONS

Suddenly a lawyer came through the crowd leading a man. Reaching his colleagues, he said, "I have found a valid witness. Listen to what he has to tell." They were very attentive as the stranger said: "Jesus is insane; He has strange ideas. I think He will try to destroy the temple because He thinks He can build a new one in three days. Only a madman could think and speak like that. You had better stop Him before it is too late." The lawyers were very thoughtful, but finally one asked, "How do you know He threatened to do as you say?" "Oh, I was there when He said, 'I will destroy this temple that is made with hands, and within three days I will build another made without hands.' Yes, that man is mad and might do a lot of damage to our temple." That piece of twisted evidence seemed irrefutable, for truly, the Lord had uttered words to that effect. Years earlier Jesus ". . . answered and said unto them, Destroy this temple, and in three days I will raise it up. Then said the Jews, forty and six years was this temple in building, and wilt thou rear it up in three days? *But He spake of the temple of His body.* When therefore He was risen from the dead, His disciples remembered that He had said this unto them; and they believed the Scripture, and the word which Jesus had said" (John 2:19-22). The smiles on the faces of the lawyers indicated they could proceed with their case. Jesus the Prisoner was not only a blasphemer; He was a mad heretic threatening damage to sacred property. He had to be restrained, and the only safe way to do this was by death.

And the high priest stood up in the midst, and asked Jesus, saying, Answerest thou nothing? what is it that these witness against thee? But He held His peace, and answered nothing. Again the high priest asked Him, and said unto Him, Art thou the Christ, the Son of the Blessed? And Jesus said, I am: and ye shall see the Son of man sitting on the right hand of power, and coming in the clouds of heaven. Then the high priest rent his clothes, and saith, What need we any further witnesses? Ye have heard the blasphemy: what think ye? And they all condemned

Him to be guilty of death. And some began to spit on Him, and to cover His face, and to buffet Him, and to say unto Him, Prophecy: and the servants did strike Him with the palms of their hands (vv. 60-65).

A TACTFUL SILENCE

"*But [Jesus] held His peace and answered nothing*" (v. 61). The court-room was filled with confusion. Everybody seemed to be speaking, and yet nobody was saying a thing! Witnesses were at variance; prosecutors were apprehensive, and the Prisoner alone seemed at ease. Something had to be done or the whole scene would become a fiasco. The high priest looked with disdain on those who were supposed to be in charge of the case; they were getting nowhere! "And the high priest stood up in the midst, and asked Jesus, saying, Answerest thou nothing? What is it that these witnesss against thee? But Jesus held His peace." It would have been unwise to say anything. The Lord knew they were not seeking truth; their question and activities were hypocritical; they had passed sentence even before the trial commenced. Whatever was said, they would misrepresent His words, distort His sayings, and with great deliberation pronounce Him to be guilty. For lesser prisoners it would have been a chance to shout; to call them hypocrites, and deny every charge made, but of Jesus it has been written, "When He was reviled, He reviled not again" (1 Peter 2:23). Jesus was aware of the words of Solomon. There is "...a time to keep silence, and a time to speak" (Eccl. 3:7).

A TREMENDOUS STATEMENT

"A time to speak." That moment was quickly forthcoming, for when a question was asked concerning His identity, the Lord was obliged to answer, "I am" (v. 62). He was not afraid of being charged with contempt of court, but He was concerned with any testimony regarding truth. When people ask for guidance in regard to divine affairs, no man is justified in withholding information. The Lord was also safeguarding Himself against accusations which could be made when, as Judge, He will preside over "The Great Assize." The high priest will not be able to say at his own trial, "When I asked for guidance, you refused to supply it." It may be safely assumed that no soul will ever be lost because God withheld soul-saving information. It is incumbent for God to send His message to perishing man, but what happens afterward is man's responsibility. When the Lord spoke of His personal return, the statement appeared to be blasphemous, and the accusers were delighted. We are confronted with one great fact. Either Jesus *was* what He claimed to be or He was the most abominable charlatan ever to walk the earth.

A TERRIBLE SIN

"Then the high priest rent his clothes" (v. 63). This garment was a sacerdotal frock; a garment with a hole sufficiently large to permit the garment being placed over the head. It had a small opening at the front of the neck; an opening resembling the neck line of a woman's blouse. Horrified, the priest lifted his hands and with brute force, tore his frock or robe into pieces. This was a sign of intense indignation, but in actuality, it was a revelation of the bankruptcy of his soul. What he did had been expressly forbidden by the laws of Moses. Leviticus 10:6 says, "And Moses said unto Aaron, and unto Eleazar, and unto Ithamar, his sons, Uncover not your heads, *neither rend your clothes; lest ye die...*" Obviously the priest had forgotten the commandment he was supposed to teach. It is of interest to note the Greek verb rendered "rent" implies violent, dramatic action. Some of the early church Fathers taught that this act typified the rending of the priesthood from Caiaphas and Jewish nation. Are we justified in contrasting the rending of the veil in the temple with the rending of the high priest's garment? The one signified an earthly priesthood was ending; the other indicated a new and a living way was being opened to the Mercy Seat — a way to be traveled by all who through the grace of God have been made kings and priests (see Revelation 5:10).

A TRAGIC SENTENCE

"And they all condemned Him to be guilty of death" (v. 64). Probably all heaven would have been thrilled by a chance to hasten to the Lord's rescue, but God's outstretched hand held them back. Strange as it might sound, this was part of the plan, foretold by the prophets. "I gave my back to the smiters, and my cheeks to them that plucked off the hair: I hid not my face from shame and spitting" (Isa. 50:6). Once the sentence had been passed, the onlookers became a mob. Jesus was slapped by the officers; His beard was torn from His face, and yet, although He possessed the ability to destroy His foes, He did nothing. "...as a sheep before her shearers is dumb, so He opened not his mouth" (Isa. 53:7).

SECTION NINE

Expository Notes on Peter's Denial of His Lord

And as Peter was beneath in the palace, there cometh one of the maids of the high priest: And when she saw Peter warming himself, she looked upon him, and said, And thou also wast with Jesus of Nazareth. But he denied, saying, I know not, neither understand I what thou sayest. And he went out into the porch; and the cock crew. And a maid saw him again, and began to say to them that stood by, This is one of them. And he denied it again. And a little after, they that stood by said again to Peter, Surely thou art one of them: for thou art a Galilaean, and thy speech agreeth thereto. But he began to curse and to swear, saying, I know not this man of whom ye speak. And the second time the cock crew. And Peter called to mind the word that Jesus said unto him, before the cock crow twice, thou shalt deny me thrice. And when he thought thereon, he wept (vv. 66-72).

Simon Peter was an unpolished diamond! He was a man of great worth, but at that particular moment, no one would have recognized his value. He made promises with great enthusiasm, but just as easily, broke them. He boasted of unfailing faithfulness to Jesus, but when pain and persecution threatened, Peter, with his brethren, fled. He insisted he was more reliable than his brethren, but when things went wrong, became worse than they. Afterward, Simon Peter would have been the first to admit he was to be distrusted; he was arrogant and a little conceited. Let us not be deceived. In spite of appearances, Simon *was* a diamond, but it took the hand of a Master Polisher to bring out the hidden beauty.

PETER DISAVOWS HIS FRIEND

It has been recorded that "they all forsook Him and fled" (v. 50). It should be remembered, that somewhere in the darkness of the city, the fleeing Simon came to a halt. His conscience paralyzed his feet. He who had promised to be loyal was running away! Peter returned, and although it is also written that he followed afar off, at least, *he was following.* He saw the crowd entering the palace of the priest, but probably felt reluctant to enter. "And Simon Peter followed Jesus, and so did another disciple: that disciple was known unto the high priest, and went in with Jesus into the palace of the high priest. But Peter stood at the door without. Then went out that other disciple, which was known unto the high priest, and spake unto her that kept the door, and brought in Peter" (John 18:15-16). What happened to John does not really concern us; we know that Peter drew near to the fire and stood among the strangers warming himself. Probably, the maid who had admitted Peter, also felt cold from standing in the draught, and coming over to the fire, recognized John's companion. Looking intently at Peter she exclaimed, "And thou also wast with Jesus of Nazareth" (v. 67). Taken off guard, Peter impulsively denied the accusation. A sudden surge of conscience smote him, and within moments he was hurrying to the exit. But, and this is an important *but*, there he stopped. The world has long since decided that had he been a prudent man, he would have continued going until he was far away. Then suddenly the crowing of a cockerel echoed through the night, and Peter trembled. He had deserted his Master and was thoroughly ashamed of himself. How could he hide when the Lord was in danger? It was unthinkable; and Peter returned to the hall. There are two sides to every picture, and before we condemn the fisherman for his denial, it might be wise to ask if we would have returned or hastened to a hiding place at the far end of the city!

PETER DENIES HIS FELLOWSHIP

When the maid saw him again, she said, "This is one of them" (v. 69). We should notice the change of direction in her subtle accusation. She knew Peter had denied identification with Christ and she could hardly call him a liar; but at least she was sure he had some connection with the friends of the Prisoner. Her words were heard by the people nearby, and Peter was becoming infuriated. "Why could not that pesky girl keep her mouth shut, and mind her own business?" Peter had spent three years in fellowship with the Master, and his language had been somewhat refined! Even although he was unaware of the change, an indescribable charm from Jesus had mellowed the rough fisherman from Galilee. Alas, everything was about to collapse! That girl was so insistent; the men were getting suspicious; Peter had to say something. He did, and his fierce remarks left no room for conjecture. He knew nothing about the Prisoner, nor any movement He had started.

PETER DEPLORES HIS FAILURE

Suddenly Peter stiffened; the cock was crowing again, and "Peter called to mind the word that Jesus said unto him, Before the cock crow twice, thou shalt deny me thrice. And when he thought thereon, he wept" (v. 72). Luke says, "And Peter went out and wept *bitterly*" (22:62). Luke uses the word *pikros* which means "bitterly, with poignant grief, anguish." Simon Peter was devastated, shattered, completely overcome by irrepressible guilt. Somewhere within the city, he broke his heart and decided his world had ended. All thoughts of forgiveness were rejected; in any case, he could never face his Lord again, and even the disciples would be angry and critical, because he had been dishonorable. Simon had promised to remain faithful even if the others failed! Yet they had not denied Jesus; he had! His tears continued to flow; Peter wished he were dead!

There remains but one thing to consider. Luke's account of this incident was given in more detail (see Luke 22:55-62). Luke mentioned one cock-crowing. Matthew agreed with Luke. The different versions are unimportant. The other writers were concerned only with the fact that Peter denied before the cock crew. Peter, the man most concerned with the incident, knew every detail. They were engraved upon his conscience. It was as though he said, "Brothers, I was there, *I know* what happened."

Some theologians offer a different interpretation. They refer to the fact that the changing of the guard was always accompanied by the blowing of a bugle. This was part of the ceremonial observance. The bugle call was known as the *gallicinium,* which in the Latin meant "cockcrow." Furthermore, in Mark 13:35, the term is used to denote *a particular watch of the night.* Sometimes a disturbed cockerel may crow all night, but generally, the cry of the bird heralds the dawn of the day. It has been suggested that the Lord referred to the blowing of that bugle, and that by so doing, was setting a precise time before which Peter would sadly fail. The traditional view is that a cockerel did crow. Peter failed to live up to expectations. His tears were insufficient to absolve him from guilt, but he discovered later that what tears could not do, the precious blood of Christ could, and did do.

HOMILIES

Attention is drawn to the fact that several homilies dealing with parallel passages of Scripture may be found in the author's companion volumes.

"Mary of Bethany...Who Did Not Wait for the Funeral," *John's Wonderful Gospel,* p.259.

"Judas...Who Gambled and Lost His Soul," *John's Wonderful Gospel,* p. 288.

"The World's Greatest Battle," *Luke's Thrilling Gospel,* p. 462.

"Simon Peter...Who Sat at Two Fires," *John's Wonderful Gospel,* p. 382.

"Christ and His Tantalizing Inconsistency," *John's Wonderful Gospel,* p. 375.

The Fifteenth Chapter of Mark

THEME: *The Death of Jesus*

OUTLINE:
I. Christ Is Condemned...*At His Trial* (Verses 1-15)
II. Christ Is Crowned...*By His Tormentors* (Verses 16-21)
III. Christ Is Crucified...*With Thieves* (Verses 22-41)
IV. Christ Is Carried...*To His Tomb* (Verses 42-45)

SECTION ONE

Expository Notes on Christ's Appearance Before Pontius Pilate

And straightway in the morning the chief priests held a consultation with the elders and scribes and the whole council, and bound Jesus, and carried Him away, and delivered Him to Pilate. And Pilate asked Him, Art thou the King of the Jews? And He answering said unto him, Thou sayest it. And the chief priests accused Him of many things: but He answered nothing. And Pilate asked Him again, saying, Answerest thou nothing? Behold how many things they witness against thee. But Jesus yet answered nothing; so that Pilate marvelled (vv. 1-5).

A SATISFIED ASSEMBLY

"And straightway in the morning" (v. 1). Let it be remembered that the leaders of the nation had been in conference all night; none had slept! Arguments, discussions, heated debates had continued hour after hour, but finally they had reached agreement on policy. This was essential because they had no power to authorize executions. Rome had taken that from them. Their verdict was final in regard to matters of religion; but sentencing a prisoner was a privilege reserved for the representatives of Caesar. It was at that point in the deliberations that the Jews had been compelled to consider a very real problem. Pontius Pilate, an idol-worshipper, had no interest whatsoever in their faith, and had they charged Jesus with religious provocation, the Governor would have either dismissed the charge, or instructed them to attend to their own affairs. If the responsibility for trying and sentencing Jesus were returned to them, they would be unable to execute the Lord, and nothing short of His death was considered satisfactory. Therefore, it became clear that any charge, to guarantee attention, would have to be based on some civil misdemeanor of such magnitude that it would appear to threaten the state (see Luke 18:31). "The Jews therefore said unto Pilate, It is not lawful for us to put any man to death." It is easy to understand from the Gospel of John, that in spite of their deliberations, the Jews did not win their case against the Lord until they emphasized this important fact. "And from thenceforth Pilate sought to release Him: but the Jews cried out saying, If thou let this man go, thou art not Caesar's friend: whosoever maketh himself a king speaketh against Caesar" (John 19:12). It would appear that the lawyers in the Sanhedrin had prepared their charge with great care. They did not wish their methods to be too conspicuous, but when they knew their arguments were of no avail, rather desperately, they reverted to what had already been decided. If Jesus were proved a menace to the Roman occupation, Pilate could not evade the issue.

THE SUBTLE ACCUSATION

"And the whole multitude of them arose, and led Him unto Pilate. And they began to accuse Him, saying, We found this fellow perverting the nation, and forbidding to give tribute to Caesar, saying, that He himself is Christ a king. And Pilate asked Him, saying, Art thou the king of the Jews? And He answered him and said, Thou sayest it" (Luke 23:1-3). "Frederic L. Godet says, 'There is a tradition quoted in the *Talmud* that forty years before the destruction of the temple, and so about the year 30 of our era, the right of pronouncing capital sentences was taken from Israel.' This would explain why the leaders of the nation thought it necessary to take their prisoner before the Roman Governor. Some writers state they wished to implicate the Gentile ruler in their affairs, so that in the event of any repercussions, they could blame him for what was essentially their crime. The charge brought against Jesus was notoriously false, for in answer to the question whether or not tribute should be paid to Caesar, the Savior had answered, 'Render unto Caesar the things which belong unto Caesar, and to God, the things which belong unto God.'... After cross-examining the Prisoner, Pilate pronounced Him innocent, and it was at this juncture the lawyers made their insidious suggestion. They knew that any man found plotting against Caesar, was commanded to commit suicide in his bath. When he failed to obey that order, he was taken to Rome and executed in the streets. When the Jewish lawyers threatened to accuse Pilate of supporting insurrection, the Governor trembled, knowing their accusations might rob him of everything he possessed" (condensed from the author's commentary, *Luke's Thrilling Gospel*, pp. 468-469).

THE SIMPLE ACKNOWLEDGEMENT

"...Art thou the king of the Jews? And Jesus answering said unto him, Thou sayest it" (v. 2). There are varying translations of the Lord's reply. *The New English Bible* says, "The words are yours." *The Living Bible* says, "Yes, it is as you say." *The Jerusalem Bible* translates it, "It is YOU who say it." Obviously the Lord remained very calm; He was aware of the importance of His answer, and therefore His reply was brief. He said all that was necessary, although John quotes Him as having said a little more. "My kingdom is not of this world, then would my servants fight, that I should not be delivered unto the Jews: but now is my kingdom not from hence. Pilate said unto Him, Art thou a king then? Jesus answered and said, Thou sayest that I am a king. To this end was I born, and for this cause came I into the world, that I should bear witness unto the truth. Every one that is of the truth heareth my voice" (John 18:36-37). Jesus drew a fine distinction between His identity and His mission. He was a king, but had temporarily laid aside the robes of His Majesty to come to earth, not as a conqueror, but as a preacher of the truth. Therefore at that point in His life, *what he had to say* was of more importance than *what He might be*. He had truth to impart; if people heard and received it they would never ask if He were a king; they would know. If they disregarded His message, they would remain uninformed.

THE STRANGE ASTONISHMENT

"But Jesus yet answered nothing; *so that Pilate marvelled*" (v. 5). The word translated "marvelled" is *thaumazein* and it means, "to wonder, to wonder at, to marvel, to admire." It supplies an insight into the character of Pilate. He questioned the Lord; he watched Him, and became aware that this Prisoner was unlike any he had ever judged.

1. *His Fearlessness*. Surrounded by enemies, with no chance to escape,

Jesus maintained His serenity, and was undaunted by the overwhelming odds arrayed against Him. When He said to the Governor, "Thou couldest have no power at all against me, except it were given thee from above," Pilate could only stare in wonderment. This Man had no soldiers, no militant supporters, no helpers of any kind; and yet He acted as though He owned the world. Everything about Him seemed unbelievably strange.

2. *His Friendliness*. The accusers claimed that Jesus made Himself equal with God; but so did Caesar. All the Roman emperors proclaimed their deity. They remained aloof, and ordinary people could only view them from a distance. Caesar expected men to placate him; to offer sacrifices of money. This Jesus, unlike Caesar, owned no palace, had no money, and never asked for it. He moved among people whom He appeared to love with genuine affection, and even when His accusers told lies about Him, the Prisoner remained calm and dignified. This was beyond the comprehension of the Roman Governor.

3. *His Faithfulness*. Jesus spoke about "Truth." Pilate was not sure what this meant, but surely it referred to some doctrine which Jesus believed and taught. Doubtless, the Governor had known others whose doctrines appeared strange; but under pressure, and with a little financial encouragement, the teachers had modified their doctrines. When death threatened, some exponents of new doctrines even renounced their faith. Yet this Jesus of Nazareth was different. Whatever He believed would be expressed to the end. Death could not frighten Him; money could not bribe Him. If His kingdom belonged in another world, then the Prisoner was an excellent example of what might be found there. The Jews suggested He was trying to be a king! Jesus did not look like a king, and yet He exhibited royalty. It was all so bewildering, and "Pilate marvelled."

Now at that feast he released unto them one prisoner, whomsoever they desired. And there was one named Barabbas, which lay bound with them that had made insurrection with him, who had committed murder in the insurrection. And the multitude crying aloud began to desire him to do as he had ever done unto them. But Pilate answered them, saying, Will ye that I release unto you the King of the Jews? For he knew that the chief priests had delivered Him for envy: But the chief priests moved the people, that he should rather release Barabbas unto them. But Pilate answered and said again unto them, What will ye then that I shall do unto Him whom ye call the King of the Jews? And they cried out again, Crucify Him. Then Pilate said unto them, Why, what evil hath He done?

And they cried out the more exceedingly, Crucify Him. And so Pilate, willing to content the people, released Barabbas unto them, and delivered Jesus, when he had scourged Him, to be crucified (vv. 6-15).

A DANGEROUS CUSTOM

History, apparently, has nothing to say about the origin of this strange custom. Probably it was some conciliative move instituted by one of the governors to gain support from people who detested Roman rule. Yet to say the least, as was evident in the release of Barabbas, the murderer, it was an action capable of producing the most serious repercussions. Any avid opponent of the Roman occupation, once set free, could resume his revolutionary practices, and people would be killed. The Jews, who enjoyed very few political privileges, apparently clung to this practice of a prisoner's release. It is necessary to understand this strange procedure as it played a very significant role in the crucifixion of the Lord.

A DIFFERENT CROWD

"And the multitude crying aloud began to desire him to do as he had ever done unto them . . . And they cried out again, Crucify Him" (vv. 8, 13). The majority of the conclusions drawn about the identity of the people in this crowd could easily be wrong. Preachers in every age have drawn attention to the fickleness of the population. It has often been said that the people who desired to crown Jesus as their king, were soon willing to kill Him. One day they shouted, "Hosannah to the Son of David," and the next, "Away with this Man." There exists the possibility that this interpretation is wrong. Who were the people in that crowd? It must be remembered that at that very early hour in the morning, all sensible folk would still be asleep. The commotion in the night had been caused by the rabble which had witnessed the arrest of Jesus. This great company had followed the arresting soldiers to the palace of the high priest, and were there to obtain the release of a prisoner. Matthew 27:15 says, "Now at that feast the governor was wont to release unto the people a prisoner, *whom they would.*" The choice of which prisoner should be liberated was made by the crowd. It is very probable that those present were ardent followers of Barabbas, and had come to obtain the release of their leader. If this were the case, it is even more noteworthy that *even they* had to "be moved, or persuaded, or influenced" by the emissaries of the Priests, before they consented to rejecting the greatest Friend ever known by the Palestinians.

A DECISIVE CHOICE

"And there was one named Barabbas, which lay bound with them that had made insurrection with him, who had committed murder in the insurrection. And the multitude crying aloud began to desire [Pilate] to do as he had ever done unto them" (vv. 7, 8). Very little is known about this criminal, but obviously he was a brigand guilty of murder. Some ancient writers mention a fanatical sect known as the Sicarii; they were famous for the daggers concealed beneath their cloaks; they were deadly assassins. Judges 3:16-26 supplies an excellent example of their *modus operandi*. It has been suggested that Barabbas was one of the leaders of these people; and that during an attack, he and some of his men had been captured by the authorities. Hence "he lay bound with them who had made insurrection with him." The desperado was obviously guilty, and no amount of legal argument could possibly gain a reprieve for this bitter enemy of Caesar. There was but one hope, and that was in taking advantage of the strange custom by which a prisoner could be pardoned. Yet no one could have imagined that the choice would be between the best and the worst of the nation's citizens. It was a choice between love and hatred, peace and war, beauty and ugliness, goodness and evil. The Healer of men was contrasted with the killer of men. Jesus had healed a woman who had suffered from a hemorrhage for twelve years; He had stopped the issue of blood. Barabbas, callously, had made blood to flow from the veins of his victims. Even his followers knew this, and were shocked by the choice confronting them. "But the chief priests *moved the people*, that he should rather release Barabbas unto them" (v. 11). The word translated "moved" is *aneseisan* which literally means "to stir up." The persuaders moved among the crowd, agitating them; urging them vehemently; reminding them that this was their only chance to secure freedom for their national hero. They may have also bribed them with money. It was a tragedy when the wrong decision was made, but we must never forget the choice has remained unchanged throughout the centuries. Men still choose between Barabbas and Jesus; between personal ambitions and the will of God. Unfortunately, with many people, the cry remains, "Release unto us Barabbas."

A DEFINITE CONCERN

"Then Pilate said unto them, Why, what evil hath He done?" (v. 14). "Pilate saith...unto the Jews...I find in Him no fault at all" (John

18:38). "I will chastise Him and release Him. For of necessity he must release one unto them at the feast" (Luke 23:16-17). It would appear that Pilate was very surprised when the mob chose Barabbas instead of Jesus. First, he pronounced a verdict of "Not Guilty;" then he offered a compromise of chastising the prisoner prior to His release. Matthew mentions another detail which might have influenced Pilate. "When he was set down on the judgment seat, his wife sent unto him, saying, Have thou nothing to do with that just man: for I have suffered many things this day in a dream because of Him" (Matt. 27:19). Pilate knew what he desired to do, but alas, had not the moral strength to do his duty. His indecision was fatal. He listened to the cries of the crowd and ignored the voice of his conscience. This always leads to disaster.

A DEADLY COLLAPSE

"And so Pilate, willing to content the people, released Barabbas unto them, and delivered Jesus, when he had scourged Him, to be crucified" (v. 15). He was a living and dying example of another truth uttered by Jesus. "For whosoever will save his life shall lose it: and whosoever will lose his life for my sake shall find it" (Matt. 16:25). His enormous guilt became a burden too heavy to carry. "We are told that within seven years of his despicable act, a broken and destitute man, removed from high office by the Governor of Syria, alone and unwanted by Caesar, Pilate went out into the darkness of the night to commit suicide. His body was found by a workman. Poor guilty man, I feel sorry for him. He met the Savior and refused to love Him. And now it is dark — awfully dark" (condensed from "Pilate's Last Chance." See the author's commentary, *Luke's Thrilling Gospel*, pp. 472-473).

A DELIVERED CHRIST

Through time and eternity, Pilate will always be known as the Judge who should have been judged! He thought more of the plaudits of men than the praise of God. He issued the order that the prisoner be scourged, and for this, will never be forgiven either by men or God. Scourging was the most terrible punishment known to men. Cicero the Roman historian said the very word "crucifixion" should be removed from the Roman vocabulary. Many men sentenced to die on a cross never survived the earlier punishment of scourging. The Roman lash was an instrument of cruelty. It was a long leather strap into which had been set pieces of sharpened bone or lead. When the whip fell upon the bared backs of prisoners, flesh was torn to shreds. The accused was placed upon a rack and both arms and legs were stretched to breaking point. Then a soldier appointed to the detestable task, whipped the prisoner into insensibility. Very often the criminal died on the rack and was spared the additional torture of crucifixion. It is inconceivable that He who made the forests should die upon one of His trees. It is beyond comprehension that, although the angels watched in horror, not one was permitted to interfere. Jesus died alone — for you and for me.

SECTION TWO

Expository Notes on the Soldiers' Treatment of Jesus

And the soldiers led Him away into the hall, called Praetorium; and they call together the whole band. And they clothed Him with purple, and plaited a crown of thorns, and put it about His head, and began to salute Him, Hail, King of the Jews! And they smote Him on the head with a reed, and did spit upon Him, and bowing their knees worshipped Him. And when they had mocked Him, they took off the purple robe from Him, and put His own clothes on Him and led Him out to crucify Him (vv. 16-20).

THE PLACE

"The word, Praetorium, denoted originally the general's tent, or military headquarters, reflecting the original meaning of the word praetor... In the lay-out of a Roman military camp, the *via praetoria* was the road that ran from the praetorium to the gate that faced the presumed enemy... The headquarters building, like the rest of the cantonment was in stone, and a residence of some consequence. In the New Testament the word signifies the Governor's official residence in Jerusalem..." (E. M. Blaiklock, *The Zondervan Pictorial Encyclopedia of the Bible*, Vol. 4, p. 833).

The soldiers involved (the whole band) were probably the palace guard housed in that part of the official residence. It is not difficult to visualize the terrible scene. Pilate, having passed sentence, commanded the officer of the guard to prepare the Prisoner for crucifixion. The statement, "And so Pilate...delivered Jesus, *when he had scourged him*, to be crucified," indicates that the Lord had already been cruelly tortured, but the soldiers intent on merriment, disregarded the physical weakness of their Prisoner, and proceeded to inflict unpardonable indignities upon the condemned. Perhaps they had no real malice; they were Gentiles far from home, and any diversion from rigorous duties was welcome. They therefore led Jesus from the audience chamber of Pilate, and somewhere nearby, perhaps in their own quarters or courtyard, continued their disgusting performance.

THE PUNISHMENT

Professor J. J. Given draws attention to the fact that "In describing this sad scene, no less than five forms of beating are mentioned by the Evangelists Matthew, Mark, and Luke. The Greek word *depontes* which means 'to skin or flay,' and then severely beat." This might refer to the abominable torture inflicted on early Christians when they were literally skinned in the process of martyrdom. Whether or not a ruthless soldier tried to skin any part of the Lord's body is open to conjecture, but the word used by Dr. Luke certainly suggests it. "The second Greek word is *etupton*. It is in the imperfect meaning 'they kept on;' or 'they continued to smite him.' The third Greek word is *paisas* which means 'to inflict blows; to strike with violence.' Matthew has the fourth and fifth words, *ekolaphisan*; 'they buffeted with *clenched fist*;' and *errapisan*, 'they struck with open palms or rods.' Mark states, 'they received Him with blows of the hand or strokes of rods.' It was on this occasion, they spat in His face and blindfolded Him, derisively bidding Him 'Prophecy, who is it that smote thee'" (condensed from *The Pulpit Commentary, Mark,* p. 331).

THE PROCESSIONAL

"And. . .led Him out to crucify Him" (v. 20). "The crown of thorns was in all probability woven from the *Zizyphus pina Christi* (the *nabk* of the Arabs), which grows abundantly in Palestine, fringing the banks of the Jordan. This plant would be very suitable for the purpose, having flexible branches, with leaves very much resembling the ivy leaf in their color, and with many sharp thorns. The pain arising from the pressure of these sharp thorns upon the head must have been excruciating" (Dr. E. Bickersteth). It is worthy of consideration that thorns never made an appearance on the earth until after man had sinned. They were evidence of man's iniquity, and therefore throughout the Scriptures were emblems of sin. When man reached for the best fruits in life, he was painfully reminded there was an enemy waiting to pierce, to hurt, to hinder. The soldiers in their ignorance did not realize the tremendous implication of their act. They were crowning the Prince of Heaven with the evidence of man's guilt. Once again coming events were casting shadows before. The Romans took the emblems; God took the actual sins of a lost world, and with them crowned His Son. "Who His own self bare our sins in His own body on the tree, that we, being dead to sins, should live unto righteousness: by whose stripes, ye were healed" (1 Peter 2:24). "And He bearing His cross went forth into a place called the place of a skull, which is called, in the Hebrew, Golgotha. Where they crucified Him, and two other with Him, on either side one, and Jesus in the midst" (John 19:17-18).

That walk to Calvary, was in some senses the longest walk ever undertaken by man. It was a journey of contrasts. The weakness of the Savior was contrasted with the wickedness of men; the tears of the women with the torture Christ endured; the distress of the disciples with the fierce determination of their Master to complete the work He had commenced. Truly, it was said, "He saved others, himself He cannot save."

> Oh, the deep deep love of Jesus;
> Vast, unmeasured, boundless, free:
> Rolling as a mighty ocean,
> In its fullness over me!

And they compel one Simon a Cyrenian, who passed by, coming out of the country, the father of Alexander and Rufus, to bear His cross (v. 21).

SIMON'S RELIGION

"...Simon a Cyrenian, who passed by, coming out of the country" (v. 21). "Cyrene was a city founded by the Greeks, upon a beautiful tableland one thousand eight hundred feet above sea level. It was the capital of the district of Cyrenaica in Africa. It was a Greek city, but contained many Jews. It was represented in Jerusalem at the Pentecost (see Acts 2:10). Simon, one of its people helped Jesus bear His cross (Matt. 27:32). Cyrenian Jews had a synagogue at Jerusalem (Acts 6:9). It was destroyed in the fourth century by the Saracens. It is waste and occupied now by wild beasts and Bedouins" (*Unger's Bible Dictionary*, p. 232). History affirms that the Cyrenian Jews were very wealthy, and this also might have applied to Simon. Their synagogue, shared with others in Jerusalem, suggests these Jews of the Dispersion had not forgotten their homeland, and probably the cost of erecting their synagogue had been paid by these patriots. Apparently, Simon had come to enjoy the Passover, and was making his way along a street, when he was apprehended by the Roman soldier. It was customary for the prisoner to carry his cross to the site of crucifixion, and the route was always the longest possible, so that every onlooker would be reminded of the folly of opposing Caesar. Four soldiers formed a square, in the middle of which the accused was made to carry his cross. Another soldier walked ahead of the group, carrying a board upon which was written the crime for which the man was about to die. Other soldiers kept the crowd at a distance to prevent a last minute rescue by friends of the condemned man. Simon apparently arrived at the precise moment when Jesus could no longer drag His cross. Even the soldiers recognized Jesus was utterly exhausted, and one of them looking around for a helper, saw Simon, and using the flat head of his spear, touched the stranger on the shoulder. This was a command which could hardly be refused; Simon was obliged to do as he was bidden.

SIMON'S RELUCTANCE

"And they *compel* one Simon...to bear His cross" (v. 21). Matthew's description of this event is very strong. He wrote, "*touton eggareusan hina aree*," that is, "they forced him; they compelled him to carry..." It is not difficult to understand the anger and indignation of this pious Jew from North Africa. He had come with fervent soul to worship the God of his Fathers, and instead, was compelled by these hateful Romans to carry the cross of a criminal! If thoughts could have killed, every Roman on the street would have died instantly. Surging emotions erupted within his soul; anger flashed in his eyes; his arms were probably lifted in protest, but the Romans held spears, against which Simon had no defense. Simon stared at the Man beneath the cross. His blood-stained body lay sprawled on the street. With bitterness in his heart, the Jew stooped to lift the cross, and perhaps, at that moment, a sigh went through Heaven. The angels were silent; their King had found a friend!

SIMON'S RESPONSE

It is impossible to describe the details of the transformation which changed the life of Simon; God has not revealed the entire story. We know what happened along the street; we are aware of what Simon saw at Calvary, and we know what happened long afterward among the members of his family in North Africa. We have, as it were, the pieces of this jig-saw puzzle, but we proceed with reverent caution to the task of fitting each piece into place. In Luke 23:26 we read that Simon was compelled to carry the cross *AFTER* Jesus. Therefore Simon was able to watch the Prisoner as He stumbled down the streets. This was imperative, for had the Prisoner fallen, he also might have tripped over the prostrate form of Jesus. Then, suddenly, the procession came to an abrupt halt; Jesus was speaking to some women, and His words, filled with pity, warned them of coming disaster (Luke 23:27-31). Afterward the procession made its way to a hill outside the city wall, and by the time the man from Africa dropped the cross to the ground, something surely was taking place within his soul. The crowd, for a time, was kept at a distance, but Simon had been made to carry his burden to the summit, and was able to see and hear everything. He was there when the Prisoner was nailed mercilessly to the cross; he listened when Jesus asked God to forgive them. Maybe the man was unaware that God always pays His debts!

SIMON'S RELATIVES

". . .the father of Alexander and Rufus" (v. 21). Many years later, Paul wrote a letter to the church at Rome. He said, "Salute Rufus chosen in the Lord, and his mother and mine" (16:13). These terms of deep affection indicate that both mother and son had become intensely precious to Paul. That lovely lady had been a mother to the Apostle, and the exemplary life of Rufus had gained for him distinction among the Christians in Rome. Probably there were many named Rufus, but everybody knew the identify of *THIS* Rufus. Cornelius, a Lapide, mentions a tradition which says that Rufus became a Bishop of the Church in Spain, and that his brother Alexander suffered martrydom. Perhaps to some readers our conclusions may appear to be conjecture, but how else may we explain the amazing transformation of a Jewish family in Cyrene? Did Simon react to the love of Jesus, and return home a Christian? Did his testimony influence his family? Did God pour into that home an abundant measure of His grace, and thereby recompense the man who had carried the cross for the Prince of Heaven? All theologians are agreed that special emphasis has been given to this particular family, because this Rufus in Rome was indeed the son of the Simon apprehended by the soldier on the road to Calvary's hill. All Christians, then, and now, would have liked the privilege bestowed on Simon the Cyrenian. Let us never forget that the same opportunity awaits us, for Jesus said, "Whosoever will come after me, let him deny himself, and take up his cross, and follow me" (Mark 8:34).

SECTION THREE

Expository Notes on the Death of Jesus

And they bring Him unto the place Golgotha, which is, being interpreted, the place of a skull. And they gave Him to drink wine mingled with myrrh, but He received it not. And when they had crucified Him, they parted His garments, casting lots upon them, what every man should take. And it was the third hour and they crucified Him (vv. 22-25).

THE PLACE OF EXECUTION...Golgotha

Throughout the last few centuries, people have become increasingly interested in the site of Golgotha, and some scholars have been very decisive in their claims. It is not of paramount importance to know *where* Jesus died; it is of great worth to know *why* He died for undeserving men and women. Today, in Jerusalem, there are two sites which claim to be authentic. "One primary claim to the site is the Church of the Holy Sepulchre, whose history goes back to the fourth century. It is within the walls of the old city today, but its supporters maintain that the New Testament city wall would place it outside the city. Because modern buildings cover all real estate in the area, no excavation is yet possible to determine where that northern New Testament wall was.

"The location of this site can be traced to the Christian Roman Emperor Constantine. Eusebius, a contemporary historian, commissioned Bishop Marcarius to find Golgotha and the Tomb. This was nearly three hundred years after the crucifixion. The Church of Constantine was then built on the site of Hadrian's Aphrodite temple, and named in honor of St. Helena, the emperor's mother. Legend has it that upon excavating for the tomb, a fragment of the true cross was found that effected miracles of healing, and thus certified the site. The tradition that this is the site is very old, but it is mostly tradition. Earlier, the pagan emperor Hadrian had deliberately obscured many Christian holy sites with his temples.

"The other major contender for the site of Calvary is known today as the Garden Tomb, or Gordon's Calvary. Suggested by Otto Thenius in 1842, General Charles Gordon declared in 1885 that this was the site of the crucifixion and burial...There are some arguments to support the location as well as some serious criticisms. A garden and a tomb (in fact several tombs) are in the vicinity. Those who contest this identification maintain that the hill was part of a ridge that is still visible on the north wall of Jerusalem adjacent to Herod's gate...A better explanation of "the place of a skull" would be that either the hill was bare rock, or it served as a cemetery. Protestants prefer the latter site, because the organization that owns the land has landscaped it to make it resemble their concept of Joseph of Arimathea's garden. The Church of the Holy Sepulchre, is, of course, a building on the top of a site. It is highly decorated and the scene of much activity. It requires a good imagination to see a garden tomb there" (R. L. Alden in *The Zondervan Pictorial Encyclopedia of the Bible*, Volume 2, pp. 773-774).

I have visited Jerusalem on numerous occasions and have examined both sites. I must admit that for me, at least, only the Tomb in the Garden fits the New Testament description. Perhaps the most convincing evidence is in the tomb itself. John describing his own experience, says, "And he stooping down, and looking in, saw the linen clothes lying; yet went he not in" (20:5). John, from *outside the tomb* was able to see the place where the Lord's body had been laid to rest. I visited many tombs during my visits to the city, but always, with the exception of the Garden Tomb, it was impossible to see from outside, anything inside. Often the burial chamber was at the end of a passage, and once inside, without a light, it was impossible to see a thing. It is interesting that John, even when he stood outside of the tomb was able to see clearly that Jesus was absent; that His garments lay where they had fallen. There are other identifying details, but this commentary is not an investigation into the pros and cons of archaeological research. It is sufficient to say that close to this tomb, there is a hill (now covered with graves and tombstones), a winepress where workers from the vineyards trampled grapes; and in yet another segment of the rocky terrain, one is able to see the outline of a skull. Let it be admitted that today the strange shape is not as clearly defined as it was when I saw its photograph fifty years ago. The action of the wind, the weather, and the vibration from the adjacent bus station, have helped spoil one of the most fascinating sights in Jerusalem. The photograph which I saw as a young man, was taken by an old Baptist minister at the turn of the century, and to say the least, it was astonishing. The shape of the skull was unmistakable; the two eye sockets were caves; the nose was a shallow ravine, and yet another cave represented the mouth. Today, small trees growing in the apertures spoil the view, but for all who believe the Bible, no other place in Jerusalem accurately describes Golgotha and the Tomb in the Garden. Formerly we were permitted into the Moslem cemetery to hold devotional meetings, but in later years, entry has been forbidden to non-Arabs. Certain lewd and irreverent young people desecrated the cemetery with acts of immorality. The Moslem elders subsequently decided to deny entry to all but members of their own fraternity. It was there, somewhere on that hill overlooking what now is a bus station, that our Lord died to redeem us from the power of sin.

THE PRICE OF EXPIATION

"And they gave Him to drink wine mingled with myrrh: but He received it not" (v. 23). It has been claimed there existed in Jerusalem a company of pious, merciful women who attended every crucifixion in order to exercise charity. They prepared a drugged wine which was a pain killer. This was offered to all criminals as an opiate. When the Lord refused to accept this gift, He demonstrated His determination to remain conscious as long as possible. What had to be endured, He was determined to endure. He never asked for mercy, and never hesitated to perform that sacrifice of which the prophets had spoken. He Who was to dispense mercy to a guilty world, never asked mercy of anyone. The hymnist was correct when he wrote "*Jesus paid it all.*" "There were two occasions on which drink was offered to our Lord during the agonies of His crucifixion. The first was mentioned by Matthew (27:34) when they offered Him wine mingled with gall. This was a stupifying liquor, a strong narcotic made of the sour wine of the country, mingled with bitter herbs, and mercifully administered to dull the sense of pain. This was offered before the actual crucifixion took place. It is to this first occasion that Mark refers... The second occasion on which drink was offered to Him was after He had been some hours on His cross. When the end was drawing near, it was given in answer to His exclamation, 'I thirst.' This drink does not appear to have been mingled with any stupefying drug; we do not read that He refused it" (*The Pulpit Commentary, Mark*, p. 306).

THE PLAN OF EXPROPIATION

"And when they had crucified Him, they parted His garments, casting lots upon them, *what every man should take*" (v. 24). It is interesting to read that whereas the soldiers were each determined to have "their pound of flesh," the officer in charge of the crucifixion had other thoughts in mind (see Mark 15:39). A Jew for the most part wore five articles of dress. He had an inner garment; a cover-all which took the shape of an elaborate robe; a girdle encircled his waist; sandals or shoes on his feet, and a turban. Four soldiers stood around Jesus during the journey to Calvary, and it was always considered customary for such guardians to share any spoils which could be salvaged from the prisoner's belongings. This was a way by which they could supplement their regular pay. It seems that because some articles were of more value than others, the men cast lots to determine which should have the inner garment, the girdle, the sandals, and the turban. The greatest prize was the Lord's robe. Somewhere that night, the lottery winner proudly displayed his winnings! It was ironic that Jesus, from His cross, could look down at gamblers and see frenzied excitement as they struggled to win His garment. They were determined to get something out of this Jesus! They did not know He had already divested Himself of Heaven's robes of majesty; that He had voluntarily descended to earth to offer the garments of salvation; the invaluable robe of immortality. What did they get out of the cross? One had a robe; others had various articles. Were they pleased with their winnings? We do not know. What have we derived from Calvary's cross and the One Who died there? This is an interesting question which should be personally answered.

And the superscription of his accusation was written over, THE KING OF THE JEWS. And with Him they crucify two thieves; the one on His right hand, and the other on His left. And the scripture was fulfilled, which saith, And He was numbered with the transgressors (vv. 26-28).

THE FAMOUS SUPERSCRIPTION

The writers of the Gospels mention the proclamation which was nailed to the cross of Christ, yet for some inscrutable reason no two are alike. Probably the complete title was, "This is Jesus of Nazareth, the King of the Jews." Apparently the authors were more concerned with what was taking place than with what Pilate had to say about it. The identification and charge of the prisoner were usually written on a piece of board, and this was carried ahead of the accused throughout the procession to the place of execution. All spectators could then see at a glance the information required. John (19:20) tells us that the accusation was written in three languages, Hebrew, Greek and Latin. This was to be expected as these were the chief languages spoken in Palestine at that time. Hebrew was the national language spoken by Jews; Latin, the tongue of the Romans, was of necessity the official language used throughout the occupying administration; and Greek was the most important of the common dialects. Thus, the announcement was made, in what was tantamount to all the languages of the world. The fact that the leaders of the nation criticized the announcement was ironical (John 19:21-22). They themselves had made the initial charge, but when their accusations came "home to roost," they complained vociferously.

The Venerable Bede, the eminent English historian and theologian (673-735), the man who was probably the greatest Anglo-Saxon scholar of his generation, wrote: "This title was fitly placed over Christ's head, because, although He was crucified in weakness for us, yet He shone with the majesty of a King above His cross. The title proclaimed that He was after all a King; and that from henceforth He began to reign from His cross over the Jews. . . Pilate was restrained from making any alteration in the title, so that it should mean anything less than this." This is truly an inspiring thought, for in spite of Jewish rejection, Christ remained, as He will forever, the God-appointed KING OF THE JEWS.

THE FLAGRANT SINNERS

Luke (23:32) tells us that the two robbers — the word used is *leestees* (Mark 15:27) and this means a "robber, a plunderer, a brigand;" accompanied Jesus on that fateful journey to the place of execution. One wonders what thoughts passed through their minds as they saw Jesus and heard His voice. They were notorious criminals. One of them heard only the jeers of the onlookers, but the other heard new sounds, and among them the voice of his conscience. Yet Matthew (27:44) reminds us that both thieves cursed the Lord. The subsequent conversion of the one thief was most remarkable, for it had been predicted by the prophet Isaiah that prior to His death, the coming Messiah would "see his seed." It is interesting that some of the early fathers of the church had their own versions of the significance of Christ being crucified between two criminals. Augustine said, "This cross, if you mark it well, was a judgment seat. For the Judge being placed in the midst, the one who believed was set free; the other who reviled Him was condemned, and thus He signified what He will do with the quick and the dead. Some He will place on His right hand, and some on His left" (Augustine, *Tract 31 in Saint Johan*).

THE FULFILLED SCRIPTURE

"And the scripture was fulfilled, which saith, And He was numbered with the transgressors" (v. 28). This, of course refers to the prediction made in Isaiah 53:12. This one statement resembles a costly diamond taken from a rare collection. All students find treasure in the writings of the prophet. For example the fifty-third chapter of Isaiah provides the following predictions. Verses 3-6 reveals the reason for His death. Verse 7 describes the silence with which He faced His accusators. Verse 9 speaks of His burial in the tomb of a wealthy man. Verse 10 describes His first convert, and the fact that He would prolong His days. He would rise again from the dead. Verse 12 indicates how He prayed, "Father, forgive them for they know not what they do." These jewels are to be found in one very small part of God's widespread diamond field. The Old Testament is filled with areas where unsurpassed wealth awaits the impoverished seeker.

And they that passed by railed on Him, wagging their heads, and saying, Ah, thou that destroyest the temple, and buildest it in three days, Save thyself, and come down from the cross. Likewise also the chief priests mocking said among themselves with the scribes, He saved others; himself He cannot save. Let Christ the King of Israel descend now from the cross, that we may see and believe. And they that were crucified with Him reviled Him (vv. 29-32).

THE MEMORY OF THE CROWD...Short-lived

It is strange to read the statements of the people who saw Jesus die. His life had been filled with many wonderful miracles; His sermons had been wonderful to hear, and yet those gloating onlookers could only mention one of His sayings. They spoke of His destroying the temple, and used His words to suit their own schemes. No one mentioned the giving of sight to the blind; the cleansing of the lepers was never mentioned, and even the feeding of the thousands apparently had been forgotten. It would have been a thrilling moment if some man had cried out in gratitude, "Thank You, Jesus, for opening my eyes," or,

"Master, I shall always be grateful that You came into my life." Alas, in the hour of His travail, He was alone. The people who owed so much, forgot even to say, "Thank You." This seems to be one of the greatest mistakes men ever make. We desperately appeal for help when we need something, but are too busy and forgetful to return thanks after God has graciously come to our aid. Luke 17:12-19 describes how ten lepers were cleansed by the Savior, yet only one returned to thank the Lord. "And Jesus answering said, Were there not ten cleansed? But where are the nine? There are not found that returned to give glory to God, save this stranger. And He said unto him, Arise, go thy way: thy faith hath made thee whole." Unlike the people who sneered at the Lord, that solitary leper would have appreciated the chorus:

> Thank You Lord for saving my soul.
> Thank You Lord for making me whole;
> Thank You Lord for giving to me
> Thy great salvation so rich and free.

THE MAJESTY OF THE CHRIST. . .Serene

It is worthy of note that throughout the ordeal of the Cross, Jesus never condemned anyone; in spite of everything said by His enemies, the Lord maintained His astonishing composure.

1. *How Terrible.*—". . .the chief priests *mocking* said. . ." (v. 31). Even in cases of extreme guilt, people usually feel sympathy for a dying man. At the time of an execution, men and women stand at the gates of the prison, either to keep a silent vigil, or to express opposition to the system of capital punishment. However guilty the criminal might be, even if men are disgusted with his acts of crime, no person hurls insults at a person about to die; blame is tempered by pity. Alas, this was not the case when Jesus hung upon His cross. Gloating over their triumph, the chief priests became slaves of their corrupt passions. Oblivious to the fact they had connived plans to destroy an innocent man, they were completely bereft of shame, and found excitement in taunting their victim. They thereby surrendered all claims to decency.

2. *How Taunting.*—". . .*that we may see and believe*" (v. 32). The ministry of the Savior had been dedicated to one purpose — that men might believe. Continually He stressed this fact, and the leaders of the nation were aware of His desires. Throughout His ministry He would have done any legitimate thing to make men believe His message. Now the chief priests were apparently suggesting a way by which His objective

could be achieved. Yet it was obvious even in those moments, had Christ done what they suggested, they would have sought other means to kill Him. The bitterness and scorn in their utterances were diabolical, and lesser men possessing the power of Christ would have obliterated them.

3. *How True.*—"...himself He cannot save" (v. 31). Modern film producers would be thrilled if they could read in the Bible how Jesus miraculously descended from the cross to destroy His tormentors. They would depict flashing manifestations of power, and portray opening heavens, devastating earthquakes, and terrified priests and people. Let it be admitted that had Jesus desired so to do, He could have easily escaped from His cross. It is because *HE did NOT descend from the cross*, that we believe in Him. In order to save others He sacrificed Himself, and that has been the secret of His invincibility. Men appreciated Him because He fed them; they followed Him because they believed in His mission; they obeyed Him because they loved Him; but they adored Him because they recognized His death was a highway to life everlasting.

THE MISERY OF THE COMPANIONS

"And they that were crucified with Him reviled Him" (v. 32). Matthew, Mark and John appear to be agreed on the fact that the thieves cursed the Lord. Luke however, mentions the conversion of one of those robbers (Luke 23:39-43). It surely would be an exciting time, if we could listen as the four authors discussed this point. Why did three of them omit the story which has thrilled the world? Why did Luke alone mention the conversion of the dying thief, and from whom did he obtain his story; since he was not there himself? Could it possibly be that Matthew, Mark and John were more concerned with what men were doing to the Lord, whereas Luke was more interested in what Jesus was doing for man? Three writers were stressing the awfulness of the torrent of guilt directed toward their Master; Luke was thinking only of the river of water of life, flowing from Calvary to any man willing to drink. Maddened by pain and angry with all who had contributed to their execution, the thieves hurled blasphemous insults against everybody. The Lord recognized their anger, but patiently awaited the fulfillment of a tremendous Old Testament prediction. Isaiah had said, "...when thou shalt make His soul an offering for sin, *He shall see his seed*..." (53:10). After "His hour of travail" the Lord was to see His first convert [child]! Therefore, with calm assurance, Jesus awaited the fulfillment of that prophecy. When the dying thief responded, the Lord said, "It is finished," and bowing His head, dismissed His spirit.

And when the sixth hour was come, there was darkness over the whole land until the ninth hour. And at the ninth hour Jesus cried with a loud voice, saying, Eloi, Eloi, lama, sabachthani? which is, being interpreted, my God, my God, why hast thou forsaken me? And some of them that stood by, when they heard it, said, Behold, He calleth Elias. And one ran and filled a sponge full of vinegar, and put it on a reed, and gave Him to drink, saying, Let alone; let us see whether Elias will come to take Him down. And Jesus cried with a loud voice, and gave up the ghost (vv. 33-37).

THE STRANGE DARKNESS... "*...there was darkness over the whole land*" *(v. 33).*

Perhaps the best commentary on this event comes from the poet who wrote:

> Well might the sun in darkness hide;
> And shut His glories in
> When Christ the mighty Maker died,
> For man, the creature's sin.

"This darkness was doubtless produced by the immediate interference of God. An account of it is given by Phlegon of Tralles, a freedman of the Emperor Hadrian. Eusebius, in his records of the year A.D. 33, quotes at length from Phlego, who says, that, 'in the fourth year of the 202nd Olympiad, there was a great and remarkable eclipse of the sun, above any that had happened before. At the sixth hour, the day was turned into the darkness of night, so that stars were seen in the heaven; and there was a great earthquake in Bithynia, which overthrew many houses in the city Nicaea.' Phelgo attributes the darkness which he describes, to an eclipse, which was natural enough for him to do...We are not informed how far the darkness extended. Dionhysius says that he saw this phenomenon in Heliopolis in Egypt, and he is reported to have exclaimed, 'Either the God of nature, the Creator, is suffering, or the universe is dissolving.' Cyprian says, 'The sun was constrained to withdraw his rays, and close his eyes, that he might not be compelled to look upon this crime of the Jews.' Chrysostom said, 'The creature could not bear the wrong done to its Creator. Therefore the sun withdrew his rays that he might not behold the deeds of the wicked''' (condensed from *The Pulpit Commentary, Mark,* p. 308).

THE STIRRING DECLARATION . . . ''My God, my God, Why didst thou forsake me?'' (v. 34).

Students should note that Mark uses the aorist tense of the Greek verb and this denotes *something completed in the past*. It should also be remembered that this cry was uttered AFTER the three hours of darkness. Whatever had taken place within the impenetrable gloom, we may never know, but it must be stressed that whatever happened — had happened: It was finished for ever! This cry was not an agonized expression of unprecedented suffering. It was a glorious cry of glad relief. There was light at the end of the tunnel! The fellowship which had been broken was now being restored, and with resurgent happiness echoing in His voice, Jesus said, ''My God, my God, why *didst* thou forsake me?'' Probably He knew the answer to His own question, and asked it, that we might be enriched by searching for the reason for His utterance. The prophet Habakkuk said, ''Thou art of purer eyes than to behold evil, and canst not look on iniquity: . . .'' (Hab. 1:13). As the storm clouds obscured the sun, so the sins of a world united to ruin an eternal fellowship. We shall never know what it meant to Jesus to be separated from His Father. He had been, as it were, in a place without God, and that experience was inexpressibly terrible. It should always be remembered that this was the price paid for our redemption. The Lord endured the darkness of separation that we might enjoy the delights of salvation.

THE SOLDIERS' DRINK . . . ''And one ran . . . and gave Him to drink'' (v. 36).

It must be remembered that the Lord had already refused the pain-killing drink offered prior to His crucifixion. The drink now given to Him was the common drink of the soldiers. It was a sour wine diluted with water according to the taste of the recipients. It was a thirst quencher, and since the Lord had already been on His cross for hours, it was understandable how He had suffered acute thirst. His throat seemed on fire; His tongue was very dry; His lips parched to the extent that He said, ''I thirst.'' That some person took a reed or cane and placing the soaked sponge on it, held it high for Jesus to moisten His lips, makes us feel envious. That unnamed person did what millions of people would have loved to do. He was another who did what he could to help the Savior. It might be a marvelous study to search through the Gospels to discover other insignificant people who played their part — however small — to assist Jesus.

THE SUBLIME DEATH...".. .He gave up the ghost, or, He dismissed His spirit" (v. 37).

Matthew 27:50 says that Jesus cried with a loud voice. Luke 23:46 repeats the statement and then adds, "Father, into thy hands I commend my spirit..." John does not mention the loud cry but draws attention to the poignant prediction in Psalm 69:20-21: "Reproach hath broken my heart; and I am full of heaviness: and I looked for some to take pity, but there was none; and for comforters, but I found none. They gave me also gall for my meat; and in my thirst they gave me vinegar to drink." Mark is content to mention that prior to death, Jesus cried with a loud voice. This is very significant, for dying people do not shout. As life subsides, vocal sounds diminish, and finally noises in the throat announce imminent death. It is thought-provoking to read that the customary weakness was not seen in the death of the Lord. Instead of getting weaker, He appeared to be getting stronger. Thus did He proclaim from His cross that He was not dying as a victim of a mob; He was laying down His life because only thus could He redeem lost sinners. His was the departure of a Victor, and not the death of a victim.

And the veil of the temple was rent in twain from the top to the bottom. And when the centurion, which stood over against Him, saw that He so cried out, and gave up the ghost, he said, Truly this man was the Son of God. There were also women looking on afar off: among whom was Mary Magdalene, and Mary, the mother of James the less, and of Joses, and Salome; (who also, when He was in Galilee, followed Him and ministered unto Him); and many other women which came up with Him unto Jerusalem (vv. 38-41).

THE DAMAGED CURTAIN... "And the veil of the temple was rent in twain" (v. 38)

There is reason to believe that the rending of the veil was the most devastating event linked with the death of the Savior. The timing of that catastrophe indicated God had been watching every detail of the drama on the hill called Calvary. The rending of the veil happened not before, nor during the crucifixion; *it came at the end*. The method of the rending indicated the power which damaged the veil came from heaven, and not from the floor. Mark has been careful to say the veil was rent from the top to the bottom. Had the break originated on earth, the priests might have held the two parts of the veil together. When God commences anything, no power on earth can prevent the completion of His project. The severity of the rending — to the bottom, meant that the Mercy Seat had become visible. Formerly, it was only seen by the High Priest, who annually, on the Day of Atonement, entered within the veil to appear on behalf of Israel. The rent veil revealed there remained no barrier between the need of man and the sufficiency of God. A private footpath had become a freeway along which all could move safely.

THE DISCERNING CENTURION... *"This man was the Son of God"* (v. 39)

The centurion, a leader of a company of one hundred men, had probably been in combat many times and was accustomed to seeing men die. He could hardly have been moved by sentiment to say, "This man was the Son of God." It was the duty of every officer in charge of executions to remain at his post until the sentence had been carried out. This man, therefore, would have been present from the beginning of the crucifixion. He would have superintended the nailing of the body to the cross; the lifting of the cross into its position on the hill, and consequently, would have heard every word uttered, and watched carefully the reactions of the Prisoner. He had come to the conclusion that no ordinary man could have acted as did Jesus of Nazareth. As a warrior, he could have withstood any harsh words or military maneuver; it was the cross which destroyed his complacency. Professor J. J. Given, in *The Pulpit Commentary (Mark*, Volume 2, p. 339), reminds his readers of the first convert to Christianity ever won in Greenland. He writes: "That mission had long been unsuccessful; the missionaries had been sorely tried. At last, disheartened they were about to leave the country, when, one day, the bandit called Kajarnack, with his followers came to rob the Mission tent. On entering he saw the missionary writing and wondered what it meant; the missionary explained to him that by the marks on the paper, he was able to read the thoughts that had passed through the mind of a man called John, who had lived hundreds of years earlier. 'Impossible' exclaimed the savage chief. The missionary who was finishing his translation of the Gospel of St. John, read to these heathen Greenlanders the record of the crucifixion as contained in the nineteenth chapter of that Gospel. The chieftain and his men were strangely interested in the narrative.

"At length, with great emotion, Kajernak cried out, 'What had the man done that they treated him so?' The missionary addressed him in reply, that man did nothing amiss, but Kajarnak has done much wrong; Kajarnak murdered is wife; Kajarnak has robbed as well as murdered; Kajarnak has filled the land with violence, and that Man was bearing the punishment of Kajarnak's sins that Kajarnak might be saved. Tears rolled down the cheeks of the rude robber-chief, and he besought the missionary to read the story again, 'for' he added, 'I too would like to be saved.' We do not wonder how the story of the cross had such a powerful effect on the first convert in Greenland.''

THE DISTANT COMPANY. . . "There were also women looking on afar off" (v. 40)

Apparently there were several women present during the death of Jesus. Mark refers to "many other women which came up with Him to Jerusalem." It is an undeniable fact the women of the New Testament were more faithful than were the men. For a while at least, most of the men were lost in obscurity, but the women never deserted their Lord. It is interesting that among that gallant company of devoted ladies, three shone as stars with unusual splendor. Mark mentions Mary Magdalene, Mary, the mother of James and Joses, and Salome. Mark also tells us that these three went to the tomb on Easter morning. Yet, one additional statement reveals the overflowing love of these remarkable female disciples. *"Who also, when He was in Galilee, followed Him and ministered unto Him"* (v. 40). As was the case with Mary of Bethany, these faithful devotees had not postponed action until they could only place floral tributes on His grave. They seized every opportunity to show their love, to help His cause; and never, even in death, were they ever tempted to abandon the Lord. This apparently has been characteristic throughout the history of the church. Men covet leadership, but dedicated women are the strength of the church; and it would be wise, if all men remembered this simple fact.

SECTION FOUR

Expository Notes on the Burial of the Lord

And now when the even was come, because it was the preparation, that is, the day before the sabbath, Joseph of Arimathaea, an honorable counsellor, which also waited for the kingdom of God, came, and went in boldly unto Pilate, and craved the body of Jesus. And Pilate marvelled if He were already dead; and calling unto him the centurion, he asked whether He had been any while dead. And when he knew it of the centurion, he gave the body to Joseph (vv. 42-45).

THE CALLOUS CUSTOM

Man's inhumanity to man has always been the most ghastly feature of history. It is to be regretted that when passions are aroused, man has the capacity to revert to animal law. This was evident in all crucifixions carried out by the Romans. Criminals executed for their crimes were left hanging on crosses sometimes for several days. Their bodies were frequently left unburied and became food for scavenger dogs. It has been suggested that Calvary's hill was littered by many skulls, and this accounted for the name Golgotha, which means the place of a skull. Jewish law considered contact with a corpse to be defilement, and therefore on the eve of any important day, they insisted that dead bodies be removed from sight. When criminals failed to die quickly, it was customary for a soldier to take an iron bar and smash the legs, so that the increasing agony would hasten the end. Today, even thoughts of these atrocities make us shudder with horror, but such were the tortures apparently awaiting the Lord. When the soldiers arrived at Jesus' cross to do what was considered necessary, they were surprised their victim had already expired, and one of them, denied the pleasure of inflicting further suffering on Jesus, plunged a spear into the body of the Lord. Thus was the scripture fulfilled which said, "A bone of him shall not be broken" (see John 19:31-37).

THE COURAGEOUS COUNSELOR

The town of Arimathea is only mentioned in connection with Joseph who gave his unused tomb to Jesus. It is thought to have been about twenty miles distant from Jerusalem, and might have been the same as the Old Testament Ramathaim, the home city of the judge, Samuel.

It appears that, although Joseph had been a citizen of that place, he eventually went to reside in Jerusalem, where he became an honorable counselor. Matthew states that Joseph was a wealthy man, and draws attention to the fact that he had prepared a tomb, specially carved from solid rock. John 19:38 tells us that Joseph was "a disciple of Jesus, but secretly for fear of the Jews." We do not know how or where this great man came into contact with Christ, but it is evident that what he heard won his affections. Alas, there is no record that he ever confessed his faith. Unfortunately, he considered it to be prudent to maintain a discreet silence, lest his position in the Sanhedrin be brought into jeopardy. Probably there were times when he felt condemned, and when he became ashamed, but apparently he had no wish to lose prestige among his eminent colleagues. It is against that setting we must consider his request to Pilate. Joseph had no idea that Jesus would rise again; it cannot be overstressed that he buried a dead Christ! There would be severe criticism and many sneers when his fellow counselors heard of Joseph's act. He had reached the place where cowardice could no longer be tolerated, and so, courageously, Joseph went to Pilate to beg the body of his Lord.

THE CLEAR CONFIRMATION

"But Pilate wondered whether Jesus was dead so soon, and having called the centurion, he asked him whether Jesus was dead. And when he learned from the centurion (that he was indeed dead), he gave the body to Joseph" (vv. 44, 45; Amplified). It is important that we recognize the surprise of Pilate when he heard of the early death of Jesus. It was so unnatural and unexpected that the Governor could not believe the report. The centurion who was summoned to appear before Pilate confirmed what had been said, but it was only then that Pilate granted Joseph's request. John 19:30 says, ". . . and He bowed his Head and gave up the ghost." The *Englishman's Greek New Testament* translates the verse, ". . . and He bowed His head and yielded up His spirit." The word translated "yielded" is *paredoken*, and this according to Thayer means, "to give over; to give into the hands of another; to give over into ones power or use; to deliver to one something to keep, use, take care of, manage." It is of paramount importance that we understand the true implication of this Scripture. Jesus did not die because excruciating agony had proved fatal. He suffered all the torture of crucifixion, but when He expired, *He did so by His own volition.* He had finished the work God gave Him to do, and having cried,

"Tetelestai" — "It has been finished," the Lord committed His Spirit into the hands of God, and deliberately bowing His head, expired. Normally, a crucified person would have lingered for many hours and sometimes even for days. It was the Lord Himself Who terminated His life — at the precise moment when He knew there was no further work to be done. This explains why Pilate was astonished and could not believe the Prisoner was already dead. Even the centurion played a part in making known the glorious news of redemption. His story not only banished the doubts of Pontius Pilate; it should banish the doubts of modern man.

THE CLAIMED CORPSE

"*. . .he gave the body to Joseph*" (v. 45). Let it be remembered that Isaiah the prophet said of the coming Messiah: "And He made His grave with the wicked, and with the rich in His death" (53:9). John (19:38-39) tells us that Joseph was accompanied by Nicodemus, when the body of the Lord was gently lowered from the cross. These two secret disciples performed a service which made them famous. The disciples could have had that experience, but alas, they were absent! At the risk of being considered irreverent, we stand as it were on the greenhill to watch as the men considered the task ahead. Did they find a ladder? Did one help the other to climb to the crossbar, and then stand patiently waiting for the Lord's body to be lowered into his waiting arms? Did the other man then jump down to assist? Perhaps even the angels were hushed, as they watched that strange funeral procession making its way to the sepulchre chiseled out of the rock. When they laid the body to rest, were the tears rolling down their faces? We do not know. However, had they known our modern chorus, they might have sung softly,

> Wounded for me; wounded for me;
> There on the Cross, He was wounded for me.
> Gone my transgressions, and now I am free:
> All because Jesus was wounded for me.

And he bought fine linen, and took Him down, and wrapped Him in the linen, and laid Him in a sepulchre which was hewn out of a rock, and rolled a stone unto the door of the sepulchre. And Mary Magdalene and Mary the mother of Joses beheld where He was laid (vv. 46-47).

THE MONUMENT IN THE STONE

The word translated "tomb" is *mneemeio* and this means more than a mere place in which a corpse is placed to rest. Thayer says it means, "a monument or memorial to perpetuate the memory of any person or thing," specifically, "a sepulchral tomb." Joseph of Arimathea had no wish to be forgotten! Travelers to the Middle East are accustomed to being shown monuments upon which are many inscriptions describing the life and deeds of the deceased. Obelisks and inscribed columns obviously had an important place in the affairs of ancient people. Joseph, a wealthy man, had created a special tomb so that, afterward, people would see it and remember. *It was to be his memorial!* When he decided that Jesus should have that tomb, Joseph indicated a change in his plans. Obviously he was no longer concerned about perpetuating his own glory. He was desirous that Jesus should never be forgotten, and thus the burial place was but a transfer of memorials from the wealthy counselor to the penniless Carpenter. It was another example of a disciple who was determined to give his best to the Lord.

THE MINISTRY IN THE SEPULCHRE

"And he bought fine linen" (v. 46). John tells us that "there came also Nicodemus...and brought a mixture of myrrh and aloes, about an hundred pound weight" (John 19:39). Luke adds, "And the women also...returned, and prepared spices and ointments" (Luke 23:55-56). Had they remembered His promise to rise again, they could have saved time, labor and money. Yet they were determined the decaying processes of corruption should be held at bay as long as possible. The Master had been beautiful in life; the women were determined He should be so in death. Doubtless their dedication arose as a sweet-smelling savor before God. They were doing what they could to preserve His loveliness.

THE MEMORIES IN THE SOUL

"And [they] rolled a stone unto the door of the sepulchre" (v. 46). "Now in the place where He was crucified there was a garden; and in the garden a new sepulchre, wherein was never man yet laid. There laid they Jesus therefore because of the Jews preparation day; for the sepulchre was nigh at hand" (John 19:41-42). Were there seats in that garden? Did the mourners sit for a time to reflect on the past? Mary

Magdalene, one of the women who had watched the interment, would never forget how she had been possessed with demons until the day she met Jesus. His amazing touch had given new life; His words had sounded like music from another world. She loved Him that first day; she would always love Him. Did the memories cause the tears to flow? The time went all too quickly; she could not stay longer, for to do so would be to invite criticism. The Great Day was at hand, and contact with tombs meant defilement. She took one last look, and beneath her breath vowed to return as soon as possible. It was as though she said, "Lord, I'll be back," but as she returned to her home, she felt a part of herself had been left behind that stone which blocked the entrance to the tomb. Wise indeed is the person who feels sad when Jesus is absent!

HOMILIES

See "Joseph, the Honorable Counselor." (1) His Startling Discovery, (2) His Secret Discipleship, (3) His Sincere Devotion, (4) His Stubborn Determination, (5) His Supreme Delight, in *Luke's Thrilling Gospel*, p. 485.
See "The Soldiers Who Crucified Jesus," *John's Wonderful Gospel*, pp. 406-408.
See "The Three Marys Who Lingered at the Cross," *John's Wonderful Gospel*, pp. 408-409.

The Sixteenth Chapter of Mark

THEME: *The Resurrection of the Lord Jesus Christ*

OUTLINE:
  I. His Arising... *To Proclaim Deliverance* (Verses 1-8)
  II. His Appearances... *To Persuade Doubters* (Verses 9-14)
  III. His Announcements... *To Provide Direction* (Verses 15-18)
  IV. His Ascension... *To Pray Daily* (Verses 19-20)

SECTION ONE

Expository Notes on the Angel's Announcement of the Resurrection

And when the sabbath was past, Mary Magdalene, and Mary the mother of James, and Salome, had bought sweet spices, that they might come and anoint Him. And very early in the morning the first day of the week, they came unto the sepulchre at the rising of the sun. And they said among themselves, Who shall roll us away the stone from the door of the sepulchre? And when they looked, they saw that the stone was rolled away: for it was very great (vv. 1-4).

THEIR WORK... They bought and brought sweet spices

"A hasty, but lavish embalming of our Lord's sacred body had been begun by Joseph and Nicodemus. They had brought "a mixture of myrrh and aloes about a hundred pound weight" (John 19:39). This would be a compound — the gum of the myrrh tree, and a powder of the fragrant aloe wood mixed together, with which they would completely cover the body, which was then swathed with linen cloths also steeped in the aromatic preparation... What had been done on the eve of the Sabbath, had been done in haste... The remaining work could be done more carefully and tenderly at the tomb" (condensed from *The Pulpit Commentary, Mark*, p. 346).

The Sabbath would have ended at sunset on the Saturday evening, and it was then the women purchased the spices with which they intended to anoint the body of their Lord. The three women probably had conversed about their needs, and planned what to do. Where and how they obtained their requirements is of no concern to us. They either paid for their goods, or went out to gather from the trees that which they needed. With loving care they prepared embalming fluids or powders, and as soon as possible proceeded to the tomb in the garden. Calvary's cross had disturbed their faith, but nothing could destroy their love for Jesus.

THEIR WALK... "*They came unto the sepulchre at the rising of the sun*" *(v.2)*

"A. R. Fausset in his *Bible Encyclopedia and Dictionary* says of the aloes, 'The more precious kind grows in Cochin China, and Siam, and is not exported being worth its weight in gold. The perfume is from the oil thickening into resin within the trunk. It is used for perfuming garments (Ps. 45:8) and beds (Prov. 7:17). It is the image of all that is lovely, fragrant, and incorruptible (Num. 24:6 and Song of Sol. 4:14).... The Jews entombed, if possible, or else interred their dead; the Rabbis alleging as a reason, 'Dust thou art, and unto dust shalt thou return! (Gen. 3:19). Even enemies received burial (1 Kings 11:15). The law ordained the same treatment for a malefactor (Deut. 21:23).... To give a place in one's own sepulchre was a special honor. So Joseph of Arimathea could not have done a greater honor to our crucified Lord's body than giving it a place in his own new tomb, fulfilling the prophecy of Isaiah 53:9" (p. 104).

Somewhere within the city, the two Marys and Salome awaited the arrival of the dawn; the night appeared to be endless. Within the garden tomb, the body of Jesus was resting where it had been placed. The women were anxious and perhaps impatient. The embalming substances were ready. It is thought-provoking to compare the times as given by the authors of the Gospels. John 20:1 says that Mary came when it was yet dark. Matthew 28:1 says the two Marys came as it began to dawn. Mark says they came at sunrise. It would appear the walk began during the predawn darkness; that the closer the women came to the tomb the less dark it seemed to be, and finally when they met the risen Christ, there was no darkness at all. They walked into the sunrise (see the special homily in the author's commentary, *John's Wonderful Gospel*, "Mary...who walked toward the sunrise" pp. 416-418).

THEIR WORRY . . . Who shall roll us away the stone? (v. 3)

It is necessary to remember that New Testament tombs did not have doors! The burial chambers were caves, and entrance was gained through an arch-like doorway. Stones of varying sizes were rolled along a runway to block the entrance, and prevent animals from desecrating the grave. Such a stone can still be seen at the Tombs of the Kings in Jerusalem. When Joseph and Nicodemus left the tomb in the garden, they had rolled into position a large circular stone which probably was six or more feet high, and of considerable weight. It would have been impossible for women to move it. It is inspiring to remember that God only expects us to do what we can. It has been well said, "Man's extremity is God's opportunity." If we proceed in the right direction, God will move all hindrances threatening to halt our progress. When God says, "Walk," it is better to obey than wait!

THEIR WONDER . . . ". . . the stone was rolled away" (v. 4)

Faith is better than fear. Had the women stayed at home debating ways and means by which to overcome their problems, they would have lost the greatest thrill of their lives. They could have waited until the disciples were awake; they could have made arrangements to have at least two of them present at a specified time to roll back the stone; they could have done many things. They preferred to go immediately. Their aim was to get as close as possible to the Lord. Slowly they walked along the darkened streets, and when at last, they turned to enter the garden, behold! the stone was rolled away! It is always a mistake to spend time dreading the problems of tomorrow. All kinds of difficulties may appear to threaten our happiness, but "If God be for us, who can be against us?" Let us walk by faith, then nothing will be able to keep us away from the Lord.

And entering into the sepulchre, they saw a young man sitting on the right side, clothed in a long white garment; and they were affrighted. And he saith unto them, Be not affrighted: Ye seek Jesus of Nazareth, which was crucified: He is risen; He is not here; behold the place where they laid Him. But go your way, tell His disciples and Peter that He goeth before you into Galilee: there shall ye see Him, as He said unto you. And they went out quickly, and fled from the sepulchre; for they trembled and were amazed: neither said they anything to any man; for they were afraid (vv. 5-8).

THE ATTRACTIVE MAN

"And entering into the sepulchre, they saw a young man. . . ." (v. 5). Matthew is more explicit in his description of that youthful angel. "And behold, there was a great earthquake: for the angel of the Lord descended from heaven, and came and rolled back the stone from the door, and sat upon it. His countenance was like lightning, and his raimant white as snow. And for fear of him, the keepers did shake, and became as dead men" (Matt. 28:2-4). Luke 24:4 says there were two angelic messengers. John 20:12 agrees with Luke.

Doubtless they were all correct. Would it be possible that even more angels were in the vicinity of that tomb? Perhaps the dazzling splendor of those heavenly beings was so overpowering, that mortal eyes momentarily became blinded to such magnificence. We read in Luke 2:13 how *a multitude of the heavenly host* rejoiced at the Savior's birth; probably all heaven rejoiced when He rose from the dead. Yet one detail invites investigation. Angels were created before Adam, and therefore, to say the least, at the time of the resurrection, they would have been four thousand years old! Mark describes the angel as being *a young man*! There are no senior citizens in Heaven, for all are clothed with the garments of eternal youth.

THE ASSURING MESSAGE

"Ye seek Jesus of Nazareth, which was crucified: He is risen; He is not here: behold the place where they laid Him" (v. 6). Christianity invites investigation. If Heaven needed to advertise its product, the empty tomb would be sufficient. There are other religious systems on earth, where exponents of their doctrines proudly draw attention to the graves of ancient leaders. Christians point to a tomb, but it is empty; its only occupant has gone! Christ is not just a figure of history, One who lived and moved among men; He is Someone to be met, to be loved, and to be enjoyed. We looked and found Him in the pages of the Bible; someday we shall see Him returning in the clouds of heaven, but greatest and best of all, we find Him in the events of daily life. There, in a most remarkable fashion, we hear His voice, feel the pressure of His hand, and know His presence. He left the tomb so that by the ministry of His Spirit, He could reside with us for ever.

THE ABUNDANT MERCY

"...tell His disciples and PETER!..." (v. 7). Somewhere within the city, Simon Peter had wept bitter tears; he had denied his Lord. Peter was utterly ashamed and felt he could no longer join his colleagues. He had miserably failed; he was a disappointment to everybody. Nevertheless, he was still a disciple. Why did the angel specially mention Peter? Would it not have been sufficient to say, "Tell the disciples?" It is worthy of attention that although Mary delivered her message, Peter had no intention of going to meet the Lord. The Lord knew this, and so went looking for His despondent friend (see Luke 24:34 and 1 Corinthians 15:5). Mercifully, God has drawn a veil over what happened when Jesus met Peter, and we have no wish to intrude. Afterward, Peter became the preacher of Pentecost. The Master Potter had taken something filled with flaws and from it made a vessel of exquisite beauty!

THE AMAZED MESSENGERS

"And they...were amazed: neither said they anything to any man; for they were afraid" (v. 8). Eventually, the women recovered from the early morning shocks. It seemed as though they had dreamed a strange dream. Was it true? Had they been fantasizing? They were too scared to tell people what had happened in the garden. Slowly, their convictions deepened; they *had* seen the angel; they *had* heard his message; and the time had arrived for action. Blessed are they who know the Gospel and hurry to proclaim its message.

SECTION TWO

Expository Notes on the Resurrection Appearances of the Lord

Now when Jesus was risen early the first day of the week, He appeared first to Mary Magdalene, out of whom He had cast seven devils. And she went and told them that had been with Him, as they mourned and wept. And they, when they had heard that He was alive, and had been seen of her, believed not. After that He appeared in another form unto two of them, as they walked, and went into the country. And they went and told it unto the residue: neither believed they them. Afterward He appeared unto the eleven as they sat at meat, and upbraided them with their unbelief and hardness of heart, because they believed not them which had seen Him after He was risen (vv. 9-14).

THE AUTHORSHIP OF THE LAST TWELVE VERSES OF MARK'S GOSPEL

We have now reached a point in the manuscript of this Gospel where a different style of writing becomes evident. Throughout the first fifteen chapters of the book, it is easy to detect the influence of Simon Peter on the descriptions supplied by Mark. Peter had been an eye-witness of most of the things mentioned in this Gospel, and therefore a feeling of participation seems to be imparted into Mark's descriptions. This style of writing abruptly ends with chapter sixteen, verse eight. The closing twelve verses appear to be the work of another man; a man who looked, as it were, from afar, and described what he saw. Throughout the centuries, theologians have debated this issue, and, from the discussions, certain suggestions were forthcoming.

1. Some teachers believe Mark wrote every word of his Gospel, and the apparent change of style might be explained by the maturing of the author.

2. Others think the original end of Mark's Gospel might have been damaged or lost. To complete the story, an unknown writer wrote the conclusion, and added it to what had been preserved from Mark's manuscript.

3. Many evangelical theologians almost ignore the apparent change, stating that since the author was but a human pen in the hands of God, his identity is of little concern. If God used Mark through the writing of the manuscript, or if at a later date, He chose someone else to complete the task, is not of preeminent importance. Since God alone is the TRUE AUTHOR, *what was said* is far more vital to us than to know *who wrote* the message. *The Pulpit Commentary* cites evidence both for and against the above suggestions, but concludes that most of the facts agree that Mark was the author of the entire Gospel.

THE DELIVERANCE OF MARY

As we have already indicated, there appears to be a new style of expression in these verses. Hitherto, Mark has been an active participant in this evangelistic game of life; now he seemingly has retired to the grandstand from which he looks upon the entire playing field. He first mentions Mary Magdalene and recalls that the Lord had banished the demons which enslaved her. John, chapter 20, adds significant details to the story. Matthew and Luke also mention the events connected with this appearance. Why did the Lord first appear to Magdalene? He could have appeared to His mother, or to Simon Peter or even to John. Was there significance in the fact that her deliverance from demons was mentioned? Mary Magdalene never forgot her debt of gratitude. She was one of the women who followed Him throughout Galilee; she ministered to Him, possibly repairing garments and cooking meals; she lingered at the cross and witnessed His burial. She became a living example of what it means to endure unto the end. Now, the Lord Who had delivered her from demons, appeared to banish her doubts, and remove any sadness filling her soul. Apart from the angelic messengers, Mary Magdalene became the first preacher of the resurrection. The unexperienced convert had become a mature saint!

THE DISGUISE OF THE MASTER

"*After that He appeared in another form unto two of them* as they walked, and went into the country" (v, 12). This, obviously, is a reference to the story told in detail by Luke (24:13-35). The word translated "form" is *morphee* which means "the form by which a person or thing strikes the vision; the external appearance." The Lord, apparently, "put on a different external appearance", and that is best rendered as a disguise! He made sure that the people walking to Emmaus would be unable to recognize Him. "*He appeared in another form.*" It would be a captivating study to search the Scriptures to find other disguises of the Lord. We have been informed that sometimes Satan appears as an angel of light to deceive, if possible, even the elect (see 2 Cor. 11:14). We know that God comes in the most unexpected manner; at the strangest times, and often is not recognized. Life-giving rain often descends from the blackest thunder clouds. The evangelism of North Africa resulted from an unexpected interruption of very successful meetings in Samaria (see Acts 8:5-40). It is probable that an unwelcome illness suffered by Paul made Timothy search for a doctor in Troas. That call from a patient meant the inclusion of Dr. Luke in the missionary party (see Acts 16:6-10). Had Daniel never been thrown into the lions den, He might not have known the protective power of His God. Had the Hebrew boys never been cast into the fiery furnace, they might never have known the companionship of the One said to be, "like the Son of God" (see Daniel 3:23-25).

THE DENUNCIATION OF THE MEN

"He upbraided them with their unbelief and hardness of heart, because they believed not them which had seen Him after He was risen" (v. 14). Frequently, during His ministry, the Lord had warned His followers that He would be crucified, and that afterward, He would rise from the dead. It is sad to relate that only His enemies remembered the prediction. Matthew wrote, "Now the next day . . . the chief priests and Pharisees came together unto Pilate, Saying, Sir, we remember that that deceiver said, while He was yet alive, After three days I will rise again. Command therefore that the sepulchre be made sure until the third day, lest his disciples come by night, and steal Him away, and say unto the people, He is risen from the dead: so the last error be worse than the first" (27:62-64). Those priests have been very attentive to the sayings of the Savior. Alas, the disciples were too concerned with unimportant things. Faith and fear cannot occupy the same temple. One must kill the other. I remember how my mother's garden was divided into two sections, both occupied by chickens. She had white fowls in the top part, and Rhode Island Reds in the lower. As a small boy I was fascinated by the respective cockerels who, beak to beak, went up and down the separating wire fence. Throughout every day they challenged each other along the barricade. Innocently, I asked my mother to open the door, and permit those birds to "have a real go." Horrified, she replied, "Son, you don't understand! Those two cockerels could not live together; one would kill the other." Later, I christened those birds, FAITH and FEAR, but fortunately, from time to time, both have appeared within my own heart. The disciples would not, could not believe, and so gently, the Lord scolded them.

SECTION THREE

Expository Notes on the Commission to Evangelize the World

And He said unto them, Go ye into all the world, and preach the gospel to every creature. He that believeth and is baptized shall be saved; but he that believeth not shall be damned. And these signs shall follow them that believe: In my name shall they cast out devils; they shall speak with new tongues; they shall take up serpents; and if they drink any deadly thing, it shall not hurt them; they shall lay hands on the sick, and they shall recover (vv. 15-18).

THE SUBLIME COMMISSION

"Go ye into all the world, and preach the gospel to every creature" (v. 15). If Christ died for all mankind, then the whole world should be made aware of the thrilling fact. It is not possible to be a healthy Christian if love for missions is unknown in the soul. An artist was to paint a picture of a dead church, and he did so in a most unusual way. He depicted an elaborate building adorned with all that wealth could provide. Its architecture was a joy to behold, and the congregation was composed of beautifully dressed ladies and elegant men. The artist depicted an overflowing congregation, a contented minister, a beautifully-robed choir, and an organ of surpassing quality. Yet in the entrance to that marvelous church, the artist painted a missionary offering box with a cobweb over the slit in the lid. The church that has no interest in missions is not a church, but a social club.

THE SIMPLE CONDITION

These verses have been debated by sects throughout the centuries. "He that believeth...believe..." (v. 16, 17). Emphasis has been placed on the rite of baptism, and some teachers affirm that unbaptized converts never find acceptance with God. They say that baptism is essential to salvation; that without it, even the foremost of Christian leaders will be rejected at the day of judgment. This is erroneous. It must always be remembered that the New Testament church knew nothing of unbaptized believers. The ordinance of believers' baptism was the appointed way by which converts told the world that *something had happened*. They had passed from death to life: from the bondage of sin to the freedom of the new life in Christ. They were not ashamed to confess their faith in Christ. To do so, therefore, they went to the rivers or seashore, so that all, who so desired, could witness their personal testimony. Therefore, it was quite natural and easily understood why the ordinance was identified with genuine faith in Christ. The dying thief was never baptized, but all who followed him into the kingdom of God were. The disciples were commissioned to take the Gospel message throughout the world, and having led people to Christ, to baptize them in the accustomed way.

It is to be noted that baptism was not mentioned in the second part of the commission. It was understood that *those who believed would*

MARK'S SUPERB GOSPEL

be baptized. The people who did not believe — obviously would not be baptized, and therefore there remained no need to mention any ordinance. Unbelievers would be rejected by God even as He had been rejected by them.

THE STARTLING CHARACTERISTICS

"*These signs shall follow them that believe...*" (vv. 17, 18). It cannot be overstressed that verse eighteen is not a license for stupidity. The signs mentioned here were, for the most part, all witnessed during the earliest beginnings of the church. God gave the gift of speaking in tongues to meet a very urgent need. Within days the multitudes attending the Feast of Pentecost were to return to distant homes. If they were to hear the Gospel, they had to hear it quickly; they had no time to attend a language school. Paul did shake off a deadly serpent (Acts 28:3-6), and tradition speaks of certain Christians who escaped death by poisoning because God protected them from the attacks of enemies. These signs were to be evidence of God's protective power, and not to be exhibitions of foolish self-confidence. Today, in certain areas, snake-charming has become part of the church service, and unlimited sessions for physical healing are held in many churches. It must never be forgotten that God can, and *does* heal the sick, but He does so according to *His will* and not because the shouts and screams of faith healers disturb the tranquility of Heaven. The signs, or gifts, as enumerated in these verses, were necessary for the establishment of the church; they attracted and indisputably served their purpose. Gardeners water their young plants until the seedlings have taken root; thereafter the watering can gradually be decreased. Thus it was when the Heavenly Gardener supervised the planting of His young church.

There is sanity and majesty about all God's commands. Some teachers stress the importance of speaking in tongues, but would abstain from drinking poison. Others lay hands on the sick, but would run for life if a serpent or snake appeared. Mark supplies a list of protective promises, but if these were meant for today's church, then every member should be prepared to take a course of snake handling! Christians should refrain from argument as to the validity or necessity for such manifestations of power; it is better to concentrate on being like the Christ Who uttered these promises.

SECTION FOUR

Expository Notes on the Ascension of Christ

So then after the Lord had spoken unto them, He was received up into heaven, and sat on the right hand of God. And they went forth, and preached everywhere, the Lord working with them, and confirming the word with signs following. Amen. (vv. 19-20).

THE CELESTIAL CORONATION

"So then after the Lord had spoken unto them, He was received up into heaven, and sat on the right hand of God" (v. 19). The writer to the Hebrews adds that Christ was then crowned with glory and honor (2:7). Heaven eagerly awaited the return of its King. The work which had been entrusted to Him had been completed, and that particular day in heaven was a time of celebration. The eternal realm echoed with acclamation when Jesus, our great High Priest, took His seat on the right hand of the Majesty on High. He had been crowned with many crowns; but then, on the day of His ascension, the glory of God, as anointing oil, covered His head. From that moment He has "ever lived to make intercession for His people" (Heb. 7:25). When God concluded the installation of Jesus as High Priest, He said, "Sit on my right hand, until I make thine enemies thy footstool" (Heb. 1:13).

THE COURAGEOUS COMPLIANCE

The disciples watched as their Master went home to heaven, then with a sigh, turned to face a needy world. They had lost their Master, but He had left them a task to perform. "And they went forth and preached everywhere." They had been given a tremendous promise. Jesus had said, ". . .I will build my church; and the gates of hell shall not prevail against it" (Matt. 16:18). As they contemplated the future, they remained undaunted. There would be hills to climb and valleys to be crossed. Unprecedented problems would arise; some brethren would become martyrs. Roman legions would thwart their efforts, but nothing would ever be permitted to destroy their zeal.

THE CONTINUING COMPANIONSHIP

"They went forth. . .*the Lord working with them.*" (v. 20). This is a fitting climax to Mark's superb Gospel. The disciples had watched the Lord's ascension to Heaven, and yet, in some strange mysterious way, knew He was still in their midst. His promise, "I will never leave you" had become a glorious reality. When they preached, He was among the listening audience; when they were hard-pressed and knew not how to proceed, He was at their side to offer advice; when they were downcast, His everlasting arms were ready to lift them to new heights of achievement. They knew that nothing — neither death, nor life, nor angels, nor principalities, nor powers, nor things present, nor things to come, nor height, nor depth, nor any other creature" (Rom. 8:38, 39) would be able to separate them from the love of God, which was in Christ Jesus. Thus did Mark terminate his manuscript. Probably he read and re-read his message, and finally, realizing there was no more to be said, wrote AMEN.

HOMILIES

Study No. 19

THE LORD JESUS IN DISGUISE

The Emmaus story is among the best known of the Scriptures, but our familiarity with its details is apt to interfere with our understanding of its more serious teaching. Four questions are suggested by this stimulating account. (1) Why were the disciples going to Emmaus? It is worthy of note that apart from their contact with the Savior, the journey was a waste of time. Their purpose in visiting Emmaus was unfulfilled, for they returned almost immediately. (2) Why did they fail to recognize the Lord Jesus? (3) Why did they enjoy the Stranger's sermon, when its opening statements charged them with great folly? (4) Why did they return at such a late hour of the night, and thus prove the inadvisability of their walk to Emmaus?

THE STRANGE ROAD

Calvary had completely ruined the hopes of the disciples. These delightful people had followed Christ, because they honestly believed He would establish the Messianic kingdom. Every day they witnessed new manifestations of power, and they never questioned the imminence of His coronation. When He surrendered to His enemies, and was led forth to be nailed to a cross, their hearts turned to stone. Weary and despondent, they began making plans for the future, and ultimately two of the company decided to return home. Their walk into the country took them away from the cross; their backs were toward the sanctuary, and every step was one taken in the wrong direction. The Emmaus road has had many travellers, for embittered men have often made a contemporary Judas an excuse for backsliding. In the greater issues of life, the Emmaus road is a cul-de-sac and not a highway.

THE STRANGE REDEEMER

"And it came to pass, that, while they communed together and reasoned, Jesus himself drew near, and went with them. But their eyes were holden that they should not know Him" (Luke 24:15-16). Had Christ revealed Himself, and commanded their return to Jerusalem, they would have obeyed instantly, but their personal difficulties would have remained. There was very much more at stake than their return to the holy city. Recurring problems had ruined their peace of mind, and a strange unrest had conquered their hearts. In order to deal with these hidden troubles, the Lord Jesus disguised Himself and drew near.

THE STRANGE REACTION

His sermon had an inauspicious beginning, and could never be a pattern for ministerial students. He began by calling His audience "fools." Yet in some mysterious fashion His message was delivered in such a delightful way that it made their hearts burn. We believe literature would have been enriched immeasurably had Christ's sermon been preserved for posterity. He systematically expounded, in all the Scriptures, the things concerning Himself, and His utterances cheered their drooping spirits. They had never heard such a message, for it suggested the cross would become a beacon from which radiant happiness would shine out to a world. They had been wrong in all their conclusions. The Lord Jesus touched the trouble-spot in their agitated souls; but without His disguise, this would have been impossible.

THE STRANGE RETURN

When Christ accepted the invitation to supper, the scene was set for their greatest surprise. As he broke the bread, "they knew Him by the print of the nails in His hands.'' Then their plans were instantly changed; they desired to rejoin the brethren. The loneliness of the road, and the darkness of the night were unable to keep them in Emmaus, for, ''they rose up the same hour and returned to Jerusalem.'' The darkness of their night of sorrow had given place to a dawn, and they desired to spend the new day in fellowship with the people of God. And as it was, so it is. Man is never so stupid as when he journeys away from the cross. A tent at Calvary is better than a palace in Emmaus (taken from the author's book, *Bible Pinnacles*, pp. 99-100).

BIBLIOGRAPHY

Augustine *Tract 31 in Saint Johan*

Barclay, William *The Daily Study Bible, The Gospel of Mark.* Philadelphia: The Westminster Press, 1975.

Bruce, F. F., ed. *The New International Commentary on the New Testament. The Gospel of Luke.* Grand Rapids: Wm. B. Eerdmans Publishing Co., 1979.

Fausset, A. R. *Fausset's Bible Dictionary.* Grand Rapids: Zondervan Publishing House.

Fuller, Thomas *Cause and Cure of a Wounded Conscience.*

Geikie, Cunningham *The Life and Words of Christ.* New York: D. Appleton and Co. 1880.

Godet, Frederic L. *Commentary on Luke.* Grand Rapids: Kregel Publications, 1981.

Josephus, Flavius *The Complete Works of Flavius Josephus.* Grand Rapids: Kregel Publications, 1960.

Lange, John Peter *Commentary on the Holy Scriptures,* vol. 8. Grand Rapids: Zondervan Publishing House, 1976.

McIntyre, W. A. *The War Cry.*

Powell, Ivor *Bible Cameos.* Grand Rapids: Kregel Publications, 1985.
—————— *Bible Highways.* Grand Rapids, Kregel Publications, 1985
—————— *Bible Pinnacles.* Grand Rapids, Kregel Publications, 1985
—————— *Bible Treasures.* Grand Rapids, Kregel Publications, 1985.
—————— *Bible Windows.* Grand Rapids, Kregel Publications, 1985.
—————— *John's Wonderful Gospel.* Grand Rapids: Kregel Publications, 1983.
—————— *Luke's Thrilling Gospel.* Grand Rapids: Kregel Publications, 1984.
—————— *This I Believe.* London: Marshall, Morgan & Scott, 1957.
—————— *What in the World Will Happen Next?* Grand Rapids: Kregel Publications, 1985.

Reader's Digest *Great Encyclopedic Dictionary.*

Ryle, J. C. *Expository Thoughts on the Gospel of Matthew and Mark.* Grand Rapids: Zondervan Publishing House, n.d.

Smith, G. A. *The Historical Geography of the Holy Land.* London: Hodder & Stoughton, 1908.

Spence, H. D. and Exell, Joseph S., eds. *The Pulpit Commentary,* vol. 16, *Mark and Luke.* Grand Rapids: Wm. B. Eerdmans Publishing Co., 1950.

Tenney, Merrill C., ed. *The Zondervan Pictorial Encyclopedia of the Bible,* 5 volumes. Grand Rapids: Zondervan Publishing House, 1975.

Thayer, Joseph H. *The Greek-English Lexicon of the New Testament.* Grand Rapids: Zondervan Publishing House, 1983.

Thomson, J. A. *The Land and the Book.* New York: Harper and Brothers, 1869.

Unger, Merrill F. *Unger's Bible Dictionary.* Chicago: Moody Press, 1957.